Home Care
Survival
Guide

Home Care Survival Guide

KAY GREEN, RN, MBA

Vice President, Ambulatory Services
Desert Hospital
Palm Springs, California

Lippincott
Philadelphia • New York

Acquisitions Editor: Susan M. Glover, RN, MSN
Developmental Editor: Renée A. Gagliardi
Project Editor: Tom Gibbons
Senior Production Manager: Helen Ewan
Produciton Coordinator: Michael Carcel
Design Coordinator: Doug Smock
Indexer: Alexandra Nickerson

Library of Congress Cataloging in Publications Data
Green, Kay, 1961–
    Home care survival guide / Kay Green.
      p.   cm.
    Includes bibliographical references and index.
    ISBN 0-397-55275-0 (paper : alk. paper)
    1. Home nursing.   I. Title.
    [DNLM: 1. Home Care Services. 2. Clinical Competence.   WY 115
G796h 1998]
RT120.H65G74   1998
362.1′4—dc21
DNLM/DLC
for Library of Congress   97-42737
                                                          CIP

9   8   7   6   5   4   3   2   1

This work is dedicated to my husband, Tam,
whose love and belief in me gave me the confidence to believe in myself,
and to my daughter Heidi, who fills my life with joy and pride.

Preface

The healthcare industry continues its struggle to meet increasing societal demands for effective, cost-efficient medical services. As a result, the practice of nursing is changing rapidly. Until the 1980s, the public and healthcare providers alike usually perceived nursing as a service performed primarily in institutional settings (e.g., hospitals, skilled nursing facilities, clinics). Nursing programs prepared their students for clinical practice in such settings. Many factors, however, including the implementation of prospective payment systems, the influence of managed care, and the growth of the aging American population, have altered these perceptions and the way nursing services are now provided. Nursing's focus has shifted from an institutionally based to a community-based model of care.

A crucial component of this shift is the enormous growth of home care nursing. Outpatient procedures that require follow-up care and medical treatments initiated and maintained in the home continue to replace extensive hospitalizations. Such procedures, however, still require highly skilled, comprehensive nursing care for clients to achieve appropriate clinical outcomes. As home care has become a major force in the healthcare industry, the need for appropriate teaching and preparation of home care nurses has increased steadily.

◆ Purpose of the Text

The primary purpose of *Home Care Survival Guide* is to prepare the nursing student, as well as the nurse experienced in other care settings, for the independent, sometimes difficult, and often surprising nature of home care practice. Although the medical conditions of most home care clients are typically less acute than those of clients found in other settings, the broad scope of responsibilities and the independent nature of home care create special challenges for nurses to meet on the job each day. This text is designed to help nurses new to home care to meet these challenges and to "survive" any crises encountered in this exciting, rewarding, and professional nursing practice setting.

The text discusses elements of home care as a career alternative for nurses. It reviews fundamental concepts of nursing care and applies them to the particulars of this unique practice. It provides practical guidelines for effective nursing care of home care clients. Each chapter differentiates home care nursing from nursing in acute care settings through a *Home Care Vs. Hospital* comparison. These comparisons highlight the special work environment and difficulties that home care nurses continually face. They are especially useful to nurses who are adapting to home care from other, more traditional settings. An entire chapter is devoted to the differences between these two types of practice settings as well.

The nature of home care stresses holism and a personalized, humanistic focus on clients. Accordingly, this book discusses throughout the significant role lay caregivers play in home care and the importance of considering cultural issues when working with clients and their significant others. The ability of nurses to form therapeutic relationships based on trust and understanding with their clients is critical to successful home care practice and to the long-term health and wellness of clients. This theme is reiterated throughout the book.

Many examples of client situations are included within the text to demonstrate specific principles of home care and to reinforce learning. The *Application to Home Care Practice* displays correlate clinical concepts within a chapter to the actual work environment of home care. *Survival Alerts* give readers pragmatic suggestions regarding complex issues they may encounter and helpful lists of points to consider when solving specific problems. In most chapters, *Home Care Conflicts* are provided to illustrate common dilemmas home care nurses often face in everyday practice. *Clinical Examples with Critical Thinking* displays within the text and *Thinking Critically in Home Care* exercises at the end of each chapter provide readers with the opportunity to integrate and apply concepts to common home care situations and predicaments.

◆ Organization of the Text

The *Home Care Survival Guide* is organized into four units. Unit 1, Introduction to Home Care, defines home care, reviews the historical evolution of home care, and discusses trends that are affecting its future. This unit highlights the special responsibilities of home care nurses by comparing typical elements of practice to acute care nursing provided in hospitals. A discussion of managed care, its impact upon the healthcare industry in general and the home care industry specifically, and its potential future influence is also included. Unit II, Knowledge Base and Skill Requirements, reviews important concepts and skills required of home care nurses: cultural adaptability, documentation skills, knowledge of client rights and responsibilities, coordination of care and interdisciplinary communication, supervision of paraprofessionals, and application of the nursing process in the home care setting. Unit III, Clinical Activities in the Home, thoroughly discusses significant clinical activities home care nurses perform: teaching, maintaining safety, equipment management, and infection control. Finally, Unit IV, Home Care Practice, examines the actual practice of home care nursing. This unit integrates the many concepts presented previously and describes the implementation of home care principles during the initial visit and in subsequent visits. This unit also considers important decisions nurses will confront when caring for clients: maintaining clients on home care service after mandated periods through recertification; discussing long-term plans with clients who are facing chronic, critical illnesses; transferring the care of clients to other, more appropriate providers; and ensuring the safe discharge of clients from home care services.

◆ Key Features of the Text

The following features of the book were developed as pedagogic aids. They illustrate concepts presented in the text and act as practical guides to assist readers in implementing them in practice:

- *Learning Objectives* (beginning of each chapter): target important points for students to master when reading each chapter
- *Key Terms* (beginning of each chapter): lists of essential terms for students to know upon completion of each chapter
- *Key Concepts* (within text): boxed information highlighting essential information for students to review
- *Application to Home Care Practice* (at least one in each chapter): displays that apply concepts discussed in the text to actual practice with clients
- *Home Care Conflicts* (in most chapters): boxed scenarios that present typical dilemmas for nurses working within home care
- *Home Care Vs Hospital* (one in each chapter): comparisons of key text points between the home and the hospital setting
- *Survival Alerts* (several in each chapter): practical suggestions pertaining to issues nurses may encounter in home care and helpful lists of pointers when facing typical problems
- *Clinical Examples with Critical Thinking* (in each chapter except Chapter 1): client vignettes based on actual home care experiences with questions and exercises for students to apply their learning
- *Post Tests:* questions for review at the end of each chapter; answers are provided at the end of the book
- *Thinking Critically in Home Care Exercises* (at the end of every chapter): questions, exercises, and considerations for students at the completion of each chapter; these exercises often build upon and reinforce knowledge that students should have mastered at the end of previous chapters as well

Additionally, a variety of tables and displays provide lists of significant issues within subject areas, criteria that can be used in the application of concepts, factors that influence home care nursing practice, and ways for nurses to enhance their performance. Each chapter includes a comprehensive list of references and suggestions for further reading. Photographs and illustrations designed to enhance understanding and capture the attention of readers are also included.

Acknowledgments

I would like to acknowledge those colleagues with whom I have worked in home care and hospice for many years, particularly Rebecca Dierker, Cheryl Hunhoff, Susan Lydon, and Lilli Melchert. These individuals have provided me with so much professional and personal support that has navigated me through the trials and tribulations of administering a home health and hospice program. I would like to thank my mentor and leader, Bob Minkin, who has given me innumerable "learning opportunities" and has been a champion for me. I would like to acknowledge the tremendous assistance and support of Tracie Simpson and Amy Love, who helped me particularly during the stressful days of this project. I am so grateful to all of my friends, family, and colleagues, whose daily contributions of encouragement and laughter helped me get through the book's completion.

I want to thank my parents, Lucy and Joe Wolterman, for their faith, integrity, strength, and unconditional love. I would like to thank the National Association of Home Care (NAHC) for its fierce advocacy of home care services for a population that cannot fight for itself. NAHC has helped the home care industry and those of us who work within it immeasurably.

Finally, thanks to members of Lippincott-Raven's Nursing and Allied Health Publishing Department: Donna Hilton, Vice President and Publisher, who first recognized the opportunity to create this book; Susan M. Glover, RN, MSN, Senior Editor, who kept encouraging me to hang in there through the long development process; and most of all, Renée A. Gagliardi, Developmental Editor, who held my hand and gently led me through the process of turning a rough orientation manual I created for my own agency into a product that hopefully will have a positive impact on the quality of home care services in other communities.

Contributor:
Jean DeLong, R.N., M.S.
Home Care Consultant
Dayton, Ohio

Contents

Unit 2
Knowledge Base and Skill Requirements   79

4

Cultural Adaptability   81

5

Documentation   103

6

Client Rights and Responsibilities   128

12
Infection Control 277

Unit 4
Home Care Practice   *301*

13
The Initial Home Care Visit 303

14
Subsequent Visits, Recertification, Transfer, and Discharge From Home Care 339

UNIT 1

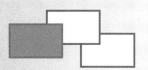

Introduction to Home Care

Home Care Overview

LEARNING OBJECTIVES

After completing this chapter, the reader will be able to:

◆ Identify the primary client populations that home care serves.

◆ Reflect upon home care's historical development.

◆ Name the regulatory bodies that establish and monitor minimum quality standards for home care agencies.

◆ Analyze national trends that are influencing home care's future.

◆ Discuss technological advances in home care.

◆ Evaluate characteristics of home care nursing practice.

◆ Assess the value of orientation and preceptorship for home care nurses.

KEY TERMS

Community Health Accreditation
  Program
Cost limit
Diagnosis related groups
Health Care Finance Administration
Health maintenance organizations
Home care
Joint Commission on Accreditation
  of Healthcare Organizations

Licensure
Medicare Conditions of
  Participation
Preceptor
Preferred provider
  organizations
Prospective payment system
Survey

ome care is an industry in which healthcare services are implemented directly in the home. The National Association for Home Care defines **home care** as "professional services provided in the place of residence on either a part-time, intermittent, hourly, or shift basis" (1995, p. 2). Typical services include professional nursing care, personal care by nursing assistants, physical therapy, occupational therapy, speech therapy, and social services. Individuals recovering from acute illnesses and chronically ill or disabled individuals whose needs cannot be met by lay caregivers are the clients that home care most commonly serves.

Aging persons who have experienced acute exacerbations of chronic diseases receive the majority of home care services. Home care is provided in various other circumstances as well, including convalescence after hospitalization, terminal illness, and chronic debilitating diseases (e.g., pulmonary diseases, congestive heart failure, and diabetes). Some home care programs are designed for the special needs of medically fragile infants, women with high-risk pregnancies, chronically ill children, clients with AIDS, and individuals with psychiatric diagnoses.

Skilled nursing is an important component of home care. Nursing services are typically goal oriented to meet specific client needs, and may be either dependent or independent. Physicians prescribe procedures, such as wound care or intravenous infusions, for home care nurses to conduct in a client's home. These functions are dependent on the physician's order. Teaching clients and their lay caregivers about disease processes and the effects and side effects of prescribed medications are independent nursing interventions that do not require physician involvement. Nurses also explain community resources—including transportation assistance, meals on wheels, free legal services, and adult day care centers—to help clients access additional services.

This chapter gives an overview of home care practice. It provides a basic understanding of the fundamental principles of this fastest growing segment of the healthcare industry. It reviews the history of home care, its recent evolution, and regulatory bodies that have affected the delivery of home care. The chapter explores national trends currently influencing home care's clinical practice and also notable technological advances in the field. Characteristics of home care and the professional lives of home care nurses are examined. A discussion of a nurse's orientation to a home care agency and the role of a preceptor (a guide who assists nurses new to home care during their period of transition) concludes this chapter.

◆ Historical Perspective of Home Care

Home care has evolved over many centuries, and its origins can be traced to well before recorded history. Prehistoric humans provided care to sick members of their tribes and families. They most likely learned to treat illnesses and injuries by observing the behavior of animals. Animals lick their wounds to remove sources of infection, eat grass and plant life that act as emetics and purgatives, and submerge inflamed wounds in water. Within the prehistoric division of labor system, men hunted for food, and women nurtured children and cared for the sick and injured of the tribe.

An individual who showed a special ability to relieve suffering and to improve the health of the sick fulfilled the role of caregiver or advisor for an entire tribe. These individuals can truly be considered the first home care providers (Donahue, 1985).

Nursing developed in Europe from the time of the Roman Empire to the Age of Enlightenment. Mary Sewell Gardner, a pioneer of public health nursing, wrote one of the first authoritative books on home care. She stated that "the true ancestors of the modern nurse are the noble abbesses and early Christian women who were trying to do for their day what the nurse of today is trying to do for hers" (1936, p. 3). Through the Middle Ages, the public viewed caring for the afflicted as consistent with Christian values. Many individuals entered nursing convents to serve God as well as the sick. After the Reformation, however, the status of nursing plummeted. In the 1700s and 1800s, European society poorly regarded the entire medical profession, which based healthcare primarily upon superstition. Working conditions within hospitals were deplorable. At the time, most of the women who entered the nursing profession were of low social standing, drunks, or prostitutes.

In the United States, charitable organizations developed visiting nursing programs in the 1800s. One of the first was the Ladies' Benevolent Society of Charleston, South Carolina, organized in 1813, which attempted to meet the needs of the infirm and poor. Many public health organizations formed in the middle to late 1800s to attend to the poverty-stricken urban populations of the Industrial Revolution. The mass influx of immigrants to the cities of New York, Philadelphia, and Boston contributed to social problems of indigence and poor health. The living conditions of these poor workers were abominable. Even very young children worked twelve to fourteen hours each day in dark factories.

Organizations concerned about poverty and public health issues proliferated during the Progressive Era of the early 1900s. These groups established Visiting Nursing Agencies (VNAs) to address some of the most profound problems of malnutrition and infectious disease afflicting American society at this time. Home care nurses provided education regarding proper diet and hygiene to the sick and their families to promote health and to decrease suffering. Often called Instructive District Nursing Associations, these organizations highlighted the significance of health education in their mission.

Over the centuries, many important individuals contributed to the evolution of nursing as a profession and to the concepts of home care. Display 1-1 discusses some of the important historical pioneers who influenced the development of home care nursing.

MODERN HOME CARE

During the early part of the twentieth century, physicians regularly visited the homes of the sick. In fact, before World War II, house calls made up the bulk of practice for most doctors. In the 1940s and 1950s, physicians began to practice in offices, and hospitals expanded their services to the public. The home care movement filled the void created by fewer house calls. Montefiore Hospital in New York City started a posthospital acute care program in 1946 that instituted the concept of convalescent home care. Similar programs quickly sprouted in towns and cities throughout the country.

Display 1-1:
Historical Pioneers in the Development of Home Care

St. Vincent de Paul organized an effort for women to visit the sick in their homes in 1617. He formed the Sisterhood of the Dames de Charité and appointed **Mademoiselle Le Gras** as a supervisor. De Paul and Le Gras possessed a philosophy of service unique for its time. They believed that interventions should focus on the causes of health problems, and that people are best served by helping them to help themselves. The public welcomed their service, which grew quickly. Lack of appropriate supervision and direction, however, caused organizational problems that ultimately doomed their efforts (Maynard, 1939). Their contribution was developing home care nursing as a vocation that provides health education and professional supervision to the sick and their lay caregivers.

Florence Nightingale had a tremendous influence on the changing image of nursing in the mid-1800s. Born in 1820 in Italy to affluent parents and raised in England, Nightingale was taught many languages and subjects by her father. Her parents were upset and concerned when she expressed, at an early age, a desire to enter the nursing field. Although her family attempted to dissuade her, Nightingale entered a 3-month training period for nursing at Kaiserwith, Germany and later studied with the Sisters of Charity in France (Donahue, 1985). Nightingale contributed significantly by improving healthcare provided in hospitals, developing appropriate educational curricula for nurses, and creating a conceptual framework for care. Her work also dramatically influenced community and home care nursing. Nightingale believed that nursing is more than just attending the sick—it is also teaching individuals the best ways to promote their own health. These beliefs are basic tenets of today's home care nursing practice.

William Rathbone, a philanthropist from Liverpool, England, assisted in advancing the notion of nursing care in the home after his dying wife received such assistance. "It is to Mr. Rathbone that we owe the first definitely formulated district nursing association and in that sense he may be called the father of the present movement" (Garner, 1936, p. 14). Rathbone wanted to develop nursing service to administer needed care to the underprivileged of Liverpool, but had difficulty finding nurses willing to do the work. In 1859, he worked closely with Nightingale to establish a school for training home care nurses and successfully introduced a home care program in Liverpool. This achievement proved that home care nursing could be effectively accomplished. Moreover, the public viewed the nurses involved in Rathbone's program as both healthcare providers and social reformers (Clemen-Stone, Eigsti, & McGquire, 1995).

(continued)

Display 1-1:
Historical Pioneers in the Development of Home Care (Continued)

Lillian Wald, a public health nurse, increased the public's awareness of the positive impact of home care efforts. She wrote two books about her experiences caring for impoverished, urban populations afflicted with illness: *The House on Henry Street* (1915) and *Windows on Henry Street* (1934). Like Nightingale, Wald came from a wealthy, well-educated family with high ideals. While attending medical school in New York City, she was asked to educate immigrant mothers regarding appropriate care for their sick families. The living conditions of these families astounded Wald. Her life and career reached a turning point when a young child asked her to visit the child's sick mother who had recently delivered a baby. The child led Wald to a sick young woman lying in a dirty bed and suffering from a 2-day-old hemorrhage. After this distressing scene, Wald decided not to return to school, but to dedicate her life to community health service. She convinced a classmate, **Mary Brewster,** to work and to live with her in a tenement house. They cared for the needy and worked for legislative and social reforms to improve living conditions. Wald is considered the founder of public health nursing and actually coined the term. In 1912, through the American Red Cross, she established the Rural Nursing Service (later called Town and Country Nursing Service) that was instrumental in providing home care nursing to areas outside large cities. Wald's legacy is her tremendous benefit in improving the health and lives of the poor and immigrants. A true reformer, Wald "opposed political and social corruption and supported those measures that would improve the health, welfare, and happiness of humanity" (Donahue, 1985, p. 348).

The Medicare program, initiated in the 1960s, introduced home care as a benefit for its participants. This development significantly affected the growth of modern home care practice, which has largely been defined by the scope of Medicare. The federal government has created standards that home care agencies must meet for Medicare reimbursement. Most other third party payors also follow these reimbursement guidelines. The home care industry continues to evolve as payors, clients, and providers gain a better understanding of the philosophy of home care: helping clients to keep themselves well.

◆ Regulations and Licensure

Both federal and state organizations regulate the home care industry. Home care agencies are required by most states to be licensed to provide healthcare services in the homes of clients. **Licensure** proves that an agency has achieved a minimum level of quality in its operations and in the qualifications of its staff. Licensure requirements vary in each state, but are generally similar to federal regulations. States define home care services and distinguish them from other home-based services, such as homemaker or housecleaning services, through licensure. The difference between home care companies and other home service agencies is that home care agencies authorize licensed professionals to deliver skilled medical services in the home.

SURVEY

Home care agencies are audited through a process known as the **survey**. Licensed healthcare providers, employed by a governmental agency, examine a home care agency's administrative and client care policies, protocols, and medical records. They evaluate the agency's compliance with regulations by interviewing clients and lay caregivers, reviewing services to a client during a home care visit, and questioning employees about their provision of services under a variety of circumstances (e.g., natural disasters, emergencies). Display 1-2 gives detailed information about the survey process.

HEALTH CARE FINANCE ADMINISTRATION

The **Health Care Finance Administration (HCFA)** is the department of the federal government accountable for the federally funded Medicare and Medicaid programs. It ensures that home care providers who access these benefits comply with appropriate regulations. The HCFA Office of Survey and Certification contracts with state health departments to perform most compliance surveys. Agencies wishing to participate in the Medicare program must comply with standards developed by the federal government known as **Medicare Conditions of Participation**. Regular on-site reviews of agency functions and client care are conducted to recertify agencies in the Medicare and Medicaid programs.

HCFA ensures that home care benefits are paid according to federally established reimbursement guidelines. Home care agencies are required to complete an annual cost report. Federal regulations specifically outline the types of costs included in this document, which HCFA uses to set Medicare reimbursement rates. Medicare reimburses providers of services up to an established regional limit, or **cost limit**. HCFA confirms that home care agencies comply with regulations for accurate and complete documentation within the cost report.

HCFA contracts with insurance companies that act as regional intermediaries for certified home care agencies. These intermediaries are responsible for processing and paying appropriate Medicare claims. Intermediaries can request medical record documentation from an agency to substantiate the appropriateness of Medicare reimbursement for healthcare services provided.

Display 1-2:
The Survey Process

STAFF INTERVIEW

During the staff interview, a reviewer is likely to question a home care nurse on the following matters:

* The processes of the agency for providing home care and planning services
* Cooperation with physicians, pharmacies, ancillary services, and community service organizations
* Methods of instructing clients and lay caregivers about procedures, including equipment management, special diets, and wound care
* Documentation methods
* Interventions performed in the home: emergency procedures, medication administration, disposal of hazardous materials, etc.
* Knowledge of safety measures
  * Equipment safety
  * Fire and electrical safety
  * Handling and disposal of hazardous drugs and waste materials
  * Adverse drug reactions
  * Personal safety

CLIENT VISITS

During visits to clients chosen at random, the reviewer will examine the following:

* Environmental safety
* Ability of clients and lay caregivers to conduct procedures taught to them by the home care nurse
* A client's awareness of rights and responsibilities and the ability to file complaints
* The ancillary services currently provided to clients, to determine their appropriateness or whether additional services are needed
* Infection control procedures
* The nurse's vehicle and bag for appropriate supplies and materials and for proper disposal of waste materials

JOINT COMMISSION ON ACCREDITATION OF HEALTHCARE ORGANIZATIONS AND COMMUNITY HEALTH ACCREDITATION PROGRAM

Many home care agencies also participate in voluntary accreditation processes offered by the **Joint Commission on Accreditation of Healthcare Organizations (JCAHO)** and the **Community Health Accreditation Program (CHAP)**. These organizations have developed more rigorous standards than the minimum quality requirements of the federal and state governments. These standards focus upon provision of clinical services and organizational processes that impact clinical services. Accreditation by one of these organizations represents an additional commitment by an agency to quality care.

◆ Reimbursement

Reimbursement issues are particularly important in today's healthcare industry, and are changing the access to and delivery of services. Reimbursement has helped home care to flourish in recent years, since it is usually more cost-effective than hospitalization and other methods of treatment. An industry-wide shift to providing services in the home that were once available only in hospitals largely can be traced to economic difficulties experienced by Medicare in recent decades. Table 1-1 outlines different methods of reimbursement.

TABLE 1-1. *Methods of Healthcare Reimbursement*

	METHOD DESCRIPTION	INCENTIVE TO PROVIDERS	EXAMPLE	PAYOR TYPES
HOSPITALS				
DRG	Flat reimbursement based on diagnosis	Encourages early hospital discharges	$7,000 for appendectomy	Medicare, Managed care
Per diem	Flat reimbursement for every hospital day	Encourages increased hospital stay	$900 per day	Managed care
HOME CARE				
Per visit	Rates for different types of home visits	Encourages high visit utilization	RN $90; PT $95; MSW $110	Medicare, Private insurance, Managed care
Per episode	Flat reimbursement for specified period	Encourages low visit utilization	$2500 for 120 day episode	Proposed by Medicare
Capitation or risk contracting	Flat reimbursement for all members of a health plan to meet all contracted health needs of membership population	Encourages providers to decrease demand of contracted health services through health promotion, early identification, and intervention with high-risk members; encourages decreased utilization of services	$6 per member per month for all home care services needed by population	Managed care

PROSPECTIVE PAYMENT REIMBURSEMENT

Medicare expenditures for hospital care increased by 19% in the early 1980s. Congress responded with the Tax Equity and Fiscal Responsibility Act of 1983, an attempt to impose a system to control the rapidly escalating tax burden used to support medical costs in the United States. This legislation implemented a **prospective payment system**. Under this system, Medicare reimburses hospitals a flat fee based on a client's diagnosis, whether the client remains hospitalized for three days or thirty days. Through **diagnosis related groups** (DRGs), hospitals are motivated to release clients as soon as possible.

The prospective payment reimbursement system has changed the face of healthcare throughout the United States. Physicians and organizations are rewarded with decreased costs and increased profits for keeping clients well and out of the healthcare system. This system encourages a distinctly different paradigm for providers who have traditionally focused upon the treatment, rather than the prevention, of illness. Prospective payment reimbursement has the opportunity to orient the healthcare industry increasingly toward health promotion. Home care, with its tradition of supporting wellness behaviors and empowering clients to manage their health independently, has the opportunity to thrive in this changing environment.

PER VISIT REIMBURSEMENT

Medicare, Medicaid, and most private insurers reimburse home care services on a per visit basis when agencies meet specified criteria. Medicare reimbursement for home care is based upon the actual costs of providing services, up to predetermined cost limits for a region. Medicare regulations specify appropriate and reimbursable costs. Private healthcare insurers occasionally pay established charges per visit, but often contract with home care agencies for price discounts on visits to beneficiaries.

The per visit method of home care reimbursement has been the method most commonly used since the 1960s. Efforts are now underway, however, to change the per visit method of reimbursement, stemming from the belief that it encourages inefficiency and overutilization. Services may be provided unnecessarily, inflating overall healthcare costs.

PER EPISODE REIMBURSEMENT

In 1995, Medicare initiated a study to evaluate how a home care per episode or case rate reimbursement system impacts client care. Within this system, an agency receives a flat payment for all home care services provided to a client over a period of 120 days, regardless of the number of visits. Although reimbursement is not dependent upon the client's diagnosis, this system is similar to the prospective payment system Medicare uses to reimburse hospitals. "Many experts advocate a 'case rate' system, akin to the way Medicare pays hospitals. Under it, a flat amount would cover the whole course of treatment for each diagnosis—motivating providers to finish treatment quickly" (Anders & McGinley, 1997). This system continues to be tested for its efficiency. Before it is extended, and per episode reimbursement replaces the per visit system, Medicare must evaluate the health outcomes of beneficiaries served in the initial study.

CAPITATION AND RISK CONTRACTING

Medicare risk contracting began in the 1990s. In this scenario, Medicare contracts with insurance companies that have met established minimum qualifications to provide healthcare to Medicare beneficiaries. Individuals with Medicare coverage have the option to "sign out" of their Medicare benefit and sign up for a commercial managed care plan instead. These commercial insurance companies are obligated to provide, at a minimum, the same benefits provided by Medicare. In turn, Medicare reimburses the private insurance companies at a price 5% less than Medicare has historically spent on beneficiaries within a specified region. The private company earns profits by negotiating discounted rates with healthcare providers, controlling the use of healthcare services, and developing capitation contracts with health-care providers.

In capitation contracts, private insurers pay a flat dollar amount per health plan member to a healthcare provider on a monthly basis. The provider is responsible for all contracted services administered to that client population. For example, a hospital signs a capitated contract to provide all acute hospitalization services for clients signed to Acme Health Plan. Five thousand members belong to the plan, and the reimbursement fee per member is $150. The hospital therefore receives a monthly check from Acme for $75,000 (5,000 x $150). If the cost of providing acute care services to these clients exceeds $75,000 in one month, the hospital suffers a financial loss. If the total cost is less than $75,000, the hospital makes a profit.

Because they are not automatically paid for their services, healthcare providers who participate in capitation contracts accept some risk of financial loss. Capitation or risk contracting is becoming more prevalent. All types of healthcare providers are signing capitated contracts, including physicians, hospitals, laboratories, radiology centers, outpatient surgery centers, and home care agencies.

One drawback of this system is that healthcare providers may be tempted to withhold needed services from clients in an effort to save money. Failure to provide appropriate levels of care for clients, however, can actually result in increased costs and potential litigation for a home care agency. For example, home care personnel neglect to visit clients an appropriate number of times to address important issues in an attempt to cut costs. As a result, these clients become acutely ill. These clients need more home care services at greater costs to the agency than if the agency had treated them appropriately in the first place.

KEY CONCEPT

Under risk contracting and prospective payment reimbursement systems, healthcare providers may be tempted to withhold needed services from clients. Failure to provide appropriate levels of care for clients can actually result in increased costs, decreased profits, and potential litigation for the home care organization.

◆ Trends in Home Care

Several trends have contributed to the growth of the home care industry (Table 1-2). Improvements in technology and the pursuit of cost-effective health plans have successfully reduced overall healthcare expenditures primarily by decreasing the frequency and duration of hospitalizations. Home care agencies can now care for individuals with complex health needs instead. Demographic shifts, including an increasing older population and changes in the traditional family structure, are adding to the importance of home care as an option for clients in need of assistance. A sense of personal responsibility for health and participation from lay caregivers are influencing individuals to receive care at home, instead of from an institution. Future political and social changes may also positively influence the expansion of home care.

TECHNOLOGICAL ADVANCES

Technological advances have contributed to changes in the healthcare environment. They have enabled services once available only in hospital settings to be provided in the home as well. Such advancements have not only reduced overall healthcare costs, but also have dramatically improved the quality of life for millions of people. Technological advances are discussed in greater detail later in this chapter.

TABLE 1-2. *The Impact of National Trends on Home Care*

TREND	IMPACT
Technological advances in medical equipment	Advanced medical technologies have allowed clients previously required to remain in institutional settings to receive necessary healthcare services at home.
Increased demand for cost-effective heathcare options	The relative cost-effectiveness of home care has resulted in an increased demand for services.
Managed care plans	Increased enrollment in managed care plans is driving healthcare services out of institutional settings and into the home.
Graying of America	As the population ages, the incidence of chronic diseases that require home care interventions is expected to increase.
Changes in family status	The number of single-person households is growing, resulting in increased reliance on organizations such as home care agencies to provide care once performed by families.
Increased self-care responsibility	Individuals are taking greater responsibility for making healthcare choices. When possible, the majority of people choose to receive healthcare in their own homes versus an institutional setting.
Increased expections of lay caregivers	As healthcare shifts to nonclinical settings, the burden of care is shifting to lay caregivers. Home care nurses need to teach sometimes complicated healthcare concepts and procedures to these individuals.

COST-EFFECTIVE CARE

In response to the demands for cost-effective healthcare, home care has experienced tremendous growth in recent decades. The number of Medicare-certified home care agencies has grown from 1,753 in 1967 to approximately 8,747 in 1995 (HCFA, Office of Survey and Certification, 1995). Furthermore, home care employment experienced an annual growth rate of 16.4% from 1988 to 1993, as compared with 4.3% for health services overall and 2.8% for hospitals (Freeman, 1995). The enormous growth of home care can be attributed to its relative cost-effectiveness. In 1995, HCFA reported that the average hospitalization cost per day was $1,810 and the average skilled nursing facility daily cost was $293. The cost of a daily home care visit was $86 (Medical Economics, 1996).

Medicare

Under Medicare's prospective payment reimbursement system, home care has become the solution for clients discharged "quicker and sicker." According to HCFA, Office of the Actuary (February 6, 1995), Medicare spent $2 billion for home care services in 1988. Since then, Medicare has experienced significant increases in home care expenditures, ranging from 18% to 50% per year. In 1994, the total cost of home care visits to beneficiaries was $12.57 billion. The Medicare program projects 21.45 billion dollars in home care expenditures in the year 2000. HCFA dramatically increased surveillance efforts on home health agencies in 1997. This occurred in response to claims of fraudulent billing practices of some home health agencies. These efforts will ensure that the anticipated growth of home health services is consistent with Medicare guidelines.

KEY CONCEPT

Home care has experienced tremendous growth with the advent of prospective payment reimbursement. Home care assists clients discharged "quicker and sicker" from hospitals under this system to ensure that discharges are safe and that clients receive needed follow-up care.

Private Industry

Private industry also endured the effects of the astronomical rise in healthcare costs that Medicare experienced in the early 1980s. Businesses traditionally have been primary consumers of health insurance products, because many companies routinely pay a large portion of premiums for workers as part of their employee benefits packages. As Medicare began to scale back reimbursement, hospitals and physicians employed cost-shifting strategies to recover the losses they experienced through participation in government programs. They began charging higher rates for reimbursement to private insurance companies. The insurance companies, in turn, increased their rates, negatively affecting the budgets of many businesses that found large portions of their operating overhead eroded by the costs of employee healthcare. Industry fought back, demanding the creation of affordable insurance products.

Managed Care Plans

The demand from the business community to lower health insurance premiums for their employees resulted in a revolution in the healthcare industry. Insurance companies responded by developing managed care plans, including **health maintenance organizations (HMOs)** and **preferred provider organizations (PPOs)**. HMOs and PPOs function under a service arrangement in which clients agree to receive medical care from specific physicians and services in designated facilities in return for lower copays or premiums. Utilization review physicians and nurses employed by these groups review the medical necessity of services provided to insurance beneficiaries. They require preapproval of physician and nursing interventions for clients in an attempt to control costs. Hospitalizations are reserved for emergencies and necessary procedures; lower levels of care (e.g., skilled nursing facilities, home care) are considered cheaper alternatives to hospitalization and are used whenever possible. Utilization control nurses investigate prices that various healthcare providers charge to ensure that providers are using the least expensive services that meet quality criteria. Many insurance companies negotiate contracts with healthcare providers; the insurance companies receive discounted prices from healthcare providers in return for the promise of a large volume of clients.

Enrollment in managed care plans has increased significantly in the last twenty years. Since 1980, participation in such health plans has quintupled from fewer than ten million members to more than fifty million (Goldsmith, Goran, & Nackel, 1995). Physicians who participate in managed care plans receive various controls and financial incentives to keep healthcare costs down. They avoid expensive hospitalizations, if possible. Declining hospital rates reflect the influence of managed care plans throughout the country. Hospital discharges are expected to decline 26%, from 32.5 million in 1995 to 24.2 million in 1999. Currently, U.S. hospitals have approximately 1.2 million hospital beds; the number of beds estimated to be needed by 1999 is 424,000 (Jenkins, 1995).

Managed care organizations consider home care to be an effective alternative to hospitalization. When hospitalization is unavoidable, utilization reviewers discharge clients from the hospital earlier and with greater assurance if qualified home care staff are available to provide the necessary follow-up procedures. Early problem identification and intervention by home care staff can reduce the incidence of rehospitalizations for clients discharged prematurely. The skills of home care professionals have evolved to provide services to highly acute client populations as well. An extensive discussion on managed care is found in Chapter 3.

KEY CONCEPT

Managed care companies use home care services extensively to prevent rehospitalizations for clients quickly discharged after their stays, and to avoid hospitalizations altogether.

THE GRAYING OF AMERICA

Another trend influencing the home care industry is the country's changing demographics—the "Graying of America." Aging baby boomers (those born between 1946 and 1964) will begin to retire in the year 2010. By 2030, persons aged sixty and older will number more than eighty-five million; the number of persons aged eighty-five and older will be approximately eight million (Fig. 1-1). The number of older minorities is expected to increase rapidly as well. While the number of older white Americans is anticipated to increase by 97% in the next thirty years, the older black population

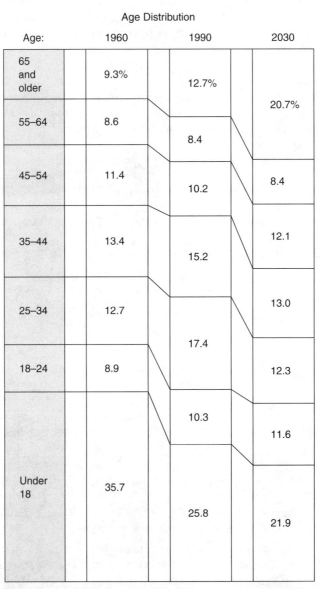

Age Distribution

Age:	1960	1990	2030
65 and older	9.3%	12.7%	20.7%
55–64	8.6	8.4	
45–54	11.4	10.2	8.4
35–44	13.4	15.2	12.1
25–34	12.7		13.0
18–24	8.9	17.4	12.3
		10.3	11.6
Under 18	35.7	25.8	21.9

Figure 1-1. The number of older adults in the United States has grown rapidly over the last 40 years. By the year 2030, adults aged 65 and older are expected to constitute more than one-fifth of the American population.

is expected to grow by 265% and the older Hispanic population by 530% (Coccimiglio, 1997). This trend significantly affects the healthcare industry, since minority groups generally have more health problems than white Americans.

As they make up a greater proportion of the population, the political influence of older adults will grow. Businesses will begin to gear products and services to meet the demands of older consumers. The home care industry can expect to benefit from these anticipated demographic shifts, because it provides services predominantly to older clients. These clients are more likely to suffer from chronic illnesses and to prefer to receive necessary healthcare services in their own homes when possible.

CHANGES IN FAMILY STATUS

The family continues to change. Single-person households are no longer a rarity. Divorce is a common social phenomenon, and blended and single-parent families are regularly encountered. As society becomes more mobile, people are geographically distanced from their extended family. Fewer possibilities for family-based support are thus available in case of illness. Sick clients separated from their loved ones often require outside services to receive necessary care. The number of older people needing assistance with basic tasks from home care is expected to double between 1990 and 2030, increasing from approximately seven to fourteen million (Government Forecasts Sharp Growth for Health Care, 1993).

K E Y   C O N C E P T

Demographic changes, including an expanding older population and a decrease in family-based support, forecast increasing home care needs for the future.

SELF-CARE RESPONSIBILITY

People are becoming more actively involved in making their own health choices, a positive development for the home care industry. When possible, most people prefer to receive care in their own homes rather than in an institution. People feel personally accountable for their own well-being and are less trusting of the medical establishment's ability to treat and prevent illness. Individuals are demanding to participate in their medical care and are developing a more sophisticated understanding of their healthcare choices. Many industries have flourished in response to the changing attitudes of society. For example, health books are increasing in popularity, vitamin sales are soaring, and people are using alternative medicine to resolve problems. Dr. Jack Kevorkian, a Michigan physician, has generated both tremendous public controversy and a loyal following in his campaign to assist those with progressively debilitating diseases to commit suicide.

Legislators have responded to the demands of their constituents and have established legal protections for the rights of individuals to make their own healthcare choices. Federal law requires healthcare providers to inform clients of their right to execute an advanced directive to predetermine health choices in the event that they become unable to communicate their wishes. Individuals want to make healthcare decisions themselves, instead of delegating them to impersonal healthcare policies or to the personal preferences of their physicians. As individuals continue to make their own healthcare choices, home care will grow. Most people are glad to have the opportunity to remain in the comfortable surroundings of their own homes while being treated for their illnesses, and home care makes this possible.

LAY CAREGIVERS

As nonclinical settings provide more healthcare services, the burden of care for the sick is shifting to lay caregivers. The relationship between a lay caregiver and a home care client varies. The lay caregiver can be a family member, friend, neighbor, church volunteer, paid caregiver, or owner of a board and care facility. One important characteristic shared by most of these lay caregivers, however, is a lack of formal training in the provision of healthcare services.

Home care professionals often rely upon lay caregivers to assist them in carrying out established medical treatment plans. Nurses must teach home care clients and their lay caregivers to perform the interventions designed to improve health or to prevent further deterioration. Clients and lay caregivers often require instruction in the scheduling, effects, and side effects of medications, early symptom identification and necessary follow-up measures, therapeutic diets, skin and wound care, safe performance of daily activities, and health promotion. Lay caregivers must sometimes learn complicated procedures, including sterile dressing changes, care of a tracheostomy, and administration of injectable or intravenous medications. Therapists often help lay caregivers learn to assist clients with exercises designed to regain strength and function and to maintain safety with mobilization. Social workers inform lay caregivers about accessing available community resources to help clients with financial, legal, or psychosocial needs. The success of a treatment plan and the ability of a client to remain in a nonclinical setting often depends upon the aptitude of lay caregivers and their willingness to accept responsibilities.

Lay caregivers struggle with many issues in fulfilling their roles. The healthcare system can be extremely intimidating. Lay caregivers often feel they do not have the necessary knowledge and skills to assist home care clients appropriately, and are afraid they will cause more harm than good. They sometimes refuse to assist with treatment plans out of fear that they will seriously injure clients.

Family Members as Lay Caregivers

Often, family members act as lay caregivers for home care clients. These individuals sometimes accept these roles by default when other options are cost prohibitive, unavailable, or undesirable. A variety of dynamics can interfere with or enhance a client's care when a family member acts as a lay caregiver. Dysfunctional family relationships are likely to worsen and can exacerbate a client's illness (Display 1-3). Substance abuse, affecting 10.5% of the American population, or 19.2 million individuals (West, 1997), can significantly affect a client's or lay caregiver's compliance with a treatment plan. Even within highly functional families (Display 1-4), the burden of providing healthcare to a spouse, parent, sibling, or other relative can be

Display 1-3:
Dysfunctional Dynamics in the Home

Often, dysfunctional patterns of interaction exist in home care settings. These patterns can either be long-standing or can develop in response to illness and disease. They can negatively affect an individual's ability to work, maintain, and nourish relationships; to keep one's identity; and to run a home. The most common dysfunctional dynamics that affect the delivery of home care service include the following:

Triangulation: difficulties, stress, or intensity between two people in a relationship that necessitates the ongoing involvement of a third person, object, issue, or group in an attempt to reduce tension. A *triangle* thus forms that stabilizes the system by reducing anxiety and tension through avoidance of direct communication.

> EXAMPLE: *Mr. and Mrs. Lewis cannot speak to one another without getting into an argument. They depend on their daughter, Phyllis, to relay their messages to each other.*

Covert roles: an individual assumes a role in order to improve a dysfunctional relationship; unfortunately, as the role is reinforced, it maintains dysfunction instead. Typical covert roles include the *mascot*, who smooths over conflicts with humor; the *family hero*, who is visibly successful and provides self-worth to the family; the *scapegoat*, whose problems or negative behavior provide a distraction and focus; and the *lost child*, who gets little attention and remains in the background.

> EXAMPLE: *Eric, a lost child, cares continually for his ailing mother, who never seems very interested in or appreciative of his efforts. Eric's mother never stops praising his older brother Tom, a successful doctor, who is the family hero.*

Unwritten rules: certain, particular rules that guide thoughts, feelings, and behaviors in relationships.

> EXAMPLE: *Some common examples of unwritten covert rules are: "Ask Mom first for what you want and she'll talk Dad into it"; "Don't talk about Aunt Martha's drinking"; and "It's not OK to get angry."*

(Adapted from Klebanoff, N. A. & Smith, N. M. [1997]. Lippincott's guide to behavior management in home care. *Philadelphia: Lippincott-Raven Publishers.*)

emotionally traumatic. When a client requires assistance with common activities of daily living, such as toileting or bathing, family members sometimes feel awkward and uncomfortable assisting their loved one with these functions.

Illness can cause major shifts in family roles, sometimes resulting in emotional turmoil for both home care clients and their caregivers. A 1996 study explored home care problems experienced by family caregivers of stroke survivors following hospital

Display 1-4:
Functional Relationship Interactions

Functional relationships adapt to changes and are not bound by rigid roles and expectations. Functional dynamics within a relationship are characterized by the following:

◆ Not keeping score or justifying one's behavior based on the past behavior of another
◆ Accepting personal responsibility, not assigning blame, and actively trying to solve problems
◆ Talking from the heart instead of lecturing
◆ Being nonjudgmental about the perceptions and feelings of others
◆ Being rigorously honest
◆ Keeping behavior and being separate
◆ Being persistent
◆ Regarding others with positive esteem
◆ Interacting within the family unit and with the community

(Adapted from Klebanoff, N. A. & Smith N. M. [1997]. Lippincott's guide to behavior management in home care. *Philadelphia: Lippincott-Raven Publishers.)*

discharge. Many of the stroke survivors experienced changes in their basic personalities, including functional, cognitive, and emotional disturbances. These changes caused tremendous stress for stroke survivors as well as for their caregivers (Grant, 1996). Data from a similar study suggest that such stressful changes in family dynamics can also result in increased health risks for lay caregivers themselves (Lichtenberg & Gibbons, 1992).

THE FUTURE

If any type of healthcare reform occurs, home care could experience significant growth. In 1994, President Clinton proposed a national health insurance plan that would have significantly changed the entire structure of the healthcare industry. Although this overhaul of the healthcare system failed to happen, future governmental actions could effect important change. Democrats and Republicans agree that long-term spending reductions in Medicare are necessary for the program to continue to meet the needs of future generations. "The $219 billion-a-year program is projected to grow at about 10 percent per year, twice the per capita growth of national income. The Medicare trustees' latest report shows that revenues from payroll taxes earmarked for hospital coverage will be insufficient by 2001" (Meyer, December 5, 1996). Attempts to reform Medicare will be a highly political process. "The elderly make up 20 percent of voters, and they are particularly focused on healthcare because of the high-decibel debate over their treasured government benefits. More than one-fifth of senior citizens polled said healthcare or Medicare is one of the top two issues that will influence their vote" (Meyer, October 5, 1996). Politically active senior citizens may force politicians to include long-term care in their election platforms.

Some type of healthcare change may occur, and cost-effective home care is likely to benefit from such reform.

◆ Technology and Home Care

Entrepreneurial healthcare companies have observed the changing healthcare environment and have developed technology to simplify services for the home previously provided only in hospital settings. Technological advances have enabled more clients to receive necessary healthcare in the community. "Nearly every method of hospital or other institutional treatment that can be made portable can be provided at home. One of the most rapidly growing areas of medical technology is the engineering and production of medical equipment tailored for use in the home" (Freeman, 1995, p. 9). In response to the deinstitutionalization of healthcare, technology has been developed for many disease processes.

MATERNAL AND NEWBORN CARE

Maternal and newborn care is one clinical area in which rapid technological advancements have flourished. Home uterine monitors allow women at risk for preterm labor, who were previously required to spend several weeks in hospitals, to remain at home until delivery (Fig. 1-2). Clients apply belts around their abdomens and telephonically transmit information from the devices to a central station where trained

Figure 1-2. Under the guidance of home care nurses, women at risk for preterm labor are able to remain at home until their delivery dates through the use of uterine monitors.

clinicians, many miles away, evaluate levels of uterine activity. Experienced obstetric nurses solicit additional information from these clients during intermittent visits and phone calls. Physicians use this information to adjust the medical treatment plan as needed. Tocolytic infusion therapy for expectant mothers is sometimes used in home care to reduce uterine activity and to prevent premature labor. Nurses must carefully monitor clients undergoing this therapy to ensure positive outcomes. These advances in technology have successfully delayed premature births in high-risk clients and have eliminated the need for the extended hospitalizations required in the past. Financial and emotional burdens for high-risk women and their families have thus been reduced, since these women can remain in their own homes.

Home phototherapy allows more families to take home their newborns with hyperbilirubinemia. Families learn how to place their infants under the lights, provide adequate hydration for their infants, and patch their infants' eyes to facilitate safe reduction in blood bilirubin levels. Home care nurses determine daily laboratory levels and perform assessments to monitor the effectiveness of home therapy.

CARDIAC CARE

Cardiac care has also benefited from advances in home care technology. Homebound clients are no longer burdened with travel to a hospital or outpatient clinic to undergo an ECG test. Portable ECG equipment allows nurses to perform the test directly in a client's home. Through telephone linkages nurses send findings immediately to a physician who interprets the results. The physician and the home care nurse thus can evaluate chest pain in a cardiac client immediately. Nurses can also provide preadmission work-ups for debilitated clients before surgery, and can perform intermittent assessments on cardiac clients to monitor their conditions.

TELEMONITORING

Telemonitoring, a relatively new technology, has the potential to revolutionize the provision of healthcare to high-risk clients with complex conditions. A specially designed computer is placed in the home of a client and in the home care agency or physician office. This system measures the client's vital signs and weight, records symptoms, and allows visual and oral interaction between the client and a physician or nurse over the monitor.

Telemonitoring is particularly useful for clients with complex medical regimens who require monitoring throughout the day. It has successfully contributed to the management of chronic diseases and conditions such as diabetes, AIDS, asthma, congestive heart failure, and high risk pregnancy. Monitoring and caring for clients with these conditions are much more cost-effective in their homes than in hospitals or healthcare facilities (Young, 1996).

EMERGENCY RESPONSE SYSTEMS

Emergency response systems have been widely used in home care for several years and have greatly enhanced the safety of many clients. These systems, which provide

Application to Home Care Practice
Telemonitoring in the Home

Mr. Davis, a diabetic client with unstable congestive heart failure and chronic obstructive pulmonary disease, is hospitalized frequently. He is noncompliant with his extensive medication regimen of 25 medication doses within a 24-hour period. A telemonitoring system is ideal for Mr. Davis. His home care nurse or physician can regularly monitor his drug compliance, frequently measure his vital signs, and identify early signs of exacerbation to provide quick and effective interventions.

a mechanism for clients to call for help if they cannot get to a phone, assist individuals who live alone or are alone in their homes for part of the day. Clients typically wear a medallion around the neck or wrist. If they fall or experience immobilizing chest pain or dyspnea, clients push a button on the medallion and thus initiate an emergency response—a call either to an ambulance or to notify a lay caregiver to check on them. Normally, operators receive initial distress calls and attempt to phone clients to ensure that they have not activated the system accidentally. Some emergency response systems have voice units that enable operators and clients to talk without the use of telephone receivers.

Distress signals are also activated when clients fail to reset units within established time frames. Such features provide additional safety checks when clients are unable to initiate distress signals themselves (e.g., when they are rendered unconscious or immobilized from a stroke or fall). If a client fails to push the reset button on the machine, a system operator phones to find out whether the client has simply forgotten or requires assistance. If a client does not respond to a call, the established response is initiated. These devices greatly protect the safety of home care clients, allowing them to be monitored without requiring hospitalization or institutionalization.

RESPIRATORY AND IV CARE

Home respiratory services have grown rapidly, largely due to advancements in technology. In 1989, $315 million were spent on home respiratory services (excluding equipment costs). By 1994, expenses increased to $1 billion and are projected to continue to grow astronomically, with expenses expected to surpass $2 billion by 1999 (Brown-West, 1996). Ventilators have become sophisticated, mobile, and easy for lay caregivers to operate, making incredible differences in the lives of ventilator-dependent clients. Thousands of individuals whose conditions once forced them to live in institutional settings are now able to live at home with the love and support of family and friends. The transportability of ventilator units allows many adults to work and to lead active, productive lives. Improved technology in ventilators and the creation of apnea monitors have enabled even chronically ill children to grow up in their own homes with the nurturing of loving parents and siblings (Fig. 1-3).

Figure 1-3. Advances in respiratory equipment allow this child to remain at home with her family while receiving nursing care.

Oxygen units are available that are extremely lightweight, giving even the highly respiratory-compromised individual the opportunity to be as mobile and independent as possible. Pulse oxymetry units were once so large they had to be rolled around on a cart. Today, hand held units enable home care nurses to check a client's oxygenation status in a noninvasive way (Carroll, 1997).

A significant example of advanced healthcare technology is the development of compact intravenous infusion pumps (Fig. 1-4). Previously, infusion pumps were bulky, heavy, and complicated to use. Infusion pumps the size of a human palm, and others that are disposable, have recently been released, permitting lay caregivers to provide safe, effective infusion therapy in nonclinical settings. Pharmacists and home care clinicians can program these devices for physician-approved dosages and infusion rates. Programming access codes within the pumps prevent clients and their lay caregivers from altering prescribed rates. Technology is currently under development that will allow programming of intravenous pumps from remote locations (Robbins, 1996).

Occasionally, clients can self-dose through a pump. For example, clients receiving continuous subcutaneous morphine infusion may occasionally need additional medication to control their pain. Infusion pumps designed for pain management allow clients to administer a bolus of pain medication. To protect clients from overdosing, the pump is programmed to limit the frequency of bolus delivery.

Tremendous advances in intravenous access devices have reduced the incidence of infection, and the devices are now easy for healthcare professionals, clients, and lay caregivers to use. New therapies are being tested in the home each year. Clients weary of hospitalization have influenced physicians and home care agencies to push established limits and to provide unorthodox treatments at home. Clients treated unconventionally often progress much better than expected in their own surroundings.

Figure 1-4. The home care nurse instructs a client on the use of an ambulatory infusion pump. (Photo courtesy of SIMS Deltec, Inc., St. Paul, MN.)

◆ Home Care Nursing Practice

Home care nursing is its own specialty and is one of the least understood practices in the healthcare system. Home care nurses have the most comprehensive knowledge of the health of their clients. When they mandate home care services, physicians routinely delegate the management of care to nurses, who perform extensive evaluations of homebound clients, recommend to physicians any additional services needed (e.g., physical therapy, home health aides, social services), and oversee entire treatment plans to ensure all goals are met. Home care nurses are responsible for maintaining the flow of communication. They must keep all disciplines involved in client care abreast of progress and alert to any changes in condition. They need to communicate with third party payors through precise documentation to justify services. Nurses must relay information to physicians and ensure appropriate involvement of community resources.

RAPPORT WITH FAMILIES AND LAY CAREGIVERS

The ability to work with families and other lay caregivers is fundamental to successful home care practice. Viewing lay caregivers as responsible participants in their clients' health is a foreign concept for many hospital nurses, who often have little or no contact with them when caring for acutely ill clients. Home care nurses, however, must involve families in the care of clients and recognize that conflicts in the home can significantly influence the course of treatment. Nurses must depend upon lay caregivers to learn and to carry out the medical treatment plan. Learning how to interact with these lay caregivers is an important skill for home care nurses to master.

INDEPENDENCE

Home care nursing is highly independent and distinct from other nursing specialties. Typically, home care nurses are responsible for a caseload of clients throughout their care. They must recognize the need for ancillary services, such as physical therapy, occupational therapy, and social services, and thoroughly understand indications for appropriate referrals to these services. Although treatment plans require a physician's authorization, physicians usually base plans on the recommendations of home care nurses and incorporate their suggestions with few revisions.

The independent nature of home care attracts many nurses to it; however, a great deal of stress often accompanies the high level of independence during employment. Although home care nurses are more independent than nurses in other settings in deciding the treatment of their clients, they also must adjust to working individually without regular peer contact and support (see Chapter 2).

KEY CONCEPT

Home care nursing is an independent practice, requiring a distinct set of skills to care for clients appropriately.

ACCOUNTABILITY

Home care nurses are highly accountable for the accurate reimbursement of services for their clients. They must be thoroughly knowledgeable of the coverage guidelines of various third party payors. Payors often review the documentation of home care nurses to determine whether a client's condition warrants the care provided. Insurance companies pay only for those services that meet coverage criteria as indicated in the documentation. Medicare, for example, holds home care agencies liable for the cost of services denied upon review. Medicare expects agency staff to be knowledgeable of the circumstances in which they can receive reimbursement. Because they perform the initial assessment of clients and primarily determine the entire treatment plan, home care nurses need a thorough awareness of coverage guidelines—or their agencies may suffer tremendous financial losses.

Home Care Vs. Hospital:
Nursing Practice

Issue	Home Care	Hospital
Role of Lay Caregivers	Nurses depend largely upon available lay caregivers to implement plans of care for clients.	Nurses perform interventions largely independent of lay caregivers.
Accountability	Nurses are accountable for developing and managing multidisciplinary plans of care and ensuring coordination of services.	Nurses are accountable for performing appropriate interventions during designated work shifts and communicating necessary information that requires follow-up.
Duration of Care	Nurses are responsible for an assigned caseload of clients throughout the course of their home care lengths of stay.	Nurse are responsible for assigned clients during designated work shifts.
Reimbursement	Nurses need a thorough understanding of reimbursement for services rendered and of documentation supporting these requirements.	Nurses have no associated responsibility.
Adaptability	Nurses must adapt and be able to perform interventions in a variety of environmental circumstances.	Nurses work in standardized and controlled environments.
Type of Practice	Nurses require generalized practice knowledge and capabilities.	Nurses have more opportunities for specialization.
Ability to Educate	Nurses must know how to educate clients and lay caregivers. Clients and lay caregivers must be able to implement plans of care independently due to lack of available professional healthcare personnel.	Nurses place less emphasis on educating clients, because professionals conduct necessary clinical interventions around the clock.
Support	Nurses have limited contact with professional peers for interaction and support.	Nurses have regular access to peers for interaction and support.

ADAPTABILITY

Adaptability to a variety of settings is essential for home care nurses. Each client's home is as different as the individuals who live there. Some homes are conducive to the easy care of a client. Others significantly challenge nurses to give services consistent with appropriate infection control and safety measures. For example, hospital nurses are used to working in clean, well-lit rooms. In home care, however, simple routines become complicated when they are conducted in poor lighting, when reaching across a queen-sized bed, or while being observed by a large dog (Carr, 1991).

KNOWLEDGE

Home care nurses must possess solid knowledge of all aspects of general nursing practice. In large medical centers or clinics, nurses often work in specialty units (e.g., oncology, orthopedics, renal, cardiac, pediatrics). Working within these environments, nurses are able to develop in-depth knowledge of disease processes associated with these specialties. In home care, however, agencies assign nurses based on geographic proximity, not by area of specialty. One home care nurse may be responsible for several clients within a specific geographic region in which multiple diagnoses from various specialties are found.

TEACHING SKILLS

Teaching plays a tremendous role in home care (see Chapter 10). Education is clearly one of the most important interventions home care nurses perform. A nurse is normally present in a client's home for one to four hours per week. For the remaining 164 hours, the client and lay caregivers must understand critical information and manage the disease process independently. Often, the most important step for clients and lay caregivers to master is knowing when to call nurses for help or advice. For example, a nurse visits a diabetic client once or twice a week, but the client can experience serious complications of the disease process anytime. This client must be able to recognize the early symptoms of a problem and know the early interventions to avoid serious complications.

KEY CONCEPT

Client and lay caregiver education is crucial in the home care setting because the nurse provides a minimal amount of clinical supervision in the home. The client and lay caregiver must understand critical information to manage the disease process independently.

ORIENTATION TO HOME CARE

Home care nursing is complicated. Nurses who enter home care practice can find it overwhelming and different from what they initially expected. Independence, broad accountability, the need to understand community resources and indications for ancillary services, pressures from managed care companies, heavy documentation requirements, client/caregiver conflicts, and productivity expectations create significant stressors for the new home care nurse. Effective education and orientation to the field are necessary to ensure a nurse's successful practice in the home. Display 1-5 is a typical program for orienting a nurse new to a home care agency.

Display 1-5:
Orientation to Home Care Nursing

A typical orientation to a home care agency includes the following processes:

- Explanation of the agency's philosophy of care, standards of practice, place within the community, and provision of services
- Distribution of the agency's policies and procedures manual. Nurses are requested to read the manual and to sign and return a form stating that they have read and understand the terms outlined within it.
- Review of documentation forms, visit reports, treatment plan forms, time cards, and other paperwork
- Discussion of ancillary services, referrals, access to suppliers and other vendors, and reliance on community organizations for support
- Review of safety measures to consider for clients, lay caregivers, and nurses themselves when providing care in the home
- Assignment of nurses to preceptors for further skill development

Preceptorship

A **preceptor**, or mentor, is very helpful to a nurse's orientation process. Preceptors are individuals who guide new home care nurses through the learning process. They oversee the learner's progress, providing assistance as needed. Preceptors can help nurses adapting to home care through a period of reality shock by providing expert advice on learning to problem-solve difficult situations independently.

Preceptors can give useful tips about the provision of effective clinical services in the home. Basic information—about accessing supplies, submitting documentation, coordinating client schedules to reduce travel time, and introducing oneself to a new client—helps to advance nurses from learners to independent practitioners. This assistance decreases burnout, improves client care, and increases job satisfaction.

KEY CONCEPT

Preceptors are extremely beneficial to nurses new to home care practice. They help to decrease burnout experienced by nurses. Preceptors contribute to improving nurses' interpersonal relationships, enhancing their client care skills, and increasing their level of job satisfaction.

Preceptor roles can be formal or informal within a home care agency. Experienced clinical nurses, staff development employees, or clinical supervisors usually fill these roles. These individuals should actively introduce new team members to everyone in the agency, educating nurses about each person's role in the organization. This instruction is extremely beneficial to new employees in gaining an understanding of internal resources and in facilitating positive interpersonal relationships. Good preceptors exhibit the qualities listed in Display 1-6.

Display 1-6:
Qualities of a Good Preceptor

- ◆ Solid clinical skills
- ◆ Positive attitude
- ◆ Effective communication skills
- ◆ Thorough grasp of home care concepts
- ◆ Problem-solving capabilities
- ◆ Good rapport with clients, families, physicians, and other employees
- ◆ Awareness of community resouces
- ◆ Empathy
- ◆ Knowledgeable documentation skills

Preceptors need to give nurses honest feedback regarding their performance, evaluating them for competency in skills conducted regularly in the home care setting. Such skills include programming portable I.V. pumps, performing venipunctures, and appropriately transporting laboratory specimens. A preceptor who finds a nurse's skills to be lacking can facilitate remedial training for the nurse to ensure that home care clients receive high standards of care.

Preceptors also help to acclimate nurses to a new organizational culture. A home care agency expresses its values and mission directly and indirectly to a new employee in many ways. New home care nurses observe an agency's methods of conflict resolution with clients and staff, relationships with physicians and community organizations, and deployment of resources to gain a better sense of the conditions under which they are expected to work.

KEY CONCEPT

Preceptors should introduce new team members to everyone in the home care agency, educating nurses about each person's function. This knowledge enhances understanding of internal resources and facilitates positive interpersonal relationships.

◆ Summary

Healthcare has experienced tremendous changes over the past several years, owing to Medicare cost-containment strategies and the advent of managed care companies. Experts predict further dramatic changes within the industry in the near future, as healthcare continues to shift to less expensive settings. Home care has grown in significance because of changes in technology, economics, demographics, and public interest in health. The role of home care nurses is central to the provision of care. Home care nursing is a unique clinical specialty, and nurses entering its practice need to develop a specific set of skills to enable the comprehensive provision of services to clients in this care setting. A preceptor program can assist individuals to fulfill their roles by reducing burnout successfully, improving client care, and increasing job satisfaction. Home care nursing is an exciting, rewarding profession that helps to meet many healthcare needs consistent with the values of its customers. It addresses many demands placed upon today's healthcare system and promises to be an integral specialty within the nursing profession for years to come.

References and Bibliography

Anders, G. & McGinley, L. Cost of medicare home visits explodes. *Wall Street Journal*, (March 6, 1997), p. A9.

Ark, P.D. & Nies, M. (1996). Knowledge and skills of the home health care nurse. *Home Healthcare Nurse, 14*(4), 293–297.

Backer, B. (1993). Lillian Wald: Connecting caring with activism. *Nursing and Healthcare, 14*(3), 122–129.

Bradley, P.J. & Alpers, R. (1996). Home healthcare nurses should regain their family focus. *Home Healthcare Nurse, 14*(4), 281–288.

Brown-West, C. (1996). Washington overview. Respiratory home care services are expanding. *AARC Times, 20*(5), 8, 88.

Caie-Lawrence, J., Peploski, J. & Russell, J. (1995). Training needs of home healthcare nurses. *Home Healthcare Nurse, 13*(2), 53–61.

Carr, P. (1991). A whole different world. *Home Healthcare Nurse, 9*(4), 6–7.

Carroll, P. (1997). Using pulse oximetry in the home. *Home Healthcare Nurse, 15*(2), 88–95.

Clemen-Stone, S., Eigsti, D.G. & McGuire, S.L. (1995). *Comprehensive community health nursing: Family, aggregate and community practice* (4th ed.). St. Louis: C.V. Mosby.

Coccimiglio, G. (1997). The uniformed elderly: A challenge for home care. *Caring Magazine, 14*(1), 12–14.

DeMeneses, M. & Perry, G. (1993). The plight of caregivers. *Home Healthcare Nurse, 11*(4), 10–14.

Donahue, M.P. (1985). *Nursing, the finest art: An illustrated history.* St. Louis: C.V. Mosby.

Fink, S. (1995). The influence of family resources and family demands on the strains and well-being of caregiving families. *Nursing Research, 44*(3), 139–146.

Freeman, L. (1995). Home sweet home health care. *Monthly Labor Review, March, 118*(3), 3–11.

Gardner, M.S. (1936). *Public health nursing* (3rd ed.). New York: Macmillan.

Garver Mastrian, K., Ritter, C. & Deimling, G. (1996). Predictors of caregiver health strain. *Home Healthcare Nurse, 14*(3), 209–217.

Gavin, M.J., Haas, L.J., Pendleton, P.B., Street, J.W. & Wormald, A. (1996). Orienting a new graduate nurse to home healthcare. *Home Healthcare Nurse, 14*(5), 381–387.

Goldsmith, J., Goran, M. & Nackel, J. (1995). Managed care comes of age. *Healthcare Forum Journal, 38*(5), 14–24.

(1993). Government forecasts sharp growth for health care industry this year. *PT Bulletin, 8*(3), 48.

Grant, J. (1996). Home care problems experienced by stroke survivors and their family caregivers. *Home Healthcare Nurse, 14*(11), 893–902.

Harris, M.D. (1994). *Handbook of home care administration.* Gaithersburg, MD: Aspen Publishers.

Health Care Finance Administration (1995). *Number of Medicare-certified home care agencies by auspice, 1967–1995.* Washington, DC: Office of Survey and Certification.

Health Care Finance Administration (1995). *Medicare home health: Visits, clients and incurred expenditures for 1989–2000.* Washington, DC: Office of the Actuary Bureau of Data Management and Strategy.

Jenkins, R. (Ed.). (1995). Hospital inpatient days expected to decrease by 34 percent over next four-year period. *Healthcare Management Team Letter, 11*(6).

Joint Commission on Accreditation of Healthcare Organizations. (1995a). *Accreditation manual for home care, volume I: Standards.* Oakbrook Terrace, IL: Author.

Joint Commission on Accreditation of Healthcare Organizations. (1995b). *Accreditation manual for home care, volume I: Scoring guidelines.* Oakbrook Terrace, IL: Author.

Lichtenberg, P. & Gibbons, T.A. (1992). Geriatric rehabilitation and the older adult family caregiver. *Neurorehabilitation, 3*(1), 62–71.

Lowes, R.L. (1996). Housecalls: Better pay may bring them back. *Medical Economics, (73)*12, 140–142, 146–148.

Maynard, T. (1939). *The apostle of charity: The life of St. Vincent de Paul.* New York: Dial Press.

Meyer, H. (1996). Campaign 1996: The scenarios. *Hospitals & Health Networks, 70*(19), 39–44, 54.

Meyer, H. (1996). Senior bashing. *Hospitals & Health Networks, 70*(23), 39–44, 54.

National Association for Home Care (1995). *Uniform data set for home care & hospice.* Washington, DC: Author.

Robbins, D. (1996). Managing information technologies: Ethical concerns. *The Remington Report, 4*(6), 36–39.

Wald, L. (1915). *The house on Henry Street.* New York: Henry Holt & Co.

Young, H. (1996). Telemedicine's future in home care. *The Remington Report, 4*(6), 20–23.

Zerwekh, J. (1995). High-tech home care for nurses. *Home Healthcare Nurse, 13*(1), 9–14.

POST TEST

1. Explain the influence of the following individuals on home care nursing:

   a. St. Vincent de Paul and Mademoiselle Le Gras

   b. Florence Nightingale

   c. William Rathbone

   d. Lillian Wald and Mary Brewster

2. List four (4) regulatory bodies that have developed standards of quality for home care services.

3. Identify three trends that are significantly changing the home care industry.

4. Describe why home care nurses depend so heavily upon the participation and support of lay caregivers.

5. Explain how preceptors can help nurses make the transition from the acute care setting to the home care setting.

THINKING CRITICALLY IN HOME CARE

1. Explain what the decrease in hospital-based services and the growth of home care and community-based nursing mean for nursing and medical educational institutions in the United States.

2. Analyze how home care nursing practice contributes to a wellness-based model of care versus an illness-based model of care.

3. Determine how the nursing profession will evolve in the next 10 years. Infer how insurance companies will also develop over this period.

2

Comparison of Home and Acute Care Nursing

LEARNING OBJECTIVES

After completing this chapter the reader will be able to:

◆ Identify the differences in power and control in hospitals versus home care settings.

◆ Discuss issues related to the environment of care in hospitals and in the home.

◆ Review the personalized and holistic nature of home care and the therapeutic relationship between the client and the nurse.

◆ Discuss the generalist nature of home care practice.

◆ Evaluate reasons why home care practice requires excellent assessment skills.

◆ Identify special concerns for teaching in the home, and compare teaching in the home with teaching conducted in hospitals.

◆ Review the role of home care nurses in making referrals to community resources.

◆ Compare the relationships between nurses and clients' significant others in home care versus the hospital.

◆ Identify opportunities and difficulties for nurses in resolving stressful or emotional issues in home care.

KEY TERMS

Generalist	Personalization
Holism	Specialization

ome care nursing is very different from nursing services in other settings. Within hospitals, clinics, nursing homes, and physician offices, the
physical environment is designed for the sole purpose of giving efficient
care to clients. Supplies are readily available. Clients are usually in hospitals
for short periods only. A nurse's contact with an individual client may last for
only a shift. Nurses have few opportunities to establish effective, therapeutic
relationships with clients. Generally, the responsibility of nurses for their clients ends when they transfer clients to the next shift.

As discussed in Chapter 1, nurses who are making the transition to home
care from other nursing practices may experience "reality shock" when facing
its unique circumstances and conditions. Display 2-1 provides a typical schedule
for a hospital nurse; Display 2-2 shows a typical home care nurse's agenda. A
comparison of these schedules serves to enhance the reader's understanding
of the differences between these types of nursing practice and the challenges
that home care nurses face daily.

This chapter discusses issues that make the practice of nursing special in
home care. To highlight these particulars, this chapter compares home care
with traditional nursing care conducted in hospitals. Issues of power and control over the client's environment, sleep and activity schedules, and food
choices differ in these two settings. This discussion explores how such differences affect nursing practice. It also includes an analysis of the personal nature of home care nursing, and the ability of nurses to address client problems
in a holistic manner. Nurses in hospitals can often develop specialized practice
when working with target client populations (e.g., in pediatrics, oncology, and
emergency services). In home care, nurses are usually required to be generalists, creating special challenges for them that are reviewed. Home care clients
are usually homebound, which limits their ability to seek healthcare. Therefore, home health nurses, as their primary contact, must develop excellent assessment skills to identify any actual or potential problems early enough for effective interventions. Teaching in home care, the role of the nurse in
identifying and referring clients to community resources, and participation of
the client's significant others are also distinct issues in home care that this
chapter explores. A discussion of the limited ability of home care nurses to
vent frustration, anger, and stress with peers, and coping mechanisms for
them to employ conclude this chapter.

◆ Power and Control

Issues of power and control differ in home care and acute care settings. In hospitals,
meals are prepared specifically to physician orders. Medications are administered
on time, and skilled personnel are available twenty-four hours a day to control every
aspect of a client's treatment. In home care, everything changes. Healthcare providers
have little control over the environment or a client's compliance with prescribed
diets and treatments. In hospitals, clients may feel too frightened to demand control
over their basic choices. At home, most clients expect full control over every part of
their lives, including medical decisions. Therefore, home care nurses must influence

	Display 2-1:
	A Day in the Life of a Hospital Nurse

07:00	Report to unit. Obtain assignments for the day. Receive report from nursing staff from previous shift.
07:20	Obtain morning vital signs and introduce yourself to your clients.
07:45	Assist in distributing diet trays. Verify that clients are receiving correct diets ordered by the physician.
08:00	Give clients their morning medications. Document that clients have taken them. Document their breakfast intakes.
09:00	Assist physicians as they perform assessments on your clients. Communicate any significant findings from your morning assessment and the night shift's report.
10:00	Review the physician's orders and ensure appropriate follow-up: notify pharmacies of new prescriptions, order and obtain labs, and implement client activity orders.
11:00	Assist clients with personal care. Ensure they have received fresh bed linens and appropriate skin care.
11:30	Eat lunch in cafeteria with other nurses.
12:00	Administer medications to clients.
12:30	Assist in verifying and distributing ordered diet lunch trays.
13:00	Document clients' lunch intake.
13:30	Complete documentation of morning assessments.
14:00	Administer client treatments as needed. Perform afternoon vitals and final client assessments as needed.
14:30	Complete the day's documentation.
15:00	Report to evening shift for follow-up on any outstanding orders, client findings, and evening treatments that are due.
15:30	Go home.

clients to self-discover the need for changes, and promote wellness through education.

Clients enter healthcare settings to receive needed services. Nurses in hospitals and other acute care settings have many conveniences at their fingertips: beds that elevate, necessary medical supplies, comprehensive and updated medical records, and clean sheets and gowns (Fig. 2-1A). The environment belongs to the providers of healthcare. An individual client spends a relatively short period of time in this environment, but the healthcare provider spends a great deal of time there. Clients often feel uncomfortable in acute care settings. They must ask someone where to find the bathroom. They hear words about their health that they do not understand, but they are too intimidated to ask for explanations. Many clients think that "everyone seems so busy," and they are right. In hospitals, nurses may have two call lights going off just when they are attending to a third client. Clients are frequently dependent upon nurses for many needs that they cannot meet themselves. Clearly, health

(*text continues on page 38*)

Display 2-2:
A Day in the Life of a Home Care Nurse

08:00   Report to the home care office. Review your caseload to determine who needs to be visited today. Plan your travel route efficiently, incorporating time requirements for certain visits (e.g.,
one client needs a morning injection) and client preferences
(e.g., another client prefers to be seen after she eats lunch).

08:30   Call scheduled clients to inform them of your expected arrival
time. Follow-up with a client you saw yesterday to find out
whether her new pain medication is working for her.

08:50   Collect all medical supplies you need for today's visits. Replen-
ish your stock of foley catheters, because two of your clients
needed changes yesterday unexpectedly.

09:00   Talk to a home health aide about specific skin care for one of
your clients. Ask her to contact you if she finds any breakdown.

09:15   Inform the agency's secretary of your schedule, load your car
with supplies, and head out for your first visit.

09:30   First client: Mrs. Jones, a newly diagnosed diabetic: You have visited her several times to teach her self-administration of her insulin injections. You question her compliance with her diabetic
diet because of her erratic fasting blood sugars and the types of
foods in her house. She swears the chocolate is for her husband
only. Her husband is emotionally supportive but wants nothing
to do with learning about diabetes and leaves the room when
you arrive. You leave a message at the doctor's office to report
the client's high blood sugar. You review with Mrs. Jones the diabetic disease process and the importance of diet. You ask Mrs.
Jones to return a demonstration of insulin injection using an
orange.

10:30   Second Client: Billy, a five-year-old receiving intravenous antibiotics once a day at home. Instruct Billy's mother to perform site
care for his Hickman catheter. She is conscientious but anxious
about learning appropriate technique. Write down the procedure
step-by-step in layman terms and promise her she won't have to
perform it independently until she is comfortable.

11:30   Third Client: Mr. Maxwell, who lives alone with three cats and a
dog. He has become very debilitated but refuses to go to a nursing home. You requested and received an order for a visit from a
social worker who is scheduled to see him tomorrow. You call
Meals on Wheels for food delivery. Home health aides are seeing
him every other day to assist him with his personal care. You
want to discuss this client with the physical therapist at the
agency tomorrow to find out if an evaluation for safety is war-
ranted. You change the dressing on a Stage II decubitus ulcer on

(continued)

Display 2-2:
A Day in the Life of a Home Care Nurse (Continued)

his coccyx. You call an equipment supply company to order an alternating pressure mattress to prevent further skin breakdown. Mr. Maxwell's son lives three hours away and promised you on the phone yesterday he would come this weekend to help. You sense a strained relationship between father and son that may impact Mr. Maxwell's willingness to accept the son's help. You plan to meet with both of them on Monday to discuss long-term plans.

12:30 Return to the office for lunch. Document the morning's events for each client.

13:30 Fourth Client: Mrs. Freed. She has terminal cancer for which you are providing supportive care. She is at high risk for skin break-down due to her poor nutritional status and appetite. She and her husband are trying to decide whether she wants to start tube feeding. You answer their many questions regarding this issue. You instruct them on how to maximize her nutritional intake. You evaluate the effectiveness of her pain medication and instruct on side effects. You suggest a social service evaluation for counseling. They agree and you call the physician for an order, which you receive.

14:30 Fifth Client: Mr. Maines. He has chronic pulmonary disease and has recently been released from the hospital after a bout with pneumonia. His newly required oxygen, which he needs almost continuously, has been a problem because he has almost tripped over the tubing several times when walking around his home. His eyesight is poor and the tubing blends into the carpet. On the recommendation of an occupational therapist, you have brought some red tape today to wrap around the tubing to facilitate his seeing it. You assess his pulmonary status and find additional fluid in his lungs. You call the doctor's office but the doctor is attending other clients. You report to the nurse at the physician's office Mr. Maines's status and ask the doctor to return your call with appropriate orders.

15:30 Return to the office to complete your paperwork. You talk to the social worker about your shared clients and the most appropriate strategies to pursue for them. You call the physical therapist to discuss whether therapy would be appropriate for Mr. Maxwell. You also receive orders from Mr. Maxwell's physician to instruct him to take an additional Lasix today and to assess him tomorrow. You follow-up with Mr. Maines's physician and call the insurance case manager to receive authorization for the additional visit.

16:30 Turn in your paperwork and go home.

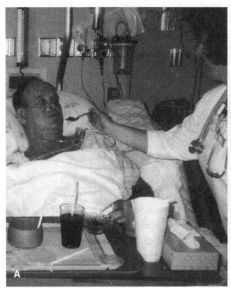

Figure 2-1. (*A*) In hospitals and other acute care settings, healthcare professionals have power and control over the environment of care. (*B*) In home care, clients are in their "castles" and are thus in a position to direct their own care.

care providers have power and control in these settings. Meals are served "on schedule." Baths are given when nurses or nursing assistants are available for assistance. Clients wear hospital gowns instead of their own robes.

In home care, clients are in their own environments—their homes and their "castles" (see Fig. 2-1*B*). Home care personnel are guests within the homes of clients and often find the tables turned. Clients know where the bathroom is and where to

Home Care Conflict:
Letting Go of Power and Control

Many nurses new to home care practice have problems in adapting to the lack of control when caring for clients in their own homes. Nurses who enter the healthcare profession to "fix" things for people become acutely aware that things will only get "fixed" if the clients themselves want them fixed. Frustration is normal. Nurses, however, must remember that they would resist attempts from others to control their lives, even for "their own good." Maintaining this perspective can help home care nurses to understand the feelings and attitudes of clients who seem resistant or noncompliant.

find their medications. Clients determine when they will eat and bathe. Nurses have very limited control over most environmental factors that may affect the health of home care clients. Clients with financial concerns may not control the temperature of their homes appropriately. They may be at risk for dehydration in hot areas or hypothermia in cold environments. Clients may not be able to afford medications or medical equipment to maintain environmental safety. Clients may have trouble leaving their homes and may miss appointments with their doctors. Doorways that are too narrow for wheelchairs may cause difficulty for clients in reaching their own bathrooms.

KEY CONCEPT

In home care, clients are in their own environments—their homes and their "castles." Home care personnel are guests within the homes of clients and often find the tables turned when dealing with issues of power and control.

◆ Holism and Personalization

Craven and Hirnle define **holism** as "the belief that people (or even their parts) cannot be fully understood if examined solely in pieces apart from their environment" (1996, p. 248). While holism is an approach used in all types of health care practice today, it is an especially important concept for home care nurses to understand and to apply when working with clients. Addressing a client's environmental, psychological, financial, and social factors can frequently be just as important to promoting recovery as treating the client's physical condition. To deal with these issues, nurses must be aware of community resources and the services of other disciplines within a home care agency (see Chapter 7). Holistic health care also means encouraging clients to assume responsibility for their own wellness.

KEY CONCEPT

Although holism is an approach used in all types of health care practice today, it is an especially important concept for home care nurses to understand and to apply when working with clients. Addressing a client's environmental, psychological, financial, and social factors can frequently be just as important to promoting recovery as treating the client's physical condition.

Health care providers working in institutions may tend to depersonalize their clients. They may find it difficult not to view a client as the "gall bladder in Room 203" instead of Mrs. McIntyre, a teacher for 30 years, who lost her husband 6 months

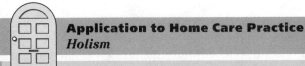

Application to Home Care Practice
Holism

Mr. Rembis, 48 yeas old, is recovering from a recent MI and quadruple bypass surgery. His physician has instructed him to limit activity to prescribed levels to promote gradual strengthening of his weakened heart. Mr. Rembis, however, has been noncompliant with these activity restrictions, resulting in many incidents of acute chest pain and visits to the emergency room.

Carol, the home care nurse, identifies several issues that are contributing to Mr. Rembis's noncompliance. Mr. Rembis has many financial concerns: sole support of his family, children in college, and high monthly mortgage payments. His father suffered from heart disease and became unable to work. His parents had a strained relationship, and his father used his diagnosis to manipulate the family's emotions. Mr. Rembis's wife and children are in denial over his condition. Knowing these financial, psychosocial, and emotional concerns, Carol can achieve a better understanding of Mr. Rembis's overall needs to create an effective and holistic plan of care.

ago, has a new grandchild, and loves to bake. Relationships between acute care nurses and clients are becoming increasingly impersonal since clients are hospitalized for shorter periods. The time available for these nurses to get to know their clients is decreasing. Nurses working within hospitals, therefore, often must remind themselves continually to treat clients in a holistic and personal manner.

Unique relationships often develop between home care nurses and their clients. Through **personalization**, nurses get to know the "whole" client. Photographs in a client's home give nurses insight into the individuals they are treating (Fig. 2-2). Home care nurses are exposed to the hobbies and relationships of their clients. They can become true advocates for their clients, giving them assistance through the maze of bureaucracy to get them what they need. Home care nurses can be tremendously creative when contacting resources and influencing clients toward positive health habits. They have the chance to touch the lives of their clients and to experience a sense of professional leadership and independence.

◆ Specialist Versus Generalist

Nurses who work in hospital settings frequently have the opportunity to **specialize** in the care of specific client populations. Hospital nurses can develop skills required by populations that are defined by disease process or age group. For example, a nurse may work in an orthopedic or a pediatric unit (Fig. 2-3). Certainly, nurses working in highly specialized units encounter new problems and issues all the time;

Figure 2-2. This home care client relaxes in the comfort of her own bedroom, with cards and photographs nearby. Such objects can provide clues about the people and things that the client holds dear.

however, they can become generally familiar with the common issues of the clients they serve. They are able to develop highly attuned skills when assessing these clients and performing common interventions.

Some home care agencies also specialize in treating specific client populations. These organizations may care for pediatric clients, clients with high-risk pregnancies, or clients requiring infusion therapy. Clearly, in these organizations, nurses must learn specialized skills to care for these populations. The vast majority of home care organizations, however, serve a broad spectrum of clients and require their nurses to develop a variety of general skills that can meet the needs of all clients. Home care thus enables nurses to develop comprehensive skills. Nurses usually have few opportunities to learn the intricacies of a specific disease process, however. As **generalists**, home care nurses need to know when and how to access specialized information to meet their clients' needs. They also must have a comprehensive working knowledge of other professional disciplines.

◆ Assessment Skills

Assessment skills needed by nurses working in acute care settings change when they move to home care. Unlike in hospital practice, where everything that happens to clients is monitored and documented (e.g., intake, output, diet, activity, visitors,

Clinical Example
with Critical Thinking

Julie Brewster, RN has worked on an orthopedic unit in a 60-bed hospital for the past 5 years. Her hospital has recently opened a home care agency and is asking for nurses interested in home care practice to apply. Julie understands the work hours are primarily during the day shift. She is tired of the rotating shift requirement in the hospital.

1. Discuss other issues regarding working conditions that Julie should consider before resigning her current position and interviewing for a home care position.
2. Identify skills that Julie might need to develop if hired for the home care position.

and blood levels), home care nurses must comprehensively evaluate a client's status based on their own observations and the reports of clients and their lay caregivers. The scope of accountability for nurses is broader in home care than in other settings, but is offset by the decreased acuity of illness found in most home care clients.

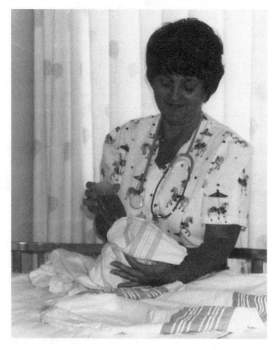

Figure 2-3. Acute care nurses often have the opportunity to specialize and to work with specific client populations, such as pediatrics.

KEY CONCEPT

The scope of accountability for nurses is broader in home care than in other settings, but is offset by the decreased acuity of illness found in most home care clients.

In hospital settings, physicians normally assess clients daily. Additionally, registered nurses perform full physical assessments during each shift. Hospital protocols ensure that significant clinical findings are detected quickly—even if one or two clinicians inadvertently miss them—because many professionals are examining clients continually.

Home care nurses must have excellent assessment skills. In home care, the primary nurse may be the only professional assessing a client's condition. No nurses from second or third shifts follow the initial assessment. A physician will not be coming by to visit the client to review whether vitals were taken. Homebound clients may see their physicians rarely. Home care nurses perform assessments intermittently (e.g., one to three times a week). A nurse's failure to discover significant clinical findings can delay a client's proper treatment and have severe consequences. If nurses fail to detect early symptoms of exacerbation, clients may progress to acute phases of illness before nurses assess them again.

In home care, nurses must perform a holistic assessment—considering not only physical, but psychological, emotional, economic, and environmental factors for their clients and lay caregivers (see Chapter 13). They must create plans of care that address critical issues of health and safety that clients and lay caregivers can manage independently. Nurses must also evaluate the progress and compliance of their clients in unconventional ways. For example, to determine a client's understanding of a special diet, a nurse may have to look through a client's refrigerator and cupboards to assess the availability of appropriate food (Fig. 2-4). Nurses may need to count a client's pills if they question medication compliance.

◆ Teaching

Client teaching in a hospital setting is sometimes ineffective. Hospital stays are typically of short duration, and clients are usually more ill while they are in the hospital than they have ever been before. Clients are often anxious about their conditions, as well as their unfamiliar surrounding and routines. They may be in pain or on pain medication, the side effects of which may decrease their level of consciousness or alertness. Such issues can inhibit a client's ability to learn and to process new information needed for independent functioning at home. Often, these learning needs initiate a home care referral in the first place. Clients may need to learn about new medication regimens or new procedures to conduct in their homes after hospital discharge.

Many individuals released from hospitals require continued "high-tech" types of services that were once considered inappropriate or impossible to perform in the home. Now, clients and their lay caregivers are expected to learn how to perform

Figure 2-4. The nurse examines a client's refrigerator to assess nutritional needs and concerns.

these skills independently. In many situations, a home care organization must become involved to ensure a client's safe discharge and follow-up after hospital care. Nurses within hospitals are generally unable to ensure that clients have developed skills to perform procedures competently. They also do not usually know whether clients have a safe environment in which to perform such procedures. Issues of compliance with newly learned techniques in complex, high-risk procedures are extremely important to the safe treatment of clients. Hospital nurses have no opportunity to monitor this important factor.

KEY CONCEPT

Many individuals released from hospitals require continued "high-tech" types of services that were once considered inappropriate or impossible to perform in the home. Now, clients and their lay caregivers are expected to learn how to perform these skills independently.

In home care, education to enable clients and lay caregivers to be independent in skills and knowledgeable in important concepts is often critical for safety. If clients and lay caregivers do not possess necessary skills or knowledge, they can perform medical treatment plans incompletely or incorrectly. Disastrous consequences to health and well-being can result. When clients are in their own homes, they are usually less anxious and less acutely ill. Such factors enhance their readiness for learning. Barriers to learning still may exist, however. As in hospitals, these barriers include the effects of medications on the medical treatment plan, the diagnosis itself, pain, and anxiety. Additionally, illness often exacerbates psychosocial issues in family systems that may contribute to learning difficulties. Sometimes, the home environment itself is not conducive to learning. Distractions, such as clutter, many visitors, and children, can impede the learning process. Teaching materials are not as readily available in homes as they are in hospitals; therefore, home care nurses must carefully plan instructional sessions to determine whether any items are needed for the learning session (see Chapter 10).

KEY CONCEPT

When clients are in their own homes, they are usually less anxious and less acutely ill. Such factors enhance their readiness for learning.

Home Care Vs. Hospital: *General Issues*

Issue	Home Care	Hospital
Power and control	Clients and their families retain power and control. The role of nurses consists of attempting to influence clients to comply with medical treatment plans.	Clients resign power and control for many issues to doctors, nurses, and hospital routines.
Holism and personalization	Nurses must become aware of the holistic needs and issues of clients to develop effective plans of care. They must develop personal, therapeutic relationships with clients to effectively influence behaviors.	Hospital nurses have little opportunity to get to know personal information about their clients. Many psychosocial issues are not evident while clients are hospitalized.
Specialist versus generalist	Home care nurses must often work as generalists. Clients are typically assigned based on geographic area. Nurses care for a wide variety of client populations.	Nurses have a greater opportunity to work with specific client populations, which allows nurses to become specialized in the skills those populations need.

(continued)

Home Care Vs. Hospital:
General Issues (Continued)

Issue	Home Care	Hospital
Assessment skills	Home care nurses must have excellent assessment skills. If nurses do not identify problems, they will potentially progress and result in serious issues for clients that would have been otherwise preventable. Nurses are the only clinicians to evaluate clients. Assessments occur infrequently, so they must be highly accurate. Nurses are responsible for identifying psychosocial needs and the need for the involvement of other disciplines.	Nurses must have highly developed physical assessment skills because of the acute conditions of their clients. If nurses do not identify problems immediately, others assess clients frequently, which facilitates early problem identification. Physicians, rather than nurses, are held accountable for identifying the need for input from other disciplines.
Teaching	Education to enable clients or lay caregivers to be independent in skills or knowledgeable in important concepts is often critical to safety. The home environment is more conducive to learning because clients are less ill and their conditions are less acute than they are in hospitals.	Performing client teaching in a hospital setting is often ineffective because of short hospitalizations, client anxiety, pain, or effects of medications, etc.
Referrals and resources	Nurses are accountable for identifying needs for assistance from other resources, and making appropriate referrals. Nurses must know indications for and payor requirements of other disciplines.	Physicians and discharge planners are primarily accountable for identifying needs for assistance from other disciplines and community resources.
Significant others	Lay caregivers have a tremendous influence on the course of care for clients. They are often responsible for performing necessary interventions in home care medical treatment plans.	Families and significant others usually do not get highly involved in the care of clients while they are in acute settings.
Stress and emotional outlets	Home care nurses must learn to practice independently without regular professional and emotional peer support. Nurses must learn to cope with stress in other ways.	Nurses usually have regular opportunities to discuss difficult situations with other nurses who can give problem-solving advice and suggestions. Nurses in institutional settings can vent a variety of emotions to their peers regularly. Discussing client care with other nurses provides an outlet for frustrations, and also an opportunity to view problems from varied perspectives.

◆ Referrals and Resources

In hospitals, physicians are generally held accountable for identifying the needs of clients that professionals from other disciplines must address. Because hospital physicians see clients every day, they become more easily aware of problems that need the specialized skills of therapists, social workers, and dietitians. Nurses can also identify these needs and may recommend a referral to a physician. A nurse may fail to identify a client's need that could be best met by a professional from a specific discipline; however, another nurse or clinician is likely to recognize the need and initiate communication with the client's physician for an order. Thus, nurses are less individually accountable for identifying these needs in hospitals than in home care.

In hospital settings, individuals who hold identified positions are usually assigned the role of evaluating client needs for community resources and making appropriate referrals (e.g., discharge planners and social workers). Their role is particularly important in the discharge planning process. The functional abilities of many clients often decrease during the course of a hospitalization. Occasionally, clients need external resources to fill gaps created by their functional deficits. Hospital nurses usually do not need to be aware of available community resources to meet these needs. If they happen to identify a client's discharge needs, nurses can communicate them to the appropriate individual who will follow through in making referrals.

Home care nurses are responsible for identifying client needs that require participation from other clinical disciplines. Physicians are often unaware of all of a particular client's problems in the home; thus, nurses are accountable for targeting needs, informing physicians, and providing professional judgment about whether a client's status warrants a referral to another clinical discipline. Nurses must be knowledgeable of payor requirements for other disciplines and ensure that they are met before initiating referrals. When providing referrals, nurses must communicate significant information to individuals performing assessments to ensure that they are prepared for the initial visit.

KEY CONCEPT

Physicians are often unaware of all of a particular client's problems in the home; thus, nurses are accountable for identifying needs, informing physicians, and providing professional judgment about whether a client's status warrants a referral to another clinical discipline.

In home care, nurses must be able to identify client issues that can be assisted through community resources, and have a working knowledge of ways to access them. Nurses in home care become aware of comprehensive and holistic issues of clients that may not be evident in hospitals. For example, a nurse may detect signs of alcohol abuse in a client during home visits, or may learn that the client is unable to purchase medications because of financial hardships. These issues and many others are often difficult to detect during the course of a short hospitalization. Home care nurses must assess the client for all potential community resource needs. Developing friendly, professional relationships with contact people within community organizations can help home care nurses facilitate access for clients to many free or low-cost services provided by nonprofit organizations. Therefore, the nursing advocacy role in home care demands effective nurses to network with organizations that can assist clients in need.

◆ Significant Others

Families and significant others of clients in the hospital usually play a small or minor role in nursing care. Visiting hours limit the presence of lay caregivers in most hospital settings. Professional clinicians provide clients with most care. Family members and others close to clients usually do not become involved in care while clients are in acute settings. Nurses may wish to include lay caregivers in client teaching, but transportation barriers or responsibilities at home or work may prevent lay caregivers from spending much time visiting clients. Hospital nurses face difficulties when attempting to assess family dynamics if lay caregivers are not readily available. They observe few family interactions in the course of short hospitalizations. Also, the acute care setting is hardly a family's natural environment for interaction. Dynamics that nurses are able to observe probably are not completely reflective of the actual home environment. Hospital nurses are thus at a significant disadvantage in their ability to incorporate potentially significant issues into the acute nursing plan of care.

KEY CONCEPT

The acute care setting is hardly a family's natural environment for interaction. Dynamics that hospital nurses are able to observe probably are not completely reflective of the actual home environment.

In home care, clients may or may not have family to help them with their activities of daily living (ADLs). If families are present, they may be ill themselves and unable to assist. Or, they may be able but unwilling to help because of past relationship problems, cultural issues, or modesty factors. Neighbors may enter the picture and play a major role in a client's care and well-being. Pets are frequently a big part of clients' lives (Fig. 2-5). For home care nurses, greeting these animals (only if they are safe and nurses are comfortable) may be appropriate in some circumstances to gain a client's trust.

Significant others can greatly influence the quality of care that clients receive; their influence can be negative or positive. Lay caregivers can be verbally, physically, or emotionally abusive or neglectful, negatively influencing a client's health. They may not administer medications, provide treatments, or prepare meals as directed. Lay caregivers may incorrectly carry out physician orders because of a lack of understanding or because of cultural and language barriers.

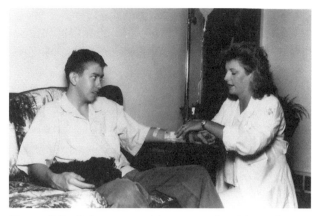

Figure 2-5. Pets can provide companionship and comfort to those receiving home care services.

Most lay caregivers are eager to learn how they can assist in promoting their loved one's recovery (Fig. 2-6). These lay caregivers can provide emotional and spiritual support, laughter, memories, and sometimes physical care unmatched by any health care professional.

◆ Stress and Emotional Outlets

In hospitals, nurses usually have regular opportunities to discuss difficult situations with other nurses who can give problem-solving advice and suggestions. If a hospital

Figure 2-6. This lay caregiver has learned appropriate foot care for her husband. She also provides the support and encouragement that accompany many years of marriage.

nurse is unable to start an IV, would like a second opinion regarding the status of a wound, or is unsure of the presence of adventitious breath sounds, assistance is only a few steps away. Nurses in institutional settings can vent a variety of emotions to their peers regularly. Discussing client care with other nurses provides an outlet for frustrations, and also an opportunity to view problems from varied perspectives. Such interaction allows nurses to learn from each other and to share ideas.

Unlike in the hospital setting, home care nurses spend most of their time away from other health care professionals. Only a few hours of every work week are actually spent in the home care office, where nurses can contact and talk with other nurses and personnel from ancillary disciplines. Home care nurses must learn to practice independently without regular professional and emotional peer support. These nurses often develop relatively close relationships with clients and lay caregivers. They often experience intense feelings when a lay caregiver's noncompliance compromises a client's health, when community agencies are unresponsive to a family's needs, when a client's clinical status fails to respond to a carefully designed plan of care, and when a client dies. They must often endure these emotions privately. Nurses working in home care may miss the peer support found in hospitals and find the adjustment challenging and stressful.

KEY CONCEPT

Home care nurses often develop very close relationships with clients and lay caregivers. They sometimes experience intense feelings when a lay caregiver's noncompliance compromises a client's health, when community agencies are unresponsive to a family's needs, when a client's clinical status fails to respond to a carefully designed plan of care, and when a client dies. They must often endure these emotions privately.

Survival Alert:

Common Stress-Reducing Mechanisms for Home Care Nurses

- ◆ Seek advice from others on how to cope, reduce stress, compromise, and negotiate.
- ◆ Solve problems methodically.
- ◆ Talk with trusted family members or friends (maintain confidentiality).
- ◆ Laugh, cry, and express other emotions honestly and safely.
- ◆ Listen to soothing music or read inspirational material.
- ◆ Find comfort in leisure and recreational activities, rest, and quiet time.
- ◆ Keep a journal.
- ◆ Exercise and play sports.
- ◆ Learn more about health and health-related behaviors.
- ◆ Meditate, pray, and participate in other stress-management activities.

◆ Summary

Hospital and home care nursing are both challenging and rewarding areas of practice. The skills needed to succeed in the home care environment, however, are unique. Clients in home care are less acutely ill than hospitalized clients, yet home care nurses have a broadened scope of responsibilities for their clients' comprehensive needs. Nurses working in home care must learn how to be effective in an environment where clients retain full power and control over all aspects of their care. Home care nursing must be very holistic in nature to adequately address issues critical to a client's health. It requires excellent assessment, teaching, and networking skills for a broad range of client populations. Significant others play a critical role in client care, and nurses must learn how to maximize their positive influences to promote health and well-being. The challenges of home care can be frustrating and demanding. For nurses seeking highly responsible, professional, independent nursing practice, however, home care is an exciting and rewarding alternative.

References and Bibliography

Alford, D. & Futrell, M. (1992). Wellness and health promotion of the elderly. *Nursing Outlook, 40*(5), 221–226.

Ark, P.D. & Nies, M. (1996). Knowledge and skills of the home healthcare nurse. *Home Healthcare Nurse, 14*(4), 293–297.

Benefield, L.E. (1996a). Productivity in home healthcare. Part one. *Home Healthcare Nurse, 14*(9), 699–706.

Benefield, L.E. (1996b). Productivity in home healthcare. Part two. *Home Healthcare Nurse, 14*(10), 803–814.

Benoit, D. & Carr, P. (1996). Partnership: The relationship between a hospital and its home health agency. *Home Healthcare Nurse, 14*(5), 388–389.

Bradley, P.J. & Alpers, R. (1996). Home healthcare nurses should regain their family focus. *Home Healthcare Nurse, 14*(4), 281–288.

Caie-Lawrence, J., Peploski, J. & Russell, J. (1995). Training needs of home healthcare nurses. *Home Healthcare Nurse, 13*(2), 53–61.

Carr, P. (1993). Beyond the hospital walls. *American Journal of Nursing, 93*(8), 14.

Craven, R.F. & Hirnle C.J. (1996). *Fundamentals of nursing: Human health and function*, (2nd ed.). Philadelphia: Lippincott-Raven.

Davidhizar, R. & Shearer, R. (1996). Using humor to cope with stress in home care. *Home Healthcare Nurse, 14*(10), 825–830.

Dossey, B.M., Keegan, L., Guzzetta, C.E. & Kolkmeier, L.G. (1995). *Holistic nursing: A handbook for practice*, (2nd ed.). Rockville, MD: Aspen Publications.

Facente, A.C. (1996). Is there life after hospital nursing? *Home Healthcare Nurse, 14*(2), 117–118.

Fisch, N. (1993). Home care nursing and psychosocial emotional needs. *Home Healthcare Nurse, 11*(2), 64–65.

Humphrey, C.J. & Milone-Nuzzo, P. (1996). *Orientation to home care nursing*. Gaithersburg, MD: Aspen Publishers.

Hunt, R. & Zurek, E.L. (1997). *Introduction to community based nursing*. Philadelphia: Lippincott.

McNamara, E. (1982). Hospitals discover comprehensive home care. *Hospital, 56*, 60–66.

Moore, S. & Katz, B. (1996). Home health nurses: Stress, self-esteem, social intimacy, and job satisfaction. *Home Healthcare Nurse, 14*(12), 963–969.

Rice, R. (1992). *Home health nursing practice: Concepts and application*. St. Louis: Mosby.

Stulginsky, M. (1993). Nurses' home health experience. Part I: The practice setting. *Nursing & Healthcare, 14*(8), 402–407.

Varrichio, C. (1994). Human and indirect costs of home care nursing. *Nursing Outlook, 42*(4),151–157.
Weishaus, G. (1997). Humor in the home care office. *Home Healthcare Nurse, 15*(4), 276–278.

POST TEST

1. Identify environmental factors in the hospital and home care practice settings that cause power and control issues to differ.
2. Discuss reasons why home care nursing practice is more personalized and holistic than hospital nursing.
3. List reasons that assessment skills of the home care nurse must be excellent.
4. Explain the differences in client teaching in home care versus acute care.
5. Discuss the significance of home care nurses having competence with community resource referrals.
6. Distinguish the roles of significant others in the home versus the hospital.

THINKING CRITICALLY IN HOME CARE

1. Assess ways and circumstances in which the personalized nature of home care can be potentially beneficial and detrimental for both nurses and clients in this setting.
2. Determine resources that nurses interested in switching to home care should access in order to make smooth transitions.
3. Home care nurses are usually expected to work as generalists. Discuss possible resources for a nurse to consult when working with the following clients:
   A. A client who is receiving chemotherapy and is taking a variety of medications that seem unfamiliar to the nurse.
   B. A client with a wound that does not seem to be healing after three weeks of care.
   C. A pediatric client with diabetes who is also lactose intolerant and allergic to many foods.

3

Managed Care

LEARNING OBJECTIVES

After completing this chapter, the reader will be able to:

◆ Discuss the reasons that managed care has become a significant force for change in the delivery of healthcare services.

◆ Identify changes that are occurring throughout the healthcare industry in response to the demands of managed care.

◆ List criticisms of managed care and ways that the market is responding.

◆ Define the use of critical pathways as a methodology to control healthcare costs while ensuring positive client outcomes.

◆ Discuss ways in which the nurse's role in home care is developing to meet the needs of managed care clients.

◆ Evaluate ways in which the healthcare environment will continue to evolve because of managed care influences.

◆ Assess the contributions that the home care industry can make in the changing managed care environment.

KEY TERMS

Critical pathways
Crosstraining
Freedom-of-choice laws
Gag rules
Health of Seniors Measure
Managed care

National Committee for
  Quality Assurance
Outsourcing
Point-of-service
Protection laws
Risk pools

T he healthcare industry is in a state of tremendous change. This transformation is redefining the practice of nursing. Managed care, which refers to processes by which payors of healthcare services attempt to achieve quality health outcomes while controlling costs, is largely responsible for this revolution. Payors achieve their goals by closely monitoring client needs, evaluating the appropriateness of medical interventions, and using the most cost-effective healthcare providers to deliver services.

This chapter discusses why managed care has become a dominant issue in today's healthcare industry, and strategies healthcare providers are adopting to respond to this rapidly changing and competitive environment. Managed care has significantly affected how home care services are provided to clients. Home care organizations are developing survival systems when faced with increasing demands for quality services at decreased costs for care. Nurses are adapting to changes in their methods of practice in home care settings, and this chapter reviews some of these changes. Critical pathways are one method of decreasing healthcare costs through standardizing care. The use of critical pathways in the home care environment is discussed. Managed care will continue to evolve and to change the complexion of clinical services provided in this country. Home care is positioned to play a tremendous role in the industry as managed care matures beyond controlling costs through utilization controls and price discounting to maintain the health and wellness of the populations it serves. This chapter concludes with an evaluation of the potential contribution of home care to the trend of wellness-focused versus illness-focused healthcare.

◆ The Managed Care Industry

In a speech made at the Healthcare Leadership Council on January 21, 1994, Hillary Rodham Clinton indicated that President Clinton believed that a revolution of the healthcare industry was needed because "he believes that our health system has become a drag on the economy." In 1996, General Motors, the largest private purchaser of healthcare in the United States, had a health bill for active and retired employees of $1200 for every car it assembled. Its healthcare costs for employees amounted to $700 more than the company spent on steel for each car it manufactured (Montague, 1997). Healthcare costs continue to rise and to consume growing proportions of the country's gross national product. In response to this growing problem, society is demanding fundamental changes in the way in which healthcare is provided. The concept of managed care has evolved to address these demands.

DEVELOPMENT OF MANAGED CARE

Traditionally, financial incentives have existed to increase the use of expensive healthcare services. When Medicare was initiated in 1965, the federal government reimbursed healthcare based upon the use of services and the cost to healthcare providers to perform such services. Medicare imposed few limits on spending, and the healthcare industry grew rapidly. Hospital stays were usually long and regularly included expensive diagnostic testing and treatments. Specialized physicians and other healthcare professionals became involved in a client's care, and nearly all services and equipment required the use of high technology. Services were reimbursed with few controls on total expenses. This system encouraged organizations to charge high rates and to use resources excessively; providing more services to their clients meant more dollars flowing into their companies.

Reform in the 1980s

In 1982, the Tax Equity and Fiscal Responsibility Act attempted to contain the uncontrolled costs of hospital services. It started a prospective payment system in an attempt to decrease the growing tax burden (see Chapter 1). Within this system, hospitals were forced to accept some financial risk for providing inpatient services to clients. Rates were developed based on average costs for hospital services for various diagnoses. A flat reimbursement schedule for established Diagnosis Related Groups (DRGs) would be used to determine reimbursement provided to hospitals each time a client was admitted to a hospital. This change forced hospitals to rethink their provision of inpatient services and to decrease their costs accordingly because of capped reimbursement.

Because of prospective payment systems, hospitals have initiated earlier discharges for clients and have decreased their use of expensive and unnecessary ancillary services and supplies. To compensate for lost revenues for inpatient care, hospitals have aggressively pursued the development of outpatient services. Home care and other outpatient services have grown significantly since the advent of DRGs to meet the needs of clients sent home quickly from hospital settings.

Businesses also experienced increases in healthcare expenses. Initially, increases in the cost of health insurance premiums were merely passed on to the customer. As competition and price-sensitivity of products continued to grow, however, businesses could no longer accept rising health insurance expenditures and remain viable. They demanded lower cost insurance products. Insurance companies responded to these demands with the advent of managed care.

KEY CONCEPT

Traditionally, financial incentives existed to increase the use of expensive healthcare services. Managed care evolved as a direct result of the refusal of taxpayers and businesses to continue to accept ever-rising healthcare costs.

THE GROWING INFLUENCE OF MANAGED CARE

In 1992, for the first time, the majority of Americans received their healthcare benefits through some type of managed care arrangement (Wolfe, 1993). Managed care continues to grow. Enrollment in HMOs is expected to experience an 8% growth rate by the year 2000, for a total of 100 million members (Managed Care Outlook, Oct. 4, 1996).

The HCFA contracts with managed care organizations (MCOs) to provide healthcare benefits to Medicare-eligible beneficiaries. Medicare reimburses MCOs on a per member, per month rate based upon average healthcare utilization in a specified region, minus 5 percent. MCOs must provide the same healthcare services that Medicare covers. In addition, they often give Medicare beneficiaries additional benefits that Medicare does not normally cover, such as pharmaceutical benefits. The federal government wants to expand the use of managed care in the Medicare program to prevent the predicted bankruptcy of the Medicare trust fund (NAHC Report, April 25, 1997).

◆ Cost Reduction Strategies of Managed Care

MCOs have predominantly achieved cost savings through two strategies: negotiating discounted pricing with healthcare providers and decreasing the use of healthcare services through utilization control measures (e.g., requiring preapproval to identify unnecessary services, and shifting services from inpatient settings to less expensive outpatient settings).

DISCOUNTED PRICING

MCOs develop contracts with physicians, physician groups, hospitals, ambulatory surgery centers, pharmacies, home care agencies, and skilled nursing facilities. Generally, healthcare providers agree to accept discounted rates for services, to follow policies for preauthorization of services, and to report utilization statistics. Physicians rarely handle the actual authorization process themselves, relying instead on registered nurses, licensed practical nurses, or trained administrative staff. These employees follow established procedures regarding treatment protocols to approve and to deny care for clients (Fig. 3-1).

Occasionally, contracts include financial incentives for healthcare providers to keep costs down. MCOs particularly target these incentives to medical groups, because of their ability to control the utilization of services and costs of care. A percentage of collected premiums are set aside in **risk pools**. At the end of a specified period, if a plan has spent more on healthcare than budgeted, money from the risk pool is used to subsidize care. Money that remains in the risk pool is shared with members of the medical group. Obviously, participants are thus encouraged to control the use of healthcare services.

One contracting strategy that MCOs use to control their financial risk of providing healthcare services is to share the risk with actual providers through capitation (see Chapter 1). In capitated contracts, healthcare providers (e.g., hospitals, physicians, home care agencies, etc.) accept a flat payment from a managed care plan on a per member, per month basis. The healthcare providers are thus encouraged to provide services to their clients as efficiently as possible to increase profits.

Figure 3-1. This nurse authorizes services for a client who is insured by a managed care health plan. (Photo by Marilu Sherer, CARING)

K E Y   C O N C E P T

One contracting strategy MCOs use to control their financial risk of providing healthcare services is to share the risk with the providers of healthcare services through capitation.

UTILIZATION CONTROL MEASURES

MCOs usually require primary care physicians to manage all aspects of a client's care and to screen all requests for healthcare services before advancing the authorization process. Clients are instructed to obtain preapproval from their primary care physicians before they go to an emergency room. Unless a situation can be clearly considered a medical emergency, most MCOs will deny hospital visits and hold clients financially responsible for payment. MCOs usually track the utilization patterns of their physicians to provide appropriate follow-up or education if they identify trends of overutilization.

In managed care, if a primary care physician approves a referral to a specialty physician for a client, the specialist provides services on a consultant basis, giving recommendations to the primary care physician who follows advice accordingly. Compare this system with the Medicare plan, in which several specialists treat clients with multiple chronic diagnoses simultaneously (e.g., a cardiologist for congestive heart failure and an endocrinologist for diabetes). Managed care plans can theoretically save money, since medical specialists often prescribe expensive diagnostic tests and treatments more liberally than primary care physicians.

MCOs often place case managers in hospitals to review and to approve the length of hospital stays and types of procedures for their members. Some MCOs are very aggressive in moving clients out of acute care settings into subacute settings or their homes. If reviews suggest that delayed services lengthened a hospital stay unnecessarily, or if clients were not discharged when they appeared medically stable, the case manager will deny reimbursement to the hospital. These managed care practices have dramatically reduced lengths of stays for clients in hospitals. "Now, it is not unusual to find HMO hospitalization rates that are not one-third, but two-thirds or three-quarters of those in the surrounding communities" (Goldsmith, Goran, & Nackel, 1995, p. 19).

◆ Criticisms of Managed Care

Although its enrollment and influence continue to grow, many criticisms have been directed against the managed care industry (Table 3-1). Managed care has been regarded as both the savior of the healthcare industry and the destroyer of quality medical services. Some individuals who joined their health plans in good faith, encouraged by advertising that presented conscientious care provided by superior clinicians, feel betrayed by this profit-oriented, multi-billion dollar industry. Similar to other new industries with no laws or regulations to guide their business practices, some managed care companies have been guilty of abuses in the name of profit. Horror stories occasionally surface in the media of a managed care plan's denial of necessary services to a client that resulted in preventable exacerbations of illness or premature death. Many such decisions by MCOs appear to be based upon their desire for financial profit rather than concern for their clients.

KEY CONCEPT

As in many new industries without laws or regulations to guide their business practices, some managed care companies have been guilty of abuses in the name of profit.

TABLE 3-1. *Criticisms of Managed Care*

Money not spent on care-related activities	Managed care funds are spent on overhead, advertising, commissions, and large salaries out of proportion with other insurance plans.
Discriminatory practices	Medicare managed care plans discriminate against older clients with multiple or severe health problems in attempts to manipulate profits.
Restrictions to healthcare providers	MCOs restrict the healthcare providers available to clients, limiting freedom of choice.
Gag rules	Gag rules prevent healthcare providers from giving clients complete information and from explaining to them all available options.
Conflict of interest issues	Physicians who receive financial incentives for limiting services may find their role as client advocate compromised.

MONEY NOT SPENT ON CARE-RELATED ACTIVITIES

One criticism of managed care is that large amounts of money are directed away from care-related activities to administrative functions. While Medicare and large insurance group plans spend only 2% and 5.5% of program costs on administrative overhead respectively, managed care plans in small group markets direct 25% or more of their program costs on overhead (Lawniczak, 1995). Generous budgets support television and radio advertisements. MCOs pay their salespeople based upon the number of enrollees they sign onto a plan. Chief executive officers of managed care companies have commanded multimillion dollar salaries. Healthcare providers and clients are critical of the use of so many premium dollars for business-related purposes while important healthcare services are often denied to customers.

DISCRIMINATORY PRACTICES

Medicare managed care plans often attempt to recruit the youngest, healthiest seniors for their plans. These plans have also been accused of enrolling members without permission and people who are incompetent. Medicare recipients who require the most frequent and expensive care are discouraged from signing onto a plan and are left in the fee-for-service Medicare program. In addition, Medicare beneficiaries have the option to disenroll from a Medicare managed care plan on a month-by-month basis. Some managed care plans encourage Medicare recipients to disenroll when they develop an expensive illness and to return to fee-for-service Medicare. These strategies increase profits for managed care companies that are reimbursed based upon the average cost of care for Medicare clients. These companies are actively manipulating their membership to include participants with the fewest expenses and to eliminate those with the highest costs. Such actions drive up costs for the routine Medicare program and subsequently for the American taxpayer (Lawniczak, 1995).

RESTRICTIONS TO HEALTHCARE PROVIDERS

Managed care achieves some of its cost savings by restricting the healthcare providers available to clients. Clients must receive services only from specific physicians, hospitals, labs, and pharmacies affiliated with a plan when they decide to enroll. Such restrictions frequently require clients to change providers they have used for years. Many employees of businesses who have purchased company-wide managed care plans are critical of this requirement. Benefits managers in companies are forced to weigh the savings they achieve by using managed care plans against employee satisfaction over issues regarding provider choice.

GAG RULES

Some managed care companies require healthcare providers to withhold information from clients regarding all potential treatment choices available to them. These orders are called **gag rules**. An MCO can terminate a physician's contract if the physician criticizes the organization in any way or informs a client of treatment options that fall outside the plan's recommendations.

CONFLICT OF INTEREST ISSUES

Another criticism leveled against managed care concerns the conflict of interest issues that arise from financial incentives for healthcare providers to withhold services. Physicians are supposed to act as advocates for their clients when accessing appropriate healthcare services. Many clients fear that physicians who receive financial incentives for withholding clinical treatments may make decisions in their own interest and thus neglect their role as advocates.

ADDRESSING MANAGED CARE CRITICISMS

Many attempts are being made to respond to the many criticisms of managed care. Legislative processes on both the state and federal levels are addressing serious issues. Accreditation processes and market forces are answering the public's demand for the accountability of MCOs for healthcare outcomes. Businesses are choosing MCOs based upon data regarding quality of services. Some employers are also addressing their concerns proactively by managing employee healthcare themselves; even under such circumstances, however, they still implement the basic concepts of managed care. Although the managed care industry needs improvements and changes, it is clearly a reality that healthcare providers must deal with to serve their clients well in today's market.

Legislative Reform

The government has responded to concerns of voters and to accusations of abuse in the managed care industry by developing legislation designed to protect the public. In 1996, Congress and twenty states mandated a minimum 48-hour hospital stay for women and infants following childbirth. In 1997, several politicians, including President Clinton, pushed for mandatory hospital stays for mastectomy clients (Kertesz, 1997). Types of proposed legislation include **freedom of choice laws** that would prohibit networks from reimbursing members of healthcare provider networks at higher levels than nonmembers, laws requiring managed care networks to admit any provider who wants to participate in a network (regardless of whether that type of provider is needed), and **protection laws** that require networks to provide justification for their exclusion or termination of a healthcare provider from their plan (Managed Care Market, 1995). "Anti-gag" legislation is also being developed in an attempt to prevent MCOs from limiting the communication between healthcare providers and the clients they serve.

Managed Care Accountability

Mechanisms to develop the accountability of MCOs for the delivery of quality medical care are underway. The **National Committee for Quality Assurance (NCQA)** has issued accreditation standards that specify minimum quality expectations for HMOs. This process is similar to the JCAHO accreditation process for healthcare providers. The government and public possess greater expectations of MCOs to display quality clinical outcomes and improved satisfaction of the members they serve. "A renewed national mandate is emerging: Maintain and improve the quality of healthcare in a measurable, demonstrative way. Lip service to quality will not be tolerated" (Solovy, 1996, p. 48) (Fig. 3-2).

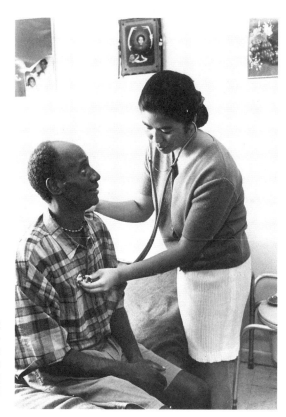

Figure 3-2. Individuals expect quality services from their providers. An increasing emphasis on managed care accountability is helping to ensure the satisfaction of consumers. (Photo by Marilu Sherer, CARING)

HCFA is requiring health plans that contract with the federal government to measure the functional abilities of the populations they serve, using a standardized tool and measuring system called the **Health of Seniors Measure**. Congress is also examining requirements for health plans to publicize the clinical outcomes of their clients, such as functional capacity and ADLs. Purchasers of health plans can thus better evaluate an individual plan's ability to help clients achieve positive health outcomes.

KEY CONCEPT

The public is demanding that MCOs display quality clinical outcomes and the improved satisfaction of their members.

Response from Businesses

Many businesses are dissatisfied with the high premiums they must pay while watching MCOs who are unable to prove quality healthcare and effectiveness for their employees earn large profits. Some employers are addressing the concerns of their workers regarding restricted access to healthcare providers. They are devising their own benefit plans and dealing with providers directly in new ways. By doing so, they hope to lower costs and to improve care, while creating a growing opening for provider-sponsored networks that are efficient (Meyer, 1996). Contracting directly with hospitals and physicians removes the network intermediary and offers employers more control to ensure quality services and employee satisfaction with their plans.

Point of Service Plans

MCOs are responding to market demands for improved choice through **Point-of-Service (POS)** plans. POS is a system in which a network of providers is available to enrollees at discounted rates. Insurance members have a primary care physician who usually refers them to specialists when necessary. What distinguishes this type of managed care product from others, however, is a member's ability to receive healthcare services outside the specified network. Members who choose to seek services outside the network will find their out-of-pocket expenses higher than if they select network providers, but can maintain coverage flexibility and a degree of personal choice.

◆ Survival Strategies of Healthcare Providers

Healthcare providers are finding it harder to refuse to participate in managed care plans. MCOs are insuring greater proportions of the population, and the market share is drifting away from providers who choose not to contract with them. Thus, many providers find they have no choice but to contract with MCOs to stay competitive. Such providers are using a tremendous range of strategies to survive the impact of managed care.

Some payors discount their healthcare services aggressively, since MCOs promise hospitals, home care agencies, nursing homes, durable medical equipment companies, and physicians additional client volume in return for low pricing. Bidding on contracts sometimes becomes highly competitive, driving the costs of services to increasingly low levels. The primary consequence for healthcare providers includes the need to reduce the costs of providing services.

Most hospitals that operate in highly managed environments are in a precarious position. The demand for hospital beds is decreasing at a dramatic rate, since outpatient settings can now provide many services once found only in hospitals. Additionally, reimbursement rates continue to decrease for services they continue to provide. Hospitals must maintain minimum volume levels to support their overhead to pay for their nonvariable expenses (e.g., electricity and building maintenance). Although revenues to hospitals are declining at alarming rates, many hospitals are unable to reduce their many fixed expenses. Hospitals that cannot adjust their costs accordingly will not be able to survive.

KEY CONCEPT

Healthcare organizations have to employ a variety of strategies to survive in the managed care environment.

INTEGRATION STRATEGIES

Healthcare providers are attempting to survive the impact of managed care by integrating some of their services with others through a variety of relationships. Integration is occurring vertically, horizontally, and on regional and national levels. Independent community providers are becoming obsolete in many communities where managed care plans dominate. Healthcare providers are selling their businesses, joining networks of similar providers, establishing joint ventures with vertical networks, and evaluating the benefits of a variety of partnerships to gain strategic advantages in the managed care contracting process. Developing these relationships can decrease overhead costs and allow providers to offer preferred pricing to MCOs. Integration also is viewed as efficient for those companies who prefer to contract with few providers.

Vertical Integration

Vertical integration (Fig. 3-3) attempts to affiliate healthcare providers along the continuum of services. For example, a hospital may participate in a joint venture with a skilled nursing facility, acquire a home care agency, or develop an ambulatory surgery center. The hospital that has developed a vertical network can provide "one-stop shopping" to MCOs. MCOs find vertical networks attractive because they simplify the contracting process and offer an implied quality advantage of continuity of care among health settings for clients.

Horizontal Integration

In horizontal integration (Fig. 3-4), healthcare providers establish relationships with similar providers to service broad geographic areas or to provide more choices for clients. Physicians are joining medical practice groups in greater numbers than ever

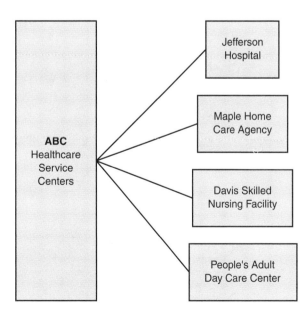

Figure 3-3. Through vertical integration, ABC Healthcare Service Centers include a hospital, a home care agency, a skilled nursing facility, and an adult day care center. Each component previously operated independently.

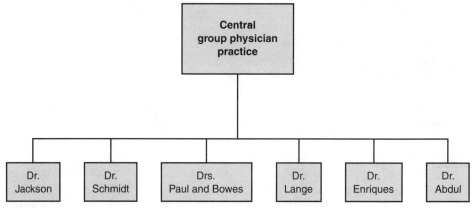

Figure 3-4. Through horizontal integration, doctors who once had individual practices have merged together to work in a group physician network.

before. Their ability to negotiate better pricing in managed care contracts increases significantly when they negotiate as a group of practitioners rather than as single physicians. Some MCOs will only contract with physician groups. Many hospitals, home care agencies, labs, and other facilities are merging in some fashion throughout the country, enabling MCOs to develop a single contract for a large geographic area.

Regional and National Integration

Integration is also occurring on regional and national levels (Fig. 3-5), allowing MCOs to develop regional and national contracts with providers. Independent healthcare providers have no opportunity to provide services for client populations served under these contracts. For example, when a hospital or provider develops a contract with a national home care organization, that organization must provide all home care

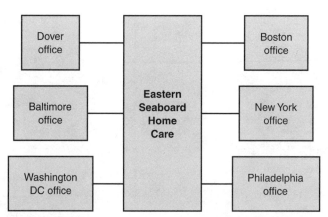

Figure 3-5. Eastern Seaboard Home Care has offices along the East Coast that provide services to clients in several cities.

services to their clients. Attempts of local agencies to establish a contract are almost impossible.

KEY CONCEPT

Managed care is forcing vertical, horizontal, regional, and national integration of healthcare providers to achieve necessary cost savings and the ability to solicit contracts successfully. Independent providers are becoming obsolete in many communities where managed care plans heavily predominate.

COST-REDUCTION STRATEGIES

All healthcare organizations working in managed care environments are examining every aspect of their operations to achieve necessary cost savings. These efforts manifest themselves in many ways. Display 3-1 discusses the effect of cost-reduction strategies on the practice of home care nursing.

Decreasing Labor Costs

The cost of labor is the largest expense for most healthcare organizations, including hospitals, clinics, and home care agencies. As executives attempt to lower operational costs to keep up with continually decreasing reimbursement, layoffs and other downsizing efforts have become prevalent. Support and ancillary personnel are often reduced or eliminated altogether.

Emphasizing Client-Focused Care

Traditional reimbursement systems based upon the cost of providing care for clients created bureaucratic organizational structures that narrowly defined employees' jobs and roles. For example, in many hospitals, the jobs of housekeepers included cleaning hospital beds, but nurses were responsible for stripping beds. Obviously, when nurses were unavailable to strip beds, delays in cleaning beds and unnecessary downtime for housekeeping staff as they waited for the opportunity to fulfill their responsibility became problematic.

Client-focused care is one philosophy that attempts to reengineer work done in hospitals to achieve cost savings and also to improve the quality of services provided. Employees in hospitals are becoming cross-trained to fulfill a variety of roles that once were specifically delegated to several individuals. Nursing assistants are being taught to perform many tasks that do not require clinical licensure.

KEY CONCEPT

Client-focused care is a philosophy of organizational structure within hospitals. Its primary goal is to organize work around the needs of clients.

Display 3-1:
Managed Care Strategies and Their Implications for Home Care Nursing

Reducing Labor Costs. Attempts to decrease labor expenses are occurring in home care. The primary strategy is to eliminate office support personnel, to enhance management, and to increase clinical productivity. Agencies are attempting to streamline paperwork and to reduce travel to achieve savings. Unfortunately, another impact of managed care is limiting the number of approved home care visits to clients. Nurses are expected to help clients achieve the same outcomes with fewer visits. Therefore, the need to accomplish more in each visit undermines the effort to improve productivity through decreasing visits.

Emphasizing Client-Focused Care The nursing profession has truly come full circle in the types of services it now provides in acute care. Forty years ago, nurses routinely provided all of the work performed in their units. Over time, various professional and nonprofessional services were gradually absorbed by "specialists" when hospitals began to receive additional reimbursement for them by Medicare. Now that reimbursement for such services has been dramatically reduced or eliminated, nurses are slowly reassuming some of these duties.

Home care nurses may need to develop skills to provide basic interventions currently performed by physical/occupational therapists and social workers. Managed care organizations will attempt to reduce costs by denying authorization for specialized services when they are not absolutely necessary.

Outsourcing Services. Organizational decisions to outsource services may affect nurses. When employees provide services, nurses can sometimes direct their work with greater ease to meet client needs. For example, a courier who is also a home care employee may more willingly shift normal routines to meet the needs of a client. A contracted worker, however, may be more rigid in following the terms and conditions of the service contract. Again, nurses are often expected to fill any service created by such agreements. Occasionally, service levels sometimes improve with contracted services, extending support for nurses.

Reducing Supplies. Limiting supply inventory is effective in reducing overall expense for any organization. Frequently, medical supplies are not always used in expected amounts. For example, a home care agency may receive an unusually large number of clients who require wound care during a given week. Occasionally, the established par levels are not adequate to meet the needs of clients who currently receive services. In this situation, nurses may not have the necessary supplies to perform the prescribed care and may have to seek supplies elsewhere. This process can be frustrating and time-consuming.

(continued)

Display 3-1:
Managed Care Strategies and Their Implications for Home Care Nursing (Continued)

Supplies may change in an attempt to reduce expense by limiting the number of contracted vendors. Nursing practice may need to change to adapt to different medical supplies.

Expanding Geographic Areas. Home care nurses are affected when they are expected to travel greater distances to cover broadened geographic areas. Obviously, the increased travel takes away time available to spend with clients. This "nonproductive" driving time can be extremely frustrating for nurses who already feel under pressure to accomplish objectives for their clients in the limited time available during visits. Also, clients sometimes need supplies that nurses do not have available in their cars. Necessary care can be significantly delayed if they must travel a great distance back to the office to acquire materials. Home care nurses must frequently obtain and deliver laboratory specimens quickly to avoid deterioration of the specimens. Even under the best circumstances, significant driving time may be involved in this process.

Outsourcing Services

Some organizations also achieve reductions in labor expenses by **outsourcing** services—purchasing services on a contracted basis from an outside vendor instead of hiring their own employees to perform these services. Food service, laundry, and housekeeping are examples of services that may be contracted out to external vendors. Professional services (e.g., social services) are also outsourced occasionally. Home health agencies may evaluate outsourcing delivery services, billing, or therapy services. Healthcare providers look for companies that can demonstrate quality at reduced costs. Companies accomplish this goal through management expertise and reduced bureaucratic systems. Theoretically, they help healthcare providers to reduce operating expenses without affecting service levels.

Reducing Supplies

Hospitals, home care agencies, clinics, and doctor's offices often attempt to decrease costs of supplies and products. Many facilities are reducing the number of supply vendors they use to demand lower prices. The impact upon nursing includes fewer choices in products available to provide care. Organizations are less likely to order the highest-quality version of a medical supply or piece of equipment in favor of a more reasonably priced version of the same item. Because nurses primarily use these supplies, their practice sometimes needs to be changed to adapt to the new materials available for care.

KEY CONCEPT

Healthcare organizations with managed care contracts that are causing reduced reimbursement may be less likely to order the "Cadillac" version of a medical supply or piece of equipment. Instead, they may obtain more reasonably priced versions of the same items. Since nurses primarily are the users of these supplies, they may need to change their practice to adapt to materials made available by the healthcare organization.

Another strategy that healthcare providers adopt is to decrease supply inventories. "Just in time" inventory is a concept that can save organizations significant dollars by maintaining minimal supply levels. Organizations establish par or minimum inventory levels based on the average amounts of supplies they have used. They spend money on supplies just before they are to use them. In this way, cash stays in the organization longer, improving the cash flow because thousands of dollars of supplies do not sit on shelves for weeks or months before they generate the revenue that covers their cost.

Expanding Geographic Areas

MCOs attempt to work with home care agencies that cover large geographic areas. This eliminates the need to develop multiple contracts with many providers. Therefore, home care agencies may feel pressured to expand their geographic area to remain competitive. Agencies are also motivated to increase their geographical coverage to capture a broader referral base. As clients with managed care plans comprise more referrals to a home care organization, the number of visits overall within the organization frequently shrinks because of the decreased visit utilization per client. Costs per visit typically increase because visits are usually longer when clients are first admitted to receive services. At this time, when clients are often the most ill, they need more education, extensive assessments, and thorough communication and follow-up. Also, because home care nurses know they must accomplish

Clinical Example
with Critical Thinking

Darlene, a home care nurse, has requested a social service evaluation for a client to help with placement in a skilled nursing facility. The client's managed care organization denies this request. The case manager says that the nurse can perform this function while providing other nursing services needed by the client. Darlene has always referred this intervention to a social worker in the past and has never participated in skilled nursing facility placement for any of her clients.

Develop a plan for Darlene to resolve this issue effectively.

necessary clinical outcomes in fewer visits, they compress more interventions into each visit. As a result, each visit takes longer.

As home care organizations experience the increasing influence of managed care, profit margins deteriorate as discounts from charges decrease revenue and longer client visits increase costs. Covering the overhead costs of the agency becomes more difficult. To survive, home care executives often realize the need to increase volume by broadening their referral base and expanding geographic coverage. They often develop branch offices to meet the needs of outlying communities.

◆ Critical Pathways

Managed care has stimulated changes in clinical practice patterns. One of the traditional hallmarks of the American medical system was the individualized practice approach to medical care. Typically, providers treated clients with very little consistency in their approaches. Pressure to reduce unnecessary expenses when providing healthcare in acute care settings stimulated the advent of **critical pathways**. Critical pathways are one approach to achieving cost-efficiency while maintaining or improving client outcomes by developing standardized practice patterns based upon best practice to reduce rates of complications and readmissions, decrease clinical errors, lower resource use, improve client education, and increase client satisfaction (Giffin & Giffin, 1994). They help to ensure the highest quality client outcomes in the most cost-effective manner. Critical pathways are also called clinical paths, clinical path guidelines, care maps, care tracks, care pathways, or case management plans.

KEY CONCEPT

Critical pathway development results in standardized practice patterns that are proven to reduce rates of complications and readmissions, decrease clinical errors, lower resource use, improve client education, and increase client satisfaction.

When developing critical pathways, physicians, nurses, and other clinicians attempt to identify the practice patterns that achieve the best clinical outcomes in the most cost-effective manner. Critical pathways are designed to recommend interventions, assessments, diagnostic procedures, consultations, referrals, medical treatments, diet, teaching, activity, and pharmaceuticals for particular diagnoses. They specify time lines to perform activities. Most critical pathways incorporate expected client outcomes or quality indicators of interventions performed. Nurses can thus evaluate variances among their clients and modify treatment plans if necessary to achieve appropriate outcomes. Variances from expected outcomes can occur for many reasons, including noncompliance or the inability to tolerate a procedure. Variances are also caused by system failures (e.g., medications not delivered on time, and clinical specialists who are unable to respond to a referral on the weekend).

Although less prevalent than in acute care settings, critical pathways have been used in home care for various diagnoses. Variances in home care are caused by a broader range of factors than those found in hospitals. According to Haidar and Grillo, the "abilities and the limitations of the client and his/her caregiver(s) can have a significant effect on the success of home therapy. Other factors affecting process and outcome . . . include environmental issues (such as the presence of a phone or the cleanliness of a home), the cognitive abilities of the patient or caregiver, psychological support systems, and physical handicaps. In the hospital setting, by comparison, these issues are of little consequence" (1997, p. 40).

KEY CONCEPT

In home care, variances from critical pathways can occur due to environmental and psychosocial issues, and due to the uncontrolled home environment. These issues are rarely encountered in hospitals.

Critical pathways can be exceptionally useful to home care nurses because of the generalized nature of this type of practice. Home care nurses see a variety of client populations; they are unlikely to know the best practice patterns for every diagnosis they encounter. Critical pathways can guide nurses to perform necessary teaching, verify correct medical treatment plans, and initiate appropriate referrals to ensure their clients achieve expected clinical outcomes cost-effectively.

KEY CONCEPT

Critical pathways can guide nurses to perform necessary teaching, verify correct medical treatment plans, and initiate appropriate referrals to ensure clients achieve expected clinical outcomes cost-effectively.

Application to Home Care Practice
Implementing Critical Pathways

Nurses caring for clients with decubitus ulcers have enormous choices regarding the use of products. Physicians often depend upon home care nurses to recommend appropriate wound care. If nurses are unfamiliar with the products that are most effective for various types of wounds, thousands of dollars can be spent on expensive wound care supplies and home visits with little improvement of the wounds. A critical pathway can help specify the most clinically effective and cost-efficient product to use for various types of wounds. It will also specify when wound care should be changed as the wound improves.

◆ The Home Care Nurse's Role in Managed Care

Home care nurses must develop a thorough understanding of managed care. They should grasp the basic elements of contract expectations for payors of clients admitted to home care services. Nurses will not be able to fulfill the roles of client advocates if they do not understand how to ensure approval and payment for needed services. Frequently, MCOs require regular reports about their clients' progress toward goals established in medical treatment plans. These reports must be provided in a timely way, or payment of services may be denied, causing clients or home care agencies to be financially liable for the cost of care. Authorizations for all services must be obtained before they are provided. Nurses must frequently justify a client's need for services to a representative of the MCO. If nurses are unable to articulate the reasons a client requires home care, services will be denied. If services are truly unnecessary, clients will suffer no negative consequences. If services are denied because of a nurse's failure to express accurately a client's needs, the client may suffer irreparable damage resulting from the inability to access appropriate care. Home care agencies usually assume full liability, because an MCO bases its coverage decision upon information received from the agency's nurse.

KEY CONCEPT

If services are denied because of a nurse's failure to express a client's needs to an MCO, the client may suffer irreparable damage resulting from the inability to access appropriate care.

COORDINATING CARE

When managed care plans cover clients, the care coordinator role of home care nursing becomes extremely important (see Chapter 7). Client outcomes need to be achieved in limited numbers of visits. When clients require multidisciplinary services, everyone involved in a client's care must coordinate their interventions with one another. Each clinician in the home must support the others' efforts. Nurses may coordinate scheduling to increase the total number of days in a week healthcare professionals visit a client. If each clinician is aware of the others' goals and knows how to help the client to reach desired outcomes, each visit can be used to reinforce teaching provided by other clinicians, or to provide an assessment of a problem that needs regular monitoring. Such interdisciplinary cooperation enhances the achievement of client goals with fewer home care visits.

CROSSTRAINING

Often, nurses need to **crosstrain**, or learn basic techniques or skills of other disciplines to manage simple client problems independently. For example, a client may need to access a variety of community resources, transfer to a skilled nursing facility, or learn energy conservation techniques. MCOs usually view some of these interventions as within the nurse's scope of practice and will not authorize personnel from specialized disciplines to perform these tasks. If a client's problems are not severe or complex, this issue is usually not a problem, but nurses must be thoroughly prepared to perform such interventions.

KEY CONCEPT

Often, MCOs view interventions typically performed by personnel from other disciplines as within the nurse's scope of practice if a client's problems are not complex or severe. As a result, they will expect nurses to perform these tasks during their visits.

APPEALING DECISIONS

If an MCO denies requested home care services and a nurse believes a client to be unsafe as a result, the nurse is responsible for aggressively seeking a reversal of this decision. Most health plans have a process of appeals that should be followed closely. If this process is not specified, is unrealistic, or requires an inordinate amount of time to achieve a resolution, nurses should simultaneously seek other ways to resolve issues. The primary care physician should be informed of the health plan's decision. If the primary physician cannot help a nurse in developing an appropriate alternate medical treatment plan that maintains the client's safety, the nurse should ask to talk with a nursing supervisor or the health plan's medical director. Nurses will find it appropriate to document all communications that occurred, the client's clinical justification for services, and specific services required in a letter sent to the health plan.

Survival Alert:
Cross Training

Home care nurses should personally facilitate cross training for basic skills of other disciplines. This effort makes a nurse an extremely valuable employee to home care agencies in managed care environments. Nurses can accomplish this task by networking with individuals from other disciplines. Questioning individuals regarding appropriate interventions for relatively simple client problems can advance a nurse's knowledge base and skill level. Nurses must understand their limitations, however, and recognize the definite indications for referrals to ancillary services. Actually observing a visit by a provider from another discipline who performs a specific intervention can greatly enhance a nurse's ability to perform expanded responsibilities independently.

Survival Alert:
Communicating with Managed Care Organizations

When communicating with MCOs, home care nurses should carefully prepare before making phone calls. Nurses should identify all home care services, supplies, and equipment that a client needs. They should review clinical documentation and prepare to report specific significant clinical findings that indicate a client's needs. They should focus on abnormal or negative findings and avoid reporting extraneous information. MCOs are typically strongly biased against intervening in psychosocial issues unless a client's primary problem is a psychiatric diagnosis, or psychosocial issues can be directly related to worsening of the client's medical condition. Unless this association can be clearly established, MCOs may deny services for clients to nurses who address multiple psychosocial issues when requesting medical services.

When requesting home care services, nurses may find it helpful to address the potential medical consequences of not providing services. For example, "If Mr. Amster is unable to get a walker, I am concerned that his unstable gait will result in a fall. Because of his diagnosis of osteoporosis, a fall could easily result in a bone fracture, and any fracture for this client will probably result in an extensive hospitalization because of his multiple medical problems." This approach helps MCOs to appreciate the potential costs of refusing services, as opposed to simply examining the costs of providing services.

Nurses should document all conversations with MCOs when requesting home care services. If services are approved, documentation is helpful in enabling home care agencies to collect reimbursement for services in the event that an MCO contends authorization was not provided. If services are denied, documentation gives proof of information given to the MCO when a determination was made to restrict healthcare services to the client.

KEY CONCEPT

If MCOs deny home care services and nurses believe the safety of their clients to be compromised as a result, nurses are responsible for aggressively seeking reversals of these decisions.

COOPERATING WITH MANAGED CARE

Overall, home care agencies will find their best interests served by developing partnership relationships with MCOs that are motivated to achieve the same objectives—positive outcomes, prevention of physical deterioration, and satisfaction of clients. MCOs, however, always wish to achieve these outcomes through providers who can perform their responsibilities cost effectively. Relationships with MCOs should be collaborative, as nurses and organizational representatives work together to develop the most cost-effective plan of care to achieve client outcomes. Agencies who have ongoing conflicts with MCOs are likely to find their contracts canceled or not renewed.

Efforts to achieve cooperation with MCOs, however, should never compromise a nurse's and home care agency's primary responsibility to ensure safe and effective care for clients. Home care organizations and their clinicians must learn to work within the restraints of managed care and to problem-solve creatively when approaching problems.

◆ The Future of Managed Care

Managed care will need to continue to provide insurance products that meet the various demands of the market. Managed care markets will evolve to the point when healthcare providers face financial risk for their cost-effective provision of services. Capitation is the contracting methodology that most effectively holds healthcare providers accountable for the cost of providing care, since providers literally face financial risk if the cost of services provided exceeds the flat reimbursement received.

Shifts in financial incentives will have dramatic implications for health systems and nursing practice within those systems. The best way to keep healthcare costs

Home Care Vs. Hospital: *Managed Care*

Issue	Home Care	Hospital
Communication with managed care organization	A primary nurse is often responsible for communication with managed care companies to report the conditions and progress of clients.	A case reviewer, primary care planner, or physician primarily communicates a client's progress to the managed care organization.
Documentation	Accurate documentation by nurses is critical for approval of reimbursement by managed care reviewers.	Managed care reviewers focus more upon physician notes.
Impact on nursing practice	Managed care companies often influence the direction of nursing tasks to include work normally performed by therapists.	Organization policy protocols determine the impact on nursing practice.
Visit authorization	Primary nurses often must track the number of visits to their managed care clients and call for authorization for additional visits.	Designated utilization review nurses or case managers within hospitals usually handle such procedural concerns.

at a minimum for an entire population is to reduce the need for such services. As the managed care population grows and capitation contracts become regular, the healthcare industry will increasingly focus upon maintaining a community's health. Health promotion, disease screening, disease management education, and community health assessments will become strategies that organizations will use to protect themselves and their members against high-cost, acute hospitalizations. The role of home care and community health nurses will increase in significance. Fewer nurses will be needed to work in hospitals, largely because of fewer hospitalized clients. More nurses will be needed to perform professional responsibilities linked to strategies for improving community and home health.

KEY CONCEPT

Changing financial incentives will force health systems to change their focus from treatment of acute illness to effective management of diseases and maintenance of community health.

◆ Summary

Home care is likely to play an important role as managed care evolves based on a capitation model. The goals and philosophy of home care nursing practice are consistent with the objectives of this changing environment. Home care services traditionally have been wellness-focused versus illness-focused. Home care nurses function in the community on a daily basis. They are aware of many important community health issues and successful strategies to manage these issues. Encouraging the public's independence in the management of health and wellness will be critical for future generations. Maximizing the independence of clients and lay caregivers is consistently a chief objective of home care practice. Many models are under investigation to identify the most effective methods for keeping populations healthy. Home care nurses will be well positioned to achieve important objectives in this changing environment.

References and Bibliography

Allen, S. (1994). Medicare case management. *Home Healthcare Nurse, 12*(3), 21–27.

Bender, A. (1997). Bringing managed care home: Strategies for success. *Home Healthcare Nurse, 15*(2), 133–139.

Brent, N.J. (1996). Managed healthcare and the home healthcare nurse in the 1990s: Selected legal implications. *Home Healthcare Nurse, 14*(2), 100–101.

Buerhaus, P. (1994). Managed competition and critical issues facing nurses. *Nursing and Healthcare, 15*(1), 22–26.

Dee-Kelly, P., Heller, S. & Sibley, M. (1994). Managed care: An opportunity for home care agencies. *Nursing Clinics of North America, 29*(3), 471–481.

Drew, J.C. (1990). Health maintenance organizations: History, evolution, & survival. *Nursing and Healthcare, 11*(3), 145–149.

Dunham-Taylor, J., Marquette, R.P. & Pinczuk, J.Z. (1996). Surviving capitation. *American Journal of Nursing, 96*(3), 26–29.

Edwardson, S.R., et al. (1988). *Impact of DRGs on nursing: Report of the Midwest Alliance in Nursing. The impact of prospective payment systems on nursing care in community settings.* Washington, DC: U.S. Dept. of Health and Human Services Publication. Division of Nursing, Jul. HRP-0907178, 61–78.

Federa, R. & Camp, T. (1994). The changing managed care market. *Journal of Ambulatory Care Management, 17*(1), 1–7.

Giffin, M. & Giffin, R.B. (1994). Critical pathways produce tangible results. *Healthcare Strategic Management, 12*(7), 17—-23.

Giuliano, K.K. & Poirier, C.E. (1991). Nursing care management: Critical pathways to desirable outcomes. *Nursing Management, 22*(3), 52–55.

Goldsmith, J., Goran, M. & Nackel, J. (1995). Managed care comes of age. *Healthcare Forum Journal, 38*(5), 14—-24.

Haidar, T. & Grillo, J. (1997). An interdisciplinary critical pathway for home intravenous antibiotic therapies. *Infusion, 3*(7), 38—-47.

Harris, M. (1996). Medicare managed care. *Home Healthcare Nurse, 14*(3), 185–187.

Jensen, L. & Allen, M. (1993). Wellness: The dialectic of illness. *IMAGE: The Journal of Nursing Scholarship, 25*(3), 220–223.

Kertesz, L. (1997). Legislative overkill? *Modern Healthcare, 27*(15), 76.

Lawniczak, J. (1995). Can managed care save Medicare? *Caring, 14*(9), 24–26, 28.

(1995). Managed Care Market. *The Case Manager, 6*(3), 16.

(1996). Managed Care Outlook, October 4, *9*(20), p. 6.

Meyer, H. (1996). The tide of times. *Hospitals & Health Networks, 70*(8), 34—-40.

Montague, J. (Ed.). (1997). Currents: Finance. *Hospitals & Health Networks, 71*(2).

Moulton, P.J., Wray-Langevine, J. & Boyer, C.G. (1997). Implementing clinical pathways: One agency's experience. *Home Healthcare Nurse, 15*(5), 343–354.

(1997). *NAHC's 1997 legal symposium and national policy conference address current issues.* NAHC Report No. 708 April 25, 1997 pp. 1, 9.

O'Rawe Amenta, M. (1996). Hospice nursing and managed care. *Home Healthcare Nurse, 14*(10), 815–816.

Pender, N., Barkauskas, V., Hayman, L., Rice, V. & Anderson, E. (1992). Health promotion and disease prevention: Toward excellence in nursing practice and education. *Nursing Outlook, 40*(3), 106–112, 120.

Rosenheimer, L. (1997). How managed care affects day-to-day operations. *Home Healthcare Nurse, 15*(4), 266–269.

Schultz, A. (1995). What is health promotion? *Canadian Nurse, 91*(7), 31–34.

Solovy, A. (1996). Business forecast: All that glitters. *Hospitals and Health Networks, 70*(8), 46–48.

Witek, J. & Hostage, J. (1994). Medicaid managed care: Problems and promises. *Journal of Ambulatory Care Management, 17*(1), 61–69.

Wolfe, G. (1993). Cooperation or competition? Collaboration between home care and case management. *Caring 12*(10), 52–54, 56, 58–60.

Zink, M.R. (1997). Key moral principles applied to managed care. *Home Healthcare Nurse, 15*(6), 423–425.

POST TEST

1. Identify forces that contributed to the development of managed care.

2. Identify common criticisms of managed care and ways currently under development to address them.

3. List reasons critical pathways can be especially useful in a home care environment to ensure the most effective, cost-efficient delivery of service.

4. Review ways in which the home care nurse's role changes in a managed care environment.

5. Provide an example of how a nurse acts as client advocate within a managed care organization.

6. Review why it is important for a home care organization to partner with a managed care organization.

THINKING CRITICALLY IN HOME CARE

1. Discuss ways that the demands of managed care are changing the overall healthcare industry. Identify industry changes that may occur as managed care evolves. Be able to explain ways in which home care may be especially affected.

2. Assess why critical pathways are especially effective in a managed care environment. Determine possible problems with the use of critical pathways and ways for nurses to avoid pitfalls.

3. Imagine that Medicare has made all of its insurance contracting into capitated arrangements with providers. In the town of Madison, the health system is a vertically integrated network that includes an acute hospital, a skilled nursing facility, ambulatory clinics, and a home care agency. This health system has full responsibility for the health of most of Madison's citizens.

   A. Explain how capitation will change the focus of Madison's healthcare.

   B. Determine ways for the health system to cooperate with local government and community organizations to improve the health of their citizens.

   C. Identify the likely role of the home care agency in such an environment and strategize coping mechanisms for home care nurses.

UNIT 2

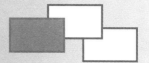

Knowledge Base and Skill Requirements

4

Cultural Adaptability

Jean DeLong

LEARNING OBJECTIVES

After completing this chapter, the reader will be able to:

◆ Understand the importance of mastering cultural diversity and diversity competence as integral functions of home care nursing.

◆ Recognize that home care nurses bring their own cultural influences to client care.

◆ Identify agency and industry resources to further develop diversity expertise.

◆ Target skills necessary to assess cultural variations in clients and lay caregivers.

◆ Use knowledge of cultural diversity in communicating with many populations.

◆ Incorporate cultural practices into nursing interventions and teaching plans.

KEY TERMS

Cultural sensitivity   Ethnicity
Culture   Race
Culture shock   Transcultural nursing
Diversity

H ome care not only requires nurses to adapt to a unique environment of practice, it also gives them the opportunity to care for persons with many different lifestyles, values, and healthcare beliefs. Nurses must use various skills to teach and to treat clients effectively, including assessment skills, interviewing skills, and knowledge of ethnic, racial, and religious behaviors and expectations. Nurses can be successful in client care when they understand cultural differences and incorporate cultural practices into home care. They must recognize that in every client situation, the culture of clients, lay caregivers, families, communities, the healthcare system, and nurses themselves must be considered.

The purpose of this chapter is to introduce home care nurses to concepts related to culture. This chapter stresses the need for nurses to be adaptable and discusses approaches for them to take when dealing with clients whose practices differ from their own. It discusses the competencies required for successful administration of home care from a culturally influenced viewpoint. This chapter presents many important skills vital to effective transcultural home care practice. It encourages nurses to build knowledge of different cultures, to develop a thorough understanding of their own culturally influenced beliefs, and to approach clients with sensitivity.

◆ Cultural Adaptability in Home Care

Culture can be defined as the shared pattern of learned behavior transmitted to others in the same group (Fig. 4-1). Culture often determines the way an individual views life, and is exhibited in the person's behaviors, actions, and attitudes. It helps people to identify "who" they are and what makes them different from others. Table 4-1 lists characteristics of culture and how people manifest these characteristics.

Home care nurses will be successful if they have a solid understanding of cultural beliefs and attitudes. Nurses bring their own individual cultural background, influenced by family, community, education, and work experience, to their clients as well. Nurses who are aware of their own cultural identity can approach client care as a mutual interaction between the nurse and client. A cultural self-assessment (Display 4-1) is helpful for nurses to conduct in order to better understand their own actions, values, attitudes, and behaviors. Effective nurses recognize that a client's ideals and values are unlikely to change and will set goals based upon the client's value system, which may differ from that of the nurse or the traditional medical establishment.

KEY CONCEPT

Nurses bring their own individual cultural background, influenced by family, community, education, and work experience, to their clients. Those who are aware of their own cultural identity can approach client care as a mutual interaction between the nurse and client.

Figure 4-1. Culture is transmitted from generation to generation and from parent to child. Culture shapes each individual's particular attitudes, beliefs, and behaviors. Values like love, concern, and caring, however, know no cultural boundaries.

TABLE 4-1. *Characteristics of Culture*

CHARACTERISTIC	EXPLANATION	EXAMPLE
Culture is learned.	Culture is inherited and taught by others. Group influences help to determine such behaviors as eating habits, style of dress, and gender roles.	The patriarchal family structure found in some Hispanic homes encourages male superiority, with females viewed as a force of bonding for the family.
Culture is shared.	Culture is not the product of individual practices but is the sum of behaviors displayed by most members of a group. Trying to change culturally ingrained behaviors in a group can be extremely difficult when the group as a whole resists such changes.	Although beliefs vary, many Asian cultures share high respect for authority and age. Some Asians may resist medical procedures such as blood drawing or surgery, believing such practices alter the body's life force.
Culture is implied.	Culture is expressed indirectly. Members of a group act in certain ways without overt direction from others. Culture comes naturally.	The preferred tone of voice, speech patterns, and social distance of individuals are often culturally determined. Most people never think consciously about these factors.
Culture is dynamic.	Culture evolves over time in response to the particulars that a group faces. It is not engraved in stone and can change to include new values, beliefs, and attitudes beneficial to the group as a whole.	Traditional family roles in many American families have changed as women continue to work outside the home and men participate in child care.
Culture is diversified.	Diversity exists within each cultural group.	Within the African-American community, economic levels, religions, and geographic origins vary.

(Adapted from Hunt & Zurek [1997], Spradley & Allender [1996], and Taylor, Lillis, and LeMone [1997]).

Display 4-1:
Cultural Self-Assessment

- Determine the influences of your own racial or ethnic background.
- Assess your patterns of communication.
- Assess your values and beliefs.
- Recognize religious and spiritual influences.
- Establish your personal healthcare beliefs and practices.
- Discuss your observations with trusted family, friends, and colleagues to determine whether your self-awareness agrees with their perceptions.
- Try to observe yourself when working with clients and lay caregivers.

◆ Diversity and Cultural Shock

The United States is a culturally diverse society. **Diversity** means that a variety of cultural patterns coexist within a designated geographic area (Spradley and Allender, 1996). Diversity encompasses race, ethnicity, socioeconomic status, religious belief, and sexual orientation. Nurses who work in home care practice are likely to encounter many of these cultural variations in their clients.

A definition of **culture shock** is "a state of anxiety experienced by people thrust into a different cultural context from their own, which can result in misunderstanding and the inability to interact appropriately" (Spradley and Allender, 1996, p. 668). Any nurse entering the field of home care practice is certain to undergo some degree of culture shock. Nurses are no longer working within the protective "cocoon" of the hospital or other acute care settings. The environment of care changes from a well organized, rigid, clean, and safe structure to an ever changing, always unique situation (see Chapter 2). Moreover, nurses will meet people whose cultural practices may not only differ from but also conflict with their own.

Transcultural nursing promotes the planning and implementation of nursing care that meets the needs of individuals and groups who represent the diverse populations within a society. Madeline Leininger, a transcultural nursing pioneer, suggests three basic approaches for nurses to consider when working with culturally diverse populations:

- ◆ Preserve beliefs that have a beneficial effect on health.
- ◆ Adapt or adjust beliefs or practices that are neutral or indifferent to the plan of care.
- ◆ Repattern beliefs that are potentially harmful to the client's health. (1978)

RACE AND ETHNICITY

Home care nurses will encounter clients from various races and ethnicities. **Race** means a group of people with distinguishing, biologically determined features (e.g., skin color). **Ethnicity** means identification with a group based on a common heritage. Traditionally, those belonging to the dominant culture of the United States have been white and middle-class. The composition of American society, however, is changing rapidly. The United States Census Bureau predicts that by the year 2080, over half of the American population will consist of individuals currently labeled as minorities. Between the years 1990 and 2030, the American Association of Retired Persons (AARP) predicts that the older white population will increase by 93%, compared with a projected increase of 328% for older minorities (Woodruff, 1995) (Table 4-2). The influence of new social groups is being felt most strongly in the sprawling urban areas of the East and West coasts, and in the growing metropolitan areas of the South (Buchwald et al., 1994). The implications for home care nursing are evident. As minority populations continue to expand, both clients and nurses will originate from diverse backgrounds. Nurses will need to become more aware of their personal biases. They will need to learn to work with and understand those who come from groups different from their own.

Application to Home Care Practice:
Cultural Diversity

Annie is an African-American home care nurse who works in a large neighborhood of New York City. Her many clients current receiving treatment include the following:

◆ John Chang, a middle-aged Asian-American receiving wound care. Mr. Chang is a practicing Buddhist. At first quiet and somewhat reserved, Mr. Chang has become more relaxed around Annie and has explained some of his religious beliefs to her.
◆ Ruth Goldstein, an older Jewish woman, who requires teaching regarding the use of an infusion pump. Ruth likes to recount her experiences as a young girl growing up in Brooklyn to Annie.
◆ Bill Dacres, a teenage African-American, who suffers from diabetes. Bill is having trouble dealing with his condition, feeling "different" from his friends at school and in the neighborhood. Annie provides Bill and his father, a single-parent, with emotional support and encouragement in dealing with diabetes along with the administration and teaching of injections.
◆ Vincent D'Allessandro, who immigrated to the United States from Italy in the 1950s, and was recently released from the hospital following bypass surgery. Mr. D'Allessandro speaks English well but sometimes has difficulty understanding terminology about his condition. His wife, Flora, a devout Roman Catholic, likes to give Annie cookies and cakes to take home to her family.
◆ Mary Mulvhille, who suffers from cancer and is being cared for by her son, Alex, and his long-time partner, Eddie. Both men provide much encouragement for Mary. They often express their worries about Mary to Annie but both are hopeful she will make a full recovery.

Clearly, Annie treats each of these clients differently, based not only on their conditions, but also on their cultural particulars. Because of her competence, friendliness, objective attitude, and genuine concern, Annie has been able to develop a unique relationship with each client and lay caregiver.

SOCIOECONOMIC FACTORS

Many home care nurses find poverty to be the most difficult cultural variation to confront. Nurses must avoid assumptions based on stereotypes when confronted with a client's socioeconomic status. Poverty does not equate with noncompliance, just as wealth does not indicate cooperation. Viewing clients from a culturally diverse perspective includes seeing beyond a client's income. A nurse may not understand why an older couple cannot afford to buy medications but can feed gourmet dog food to their poodle. The nurse may question a teenage mother who cannot afford transportation to well-baby appointments yet has a state-of-the-art stereo system in her

TABLE 4-2. *Race: Projected Increase in Population by Ethnic/Racial Background by the Year 2050*

	1990	*2000*	*2050*
European American	76%	74.4%	52%
African American	12%	13.1%	16%
Hispanic American	9%	8.9%	22%
Asian American	3%	3.4%	10%

One in four Americans will be African, Asian, or Hispanic American. English will no longer be the majority language in California. People with disabilities will make up 16% of the population.

(Source: Jamieson, D., & O'Mara, J. [1991]. *Managing workforce 2000.* Jossey-Bass.)

bedroom. Issues related to values, priorities, and knowledge of financial management need to be explored before nurses suggest any changes.

HOUSEKEEPING

In addition to socioeconomic differences, nurses must often adjust their perceptions of acceptable housekeeping standards. An older woman at risk for falls and fire due to years of clutter is unlikely to throw everything out just because her home care nurse thinks it is a good idea. Such a suggestion is more likely to cause resentment on the client's part, adding stress to the nurse–client relationship. The nurse must find ways to approach such a topic with sensitivity and to address concerns creatively and kindly. A wheelchair-bound man may not be at any health risk though his floors are sticky and he has not laundered his sheets for two months. Nurses must recognize their own biases and preferences and be able to differentiate between practices that place clients at risk and those that do not.

SEXUALITY

Attitudes about sexuality and sexual preference are also important for nurses to consider. Nurses may be exposed to sexual harassment when working within the community. They must be sure of themselves and assertive when clients or lay caregivers use inappropriate comments. Acceptance of diversity does *not* mean tolerance of rude or demeaning comments and behavior.

Objective and open-minded nurses will be most successful when caring for clients with nontraditional sexual orientations or behaviors. Nurses who cannot see past a client's homosexual relationship will not recognize the importance of working with a client's partner as the lay caregiver. A nurse who cannot handle the idea of sexual relationships outside marriage may be unable to establish a therapeutic relationship with an unwed mother. Nurses must recognize that their sexual attitudes, biases, and prejudices are readily communicated to clients through behavior, speech,

Application to Home Care Practice:
Becoming Accustomed to Neighborhood Diversity

Nurses should view each new encounter with a client as a learning experience. One of the first steps in becoming accustomed to diversity is developing a familiarity with a neighborhood. Nurses venturing into new territory may want to ask a manager or peer for details including landmarks, characteristics, directions, and safety concerns. Driving through neighborhoods can reveal information about the culture contained within them (e.g., concentrated vs. isolated; poor vs. middle income vs. wealthy; young vs. older). The number and types of houses of worship can also indicate the religions that influence a neighborhood's culture.

avoidance of certain topics, and visible comfort levels (Taylor, Lillis, & LeMone, 1997). Competent nurses approach all clients with objectivity and fairness.

◆ Culture and Home Care Competence

As populations change and people become more mobile, home care nurses are faced with an increasing demand to provide care to clients whose cultural practices are unfamiliar to them. Home care nurses may also encounter cultural differences when moving to a new community or agency. Nurses may notice differences in the

Home Care Conflict:
Sexual Orientation

Darcy, the home care nurse, has admitted Angela for wound care. During the initial visit, Angela's lay caregiver was not in the home. Darcy requests that the lay caregiver be present for teaching during the next visit. When Darcy arrives at Angela's home to conduct a follow-up visit, the client introduces Lucille as her lay caregiver and "significant other."

Darcy immediately feels uncomfortable with this situation, yet does not want to alienate Angela or Lucille. Her personal feelings are in direct conflict with her duties as a nurse. Darcy must focus on her professional role. To be a successful home care nurse, Darcy needs to remind herself of the importance of remaining nonjudgmental of others and building an empathetic, caring relationship with her clients. If she cannot reconcile her feelings toward Angela and Lucille, she will compromise both her ability as a nurse and the possible health of her client.

types of people they work with and care for as the composition of a community changes.

To provide effective home care, nurses must develop a strong set of skills to guide and direct their practice. The development of communication skills for assessment and teaching, and creativity to incorporate cultural beliefs into care planning, are essential for providing quality care. Nurses in home care often see a broad range of problems and work with many physicians whose practice patterns vary. As a result, nurses often need to develop a tremendous range of assessment, interviewing, and procedural skills. The home setting also influences successful completion of these skills. As discussed in Chapter 2, the environment is not controlled as it is in the hospital. Poor lighting may negatively influence a client's physical assessment. The social environment of clients can influence their responses to interview questions. Developing these skills is a challenge for home care nurses, who must apply them while incorporating culturally diverse techniques and encountering groups with different and new values and beliefs.

KEY CONCEPT

To provide effective home care, nurses must develop a strong set of skills to guide and direct their practice. Nurses must apply these skills, incorporating culturally diverse techniques, when encountering groups with different and new values and practices.

RAPPORT AND MUTUAL TRUST

The success of any relationship between a nurse and a client is based to some degree on the development of rapport and trust. Home care nurses must develop excellent assimilation skills that help in the establishment of effective, therapeutic relationships with clients. Many of a nurse's efforts in home care are directed toward positively influencing a client's independent health-related behaviors. Home care nurses can achieve this therapeutic relationship by displaying honesty, empathy, and caring.

To develop a trusting, mutually respectful relationship, nurses must also approach clients nonjudgmentally. Within institutional settings, healthcare professionals are often insulated from clients' lifestyles. When care is provided within clients' homes, however, nurses are exposed to many cultural differences. Any verbal or nonverbal indication that a nurse does not "approve" of a client's lifestyle can irreparably damage the therapeutic relationship, thereby rendering the nurse ineffective to influence the client's health positively. Home care nurses must show a sincere acceptance of the client as a whole person who is worthy of respect, care, and compassion despite color, religion, lifestyle, or sexual preference. Particularly in the home care setting, nurses must learn to integrate assimilation skills into all contacts with clients.

KEY CONCEPT

In institutional settings, nurses and other healthcare practitioners are often insulated from the personal lives of their clients. Home care nurses are exposed to a broad spectrum of belief systems and life-styles. They must remain nonjudgmental to provide client care effectively.

The nurse-client relationship starts before the initial visit, when a nurse reviews referral information related to socioeconomic status and makes initial contact with a client or lay caregiver(s) (see Chapter 13). An initial call to establish the first visit may reveal to the nurse that the client is not the primary decision maker in the family. For example, in some matriarchal cultures, such as the African-American culture, a decision about the visit schedule can only be made with approval from a client's wife or mother. Home care nurses can start to build rapport by attempting to schedule visits around their clients' needs.

Greeting clients at the time of the initial visit can also be critical. If nurses are unsure of cultural practices, the traditional American handshake may not be the most acceptable greeting. A simple nod of the head is a common greeting in Asian cultures. Social distance also varies, with Middle Eastern and Southern European people preferring a shorter distance between persons than Americans, and Asian and African cultures preferring a longer distance (Mitchell, 1995).

Nurses establish rapport and trust as they become better acquainted with clients and lay caregivers. Nurses must take the time to establish who the decision makers in a household are. In certain situations, assessments and teaching are futile if nurses focus on "traditional" but not "cultural" decision makers. For example, in some Hispanic cultures, the husband is the person who sets the visit time and makes introductions, while the wife remains quietly in the background. Culturally competent nurses will know to work with the wife for assessment and teaching, however, since she acts as the family's chief caregiver.

Application to Home Care Practice:
Scheduling According to a Client's Culturally Influenced Patterns

Home care nurses can start to build rapport by attempting to schedule visits around the needs of clients. For example, a white nurse may perceive 4:00 P.M. to be an ideal time to visit a client for pre-evening meal blood sugar. In Spanish cultures, however, where a siesta is routine, a more appropriate visit time may be 6:00 or 7:00 P.M.

ASSESSMENT SKILLS

Aside from the physical assessment, home care nurses must obtain information about a client's cultural background, healthcare history, and current cultural practices. Display 4-2 lists some of the items that a home care assessment may include. Assessment of the environment can also reveal information about cultural practices. Placement of a client's bed in the main dining area may reveal a family's strong need to include the client in daily activities. Conversely, seclusion of a client in a back bedroom may suggest isolation or separation from the family.

KEY CONCEPT

Aside from the physical assessment, home care nurses must obtain information about a client's cultural background, healthcare history, and current cultural practices.

INTERVIEWING SKILLS

Agencies serving large non-English speaking populations often employ interpreters and staff knowledgeable in foreign languages. Even clients who speak English fluently, however, will display variation in their responses to the nurse interviewer. Some Americans expect an immediate response to a question and are uncomfortable with long periods of silence. For others, a period of silence before a response indicates that the person being interviewed is attentive to the question. Volume of voice is also an important nursing consideration. Asian, Native American, and Latino cultures use a soft voice in conversation, whereas Mediterranean cultures speak at a louder volume, accompanied by the frequent use of gestures. Traditional American culture also expects maintenance of eye contact as an indication of listening. Home care nurses who interview Native American or Asian clients must realize that lack of eye contact does not mean that a client is uninterested or not listening (Mitchell, 1995).

TEACHING SKILLS

Home care nurses use education to help clients and families toward independent management of illness (see Chapter 10). Whether teaching is as complicated as managing total parenteral nutrition or as simple as explaining a balanced diet, nurses need an awareness of learning styles related to culture. Client education materials should incorporate a combination of illustrated and written examples. Texts should be simple or complicated enough in accordance with a client's or lay caregiver's learning level. For clients with limited mastery of English, nurses must use materials printed in native languages.

Home care nurses must recognize the importance of identifying the primary lay caregivers in a household and directing teaching toward them. For example, in Hispanic cultures, families are often large and extended. More than one person may

Display 4-2:
Cultural Considerations of the Home Care Assessment

COMMUNICATION

◆ What language/dialect is preferred?
◆ What nonverval behaviors are exhibited?

ETHNIC ORIENTATION

◆ What does the client identify as his or her ethnic origin?
◆ What are the client's values?

NUTRITION

◆ What foods does the client prefer?
◆ Does the client consider any foods taboo?

FAMILY RELATIONSHIPS

◆ Who lives in the home?
◆ What are the roles and responsibilities of family members?
◆ Who are the decision makers?
◆ What are the living arrangements?

HEALTH BELIEFS

◆ What has been the client's experience with healthcare?
◆ Does the client seek any alternative healthcare?
◆ Does the client have any special vulnerability or resistance to disease band on race (e.g., sickle cell anemia)?

EDUCATION

◆ What formal and informal education has the client experienced?
◆ What occupations has the client held?
◆ What is the client's current socioeconomic level?

RELIGION

◆ With what religious group (if any) does the client identify?
◆ Does the client believe in any specific rituals or taboos?

assume the caregiving role. Home care nurses must verify that those being taught procedures and given information are truly a client's primary lay caregivers.

KEY CONCEPT

Home care nurses must recognize the importance of identifying the primary lay caregivers in a household and directing teaching toward them.

DOCUMENTATION SKILLS

Nurses must often incorporate information about a home care client's family, cultural structure, beliefs, practices, and communication patterns into documentation. Plans of care must include cultural practices along with nursing interventions. When appropriate, the medication profile should reflect the use of herbal remedies along with prescribed drugs. The physician's plan of treatment should also contain any alternative treatments used in a client's home. Home care nurses should record conferences with other personnel and consultants involved in a client's care. For example, a nurse would document a phone conference with a pharmacist reviewing a client's medication profile and discussing the inclusion of herbal remedies within it.

PROCEDURAL SKILLS

Home care nurses who incorporate cultural practices into interventions are likely to be more successful than those who use traditional models of care only. Nurses must keep physicians appraised of any cultural practices clients use with the established plan of medical treatment. Culturally adept pharmacists should be consulted to advise nurses and clients on the use of herbal medicine along with prescription drugs.

◆ Knowledge of Cultural Differences

The more a home care nurse knows about a client's culture even before the first visit, the more likely the plan of care is to be successful. One of the best resources for home care nurses to consult is the supervisor or experienced peer. Many community service agencies also have staff experienced in working with culturally diverse populations. As a group of staff members work with a particular population, they may want

Survival Alert:

Incorporating Culturally Specific Practices Into Traditional Interventions

◆ Pain management delivered via oral medications or infusion is enhanced with the use of therapeutic massage.
◆ Acupuncture and acupressure may be used in conjunction with medication, therapy, or surgical intervention for the treatment of illnesses ranging from arthritis to gastroenteritis to migraine headaches.
◆ Asian cultures may use a procedure called moxibustion (a combination of heat and burning herbs) to treat skin disease, joint inflammation, and other chronic conditions.
◆ African-Americans believe in the use of fat to "draw out" infections. It is not uncommon to see a client wrap bacon fat around an infected extremity to treat an infection (Romero & Hoffman, 1995).

to meet regularly to share ideas and to develop a journal of tips related to that particular group. Nurses may also want to examine materials that address cultural issues. For example, The California Association for Health Services at Home offers a thirty-five-page book called *Ethnic Diversity and Hospice Care* (Young, 1996).

As nurses work with different cultural groups and talk with peers who have similar work experiences, understanding of cultural variations becomes clearer and more comprehensive. Home care nurses within an agency may find it beneficial to "pool" cultural information in written form, creating a handbook of suggestions and references specific to the populations that the agency serves (Young, 1996).

KEY CONCEPT

The more a home care nurse knows about a client's culture even before the first visit, the more likely the plan of care is to be successful. Nurses should access resources to better learn about an unfamiliar culture they will be serving.

Home care nurses have the unique advantage of being able to assess clients and their lay caregivers in their natural setting. Nurses should examine a client's communication style, family structure, nutrition, health beliefs and practices, and spirituality. By incorporating acceptable folk practices into the plan of care, nurses can successfully develop treatment plans that are individualized, meaningful, and acceptable to clients.

COMMUNICATION

Home care nurses must use effective communication to acquire relevant cultural information (Fig. 4-2). Clients may refer to symptoms of illness using slang. For example, a client may use the term "swimmy head" to describe symptoms of dizziness or "cascadin" to describe vomiting. Some clients may prefer a formal approach to communication that requires nurses to address them always in soft tones. They may expect nurses to address them by their last name rather than their first. Nurses may have to use a client's terminology when teaching procedures or interventions.

Nonverbal cultural clues are also critical to successful communication. For example, a handshake from a female nurse would be considered inappropriate when she is introduced to Orthodox Jewish or Muslim men. Asian-Americans rely heavily on nonverbal signals to demonstrate understanding and acceptance of the nurse's teaching. A gesture as simple as a bow of the head may indicate that the client is expressing agreement with the information received.

FAMILY STRUCTURE

Home care nurses must assess a client's family and kinship structure to learn the values, flow of authority, and decision-making patterns within the household. The Anglo-American emphasis on independence and individualism differs from the values

Figure 4-2. Communication presents a special challenge for a nurse who is working with a client from another culture.

of many other cultures. Consequently, some nurses may perceive the family as "too involved" or "overprotective" in certain situations. Actually, the family may be the wellspring of mutual support, security, and fulfillment for the client. Educating the entire family and including them in the plan of care may be the most culturally competent way for nurses to achieve successful compliance and positive clinical outcomes. Understanding gender roles is also critical to the success of home care nursing interventions. For example, in Muslim cultures, the husband and father is frequently the dominant figure. He must be the primary decision maker on issues concerning a family member's health. The mother is responsible for care of the children and household. In many African-American families, the mother is usually the decision maker in all aspects of care for the family.

KEY CONCEPT

The Anglo-American emphasis on independence and individualism differs from the values of many other cultures.

Clinical Examples
with Critical Thinking

1. Mrs. Lee is an 87-year-old client with a stasis ulcer of the left lower extremity. You are attempting to teach her daughter-in-law saline dressing changes. For the last 3 days, the dressing has been off the ulcer
   when you have arrived for your daily visits. The wound is clean with
   signs of granulation tissue developing. When you ask to see the old
   dressing, both Mrs. Lee and her daughter-in-law become agitated. They
   reluctantly show you the dressing, and you notice that it is covered
   with a thin paste of dark green material.

   A. Assess your immediate response to Mrs. Lee and her daughter-in-
      law.
   B. Determine your next steps in terms of the plan of care and interven-
      tions.
   C. Identify the possible resources you would need to continue to work
      with Mrs. Lee.

2. You have completed all diabetic teaching to Mr. Sanchez and his family. Mr. Sanchez is knowledgeable of his disease process and can report
   signs and symptoms of complications, but he is incapable of testing his
   blood sugar or preparing and administering insulin. He also requires assistance with most of his ADLs. At present, you are visiting him once a
   week to draw a fasting blood sugar and to supervise the home health
   aide. At 11:00 on a Tuesday morning, you receive a page from the
   home health aide who reports that Mr. Sanchez has not yet had his glu-
   cometer check or insulin. His current lay caregiver, an 18-year-old
   grandson, whom you have met previously, was just cleaning up his
   breakfast dishes when the aide arrived. The rest of the family is out of
   town for a special fiesta.

   A. Determine your initial reaction to this situation. List emergency
      steps that you would take to address Mr. Sanchez's immediate
      needs.
   B. Explain any immediate changes you would make to the plan of care.
   C. Decide what steps you may have taken to possibly prevent this
      problem.

NUTRITION

Awareness of the common foods and eating rituals of a client's cultural group can
help the home care nurse to provide appropriate nutritional instruction (see Chapter
13). For example, to help a Cuban client with diabetes, a nurse must be aware that
the typical Cuban diet is high in calories, starches, and saturated fats. The nurse
should instruct the client to use foods that are culturally acceptable, but in proportions
that would fall within dietary allowances. A nurse working with a Jewish population

Home Care Vs. Hospital:
Cultural Adaptability

Issue	Home Care	Hospital
Potential for "culture shock"	Nurses face a high potential for culture shock. They are exposed to cultural attitudes when caring for clients in their homes, extended contacts, and more frequent and personal interactions with lay caregivers and family. Nurses frequently focus interventions on changing health behaviors of clients. Such attempts fequire a thorough understanding of cultural influences that affect these behaviors.	Nurses encounter less potential for culture shock. Exposure to clients' cultural beliefs and behaviors is minimized due to relatively short contacts with clients, the acute nature of most nursing interventions, and lack of contact with the personal environment of clients.
Role of lay caregivers	The role of lay caregivers varies across different cultures. To be effective, home care nurses must understand potential cultural differences when identifying the primary lay caregivers of clients.	Hospital nurses often have limited interactions with lay caregivers during their visits to clients. Teaching is often directed toward clients and lay caregivers when they are available.
Medical treatment plan	Clients and lay caregivers may implement the medical treatment plan inconsistently, influenced by cultural beliefs (e.g., use of folk health practices, cultural food choices).	The controlled hospital environment ensures the consistent implementation of medical treatment plans.

would need to be aware of kosher laws and methods of food preparation when attempting to instruct on nutritional requirements.

HEALTHCARE PRACTICES

Nurses need to be aware of clients whose cultural background strongly affects their daily actions, health attitudes, and beliefs. They should be aware that some clients may have a "nonbiomedical approach" to illness and health practices (Buchwald et al., 1994). Display 4-3 lists some predictors of such clients. Home care nurses should realize that health beliefs may influence the types of treatments clients will accept. Nurses should ask clients to "name" their health problems and explain why the problems started. Nurses may want to explore what a client believes an illness is doing to the body, how severe the client feels the illness is, and what problems the illness has caused for the client and lay caregivers. Nurses must assess what treatments clients think will work and what fears they have about the treatment of

Display 4-3:
Possible Predictors for Clients Using Nonbiomedical Approaches

- Emigration from a rural area
- Frequent returns to the country of origin
- Inexperience with Western biomedicine and the healthcare system
- Limited formal education
- Minimal knowledge of English
- Low socioeconomic status
- Major differences in dress and diet
- Segregation in an ethnic subculture (Johnson et al., 1996)

an illness (Buchwald et al, 1994). If clients have magico-religious beliefs, they will perceive health and illness to be controlled by a god, gods, or supernatural forces. They may believe that spirits cause their symptoms and prefer to consult a voodoo healer rather than a physician for treatment. Clients sometimes use folk remedies or consult healers in conjunction with seeing a physician. They may purchase herbs, oils, powders, and religious figurines to alleviate various maladies or to drive away evil spirits.

Clients who have a holistic approach to illness and treatment believe that a balance of harmony among the elements of nature can restore health. They may also use herbs, potions, massage, acupressure, or acupuncture to treat illness.

KEY CONCEPT

Nurses should be aware that some clients may have a "nonbiomedical approach" to illness and health practices. Home care nurses should realize that health beliefs may influence the types of treatments clients will accept.

SPIRITUALITY AND RELIGIOUS PRACTICES

The religious beliefs of clients affect their responses to health, illness, birth, death, and other life events. Spiritual and religious beliefs can foster a sense of well-being and provide clients and their lay caregivers with solace and support during illness. For example, some Roman Catholics use religious articles and types of prayers in the belief that they help people to recover from illness (Fig. 4-3). Puerto Rican clients may believe that consecrated objects and ritual sacrifices may be necessary for them to recover from illness. Nurses need to focus on promoting what is best for their clients and thus should incorporate religious practices into the traditional measures used within the plan of care (Grossman, 1996).

Nurses should understand symbols in a client's home that are signs of cultural identity. For example, a Mezuza (a small piece of parchment with biblical verses)

Figure 4-3. This Roman Catholic woman prays with a rosary for recovery from illness.

at the entrance to a home is a symbol of God's law and suggests that those who live in the home practice Judaism. Some Hispanic-Americans keep shrines, religious pictures, or statues throughout their homes. These objects may symbolize identity with a particular saint and may be significant to clients in terms of praying for intercession during times of illness (Grossman, 1996).

◆ Cultural Sensitivity

Home care nurses will encounter variations in health beliefs and practices ranging from subtle (urban vs. rural) to dramatic (Asian vs. Hispanic). Nurses must recognize the importance of avoiding superficial generalizations and cultural stereotyping. The appearances and behaviors of clients are not always predictors of differences.

Survival Alert:

*Steps for Developing a
Culturally Competent Home
Care Nursing Practice*

- Determine who the family decision maker is.
- Be flexible and refrain from judging "different" behaviors.
- Examine your own prejudices and stereotypes before treating someone from a different culture.
- Remember that no matter what cultural differences you encounter, all clients have the same basic needs for safety, security, and quality healthcare.
- Find out what is culturally acceptable for the client and refrain from doing what is culturally unacceptable.
- Incorporate the client's traditional foods into diet teaching.
- Learn a few words of the client's language to help build trust.
- Schedule visits around the client's worship and holy days.
- Find culturally-same support groups for clients and lay caregivers.
- Notify your manager of a client's cultural differences so that appropriate staff can be assigned to the client (Wargo, 1996).

Cultural sensitivity means responding to people and situations with consideration, sensibility, compassion, and empathy (Hunt and Zurek, 1997). Nurses who are culturally sensitive know to address their clients with respect always. They never assume or expect clients to behave or to feel the same as they do about health, lay caregivers, the medical establishment, illness, or death.

◆ Summary

Home care nursing is a culturally diverse type of practice, because it falls outside the "traditional" care setting of the hospital, and because the client controls the environment of care. Home care nurses who are most open to differences in staff, environments, families, living situations, health beliefs, and religious beliefs will be the most successful. Nurses must always remember that a client's plan of care will be unsuccessful if it reflects only the values of the physician or the nurse. The plan must be based on the client's values, goals, and beliefs. Nurses will serve their clients well by incorporating cultural variations into traditional interventions.

References and Bibliography

Adams, R., Briones, E.H. & Rentfro, A. (1992). Cultural considerations: Developing a nursing care delivery system for a Hispanic community. *Nursing Clinics of North America, 27*(1), 107–117.

Anderson, E.T., & McFarlane, J.M. (1996). *Community as partner: Theory and practice in nursing.* Philadelphia: Lippincott-Raven.

Andrews, M.M., & Boyle, J.S. (1995). *Transcultural concepts in nursing care* (2nd ed.). Philadelphia: Lippincott-Raven.

Bernal, H. (1993). A model for delivering culture-relevant care in the community. *Public Health Nursing, 10*(4), 228–232.

Buchwald, D., Caralis, P.V., Gany, F., Hardt, E.J., Johnson, T.M., Muecke, M.A. & Putsch, R.W. III. (1994). Caring for patients in a multicultural society. *Patient Care, 28*(10), 105–120.

California Association for Health Services at Home. *Ethnic diversity and hospice care.* Sacramento, CA: Author.

Diaz-Gilbert, M. (1993). Caring for culturally diverse patients. *Nursing 93, 23*(10), 44–45.

Editors. (1994). Confronting sexual harassment. *Nursing, 24*(10), 4580.

Eliason, M.J. (1993). Ethics and transcultural nursing care. *Nursing Outlook, 41,* 225–228.

Grossman, D. (1996). Cultural dimensions in home health nursing. *American Journal of Nursing, 96*(7), 33–36.

Haggar, V. (1994). Cultural challenge. *Nursing Times, 90*(15), 71–72.

Hunt, R. & Zurek, E.L. (1997). *Introduction to community based nursing.* Philadelphia: Lippincott-Raven.

Johnson, T.H., Hardt, F.J. & Kleinman A. (1994). *Cultural factors in the medical review.* New York: Springer-Verlag.

Kavanaugh, K.H. & Kennedy, P.H. (1992). *Promoting cultural diversity: Strategies for health care professionals.* Newbury Park, CA: Sage.

Keilich, A. & Miller, L. (1996). Cultural aspects of women's healthcare. *Patient Care, 30*(16), 60–66.

Leininger, M. (1978). *Transcultural nursing: Concepts, theories, and practices.* New York: John Wiley & Sons.

Miller, M.A. (1995). Culture, spirituality, and women's health. *JOGNN, 24*(3), 257–263.

Mitchell, A. (1995). Cultural diversity: The future, the market, and the rewards. *Caring, 96*(7), 44–48.

Price, J.L. & Cordell, B. (1994). Cultural diversity and patient teaching. *Journal of Continuing Education in Nursing, 25*(4), 163–166.

Romero, H. & Hoffman, M. (1995). Cross cultural caring-Positive outcomes in Hawaii. *Caring, 96*(7), 26–30.

Rosella. J.D., Regan-Kubinski, M.J., & Albrecht, S. (1994). The need for multicultural diversity among health professionals. *Nursing & Health Care, 15*(5), 244.

Spector, R.E. (1991). *Cultural diversity in health and illness* (3rd ed.). New York: Appleton & Lange.

Spradley B.W. & Allender J.A. (1996). *Community health nursing: Concepts and practice* (4th ed.). Philadelphia: Lippincott-Raven.

Spruhan, J.B. (1996). Beyond traditional nursing care: Cultural awareness and successful home healthcare nursing. *Home Healthcare Nurse, 14*(6), 445–449.

Taylor, C., Lillis, C. & LeMone, P. (1997). *Fundamentals of nursing: The art and science of nursing care* (3rd ed.). Philadelphia: Lippincott-Raven.

Thoraben, M. (1993). Cultural sensitivity: Educating home healthcare nurses. *Home Healthcare Nurse, 11*(4), 61–63.

Wargo, L. (1996). Teach staff about cultures they might encounter to avoid friction. *Home Care Education Management,* 81–86.

Woodruff, L. (1995). Growing diversity in the aging population. *Caring, 14*(12), 4–10.

Young, M. (1996). Who wrote the book on cultural diversity? You should. *Homecare Education Management, 1*(8), 93–98.

POST TEST

1. Explain how the composition of American society is changing.

2. List the skills that home care nurses must develop to become culturally competent.

3. Identify steps nurses should take when preparing for initial visits to clients from an ethnic group different from their own.

4. Explain internal resources within a home care agency that nurses could use to develop cultural competence.

THINKING CRITICALLY IN HOME CARE

1. Examine how the population in your own community has changed in the past ten years. Discuss whether these changes have influenced or affected you.

2. Identify three community resources you believe would help foster understanding of cultural diversity.

3. Explain what steps you would take to "blend" a client's cultural beliefs into a purely medical plan of treatment ordered by a physician.

5

Documentation

Learning Objectives

After completing this chapter, the reader will be able to:

◆ State the purposes of home care documentation.

◆ Assess the ways inaccurate documentation can adversely affect the financial health of a home care agency.

◆ Identify the regulatory bodies that use documentation to evaluate home care agencies for quality and regulatory compliance.

◆ Discuss how documentation can directly influence the provision of quality home care services.

◆ Consider how documentation by home care nurses impacts payment for services provided to clients.

◆ Discuss the five coverage criteria for Medicare.

◆ Identify other sources of payment for home care services and how their coverage guidelines compare with the Medicare program.

◆ Evaluate concepts related to documentation for payment.

Key Terms

Homebound
Medicare
Medicare Certified
Peer review organizations
Quality control

Quality management
Regional intermediaries
State licensing authorities
Utilization review

Nurses new to home care often find the documentation requirements of this specialty to be challenging. Many prefer their responsibilities not to include documentation, because it can draw attention away from client care. Nurses who enter the profession out of a desire to help others and to make a positive difference in people's lives often feel pressed for time to complete all the duties necessary to best serve their clients. They sometimes resent documentation requirements, because they can be time-consuming and distracting for nurses trying to focus on treatment.

Accurate documentation by nurses, however, is a necessity in home care. Consistent documentation of a client's condition as it relates to coverage guidelines directly affects the financial stability of a home care agency. Failure to learn and apply documentation concepts is both harmful to agencies and to clients who are denied access to required services because of poor documentation. The ability of nurses to perform this responsibility efficiently and effectively is essential for the success of the home care agency, clients, and nurses themselves.

This chapter discusses the reimbursement, regulatory, quality management, communication, and legal purposes of home care documentation. It presents common interventions that home care nurses perform but often forget to document. The particular documentation requirements of Medicare, which have greatly influenced the parameters of many other third party payors, are addressed in detail. The chapter concludes with a review of the necessity for documentation accuracy for home care nurses to be effective.

◆ Purposes of Documentation

Documentation is an important component of today's healthcare system. It is a particularly critical skill for nurses to master to be successful employees for a home care agency. The survival of these agencies largely depends upon the quality of documentation in the medical records of their clients. Documentation serves many vital purposes for the well-being of clients, nurses, and agencies. It plays an important role in financial and reimbursement issues and in evaluations of an agency's compliance with regulatory and quality control measures. Documentation is also a pivotal factor in legal issues and acts as a source of communication for those involved in a home care client's treatment.

DOCUMENTATION AND REIMBURSEMENT

Documentation by home care nurses directly impacts an agency's receipt of reimbursement from insurance companies for the services provided to their clients. The medical record establishes for payors the facts about a client's health, and the services rendered by home care professionals. Payors examine these records closely to decide whether coverage guidelines are met. Clinical notes should clearly indicate a client's current clinical status, problems, and needs; issues that short-term, intermittent, skilled interventions can resolve; and expected changes in the client's condition.

Specific, objective documentation gives payors the correct information for accurate coverage decisions. Vague documentation, however, can portray an inaccurate picture of the client's status and may result in a payor's decision to deny further coverage of home care services. When an insurance company denies a home care agency reimbursement, the agency may be forced to discontinue services to clients who cannot afford to pay privately for their care. Thus, quality documentation by nurses is crucial for clients to be able to fully maximize their insurance benefits. Adherence to quality documentation also helps agencies to ensure the continued provision of necessary services to clients in their homes. Documentation for payment is discussed in further detail later in this chapter.

KEY CONCEPT

The survival of a home care agency largely depends upon the quality of documentation by its nurses in the medical records of clients.

DOCUMENTATION AND REGULATORY ISSUES

Regulatory bodies use documentation to determine the quality of services provided by home care agencies. Many types of organizations, including JCAHO and CHAP, evaluate agencies for compliance with established standards of performance used as quality indicators (see Chapter 1). Participation in these programs is voluntary, and agencies pay JCAHO and CHAP to conduct performance evaluations intermittently. These evaluations assess a home care company's policies and procedures, quality management programs, organizational structure, processes, and client outcomes. Agencies that choose to participate do so to ensure the maintenance of appropriate levels of quality. Additionally, accreditation by JCAHO and CHAP displays a high level of quality to the medical community and to insurance companies, which frequently refer clients to accredited programs only. Reviewing a home care agency's documentation comprises a significant portion of the evaluation. If documentation does not accurately and completely reflect the status of a client and the care provided, an agency may fail to obtain accreditation.

The HCFA sponsors annual surveys of Medicare-certified home care agencies to evaluate their compliance with the Medicare Conditions of Participation (see Chapter 1). Auditors review client records chosen randomly and also visit clients to determine whether these quality standards are met. Agencies unable to prove compliance with these standards can lose their Medicare certification, and, as a result, be unable to participate in the Medicare program for reimbursement of home care services. Loss of certification would mean financial ruin for the many companies that primarily serve a Medicare client population.

Peer review organizations also conduct record reviews. These companies contract with the Medicare program to evaluate providers for quality. They perform a large role in hospitals, reviewing for appropriate use of services and premature discharges. Clients who are discharged from a hospital and readmitted within thirty

Home Care Vs. Hospital: *Documentation*

Issue	Home Care	Hospital
Documentation for reimbursement	Insurance companies base decisions for reimbursement predominantly on documentation by home care nurses.	Third party payors base reimbursement decisions on numerous sources: lab reports, physician reports, consultations with doctors, and recommendations of therapists. Nursing documentation plays a less significant role than in home care.
Regulatory issues	Through review of nursing documentation, accrediting agencies evaluate the compliance of home care agencies.	Accrediting agencies and review boards evaluate compliance with regulatory issues through analysis of many different information sources.
Interdisciplinary communication	Communication among disciplines often depends upon documentation of each involved discipline's observations and relevant information.	Interdisciplinary communication often occurs verbally.

days may initiate a request for a home care record review by a peer review organization. The medical record is then examined for appropriate home care interventions in response to the identified problems of the client. Peer review organizations have the authority to issue sanctions and monetary penalties or to remove healthcare providers from the Medicare program if serious infractions are found. If the client record fails to reflect assessment findings or interventions in response to findings accurately, the home care agency may be penalized unnecessarily.

Other regulatory bodies that review home care documentation are **state licensing authorities**. Most states establish licensing criteria that must be met to operate a home care agency. For most states, these regulations are similar to the Medicare Conditions of Participation. State surveys and the Medicare compliance audit may occur simultaneously, and record review is a primary component of the state audit. Failure to pass this survey can result in the loss of the agency's license and thus the ability to provide services in that state legally.

KEY CONCEPT

Many regulatory organizations use the medical record as the basis for their determination of compliance with standards and the provision of appropriate, quality home care services.

DOCUMENTATION AND QUALITY MANAGEMENT

Individual home care agencies have developed **quality management** programs to meet regulatory standards and to improve the quality of the services they provide. Quality management programs generally consist of three distinct components:

1. Review of quality control and compliance
2. Utilization review
3. Organization performance (or quality) improvement

Various regulatory bodies conduct quality control and utilization review by examining the medical records of clients that the agency has served. During **quality control** examination, an agency's records are reviewed for compliance with specific standards. In **utilization review**, the agency's charts are examined to evaluate the appropriateness, frequency, and duration of home care services provided to clients. These audits identify quality or utilization issues of concern within the agency to quickly establish opportunities for improvement of client care. If information is inappropriately documented, the record may reflect problems that are not actually issues for client care. Time and energy may be spent trying to resolve predicaments and problems that do not actually exist.

Arguments have been made that these efforts do not actually "assure" quality of services. JCAHO and CHAP have developed standards for performance improvement that require agencies seeking accreditation to actively determine the quality issues within their own organizations. Identification of these issues helps an agency to measurably improve client care by targeting the processes within the agency itself that influence client and organizational outcomes.

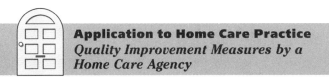

Application to Home Care Practice
Quality Improvement Measures by a Home Care Agency

A performance improvement program at the Baker Home Care Agency includes identifying clients who have experienced an inappropriate number of falls. The Baker Agency wants to record the number of falls its clients experience and compare that number with those of other home care agencies. If the number statistically exceeds that of other organizations, the Baker Agency will review literature on fall prevention programs that have been effective in reducing falls at other home care agencies. By establishing this program, the Baker Agency hopes to improve its process of identifying clients at risk for falls and to implement education and fall prevention interventions. The agency can continue to evaluate the effectiveness of these interventions and revise as needed until it achieves desired results.

DOCUMENTATION AND COMMUNICATION

Another purpose of documentation is to provide the home care nurse with an effective means of communication with other healthcare professionals. Particularly in home care, a significant amount of the communication between professionals involved in a case is written, because of the relatively infrequent opportunities for in-person discussions. Medical records that are incomplete or inaccurate can negatively impact client care. Incomplete communication of a client's condition can result in the provision of inappropriate care, which can adversely affect the client's status. If a lawsuit occurs, documentation in the medical record is the primary source of information from which a legal decision would be made.

KEY CONCEPT

Documentation in home care provides a method of communicating a client's needs to all involved disciplines. Failure to accurately and completely document in the medical record can result in uncoordinated services and have adverse consequences on client care.

DOCUMENTATION AND LEGAL ISSUES

Healthcare professionals have lost many lawsuits because medical records have failed to reflect accurately the actions taken in the care of clients. The old adage, "if it is not documented, it wasn't done" continues to apply in the courts today. Therefore, complete recording of a client's assessment and all the actions taken to address any problems is the nurse's best protection.

◆ Documenting Interventions

Nurses must remember the importance of documenting all of the interventions they perform while providing care for clients. Especially in home care, nurses are at risk of forgetting or neglecting to document certain activities they conduct that are second nature to them in hospitals and other settings. Because third party payors maintain strict rules about reimbursement for home care services, an accurate record of care is pivotal for nurses to maintain.

TEACHING

Home care nurses commonly teach in response to assessment data they have collected. Nurses frequently conduct informal teaching, such as answering clients' questions regarding their medications, while performing other interventions. Unless teaching occurs in a formal session with audiovisual tools, however, nurses often forget to document it, although teaching can be one of the most valuable services given to clients. For example, a nurse sees that a client is showing the initial symptoms

Survival Alert:

Potential Legal Problems in Documentation

Content Problems That Increase Legal Risks

• Not in accordance with professional or healthcare organization standards
• Not reflective of client needs
• Fails to include description(s) of situations that are out of the ordinary
• Overgeneralizes client assessment or nursing interventions
• Incomplete or inconsistent
• Does not include appropriate medical orders
• Implies a potential or actual risk situation
• Implies an attitudinal bias

Mechanical Problems That Increase Legal Risks

• Lines between entries
• Countersigning documentation
• Tampering
• Different handwriting or obliterations
• Illegibility
• Sloppiness (some lawyers infer sloppy care from sloppy charting)
• Dates and times of entries omitted or inconsistently documented
• Improper nurse signature or unidentifiable initials
• Transcription errors (notes made at bedside later transcribed into client record; problems include the amount of time that elapses between the event and when it is recorded, errors associated with recopying)

(Adapted from Eggland, E. T. & Heinemann, D. S. [1995]. Nursing documentation: Charting, recording and reporting. *Philadelphia: J. B. Lippincott.)*

of a potential complication. The symptoms are not significant enough to report to a physician. The nurse instructs the client on these symptoms, the related disease process, and what to do if the symptoms worsen. This teaching is a significant part of the client's treatment. The nurse must remember to include it in the documentation.

RESPONSE TO TEACHING

Nurses must also remember the importance of documenting a client's or lay caregiver's response to teaching. For example, if a client experiences an adverse event because of noncompliance, the client can claim that a nurse failed to provide adequate instruction regarding the consequences of noncompliance. Appropriate documentation of teaching and the client's demonstration of the learned procedure can later protect the nurse from litigation.

INTERDISCIPLINARY COMMUNICATION

Communication with other healthcare professionals and lay caregivers is an under-documented intervention in home care. The standard that nurses should follow when determining the significance of communication is whether client care is affected. Whenever nurses discuss potential clinical or treatment changes with others involved in a client's care, they should enter the contact into the medical record. The communication may be significant, because services are frequently coordinated through these sessions, or important instructions are given to lay caregivers. Although such interactions rarely occur at the time of primary documentation, and thus can easily be forgotten, nurses need to remember to record these discussions because they frequently result in revisions to the client's treatment plan.

KEY CONCEPT

Home care nurses should consistently document all teaching interventions and interdisciplinary communications, even when they perform these actions informally.

ACCURACY OF MEDICAL RECORD

The medical record should contain a clear picture of a client's status and services received. Documentation should be as succinct as possible, providing essential information and eliminating insignificant details. Home care nurses must document information specifically and objectively and refrain from injecting their personal opinions in the record. Extraneous information in the medical record can confuse issues and waste valuable time.

As in hospital settings, when errors in documentation occur, nurses should draw a single line through the inaccurate material, initialing above the error (Fig. 5-1). All documentation should be written in black ink, which provides the best photocopy quality. Nurses should not use correction fluid under any circumstances. If nurses make late entries in the record, they should identify them as such with the date and time.

◆ Documentation for Payment

In home care, an important function of the nurse is documentation for payment. Unlike nurses in other clinical practice settings, home care nurses must develop a comprehensive understanding of factors that impact reimbursement for services. In other practice settings, insurance companies determine payment for care by reviewing multiple sources of information to verify the client's status (e.g., regular physician notes, laboratory results, graphs of vital signs, radiology reports). In home care, however, various third party payors depend heavily upon the documentation of nurses to decide whether interventions meet their established criteria. A nurse's failure to appropriately record clinical findings can result in denial of coverage for a client. For many clients, accessing services without the financial support of insur-

---

SAMPLE OF CORRECTED DOCUMENTATION

error—vitals of different patient

1/25/98 0930 Patient complains of shortness of breath. ~~BP 156/88 P 80 R24~~ *C.H.*
BP 142/80 P 92 R 30 Productive cough clear sputum. Lung sounds-rales LLL. Notified Dr. Sandoval.

C. Hunhoff, RN

SAMPLE OF LATE ENTRY

Progress Note

Client Kevin Minden   **Date** 3/31/98   **Time** 0800
B/P 160/80   **T** 98.4 degrees **F.**   **P** 84 reg.   **R** 14

Assessment Findings 67 y.o. male. Wound at groin, 3 cm. × 2 cm., depth–2 cm. Wound bed pink and granulating—clear serous drainage saturating 3 4 × 4 gauze dressings. Sterile wet to dry dressing applied—reinforced with ABD. MSW report client will be moving to daughter's home in 3 weeks   daughter can be instructed in wound care.

R. Greenberg, RN

Late Entry: 1600 Skin, approximately 1 cm. around wound macerated and red. Client complains of pain with dressing change.

Figure 5-1. Sample correction of a charting error and sample late entry.

ance plans creates a financial hardship. Moreover, an insurance company may refuse services vital to a client's well-being. As a result, clients may suffer increased morbidity or fail to achieve functional levels that can improve their quality of life.

KEY CONCEPT

In home care, various third party payors depend heavily upon the documentation of nurses to determine whether interventions are covered within their established criteria. A nurse's failure to appropriately record clinical findings can result in denial of coverage for services to a client.

Thousands of insurance organizations include home care as a benefit within their plans. Each organization uses its own processes and criteria to determine whether home care services are covered. Nurses, however, can generally refer to some common guidelines that most organizations follow when developing home care treatment plans for clients.

MEDICARE

Medicare, the single largest payor of home care services in the United States, is a health insurance plan established in Title 18 of the Social Security Act. This national health insurance program provides coverage for persons over the age of 65 and for the disabled. HCFA determines how Medicare pays benefits and contracts with insurance companies known as **regional intermediaries** to implement benefits in various parts of the country. Home care agencies send claims to their assigned intermediary, who then determines whether services rendered meet the criteria established within Medicare. The intermediary then pays providers accordingly.

Only those home care agencies that have become **Medicare Certified** can bill the Medicare program for services. Agencies obtain certification after proving to the assigned regulatory agency that they have met Medicare Conditions of Participation. These requirements include guidelines for medical record contents, qualifications and supervision of staff, client rights, physician involvement, quality control, and utilization review.

Medicare has become the model of coverage criteria for many other third party payors of home care services. Medicaid, federally required HMOs, and most private insurances require agency providers to be Medicare certified and to follow Medicare's criteria for intermittent, skilled home care services.

KEY CONCEPT

Understanding Medicare criteria for home care services is critical for nurses. Medicare is currently the largest payor for home care. Most other payors use the Medicare guidelines as a model for their coverage criteria as well.

MEDICARE COVERAGE GUIDELINES

Medicare consists of two distinct insurance benefits: Medicare Part A, which is the hospital benefit, and Medicare Part B, which covers outpatient services. Currently, Medicare Part A pays for the majority of home care. Clients who meet guidelines for home care services receive full coverage from Medicare. The Medicare benefit has been the template that most other third party payors with home care coverage follow. Medicaid helps low income families access healthcare at costs shared by the federal and state governments. States individually determine eligibility requirements, and each implements Medicaid home care benefits differently. HMOs and PPOs develop their own criteria for approving home care services. These organizations typically attempt to manage healthcare expenses through utilization review. They provide care through specified providers within the medical system that are usually owned, contracted, or employed by the organization. Case managers or utilization review nurses may require ongoing communication about a client's status before providing authorization for coverage. Frequently, after they give verbal authorization, they will not render final payment for services until they review documentation to ensure that services were appropriate and medically necessary.

Payors generally have five primary criteria that must be met for clients to access home healthcare services:

Care is ordered by a qualified physician.
Services are required on an intermittent or part-time basis.
The client is homebound.
Services are skilled.
Services are medically necessary.

Medicare and other payors have established definitions and tests to determine whether individual clients meet these criteria (Display 5-1).

Care Is Ordered by a Qualified Physician

Payors consistently require that physicians order services and treatments given to clients in the home. Doctors of medicine, osteopathy, and podiatry can authorize home care services under appropriate circumstances. Home care nurses need to understand the types of services that require physician orders and how documentation should reflect these orders once followed (Fig. 5-2).

Physician Responsibility. For services to be covered under most insurance plans, a physician must develop a plan of treatment. Medicare requires this plan of care to include the client's diagnoses, medications, rehabilitative potential, prognosis, and the frequency and duration of required treatments and services. Physicians typically develop treatment plans immediately after home care nurses complete the comprehensive initial assessment of clients (see Chapter 13). Nurses and physicians must attempt to project home care services for the period of the medical treatment plan. Medicare allows a 62-day period, and specified orders in plans of treatment. Orders must generally include any home health services for which the home care agency wants to bill. Interventions that normally do not require a physician's authorization under a state's Nurse Practice Act may require physician orders in home care. For example, client teaching and assessment are normally considered independent nursing interventions. If third party payors are asked to pay for such services that a home care nurse conducts, however, documentation must specify that a physician authorized these interventions. Physicians generally view decisions to perform such interventions as within the scope of responsibilities of professional nurses. They usually depend upon the recommendations of home care nurses and collaborate with them to create medical treatment plans for clients.

Frequently, the plan of treatment needs to be adjusted to meet a client's evolving needs. Medications may be changed, the need for an ancillary service may be identified weeks after the initial acceptance of service, the frequency or duration of service may be modified, or interventions performed by any of the involved disciplines may need to be altered to better meet the client's needs. To meet the coverage criteria of most payors, any changes to the initial plan of treatment require physician orders for them to be covered.

The home care agency must be able to show that a physician has authorized all services for which it bills. A qualified healthcare professional typically obtains physician orders for home care services over the telephone, transcribes them onto a treatment plan, and mails them to the physician's office for signature.

(text continues on page 116)

Display 5-1:
Questions to Determine Medicare Coverage

SERVICES ARE ORDERED BY A PHYSICIAN

- Has the prescribing doctor authorized the specific home care services provided?
- Has the prescribing doctor authorized the frequency and duration of services?

SERVICES ARE PART-TIME OR INTERMITTENT

- Are nursing and home health aide services required for more than 35 hours per week or 8 hours per day?
- If skilled nursing and home health aide services are required for up to 35 hours per week, but less than 8 hours per day, does documentation support the need for the appropriateness and medical necessity of such care?

CLIENT IS HOMEBOUND

- Are absences from the home infrequent and of short duration?
- If not, are absences related to receiving medical treatment that the client cannot receive in the home?
- Does the client require the assistance of another person and/or an assistant device to leave the home?
- Is leaving the home medically contraindicated for the client?
- Do environmental factors make leaving the home difficult for the client? (for example, a wheelchair-bound client has an apartment with stairs but no elevator.)

SERVICES ARE SKILLED

- Does the client require skills of a licensed nurse, physical therapist, or speech therapist?
- If home health aides, social services, and occupational therapy are required, is the client also receiving a skilled service (i.e., skilled nurse, or physical or speech therapy)?
- If occupational therapy is necessary, was a skilled service previously involved in the client's home care treatment plan?

SERVICES ARE REASONABLE AND MEDICALLY NECESSARY

- Does the client's medical condition warrant the services that are prescribed?
- Is it reasonable to expect an adverse outcome if an intervention is not performed?
- Is the frequency of services prescribed appropriate to the severity of the client's medical condition?

Department of Health and Human Services Health Care Financing Administration					Form Approved OMB No. 0938-0357	

HOME HEALTH CERTIFICATION AND PLAN OF CARE

1. Patient's HI Claim No.	2. Start Of Care Date	3. Certification Period		4. Medical Record No.	5. Provider No.
		From:	To:		

6. Patient's Name and Address	7. Provider's Name, Address and Telephone Number

8. Date of Birth	9. Sex ☐ M ☐ F	10. Medications: Dose/Frequency/Route (N)ew (C)hanged

11. ICD-9-CM	Principal Diagnosis	Date

12. ICD-9-CM	Surgical Procedure	Date

13. ICD-9-CM	Other Pertinent Diagnoses	Date

14. DME and Supplies	15. Safety Measures:

16. Nutritional Req.	17. Allergies:

18.A. Functional Limitations

1 ☐ Amputation	5 ☐ Paralysis	9 ☐ Legally Blind
2 ☐ Bowel/Bladder (Incontinence)	6 ☐ Endurance	A ☐ Dyspnea With Minimal Exertion
3 ☐ Contracture	7 ☐ Ambulation	B ☐ Other (Specify)
4 ☐ Hearing	8 ☐ Speech	

18.B. Activities Permitted

1 ☐ Complete Bedrest	6 ☐ Partial Weight Bearing	A ☐ Wheelchair
2 ☐ Bedrest BRP	7 ☐ Independent At Home	B ☐ Walker
3 ☐ Up As Tolerated	8 ☐ Crutches	C ☐ No Restrictions
4 ☐ Transfer Bed/Chair	9 ☐ Cane	D ☐ Other (Specify)
5 ☐ Exercises Prescribed		

19. Mental Status:	1 ☐ Oriented	3 ☐ Forgetful	5 ☐ Disoriented	7 ☐ Agitated
	2 ☐ Comatose	4 ☐ Depressed	6 ☐ Lethargic	8 ☐ Other

20. Prognosis:	1 ☐ Poor	2 ☐ Guarded	3 ☐ Fair	4 ☐ Good	5 ☐ Excellent

21. Orders for Discipline and Treatments (Specify Amount/Frequency/Duration)

22. Goals/Rehabilitation Potential/Discharge Plans

23. Nurse's Signature and Date of Verbal SOC Where Applicable:	25. Date HHA Received Signed POT

24. Physician's Name and Address	26. I certify/recertify that this patient is confined to his/her home and needs intermittent skilled nursing care, physical therapy and/or speech therapy or continues to need occupational therapy. The patient is under my care, and I have authorized the services on this plan of care and will periodically review the plan.

27. Attending Physician's Signature and Date Signed	28. Anyone who misrepresents, falsifies, or conceals essential information required for payment of Federal funds may be subject to fine, imprisonment, or civil penalty under applicable Federal laws.

Form HCFA-485 (C-4) (02-94) (Print Aligned)   **PROVIDER**

Figure 5-2. Home Health Certification and Plan of Care required by Medicare.

If a complication or problem often associated with a client's diagnosis is antici-pated, the treatment plan can include an established number of "prn" or "as needed" visits to perform specific interventions. For example, a physician may include 1 or 2 prn visits per month for a client with a foley catheter, in order for the nurse to change the catheter if it leaks or becomes plugged. This preestablished order for an "as needed" visit will authorize the nurse to handle expected problems without needing to contact the physician to obtain a supplemental order.

KEY CONCEPT

To receive reimbursement from most payors, physicians are required to authorize services that nurses can normally perform independently. A collaborative relationship between the nurse and physician is necessary to establish a successful plan of treatment for a client.

Nursing Responsibility. Home care nurses must prioritize the need to collabo-rate with physicians to obtain appropriate orders for nursing visits. Third party payors will pay only for services authorized by a physician as proved through a signed doctor's order in the medical record. Though it may meet each of the other require-ments for coverage, most insurance carriers will deny coverage for a visit if a physi-cian's order for it does not exist. Physicians must designate specifically the frequency and duration of a nurse's home care visits.

Services Are Required on an Intermittent or Part-time Basis

Medicare has established that clients receive home care services on a part-time or intermittent basis and excludes the provision of continuous care services and daily visits. The Health Insurance Manual (HIM 11) has identified this type of care as beyond the scope and intent of the home care benefit (Display 5-2). The Medicare benefit specifically defines services that extend beyond the scope of intermittent care. Medicare and most insurance carriers allow daily skilled nursing visits for distinctly short periods, such as two or three weeks. If a client's clinical condition warrants daily visits beyond this period (e.g., a client requiring a daily dressing change), documentation needs to support the medical necessity of such services with a finite and predictable endpoint. Additionally, a physician must authorize continued daily visits and estimate the length of time a client will need them.

The part-time/intermittent standard is rarely an issue in the provision of home care services for most agencies. When a client requires frequent nursing interventions for dressing changes or intravenous infusions, however, services and the client's condition must be continually evaluated. Physicians should establish such interven-tions for a finite period, with supplemental physician orders granted intermittently to renew the frequency of these interventions and to predict their duration.

The Client Is Homebound

Medicare and most third party payors establish that a client is homebound based on physician certification of this status. Documentation must support this claim by

Home Care Conflict:
Nonreimbursed Services

Mrs. Watts received home care services after a total hip surgery. Two weeks after her admission to home care, her diabetes became unstable. The home care nurse informed Mrs. Watts' physician, who suggested that the nurse change the dosage of insulin. In subsequent visits, the nurse assessed Mrs. Watts for signs and symptoms of hyperglycemia and instructed her regarding diet and disease process. Medicare denied each of these subsequent nursing visits for lack of physician orders. Although the services were skilled and medically necessary, no documentation could show that the physician authorized follow-up visits.

Medicare will deny any additional services for reimbursement if physician orders are missing. For example, Mr. Stewart's doctor prescribes home care nursing visits for sterile dressing changes on a decubitus ulcer three times a week. Three weeks after the initiation of services, Mr. Stewart's lay caregiver calls the home care agency to report that the dressing has fallen off. The on-call nurse visits Mr. Stewart that evening to replace the dressing. Medicare denies this visit because it falls outside the number of visits prescribed by the client's physician. Although the visit is medically necessary, the medical record does not show Medicare criteria for physician authorization of services. A private insurance policy covers ancillary services, such as medical social services, only if interventions are performed with the *client*. Mr. Bleecker, a 42-year-old man diagnosed with pancreatic cancer, is insured by this policy. His physician gave him a prognosis of 1 to 2 weeks at the point when he became unresponsive. Mrs. Bleecker experienced difficulty coping with the burden of her husband's immediate care and the knowledge of his imminent death. The home care nurse recommended a social work evaluation that was approved by Mrs. Bleecker's physician. The social worker provided counseling to Mrs. Bleecker and initiated hospice volunteers. The social work visits were not reimbursed by Medicare, however, because services were provided not directly to the client but to his wife.

reflecting that a client cannot easily leave home to receive necessary services, and that doing so requires considerable and taxing effort. Homebound status is supported if a client's medical condition requires the use of an assistive device, special transportation, or the assistance of another person to leave the home.

Clients can be considered homebound even though they occasionally leave the home for non-medical purposes. Such absences must be infrequent and of short duration. Sometimes, clients must leave the home frequently or for extended periods to receive medical care that cannot be provided at home. For example, cancer sufferers who require daily radiation therapy can receive home care services if the other criteria of homebound status are met. Most payors continue to view these clients as homebound and qualified for home care services.

Occasionally, clients with no ambulatory problems are considered homebound,

Display 5-2:
*Definition of Part Time/Intermittent Health Insurance Manual
Rev. 277, 1996*

206.7 *Part-time or Intermittent Home Health Aide and Skilled Nursing Services.*—Where a patient qualifies for coverage of home health services, Medicare covers either part-time or intermittent home health aide services and skilled nursing services.

A. DEFINITION OF PART-TIME

Part-time means any number of days per week:

* Up to and including 28 hours per week of skilled nursing and home health side services combined for less than 8 hours per day; or
* Up to 35 hours per week of skilled nursing and home health aide services combined, for less than 8 hours per day, subject to review by fiscal intermediaries on a case by case basis, based upon documentation justifying the need for and reasonableness of such additional care.

B. DEFINITION OF "INTERMITTENT"

"Intermittent" means:

* Up to and including 28 hours per week of skilled nursing and home health aide services combined, provided on a less than daily basis;
* Up to 35 hours per week of skilled nursing and home health aide services combined that are provided on a less than daily basis, subject to review by fiscal intermediaries on a case by case basis, based upon documentation justifying the need for and reasonableness of such additional care; or
* Up to an including full-time (i.e., 8 hours per day) skilled nursing and home health aide services combined, which are provided and needed 7 days per week for temporary, but not indefinite, periods of time of up to 21 days, with allowances for extensions in exceptional circumstances where the need for care in excess of 21 days is finite and predictable.

if leaving home to receive healthcare services is medically contraindicated for them. Physicians sometimes designate clients with psychiatric conditions, for whom leaving the home is contraindicated, as homebound. A client's environment may also contribute to his homebound status.

KEY CONCEPT

Clients are considered homebound if leaving the home to receive necessary healthcare services is medically contraindicated for them.

The nurse must document findings relevant to a client's homebound status regularly throughout the home care treatment period, particularly for those clients

Application to Home Care Practice
Examples of Clients Considered Homebound

* Mr. Yum receives home care services after a prolonged hospitalization for unstable angina. He requires a neighbor's assistance to attend an appointment with his physician due to generalized weakness. An excursion to the doctor's office is physically difficult and fatiguing for Mr. Yum. He is considered homebound even though he is able to ambulate independently in his own home. Mr. Yum's poor endurance limits his ability to seek appropriate levels of medical services outside the home.
* Mrs. Giordano is still considered homebound under Medicare's definition even though she leaves her home once every 3 weeks to go to the hairdresser. As long as this outing requires the use of an assistive device or accompaniment by another person, demands considerable and taxing effort from Mrs. Giordano, and occurs infrequently, it will not jeopardize her homebound status.
* Mrs. Blair has been diagnosed with breast cancer. After chemotherapy, Mrs. Blair is certified as homebound by her physician because of her weakened immune system. It is medically contraindicated for Mrs. Blair to leave her home to have laboratory tests taken or to go to her physician's office for a clinical assessment. Therefore, home care services are covered by Medicare to provide skilled, medically necessary care to Mrs. Blair in her place of residence.
* Mr. Walthers was recently hospitalized for an exacerbation of paranoid schizophrenia. When he is discharged from the hospital, Mr. Walthers continues to be highly fearful of others. Heightened levels of anxiety when leaving his home to receive psychiatric care would ultimately slow his recovery. Home care provides necessary services until Mr. Walthers is able to return to the mental health clinic.
* Mr. Wryczensky is considered homebound because he lives on the second floor of an apartment building with no elevator and has difficulty climbing stairs.
* Mrs. Dougherty meets the requirements for homebound status because she cannot tolerate exposure to extremes in temperature due to her medical condition.

with diagnoses that do not normally cause reduced mobility. For example, a Medicare reviewer will question home care services given to a client with an injury to an upper extremity. If the client is truly homebound in this circumstance, a nurse must carefully document this finding.

Services Are Skilled

Medicare is usually the most restrictive payor in its definition of skilled services. Some payors are less stringent in adhering to the Medicare criteria, especially if they view home care as a cheaper alternative to more expensive care for the client (e.g., for a client requiring hospitalization if home care services were not available). Private insurance companies may also authorize continuous care nursing, respiratory therapy, nutritional services, homemaker services, or other interventions not usually covered under the Medicare benefit. Frequently, private insurance companies hire case managers or authorization nurses to determine the appropriateness and cost-effectiveness of services. These employees can provide phone authorization for services immediately when a client is referred to home care. This practice differs distinctly from Medicare's procedure of reviewing documentation and authorizing payment retroactively. Other insurers are much more restrictive than Medicare, allowing for only a specified number of home care visits per calendar year, or providing no home health aide services at all.

Services are considered skilled under the Medicare program if they require the interventions of a licensed nurse (Display 5-3), a physical therapist, or a speech therapist. If a client needs one of these services, Medicare may also reimburse other services, including home health aides, medical social services (Display 5-4), and occupational therapy. If a client no longer needs care from a skilled nurse, physical therapist, or speech therapist, occupational therapy may continue to be covered under the Medicare benefit. When a client no longer requires skilled services, however, Medicare will stop reimbursement for interventions by a social worker or home health aide. Chapter 7 discusses indications and referrals to ancillary services in detail.

Services Are Medically Necessary

All third party payors require that home care services provided to a beneficiary are medically necessary and appropriate to diagnosis and treatment needs. This criterion is generally considered the most difficult test for home care coverage. Even if a

---

Display 5-3:
Subpart C—Furnishing of Services

484.30 CONDITION OF PARTICIPATION: SKILLED NURSING SERVICES

The HHA furnishes skilled nursing services by or under the supervision of a registered nurse and in accordance with the plan of care.

(a) Standard: Duties of the Registered Nurse. The registered nurse makes the initial evaluation visit, regularly reevaluates the patient's nursing needs, initiates the plan of care, plans necessary revisions, provides those services requiring substantial and specialized nursing skills, initiates appropriate preventive and rehabilitative nursing procedures, prepares clinical and progress notes, coordinates services, informs the physician and other personnel of changes in the patient's condition and needs, counsels the patient and family in meeting nursing and related needs, participates in inservice programs, and supervises and teaches other nursing personnel.

(HCFA Medicare Conditions of Participation CFR 42)

Display 5-4:
Subpart C—Furnishing of Services

484.34 CONDITION OF PARTICIPATION: MEDICAL SOCIAL SERVICES

If the agency furnishes medical social services, those services are given by a qualified social worker or by a qualified social work assistant under the supervision of a qualified social worker, and in accordance with the plan of care. The social worker assists the physician and other team members in understanding the significant social and emotional factors related to the health problems, participates in the development of the plan of care, prepares clinical and progress notes, works with the family, uses appropriate community resources, participates in discharge planning and in-service programs, and acts as a consultant to other agency personnel.

(HCFA Medicare Conditions of Participation CFR 42)

client is homebound and the services ordered by a physician are considered skilled, Medicare will deny reimbursement if the client's medical condition does not appear to warrant the services provided. For example, a client's physician orders a sterile dressing change to be performed on a wound three times a week. Certainly, the criteria of physician authorization, skilled intervention, and intermittent duration of care are met. If the wound is a small abrasion, however, the intervention requested will probably not be considered a medical necessity and thus will fail to meet all of the criteria for Medicare coverage. In another case, a physician includes orders for the home care nurse to assess a client's vital signs and overall condition. If the client's condition has been and is expected to remain stable, medical justification for these services is difficult to provide for reimbursement.

When attempting to determine the medical necessity of an intervention, nurses should question whether it is reasonable to expect an adverse outcome if they do not perform the intervention. Clearly, if a client was recently discharged from a hospital with an exacerbated chronic condition, monitoring the client for a period to ensure clinical stability is considered medically necessary. Medication teaching is considered necessary for a client who is using newly prescribed drugs, but unnecessary for a client who has been on the same medications for years. What is considered medically necessary for one client is sometimes considered unnecessary for another with the same diagnosis and medical history. One factor that affects this difference is how quickly a client learns or individually responds to interventions.

OTHER PAYORS

The Medicare benefit has been the template that most other third party payors with home care coverage follow. Some payors are less stringent in adhering to the Medicare criteria, especially if they view home care as a cheaper alternative to more expensive care for the client (e.g., for a client requiring hospitalization if home

Clinical Example
with Critical Thinking

Mr. Kerkar is a 72-year-old client who was diagnosed with Parkinson's disease 3 years ago. Following a recent doctor's appointment, Mr. Kerkar's physician calls a home care agency and asks for a home care nursing evaluation to determine whether Mr. Kerkar qualifies for services under the Medicare benefit. A nurse from the agency performs a complete assessment and makes the following observations:

- Mr. Kerkar and his wife are knowledgeable about the disease process.
- Mr. Kerkar has a shuffling gait characteristic of Parkinson's disease and has fallen twice in the past month, resulting in minor cuts and scratches.
- Mr. Kerkar is becoming more debilitated and requires more assistance from his wife with his activities of daily living, such as dressing, eating, showering, etc.
- Mrs. Kerkar has healthcare problems as well, including high blood pressure and occasional angina. She has recently become highly stressed due to her husband's deteriorating physical condition and has experienced exacerbations of blood pressure and angina.
- Mrs. Kerkar does not know whether she can continue to care for her husband at home, but doesn't want to place him in a skilled nursing facility.
- Mr. Kerkar suffers from occasional depression. He does not want to leave his home, yet worries that he has become a burden for his wife. He is also very concerned about her health problems.

1. Determine whether Mr. Kerkar qualifies for home care services under the Medicare Part A benefit.
2. Be able to provide an example of effective documentation to support home care assistance if you believe it is required.
3. Evaluate what other home care services (if any) may be covered for Mr. Kerkar under the Medicare benefit.
4. Provide the documentation needed in Mr. Kerkar's record to support the medical necessity requirement for these additional services.

care services were not available). Private insurance companies may also authorize continuous care nursing, respiratory therapy, nutritional services, homemaker services, or other interventions not usually covered under the Medicare benefit. Frequently, private insurance companies hire case managers or authorization nurses to determine the appropriateness and cost-effectiveness of services. These employees can provide phone authorization for services immediately when a client is referred to home care.

◆ Accuracy of Documentation

Home care nurses frequently establish a client's eligibility for both the skilled nursing interventions that they provide and also for therapies, social services, and home health aides their clients require for optimum functioning. If a client's condition does not warrant the level, frequency, or type of service provided, reimbursement for care is denied. Sometimes, however, coverage criteria are met, but clients are denied coverage because documentation inaccurately portrays their condition or the level and type of service given. Healthcare professionals have a general tendency to document a client's status in a positive way. A client's problems, however, must be accurately reflected in the home care documentation or services will be denied.

For example, two nurses encounter and treat the same client. One documents as follows:

"Client ambulates well. No complaints. Moves all extremities. Alert and oriented. Lungs clear."

Anyone reading these notes would logically conclude that this client requires no healthcare services. Another nurse, however, examines the same client and documents the following:

"Client ambulates 20 ft. before needing to rest. Generalized weakness. Oriented, but poor short term memory, difficulty remembering instructions on medications.

TABLE 5-1. *Questionable vs. Effective Documentation*

QUESTIONABLE	EFFECTIVE
At client's request (may be questioned if client appears to be directing care)	By request of physician (if accurate; focus on the physician's directing of care)
Chronic	Acute exacerbation or acute episode
Discussed	Instructed, educated
Doing well	Comprehends (state quantitative measurements)
General weakness	Short of breath on exertion, unable to walk without assistance because of poor balance, can only sit up for 30 minutes, chair-bound, bed-bound, hemiparesis
Left home to live with son	Was removed from the home by relatives to more suitable surroundings
No change	Unresolved
Improving	Give details: improving wound decreased from 2 cm to 1 cm, continues to need instruction on safe use of walker
No complaints	Identify problems and needs: poor balance, unsteady, able to ambulate only 10 feet without tiring and becoming dizzy
No problem	No *new* problems
Not at home	Locked door, no answer
Observed	Assessed, evaluated (document specifics)

(continued)

TABLE 5-1. (CONTINUED)

QUESTIONABLE	EFFECTIVE
Reinforced	Continues to need instructions because client is slow learner because of recent stroke
Stable or stabilizing (except at discharge)	Appears to be responding to treatment, unstable, deteriorating
Noncompliant	Lack of understanding, language barrier, slow learner
No progress	Document specifics of progress (measurements, gradations, and levels): otherwise discharge (especially rehab clients)
Plateaued	Document specifics of graded progress; if no progress is demonstrated, either discharge client or place on hold and reevaluate in a timely manner
Pulse irregular	Describe pulse: bounding, weak, thready, unequal, skipped beats, bigeminal rhythm
Reviewed	Continues to need instruction because _____ (explain)
Told client to contact physician (when relates to plan of care)	Registered nurse or therapist contact physician (when relates to performance of skilled care, instabilities, deficits or significant changes in client's condition)
Accu-check (glucose) readings very inconsistent from one reading to next	Accu-check (glucose reading, range 220–460, 2 hours postprandial)
Ambulates independently, ambulates without difficulty	The ability to ambulate may bring the client's homebound status into question; therefore, the documentation must clearly indicate what makes the client homebound and should refer to specific function and affected extremities (e.g., upper, lower) or psychological instabilities that render client homebound.
Gait steady, gait steady at times	Unsteady gait, poor balance, tremors, vertigo, syncope
Intake poor, poor appetite	Describe exact intake: no solid foods, taking 2,000 cc fluid/day
Lack of description of the dimensions and drainage of wound	Wound 14 cm × 9 cm × 8 cm, with serosanguinous drainage saturating two 4 × 4 gauze dressings in 4-hr period (use consistent measurements, either centimeters or inches in accordance with agency policy)
Monitored	Evaluated, assessed
Supervised	Evaluated, instructed
Repeated instruction	Client/lay caregiver unable to give a return demonstration of previous instruction, requiring additional education/instruction
Low sodium taught	Began teaching on 2-g sodium diet (give specific aspect taught)
Diabetic diet taught	Began teaching on 1,200 cal ADA diet (give specific aspect taught)
Insulin rejection given	Nurse administered 15 units NPH insulin subcu, right deltoid area

(Adapted from MJGC Orientation Manual)

Client becomes slightly short of breath on exertion and states, 'I just do not feel well.' "

Like the adage that one individual sees a glass of water half full, while another claims it is half empty, two very different pictures have been painted of this client's status.

To provide the justification for home care services and access to healthcare resources for clients, nurses must document the status of their clients as precisely as possible. They must clearly specify reasons for ordered interventions. Documentation of conversations with other healthcare professionals, pertinent subjective statements made by clients or lay caregivers, measurable descriptions of a client's functional status and ability to learn new information presented in teaching, wound measurements, and specific descriptions of drainage and tissue help to paint a vivid picture of the client's needs for those evaluating the record for appropriateness of care provided.

Home care nurses must be careful to document all of the interventions conducted within a home care visit. Frequently, a nurse automatically performs skilled nursing interventions that are medically necessary for the client's condition, but fails to document some clinical activities. Client teaching and assessment are often second nature to experienced nurses; therefore, they may not recognize them as distinct interventions. Documentation of all skilled interventions is important for payment purposes, and also for risk management purposes in the case of litigation. Table 5-1 provides thorough guidelines for home care nurses to follow when documenting.

◆ Summary

Understanding the importance of documentation and its relationship to reimbursement issues in the home care practice setting is critical for nurses, who must develop an awareness of the types of services that clients can access through various third party payors. Medicare has developed the model that most insurers follow when determining eligibility. Understanding and applying Medicare's five basic coverage criteria when performing an initial assessment, developing a client's plan of treatment, and documenting clinical notes are vital skills for the home care nurse to acquire. Accurately describing the client's medical history, current condition, response to treatment, and any intervening factors will answer the question, "Why does this client need home care services?" When they consistently record the answers to this question in home care documentation, nurses have fulfilled this important responsibility, ensuring that their clients receive needed services.

References and Bibliography

Allen, S. (1994). Medicare case management. *Home Healthcare Nurse, 12*(3), 21–27.
Brent, N.J. (1997). The home healthcare nurse and confidentiality and privacy. *Home Healthcare Nurse, 15*(4), 256–258.
Calfee, B.E. (1996). Labor laws: Working to protect you. *Nursing, 26*(2), 34–40.
Eggland, E. & Heinemann, D. (1994). *Nursing documentation, charting, recording, and reporting.* Philadelphia: J.B. Lippincott.

Ellenbecker, C. & Shea, K. (1994). Documentation in home healthcare practice: Evidence of quality care. *Nursing Clinics of North America, 29*(3), 495–506.

Elliot, L. & Kulwicki, G. (1993). Improving patient education documentation. *Nursing Management, 24*(10), 61–62.

Gale, B.J. & Steffl, B.J. (1992). The long-term care dilemma: What nurses need to know about Medicare. *Nursing and Healthcare, 13*(1), 34–41.

Gruber, M. & Gruber, J.M. (1990). Nursing malpractice: The importance of documentation, or saved by the pen! *Gastroenterological Nursing, 12,* 255–259.

Health Care Financing Administration. (1990). *Health insurance manual* (pub No. 11—rev 277). Washington, DC: Department of Health and Human Services.

Health Care Financing Administration. (1989). *Medicare conditions of participation.* 42 CFR, Part 484 (Aug. 14). Washington, DC: Department of Health and Human Services.

House, E. (1992). Resistance to documentation—A nursing research issue. *International Journal of Nursing Studies, 29*(4), 371–381.

Iyer, P.W. & Camp, N. (1995). *Nursing documentation: A nursing process approach* (2nd ed.). St. Louis: Mosby-Year Book.

Joint Commission on Accreditation of Healthcare Organizations. (1996). *1997–1998 Comprehensive accreditation manual for home care.* Oakbrook Terrace, IL: Author.

Magliozzi, H. (1990). Home care: Charting makes it through the Medicare maze. *RN, 53*(6), 75–79.

Mandell, M. (1994). Not documented, not done. *Nursing, 24*(8), 62–63.

Marrelli, T.M. (1996). *Nursing documentation handbook* (2nd ed.). St. Louis: Mosby-Year Book.

Martin, F. (1994). Documentation tips to help you stay out of court. *Nursing, 24*(6), 63–64.

Parker, C. (1997). Charting by exception. *Caring Magazine, XVI*(3), 36–44.

Sullivan, G. (1994). Home care: More autonomy, more legal risk. *RN, 57*(5), 63–64, 67–69.

Zang, S.M. & Bailey, N.G. (1997). *Home care manual: Making the transition.* Philadelphia: Lippincott-Raven.

POST TEST

1. List five purposes documentation serves in home care.

2. Explain how and why inaccurate documentation impacts the financial health of home care agencies.

3. List four organizations that use documentation to evaluate home care agencies for quality or payment.

4. Name the most underdocumented skilled service in home care.

5. Identify how documentation can impact the delivery of quality care.

6. Discuss the reasons documentation is important from a legal perspective.

7. Evaluate the critical relationship between home care and reimbursement.

8. Determine the importance of understanding the Medicare benefit for home care nurses.

9. State the five criteria for reimbursement under Medicare.

10. List the three disciplines that are considered to provide skilled services under Medicare.

THINKING CRITICALLY IN HOME CARE

Most payors and regulatory bodies would consider the following sample documentation questionable. Revise these examples to make them more accurate and effective.

1. Sandy Jones, 48 y.o., with diagnosis of dilated congestive cardiomyopathy x 2 yrs. BP 90/50 P 98 R 24. Pulse irregular. Chronic low blood pressure. Lungs clear. No problem with respirations—pulmonary status stabilized. Condition improving. No complaints. Generalized weakness. Discussed long term plans. Discussed board and care or hospice alternatives when no longer able to care for self. Reinforced need for energy conservation techniques since client non-compliant.

   Revised documentation:

2. Mike Feldman, 77 y.o., diagnosis of osteomyelitis, status post total L. hip arthroplasty 3 months ago. Moves all extremities; alert and oriented. c/o chronic pain L. hip. IV site clear and patent. Lungs clear. Pulse regular. Patient status improved. Reinforced need for mobility and adequate diet.

   K. Senke, RN

   Revised documentation:

6

Client Rights and Responsibilities

LEARNING OBJECTIVES

After completing this chapter, the reader will be able to:

◆ Explain the significance of maintaining client rights.

◆ Identify various client rights.

◆ Evaluate the importance of maintaining confidentiality.

◆ Determine the increased risks of breaching a client's confidentiality in the home care setting.

◆ Explain how clients can waive their rights to confidentiality and, give an example of a circumstance in which they may choose to do so.

◆ Discuss client responsibilities.

◆ Consider the ways in which issues involving client rights and responsibilities can result in ethical quandaries for the home care nurse.

KEY TERMS

Advance directive
Autonomy
Beneficence
Empowerment
Ethical review committee

Home health hotline
Living will
Noncompliance
Nonmaleficence

T*he rights* and responsibilities of clients for their own health have become issues for home care nurses to consider. Traditionally, healthcare professionals viewed themselves as guardians of health for their clients and provided services in a paternalistic manner. In the past, clinicians maintained a "we-know-what's-best-for-you" manner when dealing with clients, an attitude that clients both accepted and expected. The public delegated responsibility for health to physicians. When problems occurred, people visited their doctors to be "fixed"—an idea that the medical community perpetuated.

Recently, however, society has recognized that many health problems cannot be "fixed," and individuals have developed a sense of personal responsibility for their well-being. Knowledge about the important roles nutrition and exercise play in disease prevention has encouraged many to pursue healthier lifestyles. The public continues to demand information from their physicians and insurance companies that will enable them to make health decisions consistent with their personal values. People are no longer passive recipients of healthcare, but active participants.

Home care nurses need to increase their awareness of client rights and responsibilities. This chapter helps nurses to become knowledgeable of the regulations that have been established to protect client rights and to integrate them into every aspect of home care nursing practice. Although frustration is a natural emotion when clients exercise their rights in a manner perceived to be detrimental to their health, nurses have successfully fulfilled their duties if they have maintained and protected client rights. This chapter stresses the right of all clients to be respected for the unique individuals that they are and for their ability to make choices. Along with possessing certain rights that healthcare professionals must uphold, clients also have a responsibility to comply with measures home care nurses implement to improve and to maintain their health. These responsibilities are examined in detail. Issues surrounding client rights and responsibilities can sometimes lead to ethical dilemmas for those involved in providing care. This chapter encourages nurses to become aware of the possibilities for conflict so they are prepared to face these ethical issues and to propose effective solutions.

◆ Client Rights

Congress has developed specific laws regarding the maintenance of client rights in home care, reflected in the Omnibus Budget Reconciliation Act of 1987 (OBRA-87). Failure of a home care agency to comply with these regulations is a serious offense and can result in severe consequences for the organization. Accrediting bodies such as JCAHO and CHAP also evaluate the practices of home care agencies for compliance with client rights and standards (see Chapter 5).

The fundamental concept behind all client rights is simply the basic right of a person to be treated as a unique and valued individual. Personal rights are not diminished for those requiring assistance from the healthcare system. They are as important to those experiencing illness or disability as to those enjoying full health. Although most infractions of client rights are committed innocently by well-meaning healthcare professionals, the result is a demonstration of disrespect for the client. Home care nurses need to be highly aware of client rights to maintain them consistently.

KEY CONCEPT

One concept summarizes all of the client rights: each person has the basic right to be treated as a unique and valued individual.

NOTICE AND EXERCISE OF CLIENT RIGHTS

Clients must be notified in writing and orally of their rights before or during the initial home care visit, and before any services are provided. The National Association of Home Care has issued a Homecare Bill of Rights (Fig. 6-1) that acts as a model for agencies to follow. Nurses must communicate this information in a way that each client readily understands. For clients who are hard of hearing, nurses need to verify that their clients have heard the information. For those who speak another language, nurses must make sure that clients have interpreted and comprehended information. Home care agencies must be able to show that they have informed their clients of their rights. Nurses should document that they have educated clients regarding their rights during the initial visit. Information on client rights may also require follow-up teaching beyond the first visit. Clients must be able to exercise their rights. If a client has been found unable or incompetent to make decisions independently, a lay caregiver may exercise rights on the client's behalf.

KEY CONCEPT

Nurses must communicate client rights in a way that clients easily understand before initiating any services.

THE RIGHT OF RESPECT FOR PERSONAL PROPERTY

Respect for a client's property is a particularly important issue for nurses to consider when providing care in the home. Hospitals encourage clients to leave personal property at home to avoid damage or loss. Therefore, hospital nurses rarely need to consider this issue. They have more leverage in determining what environmental adjustments will make their work most efficient and effective. Moving a bed or equipment in a hospital room is not given a second thought by either the nurse conducting a needed procedure or the client.

In the home, however, property belongs to the client. Home care nurses must develop a sense of awareness regarding this sensitive issue to demonstrate respect for personal property. Altering a room in any way may disturb a client, even when an alteration is as temporary as moving some figurines on a table while preparing

(*text continues on page 133*)

HOME CARE

BILL OF RIGHTS

Home care clients have a right to be notified in writing of their rights and obligations before treatment begins to exercise those rights. The client's family or guardian may exercise the client's rights when the client has been judged incompetent. Home care providers have an obligation to protect and promote the rights of their clients, including the following rights:

Clients and Providers Have a Right to Dignity and Respect

Home care clients and their formal caregivers have a right to not be discriminated against based on race, color, religion, national origin, age, sex, or handicap. Furthermore, clients and caregivers have a right to mutual respect and dignity, including respect for property. Caregivers are prohibited from accepting personal gifts and borrowing from clients.

Clients have the right:

◆ to have relationships with home care providers that are based on honesty and ethical standards of conduct;

◆ to be informed of the procedure they can follow to lodge complaints with the home care provider about the care that is, or fails to be, furnished and about a lack of respect for property. (To lodge complaints with us call _____);

◆ to know about the disposition of such complaints;

◆ to voice their grievances without fear of discrimination or reprisal for having done so; and

◆ to be advised of the telephone number and hours of operation of the state's home care "hot line," which receives questions and complaints about local home care agencies, including complaints about implementation of advance directive requirements.
The hours are _____ and the number is _____.

Decision-making

Clients have the right:

◆ to be notified in advance about the care that is to be furnished, the types (disciplines) of the caregivers who will furnish the care, and the frequency of the visits that are proposed to be furnished;

◆ to be advised of any change in the plan of care before the change is made;

◆ to participate in the planning of the care and in planning changes in the care, and to be advised that they have the right to do so;

◆ to be informed in writing of rights under state law to make decisions concerning medical care, including the right to accept or refuse treatment and the right to formulate advance directives;

◆ to be informed in writing of policies and procedures for implementing advance directives, including any limitations if the provider cannot implement an advance directive on the basis of conscience;

◆ to have health care providers comply with advance directives in accordance with state law requirements;

◆ to receive care without condition on, or discrimination based on, execution of advance directives; and

◆ to refuse services without fear of reprisal or discrimination.

The home care provider or the client's physician may be forced to refer the client to another source of care if the client's refusal to comply with the plan of care threatens to compromise the provider's commitment to quality care.

Privacy

Clients have the right:

◆ to confidentiality of the medical record as well as information about their health, social, and financial circumstances and about what takes place in the home; and

◆ to expect the home care provider to release information only as required by law or authorized by the client and to be informed of procedures for disclosure.

Figure 6-1. A home care bill of rights. (Reproduced with permission from the National Association for Home Care, from *Bill of Rights*. Not for further reproduction.)

Financial Information

Clients have the right:

- to be informed of the extent to which payment may be expected from Medicare, Medicaid, or any other payor known to the home care provider;
- to be informed of the charges that will not be covered by Medicare;
- to be informed of the charges for which the client may be liable;

- to receive this information, orally and in writing, before care is initiated and within 30 calendar days of the date the home care provider becomes aware of any changes; and
- to have access, upon request, to all bills for service the client has received regardless of whether the bills are paid out-of-pocket or by another party.

Quality of Care

Clients have the right:

- to receive care of the highest quality;
- in general, to be admitted by a home care provider only if it has the resources needed to provide the care safely and at the required level of intensity, as determined by a professional assessment; a provider with less than optimal resources may nevertheless admit the client if a more appropriate provider is not available, but only after fully informing the client of the provider's limitations and the lack of suitable alternative arrangements; and

- to be told what to do in the case of an emergency.

The home care provider shall assure that:

- all medically related home care is provided in accordance with physicians' orders and that a plan of care specifies the services and their frequency and duration; and
- all medically related personal care is provided by an appropriately trained home care aide who is supervised by a nurse or other qualified home care professional.

Client Responsibility

Clients have the responsibility:

- to notify the provider of changes in their condition (e.g., hospitalization, changes in the plan of care, symptoms to be reported);
- to follow the plan of care;
- to notify the provider if the visit schedule needs to be changed;

- to inform providers of the existence of any chnages made to advance directives;
- to advise the provider of any problems or dissatisfaction with the services provided;
- to provide a safe environment for care to be provided; and
- to carry out mutually agreed responsibilities.

Additional Agency Information

To satisfy the Medicare certification requirements, the Health Care Financing Administration requires that agencies:
1. Give a copy of the Bill of Rights to each patient in the course of the admission process.
2. Explain the Bill of Rights to the patient and document that this has been done.

Agencies may have clients sign a copy of the patients *Bill of Rights* to acknowledge receipt. This patients *Bill of Rights* meets Federal Medicare requirements but may not meet state requirements. Agencies should develop an addendum if needed to meet additional state requirements.

Figure 6-1. (Continued)

a dressing change. Nurses must obtain permission from clients before taking any such action. Failure to obtain this permission shows a lack of respect for property and can lead clients to believe they are not respected as individuals. Nurses must prioritize respect for the home and property of clients for whom they care. Simply by asking permission before implementing any change in a client's home, a nurse expresses respect for the property and, more important, respect for the person. Home care agencies are required to investigate all complaints regarding employees who have failed to respect a client's property.

K E Y   C O N C E P T

The failure of nurses to obtain permission to move or to handle anything in a client's home demonstrates a lack of respect for the client's property. Clients may assume that they are also not respected as individuals.

THE RIGHT TO RECEIVE FINANCIAL INFORMATION

Clients have the right to be informed orally and in writing of reimbursement provisions for the home care services they receive (Fig. 6-2). They must be informed of the extent to which third party payors, such as Medicare, Medicaid, and private insurance companies, will reimburse for services. Clients must also be informed of and consent to any financial obligations they will retain before any services are provided to them. If any monetary changes or adjustments occur during the course of care, the home care agency must notify the client as quickly as possible.

Figure 6-2. A nurse explains important financial information to a home care client. (Photo by Marilu Sherer, CARING)

If a client requires a referral to another component of the home care agency or its parent company, the attending nurse must disclose to the client the overall benefits to the organization. For example, Mrs. Seeley has been receiving intermittent nursing services through a hospital-based home care agency. The nurse caring for her identifies a need for private duty homemaker services and a walker. If the private duty and durable medical equipment companies are also owned by the hospital, the nurse must notify Mrs. Seeley of this financial relationship and the financial benefit the agency receives from the referral for these services.

Clients have the right to review all bills for the home care services they receive, even when a third party payor fully reimburses services. Home care agencies must provide copies of all bills upon the client's request to give clients the opportunity to ensure accuracy.

KEY CONCEPT
Clients have the right to be fully informed of all provisions for the financial reimbursement of home care services and financial benefits to the parent organization of referred services.

THE RIGHT TO PRIVACY AND CONFIDENTIALITY

People entering the healthcare system must fully disclose many intimate and private aspects of their lives to obtain appropriate treatment for their medical problems. Although healthcare providers may have the best interests of their clients at heart, private information divulged inappropriately can cause emotional, social, or economic injury to clients and lay caregivers. Therefore, many legal and regulatory mechanisms protect the right to confidentiality.

Legal Action

A home care agency can suffer severe consequences if it neglects to protect the confidentiality of the medical records of its clients. Most state laws treat a nurse's failure to maintain confidentiality rigidly and consider unauthorized disclosure of information in the medical record a solid basis for litigation. States often regard these mistakes as breaches of confidentiality or negligent disclosures of client information (Rozovsky & Rozovsky, 1993). Employees may also find themselves personally liable for exposing protected information to unauthorized individuals. Healthcare professionals could be sued in civil court for defamation of character or invasion of privacy. In addition, maintaining a client's confidentiality is typically included within home care agency policies; an employee's failure to comply with agency regulations can result in disciplinary action, including documented performance counseling or termination of employment.

An agency must notify clients of its policies and procedures regarding circumstances in which it discusses clinical records. For example, an agency may establish a provision to give the medical records of its clients to state or federal regulatory

Home Care Vs. Hospital:
Client Rights and Responsibilities

Issue	Home Care	Hospital
Nursing accountability for educating clients regarding rights and responsibilities	Home care nurses are primarily responsible for educating clients about their rights and responsibilities, for ensuring comprehension, and for documenting in the record that rights were discussed.	In hospitals, personnel from various departments (e.g., admitting, registration) provide clients with copies of their rights and responsibilities.
Informed consent for medical procedures	Nurses must obtain informed consent from clients for home care medical procedures.	Physicians have primary responsibility for obtaining informed consent in hospitals. Nurses must validate that informed consent was provided.
Maintaining confidentiality of medical records	Nurses create medical records in the field. They often use "field charts" on a continuing basis. Nurses are responsible for maintaining the confidentiality of this material.	Hospital personnel create and keep medical records in specific locations of the hospital.

bodies for review of compliance with quality and payment standards. Clients must be informed of this practice.

Risks

Opportunities for breach of confidentiality can occur in any healthcare setting. Home care inherently contains an increased risk of the inadvertent disclosure of protected information. For clients who receive services in hospitals or clinics, client documentation usually remains contained and protected within the confines of the physical location. Home care clients receive treatment in the community; thus, nurses often bring client information in and out of the home in order to provide safe and effective services. For example, some nurses carry pieces of the medical record to a client's home so that pertinent information is available when they perform interventions. Although this behavior is perfectly appropriate (provided the home care agency allows this practice), nurses increase their risk of accountability should client documentation be inappropriately disclosed. Careless positioning of a client's clinical record where a visiting friend or neighbor can see it clearly puts a nurse at risk of inadvertently revealing protected information.

Nurses should be keenly aware of their responsibility to safeguard clinical documentation at all times. Often, families, neighbors, and friends request information regarding clients out of a desire to help them. For example, a neighbor may want to offer emotional support to a client diagnosed with a serious illness, and a family member may wish to pay for medications or equipment. They want details of the client's condition first and ask for information from the home care nurse. A nurse who is trying to find all possible resources for the client may be especially tempted

Clinical Example
with Critical Thinking

Consider the following situations:

1. You have just received a phone call from a person who claims to be a brother of one of your clients. He says he is a physician and lives out of state. He expresses concern about the level of medical treatment his brother is receiving and questions whether he should come and visit. He starts asking you very specific questions regarding your client's condition.
   A. Assess how you should respond to the questions. Determine what information (if any) you are able to provide.
   B. Evaluate your next steps. Be able to identify the reasons for your actions within the context of client rights.
2. You have recently admitted Mrs. McClintock to home care services. The client and her family actively participate in the care planning on the initial visit. You perform intermittent skilled nursing visits to teach Mrs. McClintock and her husband about her newly diagnosed diabetes, how to self-administer insulin, and how to follow a diabetic diet. After 2 weeks of service, the client has shown appropriate technique with insulin injections and accurately verbalizes knowledge of the diet she must follow. Her blood sugars remain erratic, however, after several insulin dosage changes. Upon taking leave of the McClintocks after a regular visit, Mr. McClintock follows you to your car. He informs you that his wife has not been following the established diet plan and regularly eats candy and drinks alcohol in the evening.
   A. Identify the client rights and responsibilities involved in this situation. Determine the level of family involvement and issues involving breach of confidentiality in this situation.
   B. Assess the next steps that you should take.
   C. Decide what should be done if the client continues to ignore her prescribed diet and her blood sugars remain unstable.

to divulge details freely. Sharing this type of information, however, is clearly outside regulatory standards. The client must grant permission before any such discussions occur.

KEY CONCEPT

Sharing private information of any kind without the express permission of clients is a clear violation of the right to privacy. A breach of confidentiality that causes harm can result in liability for the nurse and the home care agency.

Some agencies allow nurses to complete documentation outside the agency's office, especially if the nurses cover large service areas and require extensive travel time to document at the agency. Nurses who document outside the office face a tremendous risk of inappropriate exposure of client information. They must take great caution when practicing in this fashion, since the healthcare professional is responsible for preventing destruction of or modification to the home care record.

Less peer support is available for home care nurses than for those in other healthcare settings because of the independent nature of this type of practice. Consequently, home care nurses may experience an increased desire to discuss a client's health with their family members, friends, and other loved ones, because fewer opportunities exist for discussion with other professionals involved in the client's care. Laws and regulations, however, deem any such unauthorized disclosure of client information as a breach of confidentiality. Such breaches are considered grounds for disciplinary action within an agency and for civil liability.

Releases

Clients may wish to waive the right to confidentiality and allow the home care agency to share clinical information. Clients often choose this option if they want an agency to bill an insurance company directly for services, because most third party payors require medical information before they authorize payment. A consent form signed by the client must be in the agency's records before it releases any information.

Frequently, an agency will ask a client to sign a release of information form during the admission process. This document specifies to whom the agency may release information. Occasionally, clients consider moving to board and care or skilled nursing facilities, especially when lay caregivers are absent, or adequate support is unavailable to help clients safely remain at home. Home care nurses are often involved in facilitating the transfer when clients decide to move. Most facilities require medical information about clients before they agree to admit them. Nurses must obtain a release of information from clients to disclose this requested information to potential facilities.

THE RIGHT TO SELF-DETERMINATION

Involvement in decision making is another important concept for home care nurses to master when considering client rights. Clients have the right to be involved with decision making related to any aspect of their care. The role of the nurse includes educating clients regarding care options. This knowledge allows clients to give informed consent for needed services. Although they can make recommendations about the care choices available, nurses must strongly communicate that final decisions are a client's to make.

Education

The responsibility of healthcare professionals to make clients aware of their conditions and to involve them in decision making is a recent development. This change has increased the level of interaction that nurses have with their clients and has allowed a "shared" responsibility for a client's health to flourish. Only a few years ago, even simple tasks, such as informing clients of their blood pressure readings, needed to be done by physicians. Moreover, clients were told their readings only upon request, because the ultimate responsibility for their health was delegated to physicians.

Changing times have led clients to view themselves as consumers within the service industry of healthcare. Subsequently, nurses are now expected to educate clients regarding treatment options available to them and the potential consequences of their various decisions (Fig. 6-3). This transition can be difficult for healthcare providers, particularly when clients make decisions nurses themselves would not choose. Healthcare providers are learning to shift their perceptions of their role from "protector" of well-being to "educator" of choices. "The ability to withhold judgment, to avoid pressure by imposing our own point of view, requires the highest degree of skill and an uncompromising respect for the rights of the individual" (Field, 1967, p. 149).

Noncompliance. Maintaining the role of educator can be extremely frustrating for nurses dealing with clients who behave self-destructively. **Noncompliance** with a medical regimen designed to improve a client's health may result in increased symptoms and a decline in well-being for the client. When clients appear unwilling to modify their behavior, though changes would dramatically improve their conditions, nurses may feel angry with them and view noncompliance as a personal failure. Case law and statutory law, however, have upheld that " . . . in all states a competent person has the right to refuse or to discontinue treatment, even if such a request is not in accordance with the home care provider's ethical or religious beliefs" (Schatzki & Tamborlane, 1988, p. 58).

Nonjudgmental Approach. Nurses must remember that *clients are individually responsible for their own treatment decisions*. The nurse's role is to inform clients of

Figure 6-3. Clients have the right to understand all of the treatment options available to them in order to receive the most appropriate care. This nurse explains some choices to a client.

options, to make recommendations, and to address possible consequences (Fig. 6-4). Nurses must demonstrate a nonjudgmental perspective when educating clients regarding their healthcare options. Clients who sense that nurses will perceive their circumstances or choices negatively may withhold information about their condition and decisions. Obviously, the nurse's ability to provide effective services will thus be compromised.

The home care nurse's ability to implement an effective plan of care depends greatly upon a client's report of symptoms and compliance with an established medical regimen. Fundamental to providing quality services in the home setting is the ability of nurses to gain the trust of their clients. Nurses can establish trust by projecting an objective, nonjudgmental attitude toward a client's choices. Otherwise, clients will be afraid to be candid with nurses, leading to inappropriate interventions.

KEY CONCEPT

The role of nurses in home care is to educate clients regarding their healthcare choices and the consequences of the decisions they make. Participation in decision making is the right and the responsibility of the home care client.

Influence

Home care nurses can positively influence the health decisions of their clients. By displaying genuine concern for an individual's health and well-being, respecting whatever decisions a client makes, providing an environment in which information can be exchanged readily, and responding to questions openly and honestly, nurses create a therapeutic relationship with clients based upon mutual respect. Clients

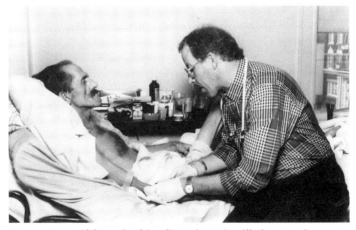

Figure 6-4. Although this client is quite ill, he continues to smoke. The nurse must remember that the client is ultimately responsible for his own health. (Photo by Marilu Sherer, CARING)

will most likely follow the advice of nurses who express genuine concern for their health and respect for them as individuals.

Nurses should consider the influence of the family and other lay caregivers when clients are making treatment decisions. Family interference can limit the ability of clients to take personal responsibility for their treatment decisions (Hospitals & Health Networks, 1993). Educating the client's lay caregivers regarding treatment options and consequences helps to make alternatives more accessible and understandable. Nurses must, however, obtain the client's consent before divulging any private information.

Developing a Plan of Care

Clients make decisions not only about treatments, but about all aspects of care. Clients have the right to refuse services. Thus, healthcare providers must involve them in all care planning decisions. Clients must have the opportunity to accept or decline all available options. Nurses should discuss specific recommendations regarding ancillary services and the time and frequency of visits with clients. Once a client, nurse, and physician have mutually agreed upon a plan, a document should be written specifying the care that is to be furnished, the types of disciplines that will furnish the care, and the proposed frequency of services to be provided. Joel Gurin, science editor at *Consumer Reports* magazine, states "Everybody should be able to get the level of explanation that is going to make them feel most comfortable, and the level of participation that's going to make them feel best" (Hospitals & Health Networks, 1993, p. 44).

Alterations to the Plan of Care

Occasionally, clients feel uncomfortable with a particular clinician or a specific plan of care. Clients should be informed upon admission to home care services of their right to request a change in personnel. Nurses must stress to their clients that no repercussions will stem from a decision to exercise this right. They must also inform clients of the right to refuse the recommendations of healthcare professionals without any fear of reprisal or discrimination. Clients must be informed of any changes to their plan of care before changes are made. They must be made aware of any necessary changes to their scheduled visits in a timely fashion. Nurses must attempt to adhere to visits initially scheduled with clients; however, if a schedule or visit change becomes necessary, nurses should notify clients when that need is identified.

Emergency Response Service

Clients have the right to predetermine whether they wish to receive emergency response services. Federal law mandates that clients be informed of their right to refuse services, including life-sustaining measures. An **advance directive** formally documents the preferences of individuals in case they become unable to inform healthcare personnel of their wishes. Nurses must inform clients of this option when they are admitted to home care service.

By using advanced directives, competent patients indicate what interventions they wish to refuse or accept should they lose the capacity to make decisions about their care. Advanced directives include conversations, written directives, living wills, and durable powers of attorney for healthcare. Advance directives are often vague and require interpretation and the development of a careplan with specific orders (i.e., No-CPR) (Chandra & Hazinski, 1994, p. 7).

Clients should discuss their wishes with physicians well before an emergency occurs to ensure that they have made an informed decision. Physicians should incorporate a client's wishes into the treatment plan and communicate them to everyone involved in the client's care. A "No CPR" or "Do Not Resuscitate" order is one mechanism by which clients inform nurses of these wishes. If no such written documentation exists, however, nurses must assume that a client wants resuscitative services and provide them in the case of an emergency.

Family Override. In emergencies, a client's family may demand resuscitative services, even with the existence of a "No CPR" order. Under such circumstances, home care nurses should initiate the emergency response to give themselves an opportunity to verify the validity of the doctor's order and to resolve the conflict with the family. If deemed appropriate, services can be withdrawn later.

Living Will. Similar circumstances exist when a living will is inconsistent with a medical treatment plan. A **living will** is one tool used to establish the desired medical services if the client becomes incapacitated (Fig. 6-5). Nurses, however, are obligated to follow physician orders, not living wills. If a conflict exists in the event of an emergency, emergency response procedures should be initiated. The living will can be interpreted later.

THE RIGHT TO RECEIVE QUALITY HEALTHCARE SERVICES

Clients have the right to receive quality healthcare services. An agency should only accept a client if it has adequate resources available to meet the client's needs. For example, an agency that admits a client who requires daily dressing changes, but has inadequate staffing to provide the necessary weekend visits, has violated this client's right to quality care. In this instance, the agency has inappropriately accepted responsibility for a client's healthcare needs while being unable to meet them. A client's right to receive quality care also means that physician orders are followed. If a client's treatment plan is revised without a doctor's authorization, quality of care can be negatively impacted.

Quality client care requires appropriately trained personnel to perform necessary interventions. If home care nurses perform procedures in which they do not demonstrate competency, a client's right to quality care has clearly been ignored. For example, an agency assigns an inexperienced nurse to a client who requires the use of an IV pump. Lack of appropriate knowledge about the use of specific IV pumps could lead the nurse to dose inaccurately or could lead to the occlusion of a line. Blood drawn by a nurse who lacks venipuncture experience may result in multiple sticks or an insufficient specimen.

The right to quality care also includes receiving education regarding potential medical emergencies and interventions that clients should perform in these emergencies. Nurses neglect their responsibility to provide quality clinical services if they do not provide clients with this important information. Because professionals assess

---

TO MY FAMILY, MY PHYSICIAN, MY LAWYER, MY CLERGYMAN
TO ANY MEDICAL FACILITY IN WHOSE CARE I HAPPEN TO BE
TO ANY INDIVIDUAL WHO MAY BECOME RESPONSIBLE FOR MY HEALTH, WELFARE OR
AFFAIRS

Death is as much a reality as birth, growth, maturity and old age—it is the one certainty of life. If the time comes when I, _____ can no longer take part in decisions for my own future, let this statement stand as an expression of my wishes, while I am still of sound mind.

If the situation should arise in which there is no reasonable expectation of my recovery from physical or mental disability, I request that I be allowed to die and not to be kept alive by artificial means or "heroic measures". I do not fear death itself as much as the indignities of deterioration, dependence and hopeless pain. I, therefore, ask that medication be mercifully administered to me to alleviate suffering even though this may hasten the moment of death.

This request is made after careful consideration. I hope you who care for me will feel morally bound to follow its mandate. I recognize that this appears to place a heavy responsibility upon you, but it is with the intention of relieving you of such responsibility and of placing it upon myself in accordance with my strong convictions, that this statement is made.

Signed _____

Date _____
Witness _____
Witness _____
Copies of this request have been given to _____
_____
_____
_____

Figure 6-5. A living will is one mechanism individuals may use to express their wishes in advance of incapacitating illness or injury.

them intermittently, home care clients must be able to identify early signs of problems independently and to perform appropriate courses of action. Without this information, a medical emergency can progress to dangerous levels before a client takes appropriate measures. For example, disastrous and unnecessary consequences can result for a diabetic client who has not been taught to recognize symptoms of insulin reaction and the appropriate response measures.

KEY CONCEPT

Nurses have neglected their responsibility to provide quality clinical services if they have not informed their clients of potential emergencies and interventions that they can perform in the event of such emergencies.

Application to Home Care Practice:
Physician Authorization for Treatment
Plan Alterations

Mrs. Harrelson is receiving home care services for a wound. Mrs. Harrelson's insurance company informs the home care agency that daily dressing changes for the wound will be authorized for 1 week only. Mrs. Harrelson's daughter, Julie, who is the lay caregiver, must learn how to perform the dressing change independently after 7 days. The physician has ordered daily visits by a home care nurse to perform the wound care and is uncomfortable with Julie assuming this duty. The agency is now placed in the situation of performing nonreimbursed services. If the nurse decreases the frequency of services without the physician's authorization, quality of care could be compromised. The nurse and agency are responsible for ensuring the safety of the client.

The home care nurse can take several courses of action to resolve this issue with the active participation of the client and her physician:

- First, the nurse can encourage the physician and Mrs. Harrelson to appeal the insurance company's decision based upon the client's clinical needs. Sometimes, nonclinicians make reimbursement decisions. Discussing the situation with a health plan's nurse, case manager, or medical director can often resolve an issue like this one quickly. Often, when an insurance company is informed of the potential consequences and costs of refusing to approve the provision of an appropriate plan of care, it quickly reverses its initial decision.
- If this course of action is unsuccessful, the home care nurse can discuss other treatment options with the physician. For example, the physician may be able to prescribe an alternative wound care procedure easier for Mrs. Harrelson or Julie to learn that still provides safe and effective treatment. The nurse may attempt to find another lay caregiver to perform the dressing change who will be more competent in learning the procedure.

If none of these options is available, and Mrs. Harrelson is unable to pay for services independently, the home care organization cannot abandon her without making arrangements for the provision of necessary services in some manner.

◆ Client Complaints

Home care agencies must have policies and protocols for the receipt and resolution of complaints from clients and lay caregivers. Upon admission to home care services, clients must be informed of these protocols. Nurses should emphasize that clients will not suffer retaliation or discrimination for voicing concerns, and that they will be notified of results if they make complaints.

Each state is required to furnish a **home health hotline**—a phone number the public can call to ask about local agencies or to lodge complaints. State agencies investigate complaints made regarding a home care agency, evaluate the agency's compliance with regulatory standards, and assess its maintenance of client rights. The state can issue citations for regulatory noncompliance. Agencies in which deficiencies and inadequacies are found are required to provide corrective action plans to ensure future compliance.

KEY CONCEPT

Nurses should stress to clients and their lay caregivers that they will not suffer retaliation or discrimination for voicing concerns and complaints.

◆ Client Responsibilities

Home care nurses should take all possible measures to ensure that they vigorously protect the rights of clients. Clients also have important responsibilities, however, that they must fulfill in order for healthcare professionals to perform their duties competently. Failure of clients to provide complete information about their health, to cooperate in maintaining a safe home environment, to inform home care personnel when they cannot keep an appointment, to adhere to an established plan of care, and to voice questions and concerns about confusing information or issues can hinder a nurse's ability to treat them effectively. The health of clients may then be unnecessarily jeopardized, and their quality of life needlessly compromised.

KEY CONCEPT

In addition to rights, clients have responsibilities that allow healthcare professionals to perform their duties competently.

COMPLETE INFORMATION

Clients are responsible for providing accurate and complete information about their health and medical history to home care staff. Failure of clients to give accurate details about their health status can result in inappropriate treatment. For example, Mrs. Dierker has kept every medication ever prescribed for her in her medicine cabinet "just in case" she experiences any of the same symptoms again. When a nurse asks to see all of her current medications, Mrs. Dierker fails to show some medications in the cabinet that she takes "now and again." As a result, the nurse receives a physician order for a medication for Mrs. Dierker that negatively interacts with another medication that Mrs. Dierker takes on occasion. Because Mrs. Dierker has never made the nurse aware of the other medication, identifying the cause of the problem should symptoms from the interaction arise would be difficult, if not impossible, for the nurse and the physician.

SAFE ENVIRONMENT

Another responsibility of clients is to help home care nurses in establishing and maintaining a safe environment. Nurses may identify health risks in the client's environment that can negatively affect the effectiveness of the care plan. Clients need to cooperate with nurses to eliminate such risks. Consider Mr. Schader, who suffers from an unsteady gait due to generalized weakness and osteoarthritis. Papers and trash clutter his home, placing Mr. Schader at a high risk of falling. In this situation, Mr. Schader is responsible for accepting the home care nurse's assistance in removing these environmental barriers that make his home unsafe.

APPOINTMENT CHANGES

Clients should inform home care nurses when they are unable to keep an established appointment. Just as clients have the right to expect planned visits and to be informed of any necessary schedule changes by home care personnel, clients must also notify home care personnel as soon as possible if they need to reschedule a visit. Failure to accept an agreed-upon appointment can interrupt the plan of care and delay or impede progress toward a client's established health goals. Moreover, if a nurse visits a client's home at a scheduled time and the client does not answer, the nurse may rightly become concerned that the client has fallen or is otherwise incapacitated. The nurse may then initiate an emergency response, such as calling police or emergency personnel to investigate. If a determination is made to break in and to attempt to locate a client who is mistakenly feared to be in danger, possible damage to the client's home and unnecessary worry, stress, and upset for all involved parties may result.

CLIENT PARTICIPATION IN CAREPLANNING

Clients should participate in their careplanning and adhere to it. Client cooperation regarding careplanning is particularly critical in the home care setting. Clients who participate in developing plans of care specifically designed to address their personal objectives for treatment are more likely to comply with actions they must perform when a nurse is not present. For example, provisions of a client's treatment plan can include eating an appropriate diet, following mobility recommendations, and taking prescription medications in a timely fashion. Clients need to understand the direct correlation between complying with the plan of care and achieving health objectives. Nurses can facilitate this understanding by actively involving clients in the careplanning process. If a client neglects a medical regimen, a nurse may continue with a home care treatment plan and be unable to identify the causes of unexpected symptoms.

REQUESTING INFORMATION

Clients are responsible for ensuring complete understanding of their medical treatment plans, and must request further explanations from home care personnel when they have trouble absorbing or understanding information presented to them. While it is a client's responsibility to voice any worries or problems to staff members, nurses

Home Care Conflict:
*Client's Failure
to Comply with
Medical Regimen*

M̲rs. Evaro, a client with AIDS, is supposed to infuse antivirals into a central line four times a day. An active person who has been resistant to the frequency of therapy, Mrs. Evaro nevertheless verbalizes understanding of the importance of treatment and agrees to administer the infusions regularly. When symptoms occur because of irregular dosing, however, the physician and home care nurse are unaware of the real cause of the problem. They inappropriately agree to change or increase the medication, believing the drugs to be at fault, instead of recognizing Mrs. Evaro's noncompliance with her treatment plan.

must consider and be on the lookout for potential difficulties. Nurses need to work with their clients to establish a comfortable atmosphere that permits the free exchange of questions and information. Nurses who seem hurried or bothered by questions may find their clients are unwilling to seek clarification or to share their concerns. Similarly, they must continually verify the level of their clients' understanding without badgering or intimidating them. Nurses who ensure that their clients truly absorb and agree to a plan of care also enhance the ability of clients to meet their responsibilities.

◆ Ethical Issues in Home Care

Nurses in the home care setting often face circumstances in which their professional duties and client rights conflict. The principle of **autonomy** allows individuals to make choices about their health and lifestyle. The tenet of **beneficence** requires healthcare professionals to protect their clients from harm and to promote their well-being. **Nonmaleficence** is the principle by which healthcare professionals avoid actions that may cause harm to clients through responsible, prudent decisions. Sometimes, these principles conflict and create ethical dilemmas for home care nurses.

A basic theoretical principle for home care nurses to follow is that of **empowerment**—maximizing the independence of clients and their caregivers. In the context of an ethical dilemma, therefore, the principle of autonomy usually predominates. Home care professionals also have a responsibility to ensure that they provide quality care.

Occasionally, a client has needs that extend beyond the capabilities of a home care agency. To maintain a client's right to quality care, an agency should refuse clients whose needs extend beyond the agency's reach; however, if an agency stops providing services, even if it cannot fully meet a client's needs, the client's health may be at even greater risk. Agencies need a process through which ethical dilemmas can be reviewed and resolved. In some agencies, an **ethics committee** reviews circumstances of dilemmas, gathers all pertinent information, and examines the rights and responsibilities of all involved parties. Some organizations request the

Survival Alert:

*Examples of Common Ethical
Dilemmas in Home Care*

1. Mr. Lydon cares for his 60-year-old wife who has Alzheimer's disease. Mrs. Lydon's dementia has become progressively worse over the past 3 years. Since Mrs. Lydon's initial diagnosis, the couple's financial reserves have rapidly diminished due to the growing costs of her care. Mr. Lydon works full-time during the day, and several people have helped him to care for his wife. Most recently, a niece has stayed with her while Mr. Lydon works. Mrs. Lydon has gradually become more combative, but is less difficult with her husband than with others. The niece has refused to care for her aunt any longer because of the stress associated with her care. Mr. Lydon does not qualify for Medicaid and morally believes such assistance is unacceptable. He is unable to afford a personal care assistant or a skilled nursing facility to attend to his wife, and adult day care is not available in his community. Mr. Lydon plans to lock his wife in the home alone while he works and to have a neighbor check on her a few times a day. This situation is clearly unsafe, but no other solutions seem available. Mr. Lydon sincerely cares for his wife and wants the best for her, but is out of ideas.
2. Mr. Jacoby is a 76-year-old diabetic. He lives alone and has no nearby family. He has recently fallen several times and has been found on the floor three times by home care personnel. He has demonstrated a general inability to care for himself through irregular meals, inadequate hydration, and poor hygiene. A board and care facility would have the capabilities to meet Mr. Jacoby's needs, but he has flatly refused such placement. Mr. Jacoby states, "I'd rather die in my own home than live somewhere else."

direct participation of clients, lay caregivers, physicians, and home care nurses to reach the most favorable conclusions for everyone. Healthcare providers must examine their professional standards of practice, community standards, client and family wishes, available resources, and legal liabilities. They should thoroughly explore all potential alternatives.

By its very definition, an ethical dilemma represents a conflict in which all alternatives are somewhat deficient or lacking. Although it provides no guarantee of a positive and desirable conclusion for all involved parties, the ethics committee's review process helps home care nurses to follow a course of action that is the most favorable.

KEY CONCEPT

Conflicts stemming from issues involving client rights are common in the home care setting. These conflicts can create dilemmas for the home care nurse. An ethics committee's review process will usually result in the most favorable resolution.

Application to Home Care Practice
Resolving an Ethical Dilemma

Ms. Jackson has multiple sclerosis and lives alone. Home health aides have visited her on a daily basis for several years to assist her with bathing and dressing. Her muscle strength has now deteriorated to the point that it is unsafe for her to live alone. Although fiercely independent, Ms. Jackson cannot afford to have a personal care assistant stay with her. Clearly, Ms. Jackson has needs that extend beyond the scope of services provided by the home care agency, yet to discontinue services would result in a highly unsafe home situation for her.

The home care nurse must consider all of the important, conflicting issues in this situation. Ms. Jackson must maintain her right to self-determination. The agency is obligated to provide care only in an environment in which it can safely meet the client's needs. Clearly, these two important objectives seem to conflict. Supporting an unsafe environment is not in the best interest of the client. Should Ms. Jackson suffer an injury, the nurse has, in effect, contributed to the negative outcome. Therefore, the nurse must understand the limitations of the services that can be provided and present the client with as many alternative solutions as possible.

The nurse may explore long-term placement in a board and care facility for Ms. Jackson, or identify support systems to provide necessary assistance. Ms. Jackson needs to be educated on the limitations of the home care organization and the rationale for these limitations. If Ms. Jackson maintains her right to choose to live in an unsafe environment, the home care agency must give her notice regarding the withdrawal of services. The agency must inform her of all possible options and should consider reporting the unsafe situation to a county or state adult protective or social service department. Although these organizations are often limited in their abilities to intervene if the client is mentally competent, they can provide the client with adequate notice to make other arrangements and give assistance in doing so, if the client so desires. Ms. Jackson and her physician should be involved in every aspect of this decision-making process. The nurse will thus avoid the ethical and legal burdens of abandoning Ms. Jackson while maintaining the integrity of the agency's policy of providing only the services for which it is equipped.

◆ Summary

Home care nurses must diligently preserve and protect client rights. Educating clients about their rights and actively maintaining them is one of the nurse's fundamental obligations. Clients need to comprehend their rights fully before they receive any services. Nurses must remember to encourage their clients to exercise rights with no fear of reprisal. They also need to provide instruction concerning client responsibilities. Fulfillment of these responsibilities is necessary for nurses to best help their clients to achieve goals established in the home plan of care. Understanding these principles enables home care nurses to protect the dignity of those they serve.

References and Bibliography

Aiken, T.D. & Castalano, J.T. (1994). *Legal, ethical, and political issues in nursing*. Philadelphia: Davis.

American Nurses Association. (1986). *Standards for home health nursing practice*. Washington, DC: Author.

Annas, C. & Glantz, H. (1986). The right of elderly patients to refuse life-sustaining medical treatment. *Milbank Quarterly, 64*(Suppl. 2), 95–162.

Brent, N.J. (1997). The home healthcare nurse and confidentiality and privacy. *Home Healthcare Nurse, 15*(4), 256–258.

Chandra, N.C. & Hazinski, M.F. (Eds.). (1994). *Basic life support for healthcare providers*. Dallas, TX: American Heart Association.

Collopy, B., Dabler N. & Zuckerman, C. (1990). The ethics of home care: Autonomy and accommodation. *Hastings Center Report, 20*(2), 1–16.

Donley, R. (1993). Ethics in the age of health care reform. *Nursing Economics, 11*(1), 19–24, 51.

Duffy, B., Brent, N.J., Pfaadt, M.J. & Rooney, A.L. (1996). What to do about Harry? *Home Healthcare Nurse, 14*(6), 421–426.

Field, M. (1967). *Patients are people: A medical social approach to prolonged illness* (3rd ed.). New York: Columbia University Press.

Fruger, A. (1993). Factors involving ethical decision making in the home setting. *Home Healthcare Nurse, 10*(2), 16–20.

Gates, M.F., Schins, I. & Sullivan Smith, A. (1996). Applying advanced directives regulations in home care agencies: Survey of home healthcare advance directives regulations in Michigan. *Home Healthcare Nurse, 14*(2), 127–133.

Humphrey, C.J. & Milone-Nuzzo, P. (1996). *Orientation to home care nursing*. Gaithersburg, MD: Aspen.

Jameton, A. (1993). Dilemmas of moral distress: Moral responsibility and nursing practice. *AWHONN's Clinical Issues in Perinatal and Women's Health Nursing, 4*(4), 542–551.

Reckling, J. (1989). Abandonment of patients by home health nursing agencies: An ethical analysis of the dilemma. *Advances in Nursing Science, 1*(3), 70–81.

Rich, P.L. (1995). Protecting patient information. *Nursing, 25*(9), 32L.

Rozovsky, F. & Rozovsky, L. (1993). *Home health care law*. Boston: Little, Brown and Company.

Schatzki, M. & Tamborlane, T.A. (1988). Negotiation strategies for conflict resolution: Within ethical and legal constraints. *Caring Magazine, 7*(4), 56–58.

Simpson, R.L. (1994). Ensuring patient data privacy, confidentiality, and security. *Nursing Management, 25*(7), 18–20.

Zang, S.M. & Bailey, N.C. (1997). *Home care manual: Making the transition*. Philadelphia: Lippincott-Raven.

POST TEST

1. Explain why it is important for home care agencies to ensure the education and maintenance of client rights.

2. Determine the client right that is more significant for nurses working in home care than for nurses working in hospitals.

3. The role of the healthcare professional has shifted away from "protecting" clients to that of _____ clients regarding their treatment options.

4. When services are fully reimbursed by a third party payor, clients have no right to be made aware of the agency's charges for care provided.
____True ____False

5. List three components of a client's right to receive quality care services.

6. List three client responsibilities.

THINKING CRITICALLY IN HOME CARE

1. During a visit, a client seems angry and informs Ruth, the nurse, that the home health aide carelessly broke a treasured crystal bowl during yesterday's services.

   A. What factors may be contributing to this client's anger?

   B. Determine Ruth's appropriate response to the client.

   C. Describe actions that Ruth should take after the visit.

2. Brian, a home care nurse, recently began a new position with Caregivers Home Health Agency. During orientation, his preceptor, Kate, is sharing specific and personal information about clients she has cared for in the past. Kate is doing so with the purpose of educating Brian about the types of clients the agency serves and performance expectations of nurses who work there.

   A. Based on the above information, decide whether or not Kate is breaching client confidentiality.

   B. Explain how Brian could intervene in this situation to prevent any disclosures of confidential information.

3. Mr. Wolfmann, 67 years old, has recently been referred to home care for treatment following a total hip replacement. He speaks only German but lives with his son Todd, who speaks fluent English and German. Fran, the home care nurse performing the initial visit, has asked Todd to interpret for them. Todd fulfilled this role during his father's recent hospitalization. As Fran explains Mr. Wolfmann's rights and responsibilities, she observes that Todd's translations are relatively succinct. She becomes concerned that Todd is not fully communicating all pertinent information to his father.

   A. Assess Fran's responsibilities in this situation.

   B. Determine ways for Fran to ensure that Mr. Wolfmann fully understands his rights and responsibilities.

   C. What are the potential consequences of poorly understood rights and responsibilities in this scenario?

7

Coordination of Care and Interdisciplinary Communication

LEARNING OBJECTIVES

After completing this chapter, the reader will be able to:

◆ Evaluate the importance of interdisciplinary care coordination.

◆ Discuss characteristics of home care that make coordination of care challenging.

◆ List indications for referrals to ancillary services, e.g., physical therapy, occupational therapy, speech therapy, social services, home health aides, and other professional services.

◆ Identify resources that are available in many communities for home care clients.

◆ Determine when interdisciplinary communication should occur.

KEY TERMS

Activities of daily living
Aphasia
Care coordinator
Case conferences
Dietitian
Home health aide

Occupational therapy
Physical therapy
Respiratory therapy
Social services
Speech therapy

To *provide* effective care in the home, nurses must learn the importance and methodology of coordinating services. To perform these functions adequately, nurses must develop excellent communication skills, a holistic perspective, and an awareness of the unique contributions of ancillary services and community resources. This chapter reviews the importance of interdisciplinary coordination in home care practice. It presents indications for referrals to ancillary services. Communities differ greatly in the breadth and scope of service organizations available to their citizens. This chapter covers some common types of services open to home care clients in many communities. It addresses the complexities of interdisciplinary communication, including the many barriers that home care providers face when treating clients. A care coordinator works diligently to overcome the difficulties of interdisciplinary communication. The chapter concludes with a discussion of the role of the home care nurse as care coordinator.

◆ Importance of Interdisciplinary Coordination

Home care clients frequently require skills from multiple disciplines to achieve the goals initially established in their plans of care. Often, many individuals are involved in carrying out a client's plan of care, including nurses, physicians, therapists, social workers, home health aides, community resource personnel, lay caregivers, and pharmacists. Even when competent, highly motivated professionals treat a home care client, disastrous outcomes can result if these individuals fail to coordinate their efforts. Communication among nurses, physicians, and other team members must be consistent and ongoing for the successful provision of home care services. All parties involved in a client's care must be aware of the client's response to treatment, and any new problems the client encounters, to provide appropriate and effective treatment (Esposito, 1994).

Consider a football team comprising highly skilled players without a coach. When a coach is not present to encourage the unique talents of each player and to develop strategies for the whole team to meet common objectives, the team is likely to lose the game. Similarly, when members of a home care team fail to coordinate their efforts, clients are likely to experience negative consequences: increased morbidity, lack of progress toward treatment goals, frustration with duplicated efforts or ignored issues, and the trauma of rehospitalization. Third party payors regard uncoordinated care as a waste of resources and money. Regulatory agencies perceive poor coordination of services as a violation of established regulations. Thus, all involved parties lose in their quest to improve a client's health and to provide the best care possible if they fail to coordinate their efforts.

KEY CONCEPT

To achieve optimal client outcomes, home care interdisciplinary teams must coordinate their provision of care. Failure to do so can result in negative consequences for all those involved.

NURSE—PHYSICIAN COLLABORATION

In home care, the roles of the nurse and the physician often overlap. Nurses and physicians share more responsibilities in home care than in other settings, where duties are more clearly distinguished. For example, in hospital settings, nurses are primarily responsible for the development of nursing plans of care, and physicians are mostly responsible for developing medical treatment plans. The blurring of such distinctions in home care demands a high level of nurse—physician collaboration.

Home care nurses depend upon physicians to approve many interventions normally considered within the scope of nursing practice. Payors almost consistently require demonstration of physician authorization for nursing services before they reimburse a home care agency for those services. In a hospital or clinic, nurses conduct client teaching independently. Although independent teaching also takes place in home care, Medicare and most other insurance carriers will not reimburse this intervention without demonstration of physician orders in the home care record (see Chapter 5). Therefore, if an agency wishes to receive reimbursement for teaching services, a physician must authorize them.

Physicians must depend upon home care nurses to guide many medical services in the home that they themselves would perform in acute care settings. They see their home care clients infrequently and rely upon the findings and interpretations of nurses to draw appropriate conclusions. Physicians frequently request and follow the recommendations of home care nurses regarding medical treatment decisions, such as wound care orders, laboratory tests, and appropriate medications.

The interdependent relationship between a nurse and a physician involved with a home care client requires a great deal of cooperation. In home care, the client's nursing and medical treatment plans closely mirror one another. Both home care nurses and physicians must work together jointly to give their clients precise and capable treatment.

K E Y   C O N C E P T

Logistical and reimbursement issues within the home care setting require an interdependent relationship between nurses and physicians. As a result, a high level of collaboration between them is essential for developing effective nursing and medical treatment plans.

ANCILLARY DISCIPLINES

Collaboration between a nurse and a physician helps to establish and to maintain an effective treatment plan for a client. Home care nurses must also work with various personnel from ancillary disciplines to coordinate additional services designed to optimize a client's quality of life. When performing a client's initial assessment (see Chapter 13), a nurse determines the type and frequency of nursing interventions to be implemented and evaluates the client for any needed ancillary services. Home care nurses must become familiar with indications for services from disciplines including physical therapy, occupational therapy, speech therapy, social services, and home health aides.

Insurance companies and Medicare have specific criteria that must be met for the rehabilitative services of physical therapy, occupational therapy, and speech therapy to be considered medically necessary. The Health Insurance Manual for Medicare (HIM11) published by HCFA (1990) specifies conditions indicative of a need for rehabilitative services (Display 7-1). Presence of one or more of these conditions, however, does not necessarily warrant a referral to a rehabilitative service. Clients must also display a reasonable potential to improve their functional status. Insurance companies often use date of onset or date of exacerbation of a chronic condition as one criterion in making this determination. Usually, individuals with a longstanding chronic condition and no recent exacerbations (e.g., CVA 3 years ago) are generally considered unable to make significant advances in their functional status. Their rehabilitative potential is usually considered poor; therefore, insurance companies usually resist covering therapeutic services for these clients. For example, a case reviewer will question the potential functional improvement of a client who has had Parkinson's disease for 4 years, and will be reluctant to approve ancillary services for this client.

Display 7-1:
Criteria to Determine the Medical Necessity for Rehabilitative Services

* Fractures or dislocations
* Orthopedic surgeries, such as joint replacements or reconstructive surgeries
* Degenerative joint or disc disease
* Rheumatoid arthritis
* Amputations
* New prostheses
* Burns with joint involvement or other involvement that reduces function
* Cerebrovascular accidents
* Multiple sclerosis
* Head injuries
* Spinal cord injuries
* Parkinson's disease
* Amyotrophic lateral sclerosis
* Neuropathies or myopathies that cause functional limitations
* Chronic obstructive pulmonary disease
* Chronic cardiac disease
* Functional limitations that require utilization of special assistive devices
* Laryngectomies or glossectomies
* Dysphagia
* Hearing loss
* Blindness

Referrals to therapy are also questioned if therapy is ordered to address generalized weakness in a client that has resulted from temporary immobility, such as following an acute hospital stay. Insurance companies regard such weakness as a transient loss of function only and expect the client's condition to improve spontaneously. Thus, they view skilled therapy services as not required, and will not reimburse them (Rice, 1994). Insurance companies occasionally make exceptions to their general rules for reimbursing ancillary services for clients with longstanding or temporary conditions. Some exceptions may include (1) therapy services to instruct new lay caregivers in safe transfer techniques; (2) therapy for clients who have experienced recent exacerbations of their chronic conditions; and (3) therapy for clients with longstanding chronic diagnoses, who did not receive therapy initially but could now benefit from instruction on techniques and equipment to maximize function.

KEY CONCEPT

To meet the comprehensive needs of home care clients, nurses must become familiar with indications for referrals to physical therapy, occupational therapy, speech therapy, social services, and home health aides.

Physical Therapy

A definition of **physical therapy** by Carr is "the assessment, evaluation, treatment, and prevention of physical disability, movement dysfunction, and pain resulting from injury, disease, disability, or other health-related conditions" (1994, p. 38). Physical therapy is clearly beneficial to clients with mobility problems, including difficulties with ambulation, transfers, or bed mobility. This service is also useful for those individuals with balance or coordination problems, or with decreased range of motion and strength. Physical therapists make useful recommendations to clients who require guidance in adapting their homes to promote safety or to increase functionality (e.g., converting stairs to a ramp to improve access; placing grab bars in a shower). Physical therapists also establish home exercise programs to enhance or to maintain a client's range of motion, muscle strength, and endurance.

Many home care clients are homebound because of mobility problems. These clients encounter significant safety risks while performing routine activities, such as ambulating within their own homes, transferring to bedside commodes, and climbing stairs to their bedrooms. Physical therapists help to evaluate a client's need for assistive devices (e.g., canes, walkers, crutches) and educate clients about their safe and appropriate use (Fig. 7-1). Physical therapists also assist clients to improve mobility and to reduce the risk of injuries resulting from accidents.

Pain management is another area in which physical therapists effectively contribute to the medical treatment plan. Their interventions include instruction in positioning and posture, relaxation techniques, massage, ultrasound, hot packs, and transcutaneous nerve stimulation therapy. Physical therapists work closely with clients and lay caregivers and require their active participation in treatment. Without cooperation

Figure 7-1. A physical therapist assists a client in the use of crutches. (Photo by Marilu Sherer, CARING)

from clients and lay caregivers, physical therapy is likely to be unsuccessful (Carr, 1994).

Occupational Therapy

Occupational therapy is most effective for clients with diseases or disabilities affecting their functional status. Occupational therapists provide services to increase a client's ability to perform **activities of daily living** (ADLs): bathing, dressing, toileting, cooking, eating, and homemaking. Occupational therapists instruct clients on techniques, equipment, and aids that can help them to overcome their disabilities. These professionals educate clients in energy conservation techniques, which are particularly helpful to individuals with reduced respiratory capacity (e.g., COPD, CHF) or with chronically compromised strength and endurance (e.g., muscular dystrophies). Occupational therapists also assist clients debilitated by illness or injury with adapting their homes to improve functionality. For example, an occupational therapist can recommend ways for a woman afflicted with early-stage multiple sclerosis to reorganize her kitchen. These suggestions can make cooking more accessible for the client and help her to continue to prepare meals (Fig. 7-2).

Occupational therapists are experts in exercises of the upper extremities and hands. They develop therapeutic exercise programs for home care clients who have experienced injury or decreased function in an upper extremity or a hand because of neurological impairment (e.g., nerve damage, CVA, brain injury). These profession-

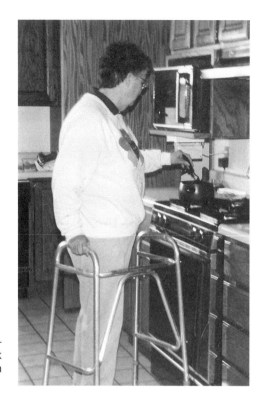

Figure 7-2. After sessions with an occupational therapist, this client can cook and ambulate around her kitchen with relative ease.

als are also trained in the application of splints, which are used to rest inflamed joints in optimal positions to prevent or to correct deformities.

Occupational therapists are knowledgeable about adaptive devices that clients can use to overcome a variety of functional deficits. Home care clients with reduced hand dexterity, strength, and sensation may become highly dependent upon others to attend to their basic needs, such as eating and dressing. A client's independence can improve dramatically by using specially designed eating utensils or devices that assist clients in buttoning clothing. Occupational therapists may also recommend ways to adapt clothing (e.g., through the use of Velcro) that enable clients to dress themselves. Occupational therapists help clients to maximize their autonomy, which can profoundly affect self-esteem and the ability to live alone.

Speech Therapy
Speech therapy is indicated for clients with illnesses or disabilities affecting their ability to communicate. Speech therapists frequently treat clients suffering from cerebrovascular accidents, head injuries, brain tumors, muscular dystrophies, hearing loss, and throat surgeries (e.g., laryngectomies, tracheostomies). Clients requiring speech therapy may experience cognitive difficulties in expressing themselves or in understanding the communication of others. They may have suffered a hearing loss, or may be physically unable to enunciate words. **Aphasia** (an indication for speech therapy) is a condition in which a client's ability to speak, to understand speech

and nonverbal communication, to read, or to write is impaired. Hearing loss represents another significant communication barrier. A client's incapacity to fully communicate with others can lead to social isolation, decreased self-esteem, depression, delayed developmental growth (in pediatric clients), disrupted family dynamics, potential for injury (because of an inability to detect warning sounds), and tremendous anxiety for both clients and lay caregivers.

Speech therapists help clients to develop their remaining communication skills and to learn compensatory communication mechanisms. Therapists instruct clients and lay caregivers in methods of augmenting communication through visual cues and cognitive retraining. Speech therapists set up a variety of communication aides and technology. They assist clients with learning sign language, obtaining hearing aides, or mastering the use of an electrolarynx. Speech therapy can help clients with no potential for actual speech to learn to communicate with others through a variety of mechanisms. For example, therapists teach clients to use a simple communication board that includes common messages they wish to communicate. Clients can point to messages on the board indicating whether they are hungry, thirsty, hot, or cold (Fig. 7-3A).

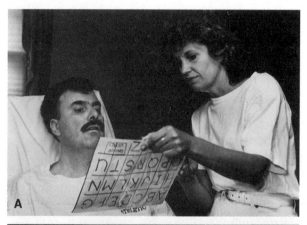

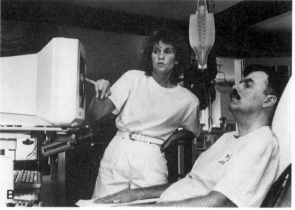

Figure 7-3. Speech therapists can help clients with impaired communication to express themselves in many ways. (*A*) Here the therapist teaches the client to use a communication board. (*B*) The therapist also instructs the client on ways to communicate via computer technology. (Photos by Marilu Sherer, CARING)

Computer technology has advanced tremendously to enable communication-impaired individuals to convey messages and relay information to others. Many telecommunication systems have been developed for people with a decreased capacity to communicate (Fig. 7-3*B*). Phones have been developed for clients with hearing loss that transcribe spoken words into written messages on a screen. Technology has developed many other systems that allow clients with no speaking ability to effectively communicate with those around them.

Speech therapists also assist clients with swallowing difficulties (e.g., dysphagia). Therapists often assist physicians with identifying the severity of a client's swallowing problem and appropriate interventions. Some clients and lay caregivers can be instructed in swallowing exercises and techniques to decrease the likelihood of aspiration while eating or drinking.

Social Services

Social services help to manage the care of clients with difficult or complicated psychosocial problems. Current research has increasingly supported the concept that psychosocial issues and emotional adjustments to medical conditions greatly affect the recovery of clients suffering from illness or infirmity (White, 1997). Failure of healthcare personnel to help clients address these psychosocial issues may undermine the success of an otherwise comprehensive home care treatment plan. Social workers provide tremendous assistance to home care clients with often painful issues that may inhibit the attainment of treatment goals.

Social workers provide invaluable assistance to the home care team. Nurses, therapists, and home health aides working in a home with complex psychosocial concerns may become frustrated with their apparent inability to help a client progress toward treatment goals. Sometimes, clients inexplicably fail to comply with instructions outlined in their treatment plans. Some lay caregivers refuse to participate in the care of a client for reasons that are not apparent to the clinicians involved. Social workers can frequently pinpoint the emotional and psychological problems that are impeding a client's progress and explain these issues to other members of the home care team. Home care nurses can develop a better understanding of a client's home situation and personal attitudes toward treatment. Nurses can then abandon their personal feelings of anger and frustration that they may otherwise direct at clients or lay caregivers for not actively cooperating. Social workers can develop plans to address these issues and can educate the rest of the home care team in ways to handle these situations appropriately.

Occasionally, clients refuse to participate in home care treatment plans because of unconscious psychological defense mechanisms such as denial. Counseling from a social worker can help clients and lay caregivers to accept lifestyle changes caused by illness or injury and ease active involvement in care. In the most difficult situations, including those outlined in Table 7-1, social workers help clients confront complex issues to improve both their emotional and physical well-being. Social workers are also frequently able to furnish objective recommendations for psychosocial interventions that everyone involved in a client's care can perform.

Frequently, social services are ordered for clients requiring assistance from com-

Survival Alert:

*Indications for Client Referrals
to Social Workers*

- ◆ Client is in an inappropriate or unsafe living situation.
- ◆ Client exhibits an unstable mental condition (e.g., depression, anxiety, phobias).
- ◆ Client has marital or family conflicts.
- ◆ Client verbalizes financial concerns.
- ◆ Client requires access to multiple or community resources that may not be immediately available.
- ◆ Client requires placement in a board and care facility or a skilled nursing facility.
- ◆ Client has a disfiguring disease or has been recently diagnosed with a chronic or terminal illness.
- ◆ Client or lay caregiver has unrealistic goals for care.
- ◆ Lay caregiver undermines the client's treatment plan.
- ◆ Client has experienced personality changes.
- ◆ Client is suffering from substance or alcohol abuse.
- ◆ Client is living with an abusive partner, parent, child, or lay caregiver.
- ◆ Client is suicidal/homicidal.
- ◆ Client is the victim of sexual assault or inappropriate sexual behavior.
- ◆ Client experiences poor compliance with home care treatment plan.
- ◆ Client is grieving.
- ◆ Client has been evicted.

munity services. Social workers are frequently experts in identifying community resources and governmental programs that give various forms of aid to clients. For example, some clients face serious financial obstacles that inhibit their ability to purchase necessary food and medications. Social workers can determine the eligibility of these clients for many federal, state, and county assistance programs (e.g., food stamps, Medicaid, social security, and WIC). They can inform clients and their lay caregivers about access to these programs. Most communities also have a variety of free or low-cost local services that benefit home care clients, including home meal delivery programs, transportation services, senior companion programs, legal assistance, and daily telephone safety checks. Businesses designed to meet the needs of home care clients include board and care homes, private duty or homemaker companies, pharmacies and grocery stores that deliver, adult day care centers, and skilled nursing facilities.

Social workers also intervene in crises. For example, referrals to social services are indicated for a home care client using an oxygen concentrator who has received a notice of imminent cancellation of utilities; a client who verbalizes an intent to commit suicide; or a client whose lay caregiver is physically abusive or negligent. Expedient interventions by social workers can frequently divert an impending crisis and establish an action plan to prevent similar crises from recurring.

Home Care Conflict:
Dysfunctional Family Dynamics Impacting A Treatment Plan

Mr. Wurtz is receiving home care services. His daughter, Carol, acts as his lay caregiver. Josephine, the nurse instructs Carol regarding medication administration. Carol verbalizes an understanding of the medications' effects and her responsibility to assist her father with the medications. In subsequent home visits, however, Josephine discovers that medications have been inconsistently provided to Mr. Wurtz, resulting in an exacerbation of his medical condition. Although Josephine reviews instructions with Carol, who again verbalizes an understanding of the importance of compliance, Carol continues to behave inconsistently in assisting her father. Based on Josephine's recommendations, Mr. Wurtz's physician orders a social work referral to identify any issues that are affecting Carol's compliance with the medical regimen.

Through an in-depth assessment of the family dynamics and history, the social worker, Michael identifies that Mr. Wurtz has a history of alcoholism and emotionally abusive behavior toward Carol. Carol resents her role as lay caregiver. She is uncomfortable with her father's dependence on her, since she perceives that he never supported her when she needed him. Although Carol does not openly express resentment and anger toward Mr. Wurtz, her passive-aggressive behavior allows her to act out years of anger toward an absent and abusive father. Michael initiates social work interventions for this family, including short-term counseling to help Mr. Wurtz and Carol to resolve this conflict. A referral to a psychologist will provide more extensive family counseling, if necessary.

TABLE 7-1. *Indications for Social Services With Examples*

INDICATOR	EXAMPLE
Client is in an appropriate or unsafe living condition	◆ Clients who have had frequent falls and live alone ◆ Clients with inappropriate temperature control in their residences ◆ Clients living in filthy conditions or in infested residences ◆ Clients living with an abusive family member or lay caregiver
Client exhibits an unstable mental condition	◆ Clients who exhibit unusual behavior ◆ Clients who are overly anxious ◆ Clients suffering from depression, paranoia, hallucinations, alcohol/drug abuse, or moodswings
Client has serious financial concern	◆ Client is unable to meet basic living or medical expenses
Lay caregiver undermines the client's treatment plan	◆ Lay caregiver provides inappropriate foods for the client ◆ Lay caregiver fails to assist the client as needed

Home Health Aides

Home health aides are taught to provide personal care to clients, helping them with ambulation and simple exercises that nurses or therapists recommend. Although members of a professional discipline (physical therapy, occupational therapy, speech therapy, or social services) will perform their own evaluations of clients and determine appropriate medical treatment plans within their scope of care, home care nurses determine the duties of home health aides. Nurses base the frequency of visits upon a client's level of functioning and the availability of a willing and able lay caregiver in the client's home. For clients with severe disabilities and marginal home support, daily visits by home health aides are often indicated. For clients who can ambulate but are unable to perform personal care independently, visits of three times a week are appropriate. Chapter 8 discusses the role of home health aides and the supervisory functions of the home care nurse in detail.

Other Professional Services

Occasionally, home care nurses identify whether their clients require interventions from professional services other than those mentioned above. **Respiratory therapists** are particularly helpful to clients with serious pulmonary conditions. For example, the parents of medically fragile children with cystic fibrosis require careful instruction on percussion and postural drainage. Children who require apnea monitors and individuals maintained on respirators in the home are strong candidates for the specialized skills and services of a respiratory therapist.

Dietitians are indicated for clients who must follow very rigid diets. Examples of clients who must follow special diets include those with unstable diabetes and those with end-stage renal disease on dialysis. Clients receiving total parenteral nutrition (TPN) and enteral nutrition also benefit from the intermittent evaluations and recommendations of a dietitian. Dietitians may also be appropriate for clients with wounds that are not healing because of low blood albumen levels.

The services of respiratory therapists and dietitians are generally provided less frequently than the services of nursing, physical therapy, occupational therapy, speech therapy, social services, and home health aides. Medicare and many insurance carriers do not directly reimburse home care agencies for theses services, and clients often cannot afford to pay for such skills independently.

COMMUNITY SERVICE ORGANIZATIONS

Each community varies in the types of services it makes available to individuals with special healthcare needs. Some localities have a wealth of organizations and programs to provide assistance to home care clients; others have very few services available. Large urban areas often contain many public and community organizations to assist the needy; however, personal, individualized support is not always available because of the large populations served in these communities. Conversely, few formal organizations may be available in isolated, rural areas, but many informal support systems may be found. Some organizations provide very specialized services; others are broader in the assistance they furnish. For example, one charity organization provides books-on-tape for blind, elderly individuals only; another organization gives

Application to Home Care Practice
Accessing Community Resources for a Client

Mrs. Plummer is a 48-year-old client with breast cancer. She receives home care nursing visits from Danielle for nutritional status elevation, assessment for infection, and instruction on medication scheduling. Mrs. Plummer has suffered serious financial difficulties due to her illness and cannot afford to purchase cosmetic pieces that would enhance her physical appearance. Her self-esteem has dwindled, leading to social isolation and depression. Danielle greatly enhances Mrs. Plummer's plan of care by contacting the local chapter of the American Cancer Society. The organization provides Mrs. Plummer with a wig and breast prosthesis and puts her in contact with Mrs. Londono, a woman of the same age who has recovered from breast cancer, for social support. These additional services significantly enhance the client's well-being and self-esteem. They attend to her emotional and mental well-being in the same way that nursing interventions treat her physical health.

food, shelter, emergency funds, and social support to anyone who can display need. Both organizations augment the care provided by home care agencies to meet the comprehensive needs of clients.

Home care nurses have access to a tremendous variety of services for the specific needs of their clients. Many towns and cities run programs in which volunteers deliver meals to homebound individuals at a low cost. Some senior centers design programs in which volunteers visit isolated clients. Many adult day care centers are lifesavers for clients whose lay caregivers must work during the day. Community service organizations fill gaps of need identified for many clients. Display 7-2 provides a detailed list of community service organizations and programs that sometimes assist in the plans of care for clients.

Developing a Community Resource Base

To meet the varied and extensive needs of home care clients appropriately, nurses must become familiar with community service organizations. Many home care agencies maintain lists of available community resources that nurses should regularly examine. Senior centers are also usually very knowledgeable about community resources available for the older populations they serve. Churches and other groups stay informed of changes in community offerings. Social workers can often give advice to nurses on many community service organizations. Phone books, public health departments, and hospital discharge planning departments are additional resources the home care nurse may wish to access to learn of available services.

Nonprofit organizations, charities, church programs, and many small businesses give services to individuals with acute and chronic health problems. Many of these programs have limited advertising budgets and remain relatively unknown to the communities they serve. Home care nurses who have developed an awareness of

Display 7-2:
Examples of Community Service Organizations

Skilled nursing facilities	Private duty companies
Board and care facilities	Church volunteers
Senior centers	Adopt-A-Senior programs
Meals on Wheels programs	Big Brother/Big Sister programs
Durable medical equipment companies	Guide dogs
American Heart Association	Hospice
Pharmacies with delivery services	American Cancer Society
Groceries with delivery services	Support groups
Beauticians/barbers that visit homes	Mobile library
Wheelchair vans	Food stamp programs
Emergency response systems	Psychologist
Free or low-cost legal services	Adult day care centers

these resources can more effectively meet their clients' needs. Maintaining and carrying a current phone list or a card file of community organizations that frequently help home care clients will aid nurses to make referrals easily while performing visits in the field.

KEY CONCEPT

The most effective home care nurses are individuals who maximize all available resources to meet the needs of their clients. Many such resources can be obtained through community service organizations.

Goods and Services

Clients often need information about suppliers of goods and services that they will continue to access long after home care services are discontinued. For example, some clients use durable medical equipment that requires continual maintenance from a reliable community vendor (Fig. 7-4). Clients with new ostomies need regular access to medical supplies. Home care nurses must stay abreast of community resources for these goods and services. Nurses best help clients by giving them a list of reliable providers and teaching them how to access these services themselves. Nurses thus encourage the independence of clients in meeting their own ongoing needs. Many organizations have brochures or other forms of promotional materials that nurses receive and can distribute to appropriate clients. If necessary, home care nurses may refer clients to service providers directly.

Although many companies that provide goods and services to clients frequently send marketing materials directly to home care nurses, nurses should not place themselves in the awkward position of "selling" clients on specific providers. Rather,

Figure 7-4. Nurses often need to direct clients to centers for durable medical equipment.

nurses should discuss with clients the different services and products that several reliable businesses offer. They should encourage clients to make their own choices about services before initiating referrals.

Support Groups

Many community support groups are available to meet the specialized needs of clients. The topics discussed in these groups are numerous and varied. Some groups specialize in support for clients with specific chronic diseases. They are beneficial to clients recently diagnosed with an illness or who suffer further deterioration related to their medical condition. Group members help newly diagnosed clients adapt to changes in health status. These organizations provide needed social encouragement to home care clients and lay caregivers who feel isolated and alone in dealing with the stresses of illness or injury. Individuals who have learned to manage their conditions successfully can act as role models in these groups. The sharing of emotions among people who truly understand what the others are confronting is an invaluable psychosocial outlet for participants in support groups.

Some organizations provide free or low-cost legal services, educational materials, financial assistance, transportation to receive medical services, or professional counseling for their members. Many nationally based organizations support current research and relay information to members. Such organizations include the American Cancer Society, American Lung Association, American Diabetic Association, and Alcoholics Anonymous. Some communities form organizations as grass-root efforts to meet specific community needs. Examples of such groups are bereavement support groups and support groups for parents of medically fragile children. These organizations act as tremendous resources for many home care clients within communities.

Board and Care

Board and care facilities benefit individuals who are primarily independent in their personal care but need assistance with cooking, cleaning, laundry, and errands. Board and care programs are also helpful to isolated individuals in need of social interaction. These facilities provide either private or shared rooms, meals, and varying levels of other services. Home care nurses should consider referring clients to a board and care facility temporarily when their current environment or situation is unsafe. One example would be a client who lives alone, receives treatment for weakness after exacerbation of a chronic condition, and lacks available support from a lay caregiver. Clients placed in short-term board and care homes usually maintain their primary residences until they have recovered and can return home.

Long-term residence in a board and care center may be the best option for clients with chronic debilitating diseases who are not expected to regain the significantly improved function that would enable them to live alone in their own homes. Individuals entering board and care facilities for periods of long duration or permanently may find relinquishing the independence of their own homes traumatic. They may feel that they are abandoning or leaving behind their memories and attachments with neighbors and friends. If possible, home care clients should be encouraged to visit available board and care facilities in their area and choose the facility that is most comfortable. Nurses should reassure clients that the same nursing and other services conducted in their homes will continue to be available when they move to board and care facilities.

◆ Complexities of Interdisciplinary Communication

Clearly, home care nurses must take the responsibility of coordinating care for their clients very seriously. Achieving this important objective represents a unique challenge. Many uncommon characteristics of home care make the successful coordination of services extremely complicated. Perhaps the most difficult aspect of home care coordination for nurses is overcoming barriers to effective communication among those treating clients.

Lack of communication among the various disciplines involved in a client's care can easily result in the application of services that directly conflict with one another. Clients and their lay caregivers often assume communication and coordination occur automatically among the professionals involved in their care. Rather than questioning inconsistencies, clients often follow directions given by the person who performed the most recent services in their home. When care providers fail to communicate,

Home Care Conflict:
Failure of Disciplines to Coordinate Efforts

Barbara, the home care nurse, tells Mr. Jordan, a CVA client, that she will arrange for a home health aide to perform his personal care. Roberto, the occupational therapist, provided instruction to Mr. Jordan on the use of assistive devices the day before, unbeknownst to Barbara. Roberto asked Mr. Jordan to perform his personal care activities independently. During his next home care visit, Roberto wonders why Mr. Jordan did not follow his instructions. He considers that Mr. Jordan might be noncompliant, never realizing that it was his own failure to update other disciplines involved in Mr. Jordan's care that has caused the confusion.

clients receive mixed messages regarding the procedures that are in their best interests. Clients can lose confidence in the judgment and competency of the home care team if repeated conflicts and miscommunications arise. Each member of a client's team must communicate regularly and often with the others to update them on the client's progress, alert them to any changes in the plan of care, and inform them of any problems or concerns. Regular communication helps to ensure that clients receive the most consistent and accurate treatment possible and demonstrates to clients competence and concern by the home care team.

KEY CONCEPT

Although various disciplines provide distinct services to clients, they are working toward common client goals. Lack of communication can cause unnecessary conflicts in treatment plans that send mixed messages to clients and lay caregivers. As a result, clients and lay caregivers can lose trust in the home care team. Therefore, regular communication is important to ensure that interventions are complementary.

BARRIERS TO COMMUNICATION IN HOME CARE

Many elements contribute to the difficulties involved in effective communication among professionals attending to home care clients. These blocks can hinder treatment goals, confuse involved participants, and potentially endanger a client's health. Nurses must become aware of barriers to communication in home care. They must find ways to overcome these obstacles to best assist their clients.

Inadequate Communication in the Home

Home care nurses see the other professionals who provide services to clients infrequently. Home care professionals rarely provide services simultaneously, because most clients do not have the endurance to withstand two or more home care visits in direct succession. In fact, nurses often design for clients a weekly schedule that staggers visits from various personnel throughout the week. Additionally, nurses may choose to spread visits from personnel throughout the week so that professionals can continually assess a client's overall status and home safety. As a result, visits generally occur at different times and on different days. Thus, few opportunities exist for those involved in different aspects of a client's care to communicate and to work in conjunction with one another.

Inadequate Communication in the Office

Home care providers also rarely have an opportunity to communicate with one another at the home care agency's office (Fig. 7-5). Most home care professionals spend very little time in the office. The bulk of their time is spent in the homes of clients or in transit. Nurses and professionals from other disciplines visit the home care agency when geographically convenient, between visits to clients. Thus, home care providers rarely see other members of the interdisciplinary team, losing additional valuable opportunities to discuss the plans of care for shared clients.

Inadequate Telephone Communication

Home care nurses are usually difficult to reach by phone or paging (Fig. 7-6). Again, they generally spend most of their time working in clients' homes or traveling. If clients call or try to page nurses while they are providing services in the home of another client, nurses cannot fully discuss issues or answer questions because of confidentiality and client relations issues. Most home care agencies thus reserve paging for urgent messages only. When home care nurses respond to pages while traveling, they must stop to find a pay phone. Calling from a public or cellular phone

Figure 7-5. Two members of a client's care team share a rare moment of discussion in the agency office. Photo by Marilu Sherer, CARING)

Figure 7-6. Home care personnel are often difficult to contact by telephone, adding to the complexities of communication in home care.

is usually inconvenient and time consuming; it also fails to lend itself to thoughtful discussion about a client's care.

Inadequate Current Medical Records

Medical records of home care clients are often less current than medical records maintained in hospitals. Home care personnel often complete various components of a client's medical record off-site. They then transport the record to an agency's office, where they review and transcribe information onto other necessary documents. In some circumstances, a week or more may elapse before part of the medical record appears in a client's chart and other care providers can review the information to best coordinate services.

Incorrect Information From Clients and Lay Caregivers

Occasionally, clients and their lay caregivers attempt to communicate the activities of various disciplines to nurses as they conduct home care visits. Although clients and lay caregivers work with the home care team to develop treatment goals, and actively participate in care planning, a lack of understanding of medical and psychosocial concepts can impede their ability to communicate information accurately. Also, clients and lay caregivers may incorrectly assume that information they communicate to one member of the home care team is shared with other personnel who need these facts to deliver services appropriately. Valuable data can thus become lost in the shuffle.

Inadequate Communication With Community Agencies

Aside from the treatment that employees of home care agencies provide to clients, community agencies and organizations not associated with home care agencies often fulfill important components of a client's plan of care. Individuals from community organizations do not formally document in the medical record. They do not communicate pertinent information to a client's primary physician. Typically, they have no professional "standards of practice" to follow. Yet, their measures can be as important to the success of a home care treatment plan as interventions that home care team members implement. Therefore, coordinating these services as well is tremendously important to successfully maintaining a client in the home.

KEY CONCEPT

Barriers to communication in home care can make the coordination of services from multiple disciplines challenging to nurses.

◆ The Role of the Care Coordinator

Every home care client requires the services of a **care coordinator**—an individual who is responsible for ensuring that the client progresses toward established goals in the home care treatment plan. This individual is responsible for coordinating all of the services that medical and community personnel furnish, and for maintaining the flow of communication among providers. These tasks can be tremendously complex and challenging when multiple disciplines and community organizations are involved in a client's treatment. Nurses usually fulfill the role of care coordinator in home care.

ACCOUNTABILITY

Various titles may be used within a home care agency to describe the role of the individual primarily responsible for managing a client's care, including "care coordinator," "case manager," or "primary nurse." Regardless of the exact title given to this individual, the home care agency must designate accountability for clients to qualified individuals who can handle coordination of the multitude of services given to clients.

GOAL SETTING

Within the care planning process, participation from clients and lay caregivers is pivotal for establishing the goals they hope to achieve with the help of the home care services they receive. Although personnel from various disciplines provide distinct services, they frequently work toward common client goals. Therefore, regular communication is important to ensure that interventions complement one another. Home care professionals must remember that they are not functioning independently but as members of a team. Then the multidisciplinary team needs to establish desired outcomes and work together to achieve them. They should integrate services

Clinical Example
with Critical Thinking

Mrs. Dennis, a 68-year-old retired nurse, lives with her 90-year-old mother, for whom she acts as primary caregiver. Mrs. Dennis, who has been a diabetic for 25 years, injured her foot while wearing a new pair of shoes. Her foot wound became infected and, after several months of treatment, gangrenous. Mrs. Dennis received a below-the-knee amputation 3 weeks ago and was discharged from the hospital 1 week ago. Home care services were immediately assigned to Mrs. Dennis. Personnel from the following disciplines perform assessments: nursing, physical therapy, occupational therapy, and social services.

Martin, the home care nurse, recommends that home health aides visit Mrs. Dennis three times a week to assist her with personal care. Martin is designated the care coordinator for this client. After personnel from each discipline have conducted their initial assessments, Martin calls the first case conference. They report the following observations:

> Nursing: The client's incision is reddened without signs of infection. Clear serous drainage from 1.5 cm. opening in incision. Blood sugar levels stable and client independent in diet and medication administration. Phantom pain in ankle of amputated leg is distressing client. Client verbalizes feelings of anxiety and depression. Elderly mother lives with the client and is independent, but unable to assist in client's care. A supportive neighbor visits regularly and assists as needed. The client states her only goal is to be able to take care of her mother again.

Nursing Concerns

◆ Potential for incisional infection, which may lead to gangrene and the need for further surgery.
◆ Anxiety and depression may inhibit active participation in an exercise program.
◆ Transfers from bed to wheelchair are unsafe; potential exists for fall and injury.
◆ Client unable to perform ADL's, and caregiver, with limited ability to assist, has care needs of her own (i.e., unable to cook).

Physical Therapy Concerns

◆ Poor upper extremity strength
◆ Fair balance during transfers
◆ Client's mother attempts to assist with transfers, but causes client to lose balance.

Social Services Concerns

◆ Elderly caregiver is at risk of developing health problems, but provides good social support to client.
◆ Client has serious financial concerns and is unable to continue to pay for prescriptions. *(continued)*

Clinical Example
with Critical Thinking (Continued)

◆ Neighbors have been visiting regularly and performing errands for client (i.e., groceries) but are leaving for the winter to visit family.

Home Health Aide Concerns

◆ Client has verbalized thoughts of suicide.
◆ Nephew visited the client one day during a home visit and "borrowed" $125.00 to make a car payment; client stated she would never see that money again.

Thought Questions

1. Assess how the concerns and issues raised by the home health aide impact the interventions of the social worker, the nurse, and the physical therapist.
2. Identify the relationship between the finding of the social worker and the nurse's plan of care.
3. List courses of action the social worker can take to support the interventions performed by the physical therapist.
4. Evaluate the types of community services that may be available to provide Mrs. Dennis with other forms of assistance.
5. Design a plan for the interdisciplinary team to address the client's goals.
6. Establish a schedule of visits and interdisciplinary communication to coordinate the plan of care for Mrs. Dennis.

whenever possible to maximize the impact of every contact with a client. For example, a nurse can evaluate a client's compliance with an exercise program that a physical therapist established. A social worker can check to ensure that a client's wound dressing is intact. A physical therapist can ask a client whether Meals on Wheels has started. Individuals should address problems as a team whenever appropriate. Information that is significant to one team member is often signicant to every team member.

INSIGHT

Frequently, the nurse who performs the initial client assessment fulfills the role of care coordinator. Home care nurses are typically responsible for developing comprehensive problem lists, plans of care, and goals. Care coordinators must obtain physician authorization for referrals to ancillary services for clients. After the members of each discipline perform their initial assessments, all personnel involved in the client's care should communicate their findings to one another to provide more comprehensive insight into a client's problems. Care coordinators can simplify this process by holding a **case conference**, during which a multidisciplinary team meets to collectively brainstorm strategies that will most effectively help clients to achieve their goals (Fig. 7-7). This process helps to ensure positive treatment outcomes, and that the goals of all involved disciplines are compatible. Care coordinators can also establish a schedule of visits at this time, staggering visits so that clients are not overwhelmed by several people performing different interventions in rapid succession. Although the team must address priority problems, clients will not fully benefit from teaching sessions and exercise programs if they are exhausted. Appropriate scheduling by the care coordinator in tandem with the multidisciplinary team can prevent problems.

KEY CONCEPT

A case conference allows the multidisciplinary team to meet and to collectively brainstorm the most effective strategies for helping clients to achieve their goals. This process helps to promote positive treatment outcomes. In addition, case conferencing ensures that the goals of all involved disciplines are compatible.

Interdisciplinary Communication

Throughout a client's treatment period, nurses must actively coordinate services and evaluate a client's progress toward goals established in the comprehensive plan of care on a continual basis. They need to facilitate the communication of appropriate information to all involved professionals (Display 7-3). For example, a home health

Figure 7-7. During case conferences, the multidisciplinary team can target strategies that will best assist the client to meet necessary health goals.

Display 7-3:
Standards of Communication

For all disciplines to function cohesively, certain standards of communication should be observed:

- Notify other disciplines of the hospitalization of a shared client as soon as it is discovered. This may save a colleague numerous attempts to contact a client.
- Integrate services to provide maximum benefit to the client (e.g., ambulation of client by the nurse, or a blood pressure check by the physical therapist).
- Problem solve jointly when appropriate.
- Notify other disciplines of plans to discharge client from services.

(Lajeunesse, D. A. [1990]. Case management: A primary nursing approach. Caring; *9(8), 13–16)*

aide discovers that a client is anxious about being a burden to his wife. Therefore, the client does not ask his wife for assistance with his exercise program. The home health aide reports this finding to the care coordinator. The care coordinator must communicate this information to the physical therapist (to potentially adjust the client's exercise program) and to the social worker (to provide counseling for the client and his wife concerning this issue). If clients are not progressing as anticipated toward established goals, multidisciplinary communication can provide a better understanding of the underlying reasons, and the plan of treatment can be altered in the most effective way.

KEY CONCEPT

If clients do not progress as anticipated toward established goals, multi-disciplinary communication can provide a better understanding of hindrances or limitations so that the plan of treatment can be altered most effectively.

DOCUMENTATION

The care coordinator should confirm that interdisciplinary communication is regularly documented in a client's clinical record. Documentation should include the disciplines involved in discussions and the results of discussions. Documentation verifies the coordination of services and interdisciplinary communication. It should display that the team made every effort to arrive at the best possible plan of care for a client. It should also show how a home care team collaborated to achieve established client goals. Demonstration of these efforts in documentation is necessary for home care agencies and employees to meet legal and regulatory record requirements (see Chapter 5).

Home Care Vs. Hospital:
Coordination of Care and Communication

Issue	Home Care	Hospital
Responsibility for identification of need for ancillary services	Home care nurses primarily identify need for ancillary services and make recommendations to physicians. Nurses must understand indications for ancillary services.	Physicians have primary responsibility to identify indications for referrals to other professional disciplines.
Coordination of care	Home care nurses are primarily responsible for coordinating all services to clients.	Physicians are primarily responsible for coordinating medical treatment plans.
Development of plan of care	Medical treatment plans incorporate all medical and nursing interventions that nurses develop and physicians approve.	Physicians develop medical treatment plans. Nurses develop nursing plans of care.
Revisions to plan of care	Clients see their physicians infrequently. Nurses usually identify and report changes in condition to physicians, who base revisions to treatment plans primarily upon recommendations of nurses.	Physicians typically assess clients once or twice a day and revise medical treatment plans based primarily upon their own observations.
Community services	Nurses need an awareness of a wide variety of community services available to meet the comprehensive long-term needs of clients: equipment, medical supplies, food, socialization, laboratory testing, personal care, etc.	Specified nurse discharge planners or social workers typically fulfill the task of identifying client needs after hospitalization. Community services are rarely accessed for clients prior to hospital discharge.

◆ Summary

Home care clients often require services from many disciplines during their treatment. Nurses must have a thorough grasp of indications for physical therapy, occupational therapy, speech therapy, social services, and home health aides to ensure that clients receive appropriate services. Nurses should also be aware of available community service organizations that can potentially meet the complex and diverse needs of home care clients. These organizations can facilitate and enhance the ability of clients to maintain independence in their own homes.

Home care professionals often seem to function independently, making the coordination of services difficult; however, home care must be coordinated for the multidisciplinary team to efficiently assist clients in achieving their goals. In many home care agencies, a nurse assumes the role of care coordinator and accepts responsibility for easing communication among professionals involved in client care.

Nurses lead the interdisciplinary and community team members to efficiently reach common objectives.

References and Bibliography

Carr, M.N. (1994). Physical therapists in home care: Yesterday, today & tomorrow. *Caring Magazine, XIII*(4), 38–40.

Esposito, L. (1994). The home care nurse as case manager. *Caring Magazine, XIII*(4), 30–33.

Harris, M.D., & Diodato, J. (1997). The medical social worker: Member of the home healthcare team. *Home Healthcare Nurse, 15*(5), 327–328.

Harris, M.D., & Kalix, J. (1997). The speech-language pathologist as a member of the home healthcare team. *Home Healthcare Nurse, 15*(1), 25–28.

Hartsell, M. & Ward, J. (1985). Selecting equipment vendors for children on home care. *The American Journal of Maternal and Child Nursing, 10*, 26–28.

Krol, M. (1993). Strategies to improve continuity of care and decrease rehospitalization of cancer patients: A review. *ONS Nursing Scan in Oncology, 2*(6), 13.

Lajeunesse, D.A. (1990). Case management: A primary nursing approach. *Caring, 9*(8), 13–16.

Lumsdon, K. (1993). Bridging the gap: Home- and community-based programs integrate acute and long-term care. *Aging Today, 76*(23), 44, 48.

Magilvy, J., Congdon, J. & Martinez, R. (1994). Circles of care: Home care and community support for rural older adults. *Advances in Nursing Science, 16*(3), 22–33.

Pokorni, J.L. & Sippel, K.M. (1997). Consultation with physical and occupational therapists to promote the motor development of young children. *Home Healthcare Nurse, 15*(5), 331–339.

Rice, R. (1994). Clinical indicators for a rehabilitation referral. *Home Care Nurse, 12*(1), 64.

White, R. (1997, January). Rural home care: Social work intervention in social isolation and safety concerns. *Caring Magazine,* 28–34.

POST TEST

1. List at least four conditions that may warrant a need for rehabilitative therapy.

2. Discuss why it is necessary for home care nurses to be familiar with community resources.

3. Explain the importance of the coordination of services in home care.

4. Give three characteristics of home care practice that make coordination of care challenging.

THINKING CRITICALLY IN HOME CARE

1. Mr. Polking is a 69-year-old client who was diagnosed with multiple sclerosis 15 years ago. Dr. Grinnel called Five Star Home Health and requested that a nurse evaluate Mr. Polking for potential home care services. The doctor states that Mrs. Polking has been calling the office almost daily, reporting a variety of vague new symptoms and a decline in her husband's functional status. Dr. Grinnel has not seen the client for over a month. She asks the nurse to evaluate the

appropriateness of nursing and therapy services. Mr. Polking has Medicare coverage.

A. Identify issues for the nurse to consider when determining appropriate therapy services for Mr. Polking.

B. Explain why it is important for the nurse to coordinate this client's medical treatment plan with Dr. Grinnel.

2. Determine the ancillary services that are appropriate for the following clients:

A. Mr. Heiman has esophageal cancer. He is 72 and has been receiving courses of radiation and chemotherapy. He is very weak and has difficulty performing ADLs and ambulating at home. Mr. Heiman is on a pureed diet but is having difficulty swallowing. His wife is an excellent lay caregiver but frequently becomes highly anxious about her abilities to care for her husband.

B. Mr. Williams is a 38-year-old man diagnosed with AIDS. He recently lost his partner of 12 years to the disease. He is showing signs of depression and has been noncompliant with his medication regimen. Mr. Williams is weak and unable to prepare meals for himself.

C. Sandy Easton is a pregnant 16-year-old with a medical history of severe asthma. After living with an aunt for several months, she has moved in with her parents following a hospitalization for premature labor. Her physician has instructed Sandy to remain in bed for the duration of her pregnancy (bathroom privileges only). Sandy's mother is concerned because her daughter has no appetite and has not gained any weight through 27 weeks of pregnancy. Sandy has suffered three serious asthma attacks since she has become pregnant. Her pulmonologist has related these attacks to emotional stress.

8

The Home Care Nurse as Supervisor

LEARNING OBJECTIVES

After completing this chapter, the reader will be able to:

◆ Distinguish between the duties of a homemaker and those of a home health aide.

◆ Identify the types of duties that home health aides perform.

◆ Explain the reasons that home care nurses supervise home health aides.

◆ Evaluate the management function of home care nursing.

◆ Discuss how nurses can give feedback to home health aides regarding their performance.

KEY TERMS

Bonded	Paraprofessionals
Custodial care needs	Personal care attendants
Home care aide organizations	Private duty companies
Homemakers	Registries
Medicaid	

Paraprofessionals, *such* as home health aides and homemakers, play a vital role in the home care industry. The nurse, acting as care coordinator, is better able to decide whether clients can remain safely in their own homes or whether they require institutional care based on the supportive services that paraprofessionals provide. Most paraprofessionals receive limited formal education and training, however; home care nurses, as the coordinators of plans of care for their clients, are responsible for supervising them. To ensure the safe care of clients, nurses must develop assignments carefully and direct the performance of paraprofessionals.

This chapter reviews the types of paraprofessionals who work with home care clients, the scope of services they provide, and the types of organizations that employ them. Third party reimbursement for some paraprofessional services is available when clients meet specified criteria. This chapter discusses payment parameters for reimbursement. Medicare-certified home care organizations are required to supervise the performance of home health aides regularly. Home care nurses are usually responsible for creating plans of care for home health aides to follow and for conducting and documenting supervision; this chapter reviews essential components of these activities. Important management concepts for home care nurses are explained. A discussion of the need to include home health aides in the overall care planning process concludes this chapter.

KEY CONCEPT

Supportive services that home health aides and homemakers provide make a difference in determining whether clients can remain safely at home or require institutionally based care.

◆ Types of Paraprofessionals

Paraprofessionals and home care aides are terms typically used to describe home health aides, homemakers, and personal care attendants. Home health aides provide "hands-on" supportive services to clients (Fig. 8-1). Their duties include helping clients with bathing, toileting, personal hygiene, ambulating, transferring, range of motion exercises, meal preparation, and feeding. Specialized home health aide activities include changing nonsterile dressings, taking a client's temperature, pulse, and respiration, and assisting clients with self-administered medications. Aides may also perform light housekeeping to maintain health and safety in the home.

Home health aides receive formal instruction regarding their role in home healthcare. **Homemakers**, on the other hand, have no formal training because their services typically do not require them to "touch" the client; that is, they do not provide "hands-on" care. Homemaker services may include housekeeping, simple meal preparation, running errands, shopping, and companionship. **Personal care attendants** are paraprofessionals used specifically by the Medicaid program,

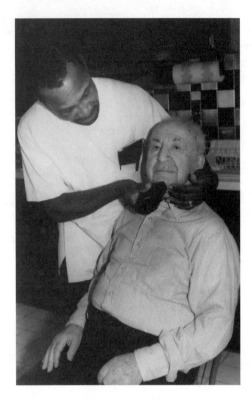

Figure 8-1. A home health aide assists this client with his grooming and personal care. (Photo by Marilu Sherer, CARING)

which is discussed later in this chapter. They can perform some, but not all, of the tasks of the home health aide.

KEY CONCEPT

Home health aides receive formal instruction in conducting personal care, assisting clients with exercises, preparing meals, feeding, light housekeeping, and performing simple skin care to maintain the health and safety of clients. Homemakers receive no formal training because their functions include no "hands-on" services.

Clients may receive paraprofessional services intermittently (e.g., three hour-long visits to perform personal care duties) or on a continuous or hourly basis (usually in 8- or 24-hour shifts). **Private duty companies**, **registries**, or **home care aide organizations** frequently provide those services conducted on a continuous or hourly basis. These companies broker the services of their employees to clients who request care. They usually screen individuals and are **bonded**, or insured, in case of unforeseen financial losses due to the actions of employees. Bonding gives additional assurance to customers should home care employees destroy or steal

Home Care Vs. Hospital:
The Home Care Nurse as Supervisor

Issue	Home Care	Hospital
Training of paraprofessionals	Homemakers and personal care assistants (Medicaid program) often have no training in the performance of their responsibilities	Nursing assistants usually receive some education and training in the performance of their duties.
Scope of paraprofessional duties	Paraprofessionals may perform all tasks of nursing assistants in hospitals PLUS meal preparation, housekeeping tasks, assisting clients with transportation, and providing general supervision for safety.	Nursing assistant duties are usually limited to assistance with personal care, collection of noninvasive lab specimens, and assistance with feeding and mobility.
Duration of supervision	Nurses direct and supervise the care paraprofessionals provide throughout the length of the home care treatment plan, typically lasting from several weeks to a few months.	Nurses usually direct and supervise during the course of their shift only.
Supervision of services provided	Nurses are able to supervise care by paraprofessionals intermittently. They provide ongoing supervision indirectly through interviews with clients and lay caregivers and assessments of clients and their environment.	Hospital nurses can easily supervise care by nursing assistants directly.
Paraprofessional care planning	Nurses must anticipate the needs of clients over several days or weeks and develop plans of care for paraprofessionals to meet these anticipated needs.	Nurses develop assignments for nursing assistants based upon the specific needs of clients each day.
Receiving client reports from paraprofessionals	Nurses usually receive reports on the status of clients and their responses to care through documentation or delayed verbal reports (unless findings are significant).	Nurses are able to receive reports about client status and responses to care during or at the end of a work shift. These reports are often given verbally.

their property. Sometimes, clients hire individuals through newspaper advertisements or through contacts with friends and neighbors. Hiring services in this manner is frequently less expensive for clients; usually, however, these workers are not bonded or insured in the event of theft or injury.

◆ Reimbursement Stipulations for Paraprofessional Services

Medicare-certified home care agencies usually provide home health aide services to clients on an intermittent basis. Medicare and some private insurance plans reimburse agencies for home health aide benefits. Under these circumstances, aides perform duties ordered by a physician and included in the medical treatment plan. Medicare has identified the specific duties that home health aides can perform. Display 8-1 outlines these duties.

A home health aide remains in a client's home for the period of time necessary to complete assigned duties in one day. Therefore, most visits last from one to three hours. The home care nurse's recommendations, based upon a client's medical and personal needs and the coverage limitations of Medicare and insurance companies, largely determine the services that the client receives.

MEDICAID

Title XIX of the Social Security Act (1966) established **Medicaid** as a state-implemented medical assistance program based on income and other criteria. Every state receives approximately 50% in matching federal funds to meet the medical needs of qualified residents. Services vary from state to state; however, home care services (e.g., nursing, home health aides, medical supplies, and medical equipment) are mandatory offerings across the entire United States.

Medicaid clients receive benefits for home care services that are similar to the parameters set by Medicare. Medicaid reimburses such services to individuals who need medically necessary care ordered by physicians. Unlike Medicare, however, Medicaid does not require clients to be homebound. Federal regulations stipulate that approved organizations provide necessary home care services to Medicaid clients.

Display 8-1:
Medicare-Approved Home Health Aide Services

- Simple exercises to extend therapy services provided to clients
- Ambulation
- Personal care
- Household services essential to home care
- Assistance with medications that are ordinarily self-administered
- Reporting changes in a client's conditions and needs
- Completing appropriate records

Personal Care Attendants

Title XX of the Social Security Act (1975) provides funding for homemaker services by personal care attendants for clients eligible for social security who meet age criteria. Organizations that primarily serve Medicaid populations typically employ attendants who have no formal training. Their employees are regularly evaluated for competency of services. Personal care attendant services (as defined by Medicaid) cannot include health-related tasks. In contrast, home health aides must perform such duties, which include changing nonsterile dressings, taking a client's temperature, pulse, and respiration, and assisting clients with self-administered medications (Surpin, Haslanger, & Dawson, 1994).

CLIENTS WHO NEED MULTIPLE SERVICES

Occasionally, clients require services from personal care attendants or homemakers in addition to the health-related services that only home health aides can provide. Home care nurses must recognize that coordination and supervision of multiple paraprofessionals are particularly important to maximize resources and to prevent unnecessary duplication of services.

Medicare and most private insurances do not pay for services to clients with only **custodial care needs** (e.g., housekeeping, meal preparation, running errands, shopping, and companionship). Unless clients qualify for some of these services under the Medicaid program, these services are usually out-of-pocket expenses for clients and their lay caregivers. Clients who privately pay for services do not have coverage determinations that limit the services they can receive. They are limited only by a home care agency's scope of service. For example, one company may refuse to allow its employees to transport clients; another company may allow workers to perform light housekeeping only (e.g., no window washing, cleaning out cupboards, etc.). These limits are highly individualized according to each company's philosophy and accepted business practices. Clients and lay caregivers must carefully select a private duty company or registry that performs all of the duties they require.

KEY CONCEPT

Home care aide organizations are highly individualized in the scope and types of services they provide. Clients and lay caregivers should select organizations that provide all desired services and that maximize third party reimbursement privileges.

Licensed and Medicare-certified home care agencies occasionally offer hourly home health aide and homemaker services as well. These services, however, are frequently provided by unlicensed, noncertified companies (e.g., home care aide agencies) that specialize in hourly nursing assistant and homemaker services. Medicare and most private insurance companies do not pay for continuous care services, since they limit their coverage to acute, short-term medical assistance. They typically consider continuous care services as long-term and/or custodial in nature.

Clients who require continuous care from paraprofessionals usually need assistance with personal care and other support. For example, a home health aide may stay with a debilitated client for 8 hours while lay caregivers work outside the home. During this time, the aide may bathe the client, prepare breakfast and lunch, help the client to eat, assist with toileting, supervise for safety, and provide social stimulation.

Aides may not be required to actively care for clients at all times. Occasionally, if a client is sleeping or wishes to watch television, an aide may read or otherwise quietly pass the time until the client needs help. For some clients, home health aides have no specific activities to perform; they are simply asked to be available if clients need them (Fig. 8-2). This scenario is common when clients are relatively independent but require supervision to ensure their safety (e.g., clients with beginning Alzheimer's disease who are alone during the day while their lay caregivers work). With other clients, aides have little free time and provide services actively throughout a shift (e.g., for a pediatric client with a brain injury who requires constant stimulation and exercise).

◆ The Home Health Aide

Home care agencies must allow only those aides who have met training and competency criteria to conduct services. Before 1989, no national standards defined the roles and responsibilities of home health aides. States differed widely in the minimum qualifications and training requirements that individuals needed to work as aides within an organization. The Omnibus Reconciliation Act of 1987 (OBRA 87) modified the Medicare Conditions of Participation, creating standards for home health aide training (Display 8-2) and competency evaluation. The revised Medicare Conditions of Participation define the term **home health aide** based on these minimum standards. Although aides must receive 75 hours of education and supervised practical training, their preparation is minimal considering the independent nature of their work.

Figure 8-2. A client and an aide share some relaxing reading time together. (Photo by Marilu Sherer, CARING)

Display 8-2:
484.36 Condition of Participation: Home Health Aide Services

(a) Standard: Home health aide training—
(a)(1) Content and duration of training. The aide training program must address each of the following subject areas through classroom and supervised practical training, totaling at least 75 hours, with at least 16 hours devoted to classroom training before beginning the supervised practical training.
(i) Communication skills.
(ii) Observation, reporting, and documentation of patient status and the care or services furnished.
(iii) Reading and recording temperature, pulse, and respiration.
(iv) Basic infection control procedures.
(v) Basic elements of body function and changes in body function that must be reported to an aide's supervisor.
(vi) Maintenance of a clean, safe, and health environment.
(vii) Recognizing emergencies and knowledge of emergency procedures.
(viii) The physical, emotional, and developmental characteristics of the populations served by the HHA, including the need for respect for the patient, his or her privacy, and his or her property.
(ix) Appropriate and safe techniques in personal hygiene and grooming, including bed bath; sponge, tub, or shower bath; shampoo—sink, tub, or bed; nail and skin care; oral hygiene.
(x) Adequate nutrition and fluid intake.
(xi) Any other task that the HHA may choose to have the home health aide perform.

(Federal Register, 1989, p.33357-8) Health Care Administration, 42 CFR Part 484

SUPERVISING THE HOME HEALTH AIDE

Home health aides are the paraprofessionals for whom home care nurses are most accountable. Regulations specify the frequency and type of direction that nurses should give to aides. Aides are usually direct employees of home care organizations that provide skilled services (e.g., nursing, physical therapy) to clients. Often, homemakers or personal care assistants are available to clients through different organizations. Although nurses are responsible for coordinating entire plans of care (including the services of paraprofessionals from other organizations), their legal obligation to **supervise** the services of home health aides employed by their own agencies is greater. Home health aide interventions are usually included in medical treatment plans. Regulatory bodies evaluate an agency's compliance with home health aide supervisory standards through documentation review and client interviews during surveys (see Chapter 5).

Management

In home care, nurses must accept the role of supervisor or manager of the care that aides give to clients. For many nurses, this role is the first supervisory responsibility of their careers. Home care nurses must understand basic concepts of management to fulfill this responsibility successfully. Management consists of four primary functions: planning, organizing, directing, and controlling (Fig. 8-3). The management process is very similar to the nursing process (see Chapter 9).

During the **planning** phase, home care nurses complete client assessments and identify the need for specific home health aide services. Nurses should prioritize each client's needs, establish goals, and determine the types of interventions necessary to achieve these goals. **Organizing** requires nurses to express the needs and goals of plans of care to home health aides, to identify the sequence of interventions to perform, and to schedule regular opportunities for interaction and discussion about client progress. **Directing** involves supervising home health aides' performance of duties. Home care nurses should teach and demonstrate procedures as needed to maintain quality care. The management function of **controlling** involves review of home health aide documentation to ensure that care is provided as planned. Controlling also means assessing the progress of clients toward their determined goals. If clients do not advance as anticipated, home care nurses revise their plans of care and initiate the management process again.

In most healthcare settings, nursing assistants frequently work side by side with registered nurses while caring for clients. In home care, however, aides conduct services for clients with little direct supervision from nurses. Registered nurses can closely manage the services of home health aides through a variety of methods to ensure that client needs are adequately met. Occasionally, nurses should directly supervise aides through supervisory visits. Nurses must also maintain continual discus-

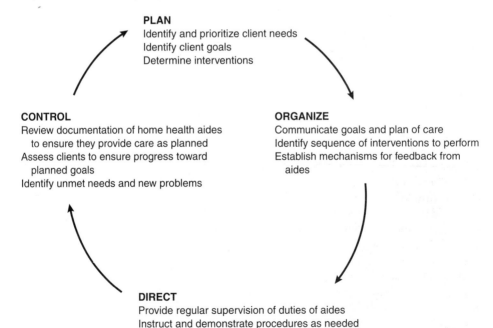

PLAN
Identify and prioritize client needs
Identify client goals
Determine interventions

CONTROL
Review documentation of home health aides
  to ensure they provide care as planned
Assess clients to ensure progress toward
  planned goals
Identify unmet needs and new problems

ORGANIZE
Communicate goals and plan of care
Identify sequence of interventions to perform
Establish mechanisms for feedback from
  aides

DIRECT
Provide regular supervision of duties of aides
Instruct and demonstrate procedures as needed

Figure 8-3. The management functions of home care nurses when supervising home health aides.

Application to Home Care Practice
Outlining Specific Duties for Aides to Perform

To ensure that aides provide care most suited to the needs of clients, nurses should specifically outline and communicate necessary interventions. A home health aide plan of care should include the exact types of personal care to be provided. For example, nurses should specify whether a shower, tub bath, assisted bath, or complete bed bath is advised for clients who need bathing assistance. Instructions should also include the frequency with which various activities are to be performed for or with clients (e.g., daily complete bed baths and a weekly shampoo).

sion with home health aides about the conditions of clients to determine whether care is appropriate or should be adjusted. Review of the documentation of home health aide visits should also be part of the management process to evaluate whether services are consistent with established plans of care. Nurses may wish to interview clients and their lay caregivers regarding their satisfaction with the services of home health aides and progress toward their goals. Nurses may find it helpful to conduct interviews soon after visits by home health aides. By doing so, nurses are better able to evaluate clients soon after services are provided. Moreover, clients will be more likely to remember visit particulars and thus will respond to questions more accurately.

KEY CONCEPT

In other healthcare settings, nursing assistants frequently work in conjunction with registered nurses while performing care for clients. In home care, home health aides provide client care with little direct supervision from nurses.

Assignments and Duties

A 75-hour training program cannot fully prepare aides for the many circumstances that can arise while they are caring for clients in the home. As healthcare continues to shift to less expensive settings, clients with extensive needs and multiple problems are receiving home care services, leading to increased reliance and pressure on home health aides. Thus, a client's primary nurse must carefully establish a home health aide service plan. The plan should clearly specify the activities to be performed and their frequency (Fig. 8-4). Nurses should identify findings, symptoms, and vital signs that aides must verbally report to them.

Home health aides are taught to comply with instructions from nurses even when clients request a change in services. Aides should not determine the most appropriate level of care for clients; that decision requires the professional judgment

Application to Home Care Practice
The Need to Ask Specific Questions During Supervisory Visits

When performing supervisory visits, home care nurses should ask clients and lay caregivers specific questions to acquire the most accurate information to improve care. Closed questions, such as "How is the aide doing?", will most likely result in general responses, such as "Fine." When nurses ask open-ended questions about specific home health duties, clients often yield information that allows nurses to update treatment plans in accordance with their evolving circumstances. An example of an open-ended statement is: "Mrs. Twane, tell me how the home health aide assists you with your exercises."

Home Care Conflict:
An Aide's Neglect of the Plan of Care

Abby is the primary home care nurse for Mr. Moore, a 56-year-old man with end-stage renal disease. Jason is the home health aide assigned to provide personal care assistance to Mr. Moore. During the course of a visit, Abby observes that Mr. Moore is unshaven and obviously has not had his hair shampooed in over a week. She reviews the home health aide plan of care and confirms that she instructed the aide to perform such activities. When Abby questions Mr. Moore, he only states that Jason has been wonderful to him. He reluctantly admits that Jason spent only 15 minutes at his home yesterday, assisting him into the shower and then leaving before Mr. Moore was finished.

Upon her return to the home care agency, Abby verifies that Jason has not reported the incident to anyone in the office or explained the reasons for his behavior. Abby addresses these issues with Jason the next morning. She states her observations of Mr. Moore's condition. She lets Jason know that Mr. Moore complimented him as well. Abby explains the reasons why leaving a weak client alone in the shower is unsafe. She reiterates the importance of completing all of the tasks outlined in the home health aide plan of care. Jason states that Mr. Moore requested only the assistance he provided and refused any other help. Abby explains that modifications to the plan of care require authorization from a licensed clinician. If Mr. Moore wants a change and refuses services, Jason must call Abby or a home care agency supervisor to report the incident immediately.

Abby confirms that Jason understands the significance of complying with the established plan of care. Jason promises to notify the agency immediately if he cannot carry out his duties for any reason.

Client Name: Jan Lacy   **Phone:** 555-2681   **Date:** 3/7/98

Address: 431 Indian Canyon Dr., Apt. 60, Palm Springs, CA 92242

Primary RN: Tracie Simpson, RN   **HHA Assigned:** Daisy Seigman, CHHA

Language Spoken: English   **Diagnoses:** Pyelonephritis 2/5/98, Multiple Sclerosis × 4 yrs

Other Members of Household: Lucy Franklin-mother Note: PCP works during the day

Directions: Take Vista Chino to Country Club, turn right on Country to Indian Canyon Dr.

and turn left, go 3 blocks, white house with tile roof on left; Note client has BIG DOG!!! Call

before 08:30 P.M. to schedule visit; request client's mom to put dog on chain.

PLAN OF CARE	FREQUENCY	SPECIAL INSTRUCTIONS
Assist client w/ bed bath	Every other day	Encourage client to perform as much
Shampoo hair	2×/wk.	of bath as possible but don't push as
Massage bony prominences		client tires easily. Report signs of redness
		or skin breakdown.
Assist to w/chair after	Every visit.	Notify nurse if client refuses to
bath using pivot transfer.		go to wheelchair.
Take vitals. TPR BP	Every visit.	Report T greater than 99.6 degrees F,
		P greater than 100 and lower than 60;
		R greater than 26, lower than 12; BP
		systolic greater than 140, lower than 100;
		diastolic greater than 90, lower than 50
Assisted active ROM	Every visit.	Perform before transferring client to
all joints		wheelchair.

Figure 8-4. A sample home health aide plan of care.

of a nurse. If an existing home health aide plan of care no longer seems appropriate or a client requests a change of services, nurses expect home health aides to communicate these findings for direction. Nurses must regularly evaluate the continued appropriateness of home health aide plans of care. Failure on the part of nurses to advance the participation of clients in their personal care at a level consistent with their increased functional capacity can lead to inappropriate dependence of clients on home health aides. The continued interventions of aides may also conflict with treatment goals that other professionals establish for clients.

Home care nurses may recommend that aides assist clients with medications.

Aides help clients to identify appropriate bottles, to retrieve the correct number of pills, to take their medications at the appropriate times of day, and to follow special instructions, such as taking medications with food. They frequently report vital clinical information about clients to nurses on days that nursing visits are not conducted. Their observations are particularly helpful to nurses who want to monitor clients closely for potential complications. For example, a client has experienced a gradual increase in blood pressure; however, it has not yet reached a level that demands medical attention. An aide can measure the client's blood pressure during visits and report readings to the nurse. The home care nurse is thus able to decide if interventions are appropriate.

Nurses must instruct home health aides to report potentially threatening changes in the conditions of clients; however, aides usually lack the essential experience and skills to identify high-risk clinical situations independently. Nurses must incorporate within plans of care important signs and symptoms for aides to relate. For example, a nurse instructs a home health aide to regularly weigh a client who suffered congestive heart failure. During a weekly visit, the aide finds a weight increase of 5 pounds. The aide must alert the nurse to this information. Unless the nurse gives specific instructions, however, the aide may be unaware that the client's weight change represents an urgent clinical situation. Nurses must incorporate in their plans of care specific findings that aides must report immediately .

Supervisory Visits

Home care nurses frequently perform necessary supervisory visits to evaluate the continued appropriateness of home health aide assignments. Nurses should also

---

Display 8-3:
Ways for Home Care Agencies and Nurse Supervisors to Encourage Home Health Aides and to Increase Employee Retention

- Allow aides to maintain flexible hours when possible. Include them in scheduling visits to clients.
- Provide mentoring by nurses and other experienced aides. Prepare aides for regularly encountered problems, possible sources of conflict, and ways to address such difficulties.
- Help aides maintain personal safety by providing escort security services in dangerous neighborhoods.
- Communicate with aides regularly. Make sure that aides are not always just reporting information to nurses, but that nurses seek out opinions and data from the aides as well.
- Always include aides in case conferences.
- Encourage aides to continue their healthcare education.
- Conduct regular performance evaluations. Ask aides in turn to rate their relationships with supervisors and with the agency overall.
- Remind aides that their services are important, specialized, necessary, and appreciated.

evaluate whether clients are receiving the benefits outlined in their plans of care. Nurses can conduct supervisory visits while aides are present or absent. A nurses will usually find it helpful to alternate the type of supervisory visits performed, as each can provide a different perspective on an aide's performance and the client's ability to attain treatment goals. Home care nurses should determine whether aides use appropriate techniques when conducting procedures. They should also assess whether aides perform duties completely and accurately, and whether clients are treated with respect and kindness.

When home care nurses perform supervisory visits without the presence of aides, clients may answer questions more openly and freely. Clients are sometimes hesitant to express their dissatisfaction with services, because they are often highly dependent upon them and may fear retribution if they verbalize service complaints. Clients may worry that home care services will be canceled or that aides will not provide optimal care because they resent complaints. Nurses should reassure clients and their lay caregivers that they need honest feedback from them to improve the services that they and other clients receive. When they anticipate conflicts and problems and provide appropriate reassurances, nurses may help allay anxiety and receive honest feedback.

KEY CONCEPT

A home care nurse can conduct supervisory visits while a home health aide is present or absent. The nurse will usually find it helpful to alternate the type of supervisory visits performed, because each visit can give a different perspective on the aide's performance and the client's attainment of goals.

Survival Alert:
Strategies for Nurse Supervisors When Addressing Conflicts with Home Health Aides

* State your position assertively, without being threatening or domineering.
* Listen to the aide's observations, opinions, and position with objectivity.
* Avoid accusations and blame. Try not to become angry or emotional.
* Reach a common understanding about the healthcare needs of clients.
* Ensure that conflicts have not arisen from faulty communication or from a lack of adequate instruction and teaching.
* Narrow the reasons for the conflict to one or two fundamental causes that can be targeted for resolution.
* Be open to alternative solutions and willing to listen to suggestions.

FOLLOW-UP OF CLIENT CARE ISSUES

Home care nurses can effectively identify significant client care issues when they directly observe visits by home health aides. Nurses should handle client care concerns promptly. When an issue needs to be corrected during a supervised client visit, a nurse should inform the aide about the issue. The nurse should instruct the aide quickly and respectfully and then continue the visit. Inappropriately reprimanding an aide in the presence of a client or lay caregivers may result in feelings of humiliation and resentment for the aide. Clients and lay caregivers may feel embarrassed or guilty about "getting someone in trouble." Clients may also lose trust in the aide's capabilities. When possible, nurses should correctively instruct aides in a private, nonthreatening environment after visits are over.

Nurses should be as specific as possible when giving performance feedback to home health aides. Most aides are anxious and eager to learn ways to care for clients more effectively. When nurses explain both the procedures to be conducted and the reasons why, aides expand their knowledge, understanding, and competence. Ongoing learning helps to make the job of home health aide interesting; interactive relationships between nurses and aides may inspire aides to stay with their jobs and perform their duties better.

Survival Alert:

Determining an Aide's Compliance with the Plan of Care During Supervisory Visits

1. Before the supervisory visit, review the home health aide's documentation of recent visits. Evaluate the aide's consistency of compliance with assignments.
2. Ask the client open-ended questions about tasks that the aide has performed. Example: What does Janis do for you during her visits? Verify reports from the client with the aide's documentation.
3. Evaluate the consistency of data the aide collects regarding the client's status (e.g., vital signs, functional status, mobility). Lack of consistency may mean falsification of documentation that warrants further investigation.
4. During the nursing assessment, examine the client for general hygiene. Consider the client's condition, frequency of home health aide visits, and environment. Examine skin integrity and look for overall signs that the aide has conducted duties appropriately. Body odor, unshampooed hair, and dirty fingernails may indicate that the aide has failed to provide appropriate care.
5. Assess the aide's relationship with the client and lay caregiver. Observe the reactions of the client and lay caregiver as they are questioned. Does the client respond to questions about the aide defensively? Fearfully? Affectionately? Respectfully? When the aide is present, do the client and lay caregiver answer questions with ease and comfort or with displeasure and timidity?

For a home health aide who has never performed a specific procedure, the nurse should demonstrate the procedure and then observe the aide's ability to perform the same duty in a return demonstration. Aides must display the ability to conduct duties in question before nurses allow them to perform such procedures independently. Examples of procedures that home health aides perform infrequently include personal care for clients receiving intravenous infusions, use of lifts, and care for disabled pediatric clients.

INVOLVING HOME HEALTH AIDES IN CARE PLANNING

Home health aides frequently spend more time with clients than any other professionals involved in their treatment plans. Consequently, clients are frequently most open with home health aides because of the personal nature of the services they provide, the great amount of time they spend with them, and their less intimidating role. Aides often obtain information from clients that is significant to the development and revision of their plans of care. Home health aides may not realize the significance of information they receive, or they may assume that clients are sharing the same information with home care nurses. As a result, aides may not volunteer pertinent information about clients to home care nurses.

Survival Alert:

Signs of a Dependent Client—Aide Relationship

* The client reports that the aide has performed many additional interventions not included in the plan of care.
* The client and the home health aide exchange many gifts or money.
* The aide visits the client outside work hours.
* The aide becomes very emotional during case conference dicussions about a specific client.
* The aide appears upset when discussing the client's discharge from home care.
* The aide consistently favors a specific client when scheduling visits, despite the obvious physical needs of other clients.
* The client becomes highly upset if the home health aide is sick or on vacation and refuses services from other aides.
* The aide is hesitant to take days off that are scheduled for visits to the client.
* Visits to the client by the aide are particularly long.
* The client knows an inordinate amount of information about the aide's family and personal life.
* The client's opinions about other home care personnel mirror those of the aide.
* When the client nears discharge, the aide reports problems that have not been observed by other personnel involved in the client's care.

Nurses should actively seek insights from home health aides regarding findings that they observe in the home. Nurses can care for clients more effectively when they work regularly with home health aides and request their ideas and opinions. Nurses will thus communicate an invaluable message—that home health aides are essential and important members of the healthcare team (Display 8-3).

◆ Summary

Home health aides play an extremely important role in home care. Nurses must work closely with aides to provide effective client care. When supervising paraprofessionals, home care nurses must ensure that appropriate care is provided to clients and that they continually revise the service plan to meet changing needs. Aides must work diligently to meet many demanding physical and social requirements for clients.

Clinical Example
with Critical Thinking

Mr. Greenwald is an 84-year-old man who had total hip replacement surgery 4 weeks ago. After a 7-day hospitalization, Mr. Greenwald went to a skilled nursing facility for 3 weeks to receive therapy and to recover from the surgical procedure. He was discharged home 2 days ago, and his physician prescribed home care visits to continue his therapy program and to evaluate his safety. Mr. Greenwald lives with his 60-year-old daughter, who manages their apartment complex. Mr. Greenwald is alone most of the day, but his daughter checks on him frequently. He is recovering slowly after surgery and states that he has not been motivated to perform the exercise program established while in the skilled nursing facility. He is developing a reddened area on his coccyx. He has a history of hypertension and chronic obstructive pulmonary disease. Showering independently is unsafe for Mr. Greenwald due to poor balance.

Develop a Home Health Aide Service Plan for Mr. Greenwald

1. Frequency of home health aide visits:

2. Interventions to be performed by home health aide:

3. Observations to report to registered nurse:

They often receive little recognition and must perform their duties with little peer interaction and support. When nurses recognize the significant role of home health aides, they provide aides with opportunities for professional growth and improved client care. They also encourage aides to be quality employees.

References and Bibliography

Burbach, A.L., Conrad, M.B., Schumacher, K.L. & Lindsay, L. (1991). Issues in home health nursing education. *Home Healthcare Nurse, 9*(4), 22–28.

Burbridge, L.C. (1993). The labor market for home care workers: Demand, supply, and institutional barriers. *The Gerontologist, 33*, 41–46.

De Savorgnani, A.A., Haring, R.C. & Galloway, S. (1992). A survey of home care aides: A personal and professional profile. *Caring, 11*(4), 28–32.

Ditson, L.A. (1994). Efforts to reduce homemaker/home health care aide turnover in a home care agency. *Journal of Home Health Care Practice, 6*, 33–44.

Douglas, L.M. (1992). *The effective nurse: Leader and manager* (4th ed.). St. Louis: Mosby-Year Book.

Guariglia, W. Sensitizing home care aides to the needs of the elderly. *Home Healthcare Nurse, 14*(8), 619–623.

Hagenow, N.R. & McCrea, M.A. (1994). A mentoring relationship: Two viewpoints. *Nursing Management, 25*(12), 42–43.

Harris, M. (1994). *Handbook of home healthcare administration*. Gaithersburg, MD: Aspen.

Jorgensen, C. & Young, B. (1989). The supervisory shared home visit tool. *Home Healthcare Nurse, 7*(3), 33–36.

Keenan, M. & Hurst, J.B. (1994). *A skills workbook for leading and managing in nursing*. St. Louis: Mosby.

Kennedy-Malone, L. (1996). The stay or stray phenomena: Reflections of home care aide fulfillment. *Home Healthcare Nurse, 14*(2), 103–107.

Surpin, R., Haslanger, K., & Dawson, S. (1994). Quality paraprofessional home care. *Caring, 13*(4), 12–22.

Walter, B.M. (1996). Home care aide retention: Building team spirit to avoid employee walkouts. *Home Healthcare Nurse, 14*(8), 609–613.

Wranesh Cook, M.L. (1997). Understanding the aide/family caregiver relationship. *Home Healthcare Nurse, 15*(1), 57–63.

POST TEST

1. Explain the difference between the role of a home health aide and that of a homemaker.

2. List duties that a home health aide may perform (as defined by Medicare).

3. Identify the purpose of supervisory visits.

4. Explain the management process and how it relates to the supervisory role of the home care nurse.

5. Discuss how nurses should give feedback to home health aides.

THINKING CRITICALLY IN HOME CARE

1. Mrs. Sorrentino, an 86-year-old widow, is diagnosed with coronary artery disease, congestive heart failure, and angina. Dan is the nurse managing her home care. Mrs. Sorrentino lives alone in an apartment complex for senior citizens. She is forgetful and often neglects to take her scheduled medications, which has led to four recent and preventable hospitalizations. The manager of the complex reports that Mrs. Sorrentino has recently failed to come down for meals in the cafeteria. He also reports that Mrs. Sorrentino does not change out of her bed clothes and has stopped participating in the social activities the complex offers. He reports, "I'm not sure she still belongs here. She's not taking care of herself anymore, and I'm not running a nursing home."

    Marla, Mrs. Sorrentino's granddaughter and primary lay caregiver, lives in another state. She has informed Dan that she will gladly pay for any services her grandmother needs to delay nursing home placement for as long as possible. Dan's agency provides hourly homemaker and home health aide services.

    A. Determine the types of services that Dan should include in a plan of care for Mrs. Sorrentino.

    B. Identify interventions that Dan should implement to maximize Mrs. Sorrentino's health and function.

    C. Indicate instructions that Dan needs to include in the home health aide's plan of care. What sorts of concerns should the aide report to him immediately?

    D. Summarize how Dan can best fulfill the management functions of planning, organizing, directing, and controlling when working with the paraprofessionals who assist Mrs. Sorrentino.

2. During a visit, Kia, a home care nurse, discovers that a home health aide has been advising a client to use a variety of products (e.g., vitamins, minerals, and herbs) from a natural food store to resolve some of the client's physical ailments.

    A. How should Kia respond to the client when given this information?

    B. Determine additional information that Kia should obtain from the client.

    C. Explain the best ways for Kia to follow up with the aide.

    D. Identify other actions for Kia to perform.

3. Chris is a 3-year-old boy with severe brain damage that resulted from a near-fatal drowning 2 months ago. Chris's mother, Dawn, is highly critical of the around-the-clock care given by home health aides, who help Chris with frequent exercises, stimulation, and personal care. Dawn verbally abuses the aides and causes them to refuse further assignments with Chris. The home care agency is finding it difficult to locate staff willing to care for Chris. Without home health aide services, however, the boy will live in an unsafe environment. Stella is the nurse who is managing Chris's plan of care.

A. Explain ways for Stella to intervene with home health aides to minimize further tensions.

B. Target how Stella can appropriately discuss the situation with Dawn. Determine measures that Stella may be able to take to help Dawn manage her behavior more appropriately.

9

The Nursing Process and Home Care

LEARNING OBJECTIVES

After completing this chapter, the reader will be able to:

◆ Identify components of the nursing process.

◆ Discuss the nursing process and its relation to home care practice.

◆ List the phases of the home care visit.

◆ Apply components of the nursing process to the home visit.

◆ Explain appropriate preparation for a home visit.

◆ Articulate issues significant to the performance of the home visit.

◆ Describe the post-visit responsibilities of the nurse.

KEY TERMS

Assessment	Outcome criteria
Evaluation	Outcome identification
Follow-up	Performance
Implementation	Planning
Nursing diagnosis	Preparation
Nursing process	

Home care visits, the personal contacts between nurses and clients, represent the basic building blocks for a treatment plan. After all, bringing healthcare services to clients is what home care is all about. Mastering the performance of the visit is critical to a nurse's success in home care. Nurses who cannot effectively carry out visits will not be competent in the home care practice setting.

Fundamental to successful home care is a thorough understanding of the nursing process. Consistent application of the nursing process is critical to safe and effective care for clients. The nursing process provides the conceptual framework for all aspects of interaction between nurses and those they serve. The independent nature of home care requires the use of the nursing process to ensure that healthcare needs of clients are continually and competently addressed. Failure to adequately comprehend and apply the nursing process in the home can lead nurses to inappropriate care delivery and poor clinical outcomes for their clients.

This chapter provides a brief review of the phases of the nursing process and shows how to apply these phases in home care nursing. The nursing process is conducted during home visits. Visits have their own distinct phases that must be completed to ensure the proficient delivery of care to clients. This chapter discusses each of these phases and links them to vital components of the nursing process.

KEY CONCEPT

Mastering the performance of the home care visit and applying components of the nursing process within it are critical to a home care nurse's career success.

◆ The Nursing Process

The **nursing process** is an invaluable conceptual framework used in all types of nursing practice, including home care. Alfaro-Lefevre defines the nursing process as "an organized, systematic method of giving goal-oriented, humanistic care that's both effective and efficient . . . It's organized and systematic . . . It is humanistic in that the plan of care is developed and implemented in such a way that the unique interests and ideals of consumers and their significant others are given great consideration" (1994, p. 3). In short, the nursing process helps to ensure that clients receive healthcare that is appropriate and suited to their particular needs.

In home care, nurses are accountable for identifying the significant healthcare issues of their clients. Nurses perform the initial home care assessment; as a result, they are ultimately responsible for subsequent services that clients receive. Physicians rarely see clients in their homes; therefore, they may never be able to fully identify the full spectrum of needs and problems that clients face. Consequently, physicians depend upon evaluations by nurses to provide appropriate orders for services. If

Display 9-1:
The Nursing Process in Home Care

ASSESSMENT

- Subjective perspective of health and illness
- Psychosocial support
- Medications
- Physical assessment
- Environment
- Nutritional factors

NURSING DIAGNOSIS

OUTCOME IDENTIFICATION

- Targeting strengths and weaknesses
- Establishing goals and objectives

PLANNING

IMPLEMENTING INTERVENTIONS

- Teaching
- Technical skills
- Coordination of services

EVALUATION

- Referral to appropriate disciplines and community services
- Client response to interventions
- Appropriateness of plan of care
- Effectiveness of plan of care
- Progress toward established goals

nurses fail to perform all phases of the nursing process completely, they will not address the overall needs of clients. Exacerbations of problems and barriers to maximizing health and function will be the unfortunate results (Display 9-1).

KEY CONCEPT

The independent nature of home care practice requires the consistent application of the nursing process to ensure that the healthcare needs of clients are consistently and competently addressed.

STEPS IN THE NURSING PROCESS

The following phases constitute the nursing process (Fig. 9-1):

1. Systematic **assessment** of a client's health and factors influencing health
2. **Nursing diagnosis** of the client's health problems and responses to actual or potential health concerns
3. **Outcome identification**, or the formulation and documentation of a client's strengths, weaknesses, and goals for care and **planning** strategies to reduce client problems
4. **Implementation** of planned interventions
5. **Evaluation** of the effectiveness of the plan of care, responses of the client to interventions, and progress toward goals

Assessment

Taylor, Lillis, and LeMone define assessment as "the systematic collection, validation, and communication of client data" (1997, p. 225). Nurses use the data collected to learn information about the patterns of health and illness for clients and lay caregivers,

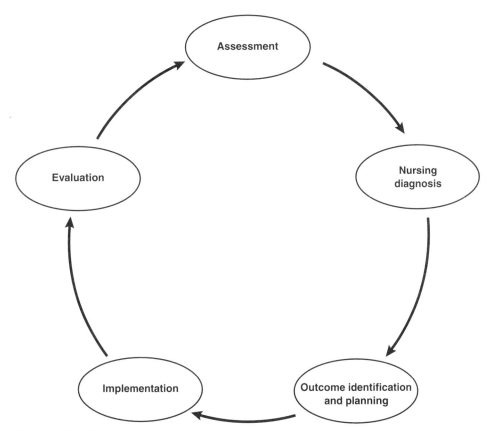

Figure 9-1. The nursing process.

and their strengths, weaknesses, coping abilities, and risk factors (Wilkinson, 1996). Nurses gather this data through observation, interview, examination, and interpretation (Craven & Hirnle, 1996).

Nursing Diagnosis

Nursing diagnoses are developed and prioritized from conclusions based upon complete assessment data. Nurses analyze and cross-reference data for patterns, trends, and common contributing factors. Diagnosis is extremely important for two main reasons: identified problems during this phase become the basis for a client's plan of care, and targeted strengths become invaluable when deciding effective nursing interventions (Alfaro-Lefevre, 1994). When formulating diagnoses, nurses must take into consideration ways to maximize a client's strengths and reduce weaknesses.

KEY CONCEPT

Nursing diagnoses should be developed and prioritized from conclusions based upon complete assessment data that nurses analyze and cross-reference for patterns, trends, and common contributing factors.

Outcome Identification and Planning

In the outcome identification and planning phase of the nursing process, nurses develop client-specific goals that are measurable and specifically address each of the targeted nursing diagnoses. Goals are used to measure the effectiveness of the nursing plan of care. Nurses must actively involve clients in the development of goals. They should also evaluate the goals, considering the data collected during assessment and conclusions drawn from the client's strengths and weaknesses. Nurses must ensure that clients can achieve goals realistically.

Next, **outcome criteria**, or measurable actions and circumstances that demonstrate the achievement of goals, are developed. Outcome criteria should answer the following questions:

Who (subject) is expected to achieve the objective?
What actions (verbs) must be performed?
Under what circumstances (conditions) should the individual be performing the actions?
How well (criteria) should the individual be performing the actions?
When (specific time) is the individual expected to perform the actions while meeting specified criteria? (Alfaro-LeFevre, 1994; Craven & Hirnle, 1996)

KEY CONCEPT

Nurses should evaluate the goals of their clients, considering data collected during the assessment and conclusions drawn from the strengths and weaknesses of clients to ensure that they can achieve goals realistically.

Application to Home Care Practice
Outcome Criteria

An example of one outcome criterion that nurses may develop for a home care client with a nursing diagnosis of "knowledge deficit of medication regimen" may be written as follows: The client (subject) will verbalize (verb) effects and side effects of all prescribed medications (under what circumstances) accurately and completely (how well) by March 17, 1998 (when).

When planning, nurses identify and document interventions that can help clients to achieve their individualized goals. Interventions should be within a nurse's scope of practice. Nurses must target them at specific or potential problems of clients, guided by the nursing plan of care. They should include clients in this process and obtain their consent to all planned interventions. Nurses should consider each client's circumstances when deciding which interventions may be the most effective. Often, multiple interventions are necessary for clients to achieve desired outcomes. After developing an overall strategy, nurses stage the timing and sequence of interventions to maximize the plan of care's effectiveness.

Implementation

Implementation occurs when nurses perform the interventions included in a client's plan of care. The implementation phase of the nursing process consists of reassessment of a client's status and problems, prioritization of problems and interventions, completion of nursing interventions, and documentation of interventions and client responses (Craven & Hirnle, 1996). Reassessment occurs at the beginning of each nursing interaction with clients to verify that interventions are still relevant. If a client's condition has changed, nurses may need to reprioritize diagnoses and planned interventions. When they definitely establish a client's condition and needs, nurses conduct interventions using appropriate communication techniques, skills, necessary supplies, and equipment. They observe the client's responses to interventions and conclude this phase of the nursing process with documentation.

Evaluation

Evaluation is the last phase of the nursing process. The purpose of evaluation is to determine the effectiveness of nursing interventions in helping clients to achieve their goals. Nurses evaluate by collecting information to establish whether clients are progressing toward their developed measurable outcomes. If clients are not meeting their goals, nurses should consider issues that may be impeding progress. They must examine the appropriateness of planned interventions for achieving goals effectively, the techniques or skills used during implementation, and the validity of the goals and outcomes themselves. Nurses should then decide whether the original goals are realistic and achievable. Evaluation may lead to changes in the goals and outcomes, revisions to the plan of nursing care, modifications of techniques used in the implementation process, or attempts to remove other barriers that are impeding a client's progress. Conclusions that nurses draw from evaluating must be documented completely in the record.

THE NURSING PROCESS IN HOME CARE

The nursing process is applied in home care during the phases of the home visit. Home care clients are less accessible to nurses than clients in other practice settings. Therefore, distinct differences exist in how nurses carry out the nursing process. The time that home care nurses spend with clients is relatively brief. Therefore, they must learn how to conduct the nursing process efficiently. Many other variables may affect the effectiveness of the nursing process in home care, including the uncontrolled environment of care, less access to clinical resources (e.g., supplies, equipment, and materials), heavy reliance on subjective data, and inaccurate reporting from clients and lay caregivers about clinical history and significant issues that arise between visits.

Home care nurses must also consider reimbursement limitations when developing plans of care. Payors may approve a limited number of visits for specific diagnoses. Unless compelling reasons exist, nurses must adapt plans of care to fit within the constraints of insurance companies. Such issues create challenges for home care nurses as they attempt to help clients achieve health goals through the nursing process.

◆ Applying the Nursing Process to the Home Care Visit

Nurses perform components of the nursing process throughout the course of home care treatment for clients. Systematic assessment, development of nursing diagnoses, negotiation with clients regarding measurable outcomes, planning care, implementation, and evaluation are usually fulfilled during the initial visit. Assessment, implementation, and evaluation are commonly repeated during subsequent home care visits. When nurses encounter new or previously unidentified problems during subsequent visits, however, they must begin the entire nursing process again.

All home care visits consist of three phases: preparation, performance, and follow-up. Each phase must be consistent and comprehensive to render a visit that is cost-effective and beneficial to clients. Discussion of these phases in this chapter, integrating the components of the nursing process, provides the knowledge base and skills necessary for successful home care visits. Chapters 13 and 14 show how to apply this knowledge in actual practice.

PREPARATION

During the **preparation** phase, nurses lay the groundwork to ensure successful, goal-directed interventions for clients. They review clinical records, collect supplies and equipment, coordinate schedules, and ready clients for the home visit. Appropriate preparation is necessary for every successful home visit. Nurses who fail to prepare their visits carefully may appear disorganized and inept, thus contributing

Survival Alert:

Preparing Appropriate Supplies and Equipment for Home Visits

Failing to prepare for the unexpected can result in delayed services, unnecessary travel, and loss of time. When preparing for visits, home care nurses should collect appropriate supplies for emergencies and other unexpected events (e.g., a sterile field is not maintained, the first attempt to insert a catheter or draw a lab specimen is unsuccessful). Nurses should anticipate things that can go wrong and make necessary backup plans. Although they should be appropriately prepared for unexpected events with additional supplies, maintaining inordinately high levels of supplies/equipment can lead to wastage. This occurs if a nurse is overly anxious about unanticipated client needs.

to a client's loss of confidence in their abilities. If, for example, nurses lack necessary supplies, appear unsure of the purpose of a visit, or seem unfamiliar with previous assessment findings, they may lose credibility in their relationships with clients. The quality of the therapeutic relationship is among the most significant factors that influence a nurse's effectiveness in implementing the positive health behaviors of a client. Therefore, preparation is a particularly critical component of every home care visit.

KEY CONCEPT

During the preparation phase, nurses establish the groundwork that ensures successful, goal-directed interventions for clients.

Beginning of Assessment

When nurses are adequately prepared for home care visits, they have also partially completed the **assessment** phase of the nursing process. Data collection helps nurses to complete the remaining steps of the nursing process successfully. Nurses may examine recent lab results, investigate findings from the last physician appointment, and review clinical notes from the last hospitalization. The compilation of this information provides a context for the client assessment that nurses perform in the home (see Chapter 13).

PERFORMANCE

The next phase of the home care visit is **performance**. During performance, personal contact with a client occurs. When beginning visits to clients, nurses should initiate nonthreatening verbal exchanges with clients on neutral subjects to create a friendly atmosphere. They should try to make clients feel comfortable and relaxed.

Informal discussion acknowledges acceptance and concern for a client as a whole person. Continuation of assessment, diagnosis, outcome identification, planning, and implementation are the components of the nursing process that nurses apply during the performance phase of visits.

Continuation of Assessment

Assessment continues during the visit's performance phase. Nursing assessment in the home consists of the interview (the client's subjective perspective of health, illness, psychosocial support, and health history), physical assessment, environmental assessment, review of medications, and review of nutritional factors (see Chapter 13). Data collected during the assessment are interpreted and integrated in a meaningful way to help nurses in directing and prioritizing care (Fig. 9-2).

In home care, nurses can actually observe a client's routine in the home and identify actual needs. Thus, a nurse can develop a more effective plan of care than is possible in many institutional settings. In most other healthcare settings, nurses formulate interventions based upon needs that they assume clients will have in their day-to-day functioning. These assumptions may or may not be accurate, which influences their effectiveness. Nurses providing care in institutional settings must depend upon clients to reveal important information. For example, a nurse working in an acute care setting assesses that Mr. Sampson lacks knowledge of an appropriate diabetic diet. As a result, the nurse formulates the plan of care to include thorough instruction regarding a diabetic diet for Mr. Sampson. At home, however, Mr. Sampson's wife prepares all of his meals, a fact that Mr. Sampson unfortunately neglects to mention. To achieve the desired outcome, interventions would have been more appropriately directed to Mrs. Sampson.

KEY CONCEPT

Home care nurses have rare opportunities to watch clients function in their own environments. They have special opportunities to conduct comprehensive assessments.

Figure 9-2. The nurse takes the client's blood pressure and records findings during assessment, part of the performance phase of the home care visit. (Photo by Marilu Sherer, CARING)

Nursing Diagnosis

Nursing diagnoses for home care clients, formulated from data collected during assessment, should include actual and potential health problems, probable causes or contributing factors, and associated signs and symptoms. Nurses should validate their conclusions with clients. Nurses can identify probable causes and contributing factors of actual or potential problems more easily in home care than in other settings. Clients and lay caregivers are usually less anxious in their own homes. Additionally, nurses can observe them in their natural setting and, as a result, witness their honest and customary interactions with and reactions to one another. Nurses in acute care settings must often draw conclusions about issues that contribute to a client's condition with little information about the client's personal life or influences. Contact with clients and their lay caregivers is often transient. Clients are often in crisis, and the environment in which clients and their significant others interact is artificial (see Chapter 2).

KEY CONCEPT

Observing clients in their own environment allows home care nurses to identify probable causes and contributing factors of actual or potential problems more easily than in other healthcare settings. Home care nurses are thus able to more accurately develop nursing diagnoses.

Outcome Identification and Planning

During **outcome identification**, nurses should identify a client's strengths and weaknesses to prioritize problems and to formulate the plan of care. Strengths and weaknesses should reflect the broad scope of intervening factors involved in the

Application to Home Care Practice
Formulating Appropriate Nursing Diagnoses in Home Care

Ramon, a pediatric client with asthma, has had multiple emergency room visits and hospitalizations. Paula, the nurse in the emergency department of a hospital, develops a nursing diagnosis of "knowledge deficit of the established therapeutic regimen" for Ramon's mother. Ramon is referred to home care. Charles, the home care nurse, observes Ramon's interactions with his mother and other family members during his visits. He notes that the family interactions seem to indicate a lack of acceptance of Ramon's chronic diagnosis. As a result, he established a nursing diagnosis of "ineffective denial" of the child's condition. Charles can now develop goals and plan interventions that will more adequately address the true needs of Ramon and his family.

Application to Home Care Practice
Using Strengths and Weaknesses in the Plan of Care

Mrs. Berk is frequently anxious, a condition that aggravates her hypertension. She states that petting her cat decreases her distress and probably lowers her blood pressure as well. This coping mechanism is a strength for the nurse to consider when developing Mrs. Berk's plan of care. The nurse should encourage Mrs. Berk to spend time with her cat when she begins to feel stressed or worried.

provision of home care services. Home care nurses must develop goals that are specific and client-oriented. Nurses create goals from diagnoses. Goals may include short-term objectives and should reflect a client's personal preferences and lifestyle. They may be related to health promotion, maintenance, or restoration, or to quality of life. The process of establishing goals gives clients and nurses a clear direction for care. Goals act as milestones that illustrate a client's progress. They show the effectiveness of nursing interventions and influence clients to improve their health behaviors.

KEY CONCEPT

The process of establishing goals gives clients and nurses a clear direction for care and provides milestones that illustrate progress.

Home care nurses are accountable for the development of a comprehensive **plan of care** for clients. Particularly in home care, nurses can perform a thorough analysis of a client's medical, psychosocial, emotional, and spiritual needs and develop strategies to meet these needs. Home care clinicians must consider interventions that are most effective in addressing identified nursing diagnoses. Aside from nursing services, a client's plan of care often includes referrals to ancillary services and community resources (see Chapter 7). Home care agencies often provide many ancillary services directly. In addition to identifying specific nursing interventions to be conducted during the initial visit, the planning phase of the nursing process in home care also includes the development of the schedule for subsequent visits.

Using the nursing process, nurses should include input from clients and their lay caregivers when developing plans of care. In home care, a client's ongoing decisions, actions, and behaviors affect the attainment of goals more than nursing procedures do. Thus, clients must actively participate in their plans of care if they need to change health behaviors. Home care nurses who achieve the most positive client outcomes are usually effective agents of change for clients. Involvement of clients in decision-making related to their health goals is an essential change strategy.

If clients are unwilling to adopt wellness behaviors or refuse to practice strategies to manage their health better, their status will most likely not improve. Nurses expect many home care clients to take their medications regularly, to follow prescribed diets, to be alert for signs and symptoms of disease, to report problems, to maintain established exercise programs, or to perform any number of medical interventions. Clients will not achieve the goals and objectives established in their plans of care unless they execute such activities.

KEY CONCEPT

In home care, a client's ongoing decisions, actions, and behaviors affect the attainment of goals more than nursing procedures do. Therefore, nurses must actively involve clients in planning care.

Implementing through Interventions

Implementing the nursing process in home care involves many interventions (see Chapter 13). Cognitive skills include management and leadership skills, coordination of ancillary services, and referrals to community organizations. Psychosocial skills involve communication, counseling, and teaching. Technical skills encompass wound care, infusions, medication administration, and venipunctures. Interventions sometimes include changing a client's home environment, which often plays a critical role in the success of the plan of care. For example, an immunocompromised client may be at risk in a home that is frequently overcrowded with visitors. The home care nurse may take actions to reduce the number of visitors while the client is most likely to be at risk.

Survival Alert:

Common Nursing Interventions Implemented in Home Care

- ◆ Teaching
- ◆ Performing technical procedures or skills (e.g., wound care, injections)
- ◆ Counseling
- ◆ Communicating verbally and nonverbally to develop or to improve the therapeutic relationship
- ◆ Coordinating or supervising care
- ◆ Altering the client's environment
- ◆ Coaching clients in the performance of procedures
- ◆ Acting as a client's advocate
- ◆ Acting as role model for clients and lay caregivers
- ◆ Referring clients to appropriate ancillary services and community organizations

FOLLOW-UP

The final stage of the home care visit is **follow-up**. The scope of the home care nurse's responsibilities extends beyond procedures conducted directly in the home. Nurses must also perform many follow-up activities to fulfill all of their obligations to their clients. Several such follow-up duties for appropriate client care include those outlined in Display 9-2.

Follow-up activities are important not only for appropriately completing the home visit, but also for expressing pertinent findings related to a client's care. A nurse's failure to execute necessary follow-up components can result in uncoordinated efforts by the interdisciplinary team. If nurses neglect to document or to convey relevant information to appropriate parties, they could compromise a client's care.

KEY CONCEPT

A nurse's failure to execute the necessary components of the follow-up phase may result in uncoordinated efforts by the home care team and may interrupt a client's progress toward established goals.

Evaluation

Home care nurses conduct the **evaluation** phase of the nursing process with every client visit. Nurses should evaluate the plan of care for continued appropriateness based upon new assessment information, revising or reprioritizing the plan as needed. The plan of care has the potential to change with every client contact, if assessment findings require revisions. Nurses should evaluate clients for their responses to interventions (e.g., understanding of teaching, and toleration of treatments with minimal discomfort). Nurses should also consider the effectiveness of the approaches of

(*text continues on page 215*)

Display 9-2:
Follow-Up Activities in Home Care

- ◆ Phoning the client's physician to report any unexpected assessment findings and to collect any additional treatment plan orders as indicated
- ◆ Revising the plan of care to reflect changing client needs
- ◆ Making referrals to community organizations to contact appropriate support systems for the client
- ◆ Communicating pertinent information to other healthcare providers involved in the client's care to coordinate efforts
- ◆ Documenting findings, interventions, and responses of the client during the visit
- ◆ Cleaning equipment as needed

Clinical Example
with Critical Thinking

M r. Cebula, 62 years old, was diagnosed with metastatic prostate cancer 3 months ago. He lives with his wife and his extended family—two brothers and three adult children live in the area. He must receive chemotherapy and radiation therapy with limited success. Mr. Cebula just completed a course of chemotherapy. His physician referred Mr. Cebula to home care with orders for the nurse to monitor his nutritional and hydration status, to evaluate pain, to assess for signs and symptoms of infection, to perform venipunctures twice a week to monitor blood count, and to identify potential community services for support.

Tom, the home care nurse, prepares for the initial visit by obtaining Mr. Cebula's most recent laboratory values. Tom talks to the social worker who has worked with the client in the clinic and discovers that the family is concerned about Mrs. Cebula's ability to consistently care for her husband because of his deteriorating condition. When Tom calls to schedule the visit, Mrs. Cebula seems highly anxious and tells Tom that her husband's pain is not being controlled with the medication. Tom adjusts his schedule to visit Mr. Cebula first, in order to evaluate his pain and to reduce Mrs. Cebula's anxiety. He prepares for the visit by gathering supplies necessary for the venipuncture, pulling teaching guides about post-chemotherapy care, obtaining brochures regarding private duty services available in the area, and formulating an admission packet complete with forms necessary to accept the client to home care.

When Tom arrives at the scheduled visit time, Mrs. Cebula, a thin, frail, elderly woman who appears distressed, meets him at the door. She rushes Tom into the bedroom to see her husband. Upon reviewing her client's rights, Tom completes the assessment and identifies the following:

Subjective Clinical Findings

* Pain level 7 on a 1–10 scale in the back, ribs, and shoulders.
* Complains of nausea. Has only taken sips of water for 2 days.
* Expresses concerns about being a burden to his wife and family.
* Family members work during the day and come by every evening.
* Refuses further courses of chemotherapy.
* Client expresses concerns about becoming addicted to pain medication.
* Complains of severe fatigue, particularly after walking.

Objective Clinical Findings

* Skin turgor poor. Dry mucous membranes. Eyes sunken.
* Ambulates with assistance from wife; unsteady gait, almost collapsed upon walking 15 ft. to restroom.
* Facial grimaces with movement.

(continued)

Clinical Example
with Critical Thinking (Continued)

Thought Questions

1. Based on the assessment data, list any ancillary services or additional community services that should be considered as potentially beneficial for Mr. Cebula.
2. Mr. Cebula is experiencing a relatively high level of pain. Mrs. Cebula is highly anxious. Consider how Tom should involve the client and his wife in planning care.
3. Review the accompanying plan of care that Tom has begun to complete. From the information provided, continue to formulate nursing diagnoses, goals, and considerations for implementation and evaluation.

Nursing Plan of Care pg 1 Client Name <u>Mr. Cebula.</u>   **Date** <u>1-25-98</u>

Assessment	Plan Nursing dx.	Implementation	Evaluation
1. Skin turgor poor. Dry mucous membranes. Eyes sunken.	Fluid Volume Deficit due to nausea caused by chemotherapy.	Call physician to obtain Rx for antiemetic. Instruct re: need for adequate fluid intake. Assess for S/S dehydration. Venipuncture 2 × wk blood counts. Assess need for home infusion.	Medication effective? Decreased S/S dehydration Lab results normal? Pt/PCP verbalizes need for adequate hydration.

Goals. 1. Mr. Cebula will drink 2000 cc of liquids every day within 48 hrs.
2. Mr. and Mrs. Cebula verbalize the need for adequate fluid intake.
3. Mr. Cebula will report reduced nausea within 24 hours.

Assessment	Plan Nursing dx.	Implementation	Evaluation
2. Pain level 7 on a 1–10 scale in the back, ribs, and shoulders. Grimace with movement.	Alteration in Comfort: pain due to disease process, CA bone.	Discuss the client's fear of addiction; instruct on need to take med regularly to keep pain under control. Assess effectiveness of pain med.	Pain med taken regularly? Pain level on a 1–10 scale Nonverbal indications of pain? Location, description, duration, description, intensity of pain.

(continued)

Clinical Example
with Critical Thinking (Continued)

Goals. 1. Mr. Cebula will report consistent pain levels of 4–5 within 48 hours and 1–3 within 1 week.
2. Mr. Cebula will demonstrate appropriate utilization of pain medication.
3. Mr. Cebula will verbalize effectiveness of pain medication.
4. Mr. Cebula will have reduced signs of pain with movement.

Assessment	Plan Nsg. Dx.	Implementation	Evaluation

Goals

Assessment	Plan Nsg. Dx.	Implementation	Evaluation

Goals

Issue	Home Care	Hospital
Assessment	Nurses perform assessments very independently. They have little opportunity to review findings with other clinicians. To collect pertinent data, they rely heavily on reporting from clients and lay caregivers. They have less access to diagnostic tools. Variables in the home environment often contribute to problems in performing complete assessments.	Nurses can confirm assessment findings with other clinicians easily. They can review data from previous nursing assessments, physician assessments, and clinical laboratory and radiologic reports. They largely focus on acute diagnoses and target their assessments for those conditions.
Diagnosis	Nurses often must develop nursing diagnoses based on old laboratory findings, physician assessments/conclusions, and recollections of diagnostic and symptom history by clients. Nurses must depend upon clients for information about intake and output, activity level, etc. Nurses are able to observe the home environment and psychosocial influences directly, which is helpful in formulating accurate diagnoses.	Nurses are able to develop nursing diagnoses based upon accurate data regarding the physical status of clients. Nurses, however, must make assumptions about the home environment of clients and related psychosocial issues that are often inaccurate.
Outcome identification	Client participation is extremely important for the achievement of desired outcomes of care. Many outcomes depend upon active participation in planning care from clients and lay caregivers. Outcomes are usually long-term in nature.	Clients are usually too acutely ill to actively participate in identifying desired health outcomes. Nurses usually target health outcomes toward stabilizing the acute conditions that led to hospitalization. Outcomes are usually short-term in nature.
Planning Care	Plans of care are heavily influenced by the availability of reliable lay caregivers, the home environment, and limitations imposed by third party payors. Most care is delivered by lay caregivers or clients themselves. Nursing interventions are usually directed at teaching individuals to perform their own care and influencing them to comply with and to maintain positive health behaviors. Plans of care are usually designed for long-term application (e.g., several weeks to a few months).	Most care is delivered by clinicians employed by the hospital. Plans of care incorporate mostly technical interventions and usually are designed for short durations (i.e., lengths of hospital stays).

(continued)

Home Care Vs. Hospital:
Nursing Process (Continued)

Implementation	Nurses encounter inconsistent home environments with highly variable noise levels, cleanliness, and distractions that can make implementation of plans of care difficult. Nurses face delayed or no access to assistance from other professionals. Supplies and equipment are usually limited to what nurses bring with them on visits. Nurses often must improvise to complete necessary interventions successfully.	The clinical environment supports easy implementation of interventions. Supplies and equipment are readily available and easily accessible, even if not identified beforehand.
Evaluation	Evaluation by nurses often depend upon subjective reports from clients and lay caregivers about symptoms. They must rely on the honesty of clients and lay caregivers about their adherence to treatment plans. Nurses also must evaluate based on reports and information about client progress from ancillary services.	Nurses can evaluate primarily through direct nursing observations, laboratory studies, and other objective measurements.

interventions as well. For example, they should question whether clients would benefit more from written rather than spoken instructions. They should determine whether clients experience more discomfort during dressing changes when they are tired. Continual evaluation of the appropriateness and effectiveness of treatment plans helps to ensure that clients meet their goals.

KEY CONCEPT

Nurses should continually evaluate plans of care for appropriateness and effectiveness to ensure that clients meet their goals.

◆ Summary

Effective performance of the home visit is the single most important skill for home care nurses to learn. Competent home care nurses use the organized approach of the nursing process as a conceptual framework for the performance of their responsibilities. The specific phases of the visit, incorporating each component of the nursing process, must be completed to serve home care clients appropriately. Thorough understanding and practice of the nursing process and the phases of home visits enhance a home care nurse's proficiency and help clients to advance on the road to wellness.

References and Bibliography

Ackley, B.J. & Ludwig, G.B. (1995). *Nursing diagnosis handbook: A guide to planning care* (2nd ed.). St. Louis: Mosby.

Alfaro-LeFevre, R. (1994). *Applying nursing process: A step-by-step guide* (3rd ed.). Philadelphia: J.B. Lippincott.

Bates, B. (1995). *A guide to physical examination and history taking* (5th ed.). Philadelphia: J.B. Lippincott.

Bulcheck, G.M. & McCloskey, J.C. (1992). *Nursing interventions: Treatments for nursing diagnoses* (2nd ed.). Philadelphia: W.B. Saunders.

Carpenito, L.J. (1995). *Nursing care plans and documentation* (2nd ed.). Philadelphia: Lippincott-Raven.

Carpenito, L.J. (1995). *Nursing diagnosis: Application to clinical practice* (6th ed.). Philadelphia: Lippincott-Raven.

Christensen, P.J. & Kenney, J.W. (1994). *Nursing process: Application of conceptual models* (4th ed.). St. Louis: Mosby.

Craven, R.F. & Hirnle, C.J. (1996). *Fundamentals of nursing: Human health and function* (2nd ed.). Philadelphia: Lippincott-Raven.

Dolan, G. & Pachis, K. (1990). Evaluation of home visits using nursing process approach. *Journal of Community Health Nursing, 7*(2), 69–75.

Frisch, N. (1993). Home care nursing and psychosocial-emotional needs of clients: How nursing diagnosis helps to direct and inform practice. *Home Healthcare Nurse, 11*(2), 64–65, 70.

Gage, M. (1994). The patient-driven interdisciplinary care plan. *JONA, 24*(4), 26–38.

Gordon, M. (1994). *Nursing diagnosis: Process and application* (3rd ed.). St. Louis: CV Mosby.

Marrelli, T.M. & Hilliard, L.S. (1996). *Home care and clinical paths*. St. Louis: Mosby.

Mignor, D. (1996). Management and evaluation of a care plan. *Home Healthcare Nurse, 14*(3), 163–165.

O'Neill, E. (1996). An exploratory study of clinical decision making. *Home Healthcare Nurse, 14*(5), 363–368.

Sundeen, S.J., Wiscarz, S., DeSalvo-Rankin, E.A. & Cohen, S.A. (1994). *Nurse-client interaction: Implementing the nursing process* (5th ed.). St. Louis: Mosby.

Taylor, C., Lillis, C. & LeMone, P. (1997). *Fundamentals of nursing: The art and science of nursing care* (3rd ed.). Philadelphia: Lippincott-Raven.

Wilkinson, J.M. (1996). *Nursing process: A critical thinking approach* (2nd ed.). Menlo Park: Addison-Wesley.

POST TEST

1. Explain the components of the nursing process.
2. List three activities that nurses complete during the preparation phase of the home visit.
3. Target ways that home care nurses are better suited for performing more thorough assessments and formulating more accurate nursing diagnoses than nurses in other healthcare settings.

4. Identify reasons for the importance of including clients and lay caregivers in goal formation and care planning.

5. List activities that nurses conduct within the follow-up phase of the home visit.

THINKING CRITICALLY IN HOME CARE

1. Performing the steps of the nursing process can be more challenging in the home care setting than in others. The nursing process, however, can also be applied more effectively in home care than in other settings. Based on the information in this chapter, as well as your knowledge of the differences between home and acute care settings, identify some distinctions in home care here:

	More Challenging	More Effective
Assessment		
Diagnosis		
Outcome Identification/ Planning		
Implementation		
Evaluation		

2. A nurse is attempting to complete the preparation phase of an initial visit to a client. The physician's referral included minimal information as follows:

Henry Busse
223 4th Street
Jacksonville, MO
Phone: 555-2457
DOB: 11/5/23   Dx: CHF, pacemaker
Lives alone.
Dr. Pratt
Orders: Evaluate for home health services. Needs foley catheter for incontinence.

A. Determine the best ways for the nurse to complete the preparation phase of the initial visit. Be sure to incorporate the assessment component of the nursing process into your response.

B. How can the nurse begin to develop a therapeutic relationship with this client while gathering initial information in the initial phone contact?

UNIT 3

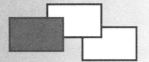

Clinical Activities
in the Home

10

Client Teaching

LEARNING OBJECTIVES

After completing this chapter, the reader will be able to:

◆ Discuss the importance of client teaching in home care.

◆ Identify adult learning principles for nurses to use while teaching clients in the home.

◆ State the components of a client teaching session.

◆ Apply teaching techniques that are effective in helping clients to retain material.

KEY TERMS

Adult learning principles	Learning readiness
Affective teaching	Maslow's Hierarchy of Needs
Cognitive teaching	Motivation
Domains of knowledge	Psychomotor teaching

Client teaching is one of the most critical nursing skills in home care. Unfortunately, many nurses underappreciate the value of teaching. Effective teaching can help clients to change their health behaviors. The primary role of home care nurses involves empowering clients to manage their own disease processes. Nurses achieve this objective by teaching clients effective disease management strategies. When clients and their lay caregivers understand disease processes and medical treatment plans, they are usually capable of managing them independently. Through teaching, nurses enable clients to maintain wellness behaviors that maximize their health. Clients are then better able to identify early problems on their own and to perform necessary follow-up measures.

In home care, most clients or their lay caregivers must learn how to execute prescribed medical treatment plans. Medical regimens range from simple (e.g., learning the effects and side effects of prescribed medications) to complicated (e.g., sterile dressing changes, maintenance of central venous catheters, or TPN infusions). Inadequate teaching can have disastrous results. An inappropriate injection site can result in paralysis. Poor sterile technique can cause a life-threatening systemic infection. Skillful teaching is required to ensure that clients and lay caregivers are knowledgeable and competent in performing tasks and to prevent potentially adverse outcomes. Home care nurses function as teachers, counselors, and cheerleaders for clients and lay caregivers who attempt to become proficient in their new and often intimidating responsibilities. Nurses must apply proven teaching concepts and instructional methodologies to ensure that their "students" have the skills to fulfill these responsibilities appropriately.

This chapter identifies reasons why teaching plays such a significant role in home care nursing. Nurses must be knowledgeable of necessary conditions for the reimbursement of nursing visits in which teaching is the predominant intervention. They also must document teaching interventions competently to ensure payment for services provided to home care clients with learning needs. This chapter reviews these issues. Home care nurses should understand and apply significant concepts of knowledge and learning to effectively assist clients to gain needed skills. These concepts and their application to home care practice are discussed. Learning is enhanced when the instructional session is appropriately implemented. This chapter includes a review of the correct performance of an instructional session.

KEY CONCEPT

The primary role of home care nurses is to empower clients to manage their own disease processes. Nurses accomplish this objective by teaching clients effective disease management strategies.

◆ Value of Teaching

Client teaching addresses many important issues. Teaching helps clients and lay caregivers to develop the confidence and skills essential to independent functioning in the home. It encourages clients to assume responsibility for their own health. Teaching increases their awareness of disease processes and treatment plans and helps them to accept their illnesses. When clients understand the rationales for their medical treatment plans, they are more likely to comply with them.

KEY CONCEPT

Teaching encourages clients to take responsibility for their own health.

Home care clients and their lay caregivers must understand their diagnoses, early symptoms of exacerbations, and appropriate self-care. This information can make the difference between wellness and acute illness or death. Home care nurses spend relatively short periods of approximately one to three hours per week with each of their clients. For the remaining 165 hours in the week, clients and lay caregivers are responsible for providing any necessary care and for identifying changes in condition that warrant immediate interventions. For example, a nurse visits a diabetic client three times a week. The client, however, can experience a dangerously high blood sugar level two hours after the nurse walks out the door. The client or lay caregiver must be able to recognize beginning symptoms of a problem and understand appropriate early interventions. This problem is not encountered in the hospital or in other acute-care settings where experienced healthcare professionals continuously monitor clients (see Chapter 2).

KEY CONCEPT

Because of the limited time home care nurses spend in the residences of clients, teaching is critical. Clients and lay caregivers must learn to manage potential problems effectively and independently, because nurses are usually not present in the home to address them.

REIMBURSEMENT AND DOCUMENTATION

Client teaching is considered a valid skilled nursing intervention by all third party payors. Although it is one of the most valuable nursing procedures in home care, nurses often neglect to document it in the medical record (see Chapter 5). Informal teaching occurs frequently during other interventions (e.g., answering clients' questions about their medications). Unless they conduct formal teaching accompanied by the use of audiovisual tools or printed materials, however, nurses frequently forget to acknowledge it as a skilled intervention. Display 10-1 lists teaching interventions that Medicare reimburses.

Display 10-1:
Medicare Guidelines for Teaching and Training

Teaching and training activities that require the skills of a licensed nurse, include, but *are not limited to* the following:

+ Teaching the self-administration of injectable medications, or a complex range of medications
+ Teaching a newly diagnosed diabetic or caregiver all aspects of diabetes management, including how to prepare and administer insulin injections, how to prepare and follow a diabetic diet, how to observe foot-care precautions, and how to observe for and understand signs of hyperglycemia and hypoglycemia
+ Teaching self-administration of medical gases
+ Teaching wound care when the complexity of the wound, the overall condition of the patient, or the ability of the caregiver makes teaching necessary
+ Teaching care for a recent ostomy or when reinforcement of ostomy care is needed
+ Teaching self-catheterization
+ Teaching self-administration of gastrostomy or enteral feedings
+ Teaching care for and maintenance of peripheral and central venous lines and administration of intravenous medications through such lines
+ Teaching bowel or bladder training when bowel or bladder dysfunction exists
+ Teaching how to perform the activities of daily living when the patient or caregiver must use special techniques and adaptive devices due to a loss of function
+ Teaching transfer techniques, e.g., from bed to chair, which are needed for safe transfer
+ Teaching proper body alignment and positioning, and timing techniques of a bed-bound patient
+ Teaching ambulation with prescribed assistive devices (such as crutches, walker, cane, etc.) that are needed due to a recent functional loss
+ Teaching prosthesis care and gait training
+ Teaching the use and care of braces, splints, and orthotics and associated skin care
+ Teaching the proper care and application of any specialized dressings or skin treatments (for example, dressings or treatments needed by patients with severe or widespread fungal infections, active and severe psoriasis or eczema, or skin deterioration from radiation treatments)
+ Teaching the preparation and maintenance of a therapeutic diet
+ Teaching proper administration of oral medication, including signs of side effects and avoidance of interaction with other medication or food.

(Health Care Financing Administration. [1990]. *Health insurance manual* (pub. No. 11–rev. 229). Washington, DC: Department of Health and Human Services, p. 14.14–14.15.)

Client teaching is an intervention that home care nurses can and should independently implement when appropriate. If teaching is the only "skilled" and "medically necessary" intervention that a nurse performs during a visit, however, criteria for reimbursement must be present and adequately reflected in documentation. Although payors recognize the importance of teaching and are willing to reimburse visits in which it is the only skilled nursing intervention performed, they will refuse to cover teaching in many circumstances. Teaching must meet the routine criterion of being "medically necessary." Therefore, payors will not consider it reimbursable unless a client's clinical condition is likely to deteriorate without it. For example, teaching a bed bound client's lay caregiver about skin pressure relief and signs of skin breakdown is necessary to prevent the deterioration that often occurs when clients are immobile. Teaching that is provided for an issue that does not present a potential or actual problem, however, will be considered unnecessary. For example, a nurse teaches about a balanced diet to a client who has no actual or potential nutrition problems. If this nutritional teaching is the primary reason for the nursing visit, the insurance company will not reimburse for it.

Payors will not cover visits to reinforce client teaching that nurses have previously provided unless they clearly document remaining knowledge deficits. Payors assume that clients or lay caregivers comprehend information given to them and are able to demonstrate applicable skills, unless the nurse's documentation specifically indicates otherwise. Teaching may not be reimbursable if clients or lay caregivers fail to demonstrate reasonable potential to learn and to apply new information. Learning deficits are one barrier that nurses must assess before teaching begins. For example, teaching is unlikely to help clients who are disoriented, or who demonstrate poor short-term memory, to achieve the medically necessary result of managing aspects of their disease processes. Therefore, payors will be reluctant to reimburse for teaching sessions in which designated individuals fail to demonstrate good potential to learn, retain, and apply information. Similarly, payors find it unreasonable to reimburse teaching of new skills to individuals who are physically incapable of performing them. For example, instructional sessions in the administration of antibiotic therapy infusions and maintenance of a central line are inappropriate for individuals with poor motor skills or bad eyesight.

Home care nurses must understand limitations to reimbursement of client education. Occasionally, nurses may believe education to be reasonable and medically necessary for certain individuals, even though some barriers exist to their learning and applying the information. In these situations, nurses must critically evaluate everything that has been documented about a client and directly address any issues that payors are likely to consider questionable. Nurses may target a client's limitations through compensatory strategies designed to circumvent obstacles to learning or applying the new information. For example, for clients who have poor short-term memory, nurses can develop environmental cues to remind clients of necessary information or actions to take. For clients with poor fine motor skills, nurses may educate them in the use of devices that help them to perform certain tasks. Under these circumstances, most payors will consider education to be appropriate; however, nurses must carefully document such actions to clarify issues for payors.

◆ Domains of Knowledge

Too often, home care nurses become frustrated when clients or lay caregivers do not seem to learn information they provide during instructional sessions. A nurse may attribute an individual's problem in comprehending information to learning deficits. In fact, the instructional approach that the nurse has taken may be the cause of difficulty. In order to become effective teachers, home care nurses must understand basic concepts of how learning occurs.

In 1956, Bloom conceptualized three **domains of knowledge** through which learning occurs: cognitive, affective, and psychomotor.

Cognitive learning involves rational thought. **Cognitive teaching** involves sharing facts and information. Nurses direct their objectives toward helping individuals to understand the information provided, and not to just memorize facts. Nurses attempt to assist clients with applying their learning to appropriate situations.

Affective teaching in home care involves changing a client's feelings or attitudes about health behaviors. Clients may cognitively understand the facts and concepts regarding their disease processes and medical treatment plans, but have negative belief systems about the desired behavior change. Nurses must address these feelings for clients to apply their knowledge to necessary health behaviors.

Psychomotor teaching refers to developing physical skills, such as muscular movements, associated with the performance of a behavior (e.g., performing wound care, applying appropriate body mechanics when lifting, ambulating with crutches, breastfeeding, and disposing of infectious wastes). When clients must learn new behaviors, psychomotor learning is required. Allowing clients to practice skills that have been demonstrated to them is the most effective teaching methodology in this type of learning (Craven & Hirnle, 1996).

Home Care Conflict:
*Failure to Apply All
of the Domains
of Knowledge*

When teaching appears to be ineffective, nurses should evaluate whether they have applied all of the necessary domains of knowledge for students to achieve desired outcomes. Frequently, learning must occur in more than one knowledge domain. For example, a nurse who must teach Mr. Clifton to perform a Phase I cardiac exercise program after a myocardial infarction must apply all three learning domains. Mr. Clifton may learn procedures cognitively and develop appropriate psychomotor skills to perform the necessary exercises. If he has not accepted that exercise will improve his health status, however, his compliance with the exercise program is unlikely. Affective learning has failed to occur. Alternatively, Mr. Clifton may affectively accept the new information but may lack the cognitive or psychomotor skills to perform the necessary exercises.

> **Display 10-2:**
> *Adult Learning Principles*
>
> ◆ Adults need to participate in and direct the learning process
> ◆ Adults are usually motivated by practical reasons to learn new information.
> ◆ Adults learn more effectively if past experiences are integrated into the instructional process.
> ◆ Adults who put new information to immediate use can retain it better.
> ◆ Adults need clear, specific feedback in the instructional process.

◆ Adult Learning Principles

Although home care nurses provide services to all age groups, they direct most efforts at client education toward adults. Pediatric clients live with adult lay caregivers. While nurses may include both pediatric clients and their adult lay caregivers in instructional sessions, they target teaching primarily to the adults, because they are ultimately responsible for the care of the children. Therefore, competence in educating adults is important for home care practitioners.

Teaching techniques that are typically successful with children are not as effective with adults. By applying known **adult learning principles** (Display 10-2), nurses increase the likelihood that adult clients will appropriately integrate concepts into behaviors that positively influence their health and wellness.

ADULTS NEED TO PARTICIPATE IN AND DIRECT THE LEARNING PROCESS

Mature learners need some sense of control in the instructional process. Nurses can give clients this feeling in several ways. They should provide clients with an opportunity to actively participate in establishing goals they hope to achieve during the educational sessions. This measure also serves to increase a client's responsibility in the learning process. Nurses should also request feedback from clients throughout the instructional process. By doing so, home care nurses can validate that information is pertinent to each client's condition and that teaching techniques are effective. Feedback can also establish that clients are progressing appropriately toward achieving their learning goals. Nurses should give clients several opportunities to direct the teaching process as well.

ADULTS ARE USUALLY MOTIVATED BY PRACTICAL REASONS TO LEARN NEW INFORMATION

Adults usually want to learn new health behaviors so that they can accomplish defined objectives. For example, Jason Gilbert wants to learn exercises to improve his mobility so that he can go to the grocery store by himself. Amy Pyle wants to eat appropriate foods to reduce the painful swelling in her legs that prevents her from going to her weekly bridge game. Effective teaching plans by nurses address these and other practical needs.

Home care nurses should try to associate all health education with its practical application in a client's everyday life. If clients do not understand how information affects their normal routine or lifestyle, they may "tune out" during sessions in which nurses cover vital material. Nurses should take the time to introduce each new concept by reviewing how the information will be useful to a client. For example, a client who can discuss the significance of preventing a painful, inconvenient exacerbation, and who understands how early symptom identification and appropriate responses can prevent progression, will probably listen actively to teaching about the disease process. Effective home care nurses present necessary health information that achieves pragmatic client objectives. Clients may not care if their diseases progress in the abstract sense; they will most certainly care, however, if disease progression means no longer driving to visit their children on Sundays. Nurses should relate all teaching to what is important to their clients.

ADULTS LEARN MORE EFFECTIVELY IF PAST EXPERIENCES ARE INTEGRATED INTO THE INSTRUCTIONAL PROCESS

Clients often experience anxiety when they realize that they must learn new information. High levels of anxiety can impede learning. Nurses must remember that adults have rich experiences that they can draw upon to simplify learning. These experiences also give nurses an opportunity to acknowledge and respect a client's wealth of knowledge. Home care nurses are thus able to build rapport with clients, which also enhances teaching effectiveness. Nurses should relate new information or skills to past experiences or skills with which the client was successful. By doing so, they can increase a client's confidence, make the information seem less intimidating, and encourage an environment for learning. Nurses thus establish the learner's knowledge baseline and ease mastery of complicated issues.

ADULTS WHO PUT NEW INFORMATION TO IMMEDIATE USE CAN RETAIN IT BETTER

This concept is particularly important when teaching clients or their lay caregivers how to perform technical procedures. Procedures can be very simple and present little risk to clients or they may be medically complex, with a high potential for risk to clients. Healthcare professionals often acquire some procedural skills through special classroom training and formal certification programs. Yet, home care nurses must instruct individuals who have no background in healthcare. Allowing individuals to participate in procedures soon after nurses teach them helps learners to commit newly introduced concepts to long-term memory.

KEY CONCEPT

Allowing clients and lay caregivers to demonstrate new skills immediately after instruction is particularly important for nurses when teaching technical procedures.

Application to Home Care Practice
Building Upon a Learner's Knowledge Base

Mrs. Boyde is the primary lay caregiver for her husband, who recently suffered a CVA. She needs to learn how to administer a tube feeding infusion through a Dobhoff tube. Mrs. Boyde feels overwhelmed with learning how to operate the infusion pump and the steps involved in setting up the feedings. She repeatedly indicates to Lori, the home care nurse, that she will never be able to learn everything she has to remember. Mrs. Boyde has indicated in previous conversations with Lori that she loves to sew and has shown Lori garments she made recently.

In order to demonstrate to Mrs. Boyde her ability to learn this new skill, Lori takes advantage of Mrs. Boyde's previous experiences in learning and developing competency with sewing. Lori correlates the many steps required in sewing to the skills Mrs. Boyde will learn for the tube feeding infusion. She reminds Mrs. Boyde of how she uses a sewing machine and relates this ability to learning how to use the infusion pump. She discusses the many steps of a pattern, and how Mrs. Boyde would similarly follow written steps in setting up the infusion. This approach acknowledges skills that Mrs. Boyde has developed as a seamstress and associates them with similar types of skills that she needs to develop competency in the procedure. Such an approach enhances Mrs. Boyde's self-esteem and therefore reduces her anxiety about learning the procedure by helping her to recognize existing skills and competencies.

By verbally informing clients regarding a procedure and its purpose, demonstrating the procedure, and asking for a return demonstration, nurses provide a supportive and safe course of learning. Depending upon the risk and complexity of the procedure, return demonstrations may be done in smaller, more manageable components. For example, when teaching a lay caregiver to perform a sterile dressing change for a client, a nurse may instruct about appropriate hand washing to maintain infection control techniques (see Chapter 12) and about applying sterile gloves during the initial visit. In subsequent visits, the nurse may then introduce the lay caregiver to additional components of the procedure.

Early return demonstrations typically require a large amount of verbal cuing by nurses (Fig. 10-1). The need for continual instruction should gradually decrease, allowing clients or lay caregivers to gain independence in procedures. Written instructions are also useful for learners, particularly when performing skills without a nurse's supervision for the first few times. Clients and lay caregivers who have an opportunity to apply newly learned information better understand and carry out concepts.

ADULTS NEED CLEAR, SPECIFIC FEEDBACK IN THE INSTRUCTIONAL PROCESS

When people are exposed to new concepts, they are usually uncertain and anxious about whether they are doing things "right." Nurses who recognize and acknowledge

Figure 10-1. The nurse verbally cues this client as he conducts a return demonstration of a procedure she has taught him. (Photo by Marilu Sherer, CARING)

the progress of clients in the learning process help them to develop a sense of accomplishment in the things they have learned already and build confidence for the rest of their instructional objectives. Feedback should be as specific as possible. For example, telling a client "You're doing so well with the diabetic instructions" is much less informative and useful to a client than saying, "You are making real progress in learning how to draw up insulin. Today, you drew up the right dose and I made only one comment to remind you to mix it." Specific, individualized feedback informs learners of their accomplishments and reminds them of what still needs to be achieved in a supportive way.

KEY CONCEPT

When nurses recognize and acknowledge the progress of clients in the learning process, adults develop a sense of accomplishment in what they have learned already and the confidence to learn the rest of their instructional objectives.

◆ The Nurse–Client Relationship and Its Impact on Learning

Teaching that nurses perform in the home is generally goal-directed. Nurses usually seek specific objectives: preparing clients to think critically if symptoms of their disease develop; changing behavioral patterns (e.g., dietary habits, exercise, and stress reduction); and developing new skills (e.g., performing a medical procedure). They teach interventions that allow clients to acquire new information in order to make independent decisions that will positively influence their health. In one way or another, nurses attempt to change a client's present and future behavior through teaching. While nurses can never "force" clients to change, health teaching involves both providing new information in effective ways, and influencing clients to consistently and appropriately use the information they learn.

TRUST

The ability to influence a client relates directly to the quality of the relationship between the nurse and the client. First, clients must trust the knowledge of nurses. Usually, clients inherently believe that nurses are knowledgeable and competent because of their thorough licensing and educational requirements. This trust can be tainted, however, if nurses provide information that is inconsistent with information clients receive from other healthcare professionals (e.g., physicians, nurses in a hospital or doctor's office, etc.). If conflicts arise, nurses should attempt to clarify the facts that they are communicating, particularly if their information is inconsistent with that of a client's physician. Sometimes, clients perceive information to be inconsistent when, in fact, it is simply communicated in two different ways. Nurses must make every attempt to clarify important discrepancies in the information that they provide to clients to maintain trust.

Home Care Conflict:
Addressing Inconsistent Information for Clients

David, the client, questions the home care nurse's instruction about appropriate exercise. His impression from talking with Dr. Martino, his physician, was that he should limit activity.

Jill, the nurse, calls Dr. Martino to check this information. During the phone call, Jill discovers that Dr. Martino instructed David that he would be weak after his surgery. She encouraged David to get enough rest and not to push himself. This instruction addressed David's active and pressured social schedule; however, Dr. Martino did not believe that David needed to restrict all exercise. Jill wished to remind David to exercise to tolerance, to retain appropriate mobility and strength. She certainly did not advocate overexercise.

A true discrepancy did not exist between the information provided by the home care nurse and the client's physician. David's perceptions indicated one to him. By clarifying the information with Dr. Martino and explaining their conversation to David, Jill resolved the issue. David was able to resume a modified exercise program to regain strength following surgery.

RESPECT

The nurse–client relationship is positively affected when clients perceive that nurses care, are concerned, and respect them as individuals. When clients feel that nurses do not care about their needs or do not demonstrate respect, however, the therapeutic relationship quickly deteriorates. Clients who sense that nurses lack concern about individual needs will not count on nurses to do everything possible to detect and address them.

Clients may construe lack of caring and concern from actions that home care nurses may consider minor. For example, clients may believe that nurses who fail to remember significant information they provided in earlier visits do not consider these issues important enough to remember. Clients may feel that nurses who appear to rush through visits have more important things to do or more important people for whom to care. Nurses who forget to follow through on commitments made to clients may also disappoint or offend clients. Clients who believe that they are not respected as individuals or treated as adults may feel resentment toward nurses. Nurses may communicate disrespect to clients by mispronouncing names after having been corrected, by being late for scheduled visits without calling to alert clients, by failing to respect property, by ignoring cultural or spiritual differences, or by inappropriately addressing clients (e.g., calling clients "honey" or "sweetie").

RECOGNITION AND ACKNOWLEDGMENT

The teaching process can greatly enhance the therapeutic nurse–client relationship. Small efforts can significantly contribute to better relationships, which further increase the ability of nurses to influence health behaviors positively. Nurses should acknowledge a client's feelings of anxiety, loss, and anger about lifestyle changes that result from new health behaviors. They can also greatly strengthen the relationship by acknowledging and recognizing small and large achievements that clients make in the learning process. Integrating personal goals of clients in teaching and charting progress toward these goals demonstrates care, concern, and respect for individuals. Initial teaching sessions that are successful can improve the effectiveness of subsequent sessions, as clients learn to trust and believe in the sincere efforts of nurses to improve their health.

◆ The Teaching Session

Informal teaching occurs regularly in home care. Nurses provide information to clients during assessments, while performing clinical procedures, or when answering questions while walking with clients to the door. Generally, informal teaching consists of relatively simple concepts that can be explained and understood in brief comments. Often, however, home care clients must also learn complex concepts about the pathophysiology of their disease processes or intricate medical procedures. When nurses expect learning to be challenging for clients, they must recognize the importance of carefully creating teaching sessions that enhance a learner's ability to

---

Display 10-3:
Steps of Client Teaching Sessions

1. Preparation
2. Learner assessment
3. Development of learner objectives
4. Development of the teaching plan
5. Implementation of the instructional session
   a. Subject introduction
   b. Instruction
   c. Summary of new information
6. Evaluation of learner outcomes
7. Documentation

---

concentrate and to practice new skills. Display 10-3 outlines the steps of the teaching session.

PREPARATION

Preparation for teaching sessions is critical to helping clients grasp complex concepts and skills. Appropriate preparation enables nurses to provide new information to clients as efficiently and effectively as possible. When planning educational sessions, nurses must consider key elements that can positively or negatively influence the learning process (Display 10-4). They should determine how positive influences can be maximized to facilitate learning and how negative influences can be minimized to decrease their effect on learning. Key elements to be considered in the preparation process include environment, communication, instructional methods, and learning aids.

Environment

Nurses should make the home environment as conducive to learning as possible. Though nurses have limited control over a client's home environment, they should attempt to reduce and to eliminate distractions during instructional sessions. Learning rooms should have adequate lighting, good ventilation, and a comfortable temperature. Uncomfortable environments can impede necessary learning.

Communication

How nurses communicate during teaching sessions directly affects the learning that occurs. Nurses must be careful to use nontechnical language, because medical jargon and abbreviations can confuse or intimidate clients and lay caregivers. Learners may be afraid to ask nurses to clarify unfamiliar terms for fear of appearing "stupid." Nurses should convey a confident understanding of material without communicating a sense of superiority over learners. They should readily welcome questions and explain concepts. Nurses should speak clearly and at a steady pace, not too fast or too slow. They should maintain eye contact with clients and lay caregivers when

> **Display 10-4:**
> *Questions to Ask When Developing a Teaching Plan*
>
> ◆ What are the client's knowledge deficits?
> ◆ In what order should these knowledge deficits be addressed?
> ◆ Should any barriers or special issues that interfere with learning be addressed in the teaching plan? (e.g., difficulty concentrating, pain, cultural issues, language, hearing loss, poor eyesight, literacy, psychomotor limitations)
> ◆ In which domains of knowledge will learning need to occur? (cognitive, affective, psychomotor)
> ◆ What are the client's learning goals?
> ◆ What is the client's readiness to learn new information? Is the client motivated to learn new information and comply with new health behaviors?
> ◆ What practical issues in the client's life will the teaching address?
> ◆ How can the client be assisted to use the information received in the teaching sessions immediately?
> ◆ How can environmental factors influence the learning process? Can negative factors be eliminated or reduced for the learning session?
> ◆ Are learning aids or materials available that can assist in the teaching process and enhance or reinforce client learning?
> ◆ How will learning be evaluated?
> ◆ What issues should be thoroughly incorporated in the documentation to address applicable reimbursement issues?

speaking and use gestures as appropriate. They should avoid distracting words and phrases (e.g., 'uhm', and 'you know').

For a client who does not speak English fluently, teaching is ideally performed by a nurse fluent in the client's primary language. Unfortunately, home care agencies do not always employ nurses who are knowledgeable in the wide variety of languages that may be spoken by clients. Therefore, interpreters are often necessary to communicate with clients. If possible, interpreters should have knowledge of the medical terminology that is used with clients. Nurses should schedule longer visits than usual when accompanied by interpreters to allow for the repetition of information that occurs during translation. They should provide written teaching materials in languages spoken by the client populations of the home care agency. Professionally translated teaching materials can help to clarify and reinforce the teaching these clients receive.

Methods and Learning Aids

Individuals learn in different ways. Thus, nurses should use a variety of teaching techniques to stimulate as many senses as possible. A variety of methods also encourages retention of material. Nurses may believe verbal instruction alone to be the most efficient way to share large amounts of information. Educational research has shown, however, that people remember 10% of what they read, 20% of what they

Survival Alert:
Environmental Factors that Impede Learning

- Poor lighting
- Poor ventilation
- Noise
- Room too hot
- Room too cold
- Visual distractions (e.g., clutter, windows)

hear, 30% of what they see, 50% of what they hear and see, 80% of what they say, and 90% of what they say and do (Patterson, 1962). Nurses can combine the techniques listed in Display 10-5 with verbal instructions to teach effectively. Home care nurses can also make teaching sessions more interesting for learners by varying these teaching techniques.

KEY CONCEPT

Individuals learn in different ways. Nurses will find a variety of teaching techniques useful to best stimulate a client's senses and ability to retain material.

LEARNER ASSESSMENT

In this phase, nurses determine knowledge deficits by assessing the current understanding of clients and lay caregivers. Nurses should evaluate their readiness to learn and their past experiences to build upon within the session. Such information increases a nurse's efficiency in teaching new material.

Display 10-5:
Techniques to Incorporate Into Learning Sessions

- Providing written instructions
- Having clients write down verbal instructions
- Demonstrating procedures
- Supervising return demonstrations
- Asking open-ended questions
- Using pictures or simple diagrams
- Using videos

Learning Needs

Clients may have knowledge deficits in a number of areas. Nurses should develop learning needs by identifying information that clients require to function as independently as possible. They should enhance critical thinking skills so clients can respond appropriately when problems arise. When home care nurses perform visits, they identify learning needs in clients through many avenues. Clients may communicate misinformation they have received about important health issues. They may verbalize or illustrate noncompliance with aspects of their medical treatment plans. Nurses may find needs for community resources, but clients may be unaware of their availability, or how to access assistance. Clients may demonstrate inappropriate technique with clinical procedures or skills. They may have a new diagnosis or medication about which they need instruction.

Teaching can often occur quickly and informally when clients have good learning potential and their learning needs are elementary and straightforward. For example, if a client asks a nurse about the purpose of a medication, the nurse should answer the question immediately and simply. Nurses should avoid providing too much information in this manner, however. Although each concept may seem straightforward and elementary, clients may become confused and overwhelmed if too many pieces of information are provided in the course of one visit. Learning needs must be triaged as well, to avoid overload. When possible, nurses should include related concepts in formal instructional sessions. For example, a nurse may provide a client with thorough information about medications during a teaching session that covers the disease process. After identifying complex learning needs, nurses should carefully follow each step of developing a comprehensive teaching session.

Learning Readiness and Learning Barriers

Readiness significantly affects the learning that occurs during a teaching session. **Learning readiness** involves such factors as a client's motivation to learn new information, learning potential, environmental factors, physiological issues, and psychosocial factors (Hunt & Zurek, 1997). Many influences upon clients can create barriers to their ability to learn new information. Nurses must carefully assess learning barriers for clients, such as difficulty hearing or seeing, or an inability to read. Clients may not volunteer such information, out of embarrassment or fear; nurses must be careful to consider such barriers when developing a teaching plan.

Motivation.   "Motivation is a key ingredient in learner outcome achievement and can be more important in successful learning than intelligence or formal education" (Zastocki & Rovinski, 1989, p. 2). **Motivation** refers to personal incentives to learn a particular concept or skill. It affects the learning process enormously. Motivation to learn increases when individuals recognize practical reasons to know information.

Inadequate knowledge may result in conditions or exacerbations of conditions that cause debilitation, pain, dependence upon others, body image changes, and social isolation. Awareness of these potential undesirable consequences may motivate clients to learn and to practice skills and behaviors that effectively prevent them. Many factors can inhibit a client's motivation to learn, including denial, depression, and secondary gains of illness. If these issues negatively impact a client's

Survival Alert:
Barriers to Learning

- Language barriers
- Cultural differences that affect the interpretation of information provided
- Learning disabilities
- Written material inappropriate for a client's reading level
- Illiteracy
- Hearing loss
- Decreased visual acuity or blindness
- Inability to concentrate
- Disorientation
- Pain
- Respiratory distress
- Emotional distress
- Effects of medications or medical treatments
- Sleep deprivation
- Information presented at a pace not appropriate for client (e.g., too slow, so client loses interest, or too fast, so client cannot keep up)
- Poor therapeutic relationship with clinical instructor

Affective Barriers

- Cultural issues—health behaviors not consistent with cultural norms
- Secondary gains associated with being ill (e.g., added care and concern from family, drug-seeking behavior)
- Denial of illness or disability
- Body image issues—effects of new health behaviors or treatments on appearance
- Depression—feelings of hopelessness or powerlessness; client may want to die
- Perceived consequences of noncompliance more acceptable than changing health behaviors
- Social issues—fear of lack of acceptance or humiliation if new health behavior adopted
- Client perceives that nurse is judgmental toward him or her
- Past negative experiences
- Poor therapeutic relationship with clinical instructor

Psychomotor Barriers

- Poor mobility or balance
- Poor eye–hand coordination
- Poor fine motor skills
- Paralysis or paresthesia
- Tremors
- Muscular weakness
- Poor endurance or strength
- Dyspnea

motivation, even the most skillful teaching methodologies will fail to help clients attain learning objectives.

Compliance. Nurses should evaluate a client's history of compliance and noncompliance with medical regimens. Evaluations should occur in a nonjudgmental way, or clients may resist answering questions honestly about their history of noncompliance. Evaluating reasons for noncompliance in the past may lead to some insights about how nurses should develop teaching plans to promote optimal compliance.

Literacy Level. When written materials are an important component of a teaching plan, a client's literacy level can significantly affect the ability to learn. The potential impact of literacy issues on client teaching is significant. One out of every five Americans reads at the fifth grade level or below (Falvo, 1994). Many written teaching materials, however, are targeted for individuals with reading levels well above that of the fifth grade. Nurses may unwittingly provide clients who are illiterate or have low literacy levels with materials that are essentially useless to them. Clients often do not admit to nurses that the written materials are inappropriate for them out of shame or embarrassment. Thus, when possible, nurses must evaluate the literacy level of clients to ensure that teaching methodologies are appropriate. Materials should be available that are targeted for lower reading levels. Nurses should also supplement written materials with other forms of education, such as verbal information, pictures, models, demonstrations, and return demonstrations.

Health Status. The health status of clients can significantly impact their ability to learn. Clients will not be able to retain information if they are experiencing severe pain, dyspnea, nausea, or fatigue. Some medical conditions affect an individual's short or long term memory and ability to concentrate. Clients may not be able to learn new psychomotor skills if they have musculoskeletal abnormalities, poor coordination, or problems with their hands. They may also have sensory deficits that impact their ability to learn new information. For example, clients with hearing loss, decreased visual acuity, or paresthesia may experience severe difficulties in learning new skills or acquiring knowledge in instructional sessions.

DEVELOPMENT OF LEARNER OBJECTIVES

Independent critical thinking that empowers clients to manage their disease processes or to perform necessary skills and procedures depends upon a thorough knowledge of concepts that are related to issues being addressed. Client goals usually reflect the need for independence. Nurses develop learning objectives to chart a course of milestones that help clients reach goals in knowledge (cognitive learning), acceptance (affective learning), and skills (psychomotor learning) needed for independence. Home care nurses create objectives when they develop goals that identify specific behaviors for clients to perform that demonstrate measurable progress. Objectives often reflect incremental steps toward goals and are updated as clients achieve them.

Written objectives must include specific components useful in allowing nurses and clients to evaluate the effectiveness of the teaching performed. They should

Home Care Vs. Hospital:
Teaching

Issue	Home Care	Hospital
Application of learned material	Often, clients must learn and apply new information immediately after teaching sessions. Clients and their lay caregivers are usually responsible for implementing most components of the treatment plan and must be competent to do so.	Clients do not usually put teaching conducted in hospitals to immediate use. Licensed healthcare professionals regularly perform assessments, so it is less critical for clients to immediately absorb and apply concepts.
Learner readiness	Clients are in the comfortable, familiar surroundings, of their homes, which usually minimizes some of the psychological barriers clients face in acute care settings. Clients are also less acutely ill and less symptomatic, causing fewer physiological learning barriers.	Clients usually encounter greater learning difficulties in hospitals. Hospitals are stressful, unfamiliar settings. Illnesses are more acute, which adds psychological and physiological barriers to processing new information.
Reimbursement/ documentation	Education is often the primary purpose for home care services. Thus, nurses must ensure that appropriate physician orders and documentation support the need for teaching. They must also accurately demonstrate the outcomes of client education in documentation.	Client education is never the primary purpose for hospitalization. Therefore, reimbursement is generally unrelated to the client teaching. Documentation of teaching primarily functions to communicate to other caregivers teaching interventions performed and to protect the hospital against litigation.
The teaching session	Nurses have limited control over the environments in which they teach. Potential for numerous distractions is high (e.g., noise, people, lighting, ventilation, temperature, etc.). Nurses have less access to teaching materials and equipment that may enhance learning.	Nurses may be distracted by the needs of multiple clients for whom they are responsible. Nurses have better access to available teaching materials and equipment (e.g., videos, models). Hospitals may employ designated client education personnel (e.g., diabetic educators). Nurses have good control of the teaching environment.
Evaluation of learner outcomes	Nurses are better able to evaluate application of new information by learners. They can observe client and lay caregiver compliance with clinical procedures and their application of concepts through problem identification.	Nurses cannot fully evaluate the effectiveness of the teaching they perform because of relatively short hospital stays. Clients apply many teaching concepts, behaviors, and skills only after discharge.

include a subject (the client or lay caregiver), an action verb, performance criteria, and a target date for accomplishment. For example: the client (subject) will perform (action verb) a sterile dressing change independently without verbal cuing (performance criteria) by January 5, 1998 (target date for accomplishment) (Hunt & Zurek, 1997). These objectives are used during the evaluation process to enable clients, lay caregivers, and nurses to assess progress of learning and to establish continued learning needs. Nurses should attempt to develop reasonable objectives in appropriate time frames for clients or lay caregivers. By doing so, they can prevent discouragement if clients or lay caregivers do not reach their goals quickly. The achievement of objectives gives nurses the opportunity to recognize the accomplishments of learners. A sense of mastery provides learners with empowerment to develop new skills and to absorb new concepts. Nurses should formulate objectives that facilitate the learning process for clients, particularly when concepts or skills are complex.

DEVELOPMENT OF THE TEACHING PLAN

Home care nurses should develop teaching plans that meet the unique learning needs of each client. Nurses and clients should collaborate to establish desired outcomes from teaching. Once nurses identify a client's learning needs and teaching objectives, they should organize the material to be covered in the instructional sessions. Teaching tools, such as brochures, diagrams, pictures, anatomical models, demonstrations, and return demonstrations, can help to educate clients. Nurses should sequence material to reflect the urgency of a client's problems, the goals of teaching, and a client's readiness to learn.

Maslow's Hierarchy of Needs

Nurses should refer to **Maslow's hierarchy of needs** when developing a teaching plan. A pyramid symbolizes Maslow's concepts (Fig. 10-2). A core concept in Maslow's theory is that people cannot meet higher level needs until they fulfill their lower level needs. This idea significantly influences the success of a client's learning. Nurses must structure teaching plans to address the level of needs that clients are attempting to fulfill. If they do not, even the most creative teaching plans will be ineffective.

Home care nurses should understand Maslow's Hierarchy of Needs for insight into the ability of clients to learn new information, and to develop appropriate teaching plans. If nurses are unaware of these needs, they can easily become frustrated with an apparent lack of progress or inability to learn. By investigating possible reasons for a client's failure to learn based on Maslow's theory, nurses can provide or initiate referrals for interventions that help clients to meet their basic human needs and gain independence in their care. Nurses should consistently consider the human needs of their clients that motivate their behavior. These needs should be considered to prioritize learning goals, to plan interventions, and to motivate clients. Maslow's hierarchy can be used to develop teaching plans that effectively address issues most significant to clients, and issues that enhance their readiness to learn new information and to perform new skills.

Self-actualization
Need to be self-fulfilled,
learn, create, understand,
and experience one's
potential

Self-esteem
Need to be well thought of by
oneself as well as by others

Love
Need for affection, feelings of
belongingness, and meaningful
relations with others

Security and Safety
Need for shelter and freedom from
harm and danger

Physiological
Need for oxygen, food, water, rest and
elimination. The need for sex is unnecessary for
individual survival but it is necessary
for the survival of humankind

Figure 10-2. Maslow's hierarchy
of needs.

KEY CONCEPT

In Maslow's theory, unmet needs can motivate clients to learn health behaviors that address these needs. Lower level needs that remain unmet may inhibit learning.

Physiologic Needs. The bottom of the pyramid represents an individual's physiological needs: food, water, and shelter. The health of clients who have recently experienced an acute phase of an illness is most likely still to be fragile. These clients may have many physiological needs that nurses need to address. They can feel greatly motivated to learn measures to resolve their health problems. Home care nurses must be aware of some basic physiological needs clients may have when returning home from the hospital. Nurses may not consider verifying that food is in the house or that a furnace works in the dead of winter to be typical nursing interventions. Unless they address these basic needs in home care, however, other more "typical" interventions will be ineffective.

Safety Needs. The second level of the pyramid in Maslow's theory is an individual's safety needs. Clients are often concerned about immediate personal safety issues. For example, they may fear falling when using new assistive devices. Preoccupation with safety issues may distract clients from other important goals they need to achieve (e.g., following their medication schedules). Although many issues may equally affect their safety, perceived threats most often motivate the behavior of clients. Home care nurses must be sensitive to their clients' safety concerns and address them as effectively as possible before moving to other issues. Nurses can increase motivation to learn health behaviors by increasing perception of safety needs. For example, home care nurses may instruct clients about the risk of falling in the shower and the injuries that they might incur. Clients may then be encouraged to learn safety procedures and appropriate use of equipment while showering to prevent accidents.

Social Needs.   The third level in Maslow's pyramid represents an individual's social needs. People usually meet social needs through family, friends, neighbors, and coworkers. For some clients, pets help to meet social needs. Nurses may find that clients' unmet needs of love, belonging, or security may affect their teaching plans. Clients may fear that lay caregivers will no longer accept and love them because of their illness or disability (Fig. 10-3). Such anxieties can impede a client's ability to learn necessary medical treatments. For some clients, interaction with home care staff meets some of their needs for social acceptance and belonging. Nurses can help motivate home care clients to learn by showing acceptance of clients and positively reinforcing a client's self-image and progress. Sometimes, clients disregard new information because they realize that gaining independence may result in discharge from home care services. These clients often fear the loss of social support that home care provides for them. Nurses must build solid relationships with clients without encouraging dependence or helplessness.

Figure 10-3. To promote a client's social needs and to instruct effectively, the nurse may find it helpful to include lay caregivers in teaching sessions.

Self-Esteem Needs. The fourth level of Maslow's Hierarchy of Needs is self-esteem. Clients with low self-esteem may not respond to new information as readily as others because they may believe themselves incapable of learning it. Nurses should be sensitive to clients who reflect esteem problems that may hamper teaching plans. Building confidence is often an important nursing intervention. Sometimes clients have good overall self-esteem but feel inadequate in learning medical information. Nurses can positively influence confidence by applying the adult learning principles. Using these effective teaching techniques allows clients to develop their understanding of disease processes and treatment plans, and increases their feelings of control in regaining wellness. Nurses thus enhance the esteem of clients as they become proficient with technical procedures and confident in managing their diseases.

Self-Actualization Needs. Self-actualization, the top level of Maslow's pyramid, means the fulfillment of one's potential. It addresses both the need of humans to maximize all of their qualities and abilities, and the psychological well-being that

Clinical Example
with Critical Thinking

Mrs. Lundon was recently discharged from the hospital with a colostomy. She lives with her elderly husband, who seems emotionally distant and leaves the room every time Bill, the home care nurse, comes to visit. Mrs. Lundon is highly anxious and avoids looking at the stoma. Once, when Bill assisted Mrs. Lundon to empty the colostomy bag, she commented: "Look at this! It's absolutely disgusting." During an interview Bill learns that Mrs. Lundon has been eating minimally to reduce output in the colostomy bag. The skin surrounding the stoma is beginning to become red and excoriated. Bill has attempted to teach Mrs. Lundon about the care of her colostomy, but she seems to retain very little information from week to week.

1. Identify Mrs. Lundon's learning needs.
2. Using Maslow's hierarchy of needs, evaluate Mrs. Lundon's unmet needs.
3. Assess ways that Bill can attempt to address these needs.
4. Indicate the adult learning principles for Bill to use with Mrs. Lundon to increase teaching effectiveness.

Develop a teaching plan for Mrs. Lundon:

Problems/Knowledge Deficit:
Teaching objectives:
Teaching subjects/material to be covered (list in sequence teaching that should be performed):
Teaching materials/tools:

emanates from these accomplishments. When each of the lower level needs are met, clients are motivated by the opportunity to fully explore their purpose in life. They can identify activities and circumstances to pursue that bring them joy and satisfaction in life. Nurses can encourage clients to develop goals that meet these self-actualization needs. For example, a client wishes to regain independence to spend time developing close relationships with her grandchildren. She wants to leave a loving memory by which they can remember her after she dies. Self-actualization needs motivate this client to build her strength through proper nutrition and paced activities.

IMPLEMENTING THE INSTRUCTIONAL SESSION

The implementation phase of teaching follows a three-step process: introducing the subject, instructing about the topic, and summarizing the newly taught information. During the introduction of the subject, nurses should present topics to be taught and discussed in summary fashion. During instruction, home care nurses implement the established teaching plan, including any necessary revisions to the plan based on client and lay caregiver participation and learner readiness. When summarizing new information, nurses should review and recapitulate the main points covered in teaching sessions.

EVALUATION OF LEARNER OUTCOMES

Nurses should evaluate the effectiveness of the teaching plan by assessing the learner outcomes that they developed with learners earlier. They can do so by asking open-ended questions to evaluate a learner's understanding of concepts, or by observing an individual's performance of newly learned skills. Nurses should discuss the progress that clients have made toward mutually established goals and begin to plan the next teaching intervention.

DOCUMENTATION

Finally, home care nurses must document client teaching. They should note a client's progress toward established outcomes. Clients and lay caregivers who are learning complicated procedures will require several sessions to master the skills they are learning. Documentation should specifically reflect how much competence learners have achieved, along with any remaining deficits. Nursing notes should indicate any barriers to an individual's learning (e.g., difficulty hearing, or short-term memory deficit) or ability to perform procedures (e.g., arthritis).

◆ Summary

Client teaching is one of the most important interventions that home care nurses perform. Although the role of teacher can sometimes be frustrating for healthcare professionals, it also can be very rewarding. Nurses can see the direct results of their interventions when they observe an anxious client or lay caregiver who is hesitant to participate in necessary care become a person who can perform new skills

Survival Alert:
Reimbursement for Teaching

Payors will not reimburse home care visits to provide teaching regarding insulin administration if previous documentation is similar to the following: "Mrs. Timmerman instructed about insulin administration for 3 y.o. daughter, Alicia." Subsequent teaching sessions will be reimbursed more readily if previous documentation has been more inclusive of all circumstances related to teaching Mrs. Timmerman, as follows: "Mrs. Timmerman instructed about insulin administration for 3 y.o. daughter, Alicia. Mrs. Timmerman unable to accurately draw insulin dose independently—difficulty reading and understanding calibrations of syringe and relating them to dosage. Able to accurately draw dosage with verbal cuing. Able to competently inject insulin in appropriate sites, but on questioning, was unable to recall appropriate rotation sites for injections and the rationale for rotating sites. Needs further instruction on accurate dosing and rotation of injection sites."

confidently and independently. Gaining competence in teaching enables home care nurses to profoundly improve the health and well-being of clients served in this often challenging setting.

References and Bibliography

Babcock, D.E. & Miller, M.A. (1994). *Client education: Theory and practice*. St. Louis: Mosby.

Barnes, L.P. (1994). Useful tools in patient teaching—Interviewing skills. *MCN, 19*(5), 289.

Bloom, B.S. (1956). *Taxonomy of educational objectives: The classification of educational goals*. New York: David McKay.

Bradley, P.J. & Alpers, R. (1996). Home healthcare nurses should regain their family focus. *Home Healthcare Nurse, 14*(4), 281–288.

Canobbio, M.M. (1996). *Mosby's handbook of patient teaching*. St. Louis: Mosby.

Craven, R.F. & Hirnle, C.J. (1996). *Fundamentals of nursing: Human health and function* (2nd ed.). Philadelphia: Lippincott-Raven.

Doak, C.C., Doak, L.G. & Root, J.H. (1995). *Teaching patients with low literacy skills*. Philadelphia: Lippincott.

Duffy, B. Using a creative teaching process with adult patients. *Home Healthcare Nurse, 15*(2), 102–108.

Falvo, D. (1994). *Effective patient education: A guide to increased compliance*. Gaithersburg, MD: Aspen.

Hunt, R. & Zurek, E.L. (1997). *Introduction to community based nursing*. Philadelphia: Lippincott-Raven.

Hussey, L.C. (1994). Minimizing effects of low literacy on medication knowledge and compliance among the elderly. *Clinical Nursing Research, 3*(2), 132–135.

Knowles, M.S. (1984). *The adult-learner: A neglected species* (3rd ed.). Houston: Gulf Publishing.

Maslow, A. (1968). *Toward a psychology of being* (2nd ed.). New York: Van Nostrand-Reinhold.

Patterson, O. (Ed.) (1962). *Special tools for communication*. Chicago: Industrial Audio-Visual Association.

Price, J.L. & Cordell, B. (1994). Cultural diversity and patient teaching. *Journal of Continuing Education in Nursing, 25*(4), 163–166.

Schonely, L. (1994). Teaching in the affective domain. *Journal of Continuing Education in Nursing, 25*(5), 209–212.

Seley, J. (1994). Ten strategies for successful patient teaching. *American Journal of Nursing, 94*(11), 63–65.

Wong, M. (1992). Self-care instructions. Do patients understand educational materials? *Focus on Critical Care, 19*(2), 47–49.

Zastocki, D.K. & Rovinski, C.A. (1989). *Home care: Patient and family instructions.* Philadelphia: W.B. Saunders.

POST TEST

1. Briefly explain why client teaching is such an important intervention in home care nursing.

2. List three adult learning principles that should be integrated into client teaching.

3. Identify five primary components of a client teaching session.

4. Give four examples of teaching techniques that home care nurses can use to stimulate various senses and enhance retention.

5. Nurses will find the use of a great deal of medical jargon beneficial while instructing clients, because this builds clients' confidence in nursing expertise.
   _____True   _____False

THINKING CRITICALLY IN HOME CARE

Mr. Marcello is a 94-year-old gentleman diagnosed with severe osteoporosis and pathologic fractures of the spine. He is in severe, constant pain. His physician has recommended a consultation with a home care nurse. Dr. Neumann initiated a low dose, subcutaneous infusion of morphine sulfate to manage Mr. Marcello's pain. Mr. Marcello lives with a 50-year-old paid caregiver, Josephina, whose primary language is Spanish. Josephina seems to understand English. She has worked for Mr. Marcello for 15 years. They appear to have a close, caring relationship. Josephina is very conscientious and accurate when providing his care. She is very intimidated by learning about the use of the infusion pump and subcutaneous needles. Mr. Marcello is physically unable to perform the procedure himself.

A. Based on the information in this chapter, assess how the nurse can help Josephina to overcome her intimidation in working with the infusion pump and needles.

B. Because of a potential language barrier, explain ways for the nurse to verify Josephina's understanding of teaching conducted in English.

C. Determine which needs from Maslow's hierarchy will be met for Mr. Marcello when Josephina learns how to provide this care.

D. What would be appropriate learning objectives for Josephina? for Mr. Marcello?

11

Safety and Equipment Management

LEARNING OBJECTIVES

After completing this chapter, the reader will be able to:

◆ Explain the role of home care nurses in evaluating and enhancing client safety.

◆ Understand the importance of assessing conditions and remaining alert for signs of abuse in clients.

◆ Appreciate the special safety considerations for homes with children and for pediatric clients.

◆ State key factors in examining a client's environment for safety hazards.

◆ Discuss safety considerations of medical equipment used in the home.

◆ List actions nurses can take to protect their personal safety while performing their home care duties.

KEY TERMS

Abuse	Side rails
Cane	Trapeze
Crutches	Walker
Lift	Wheelchair

247

H ome care nurses must become aware of safety factors for their clients and for themselves. They are confronted with a unique set of safety issues that differ from those found in other types of nursing practice. The homes of clients are not fully equipped to provide healthcare. Safety features commonly found in institutional settings are usually missing in homes. Moreover, home care nurses do not have immediate access to assistance from other personnel, which can increase risks for both clients and nurses. For example, consistently maintaining home safety for medically fragile pediatric clients presents a challenge to home care nurses and to lay caregivers, who lack the constant availability and support from clinicians found in institutional settings.

The safety of home care clients is often at risk due to impaired cognition, mobility, and functional ability. The consequences of falls, injuries, and accidents can be extremely debilitating for older clients. Nurses are responsible for assessing potential environmental hazards and attempting to minimize risks by instructing clients and lay caregivers appropriately.

Nurses who work in home care must recognize personal safety issues that are seldom encountered in institutional settings. Examples of issues for home care nurses to consider include travel in dangerous neighborhoods, homes with potentially dangerous pets, clients and lay caregivers with histories of violent behavior or with unstable psychiatric conditions, and clients who openly display weapons.

This chapter reviews safety issues for nurses to be aware of when caring for clients in the home. Nurses can perform many interventions to enhance the safety of their clients, and this chapter incorporates key factors for nurses to address when fulfilling their responsibilities. Important considerations for nurses dealing with abusive situations in the homes of clients are detailed. The special safety factors that nurses must apply in homes with children and for pediatric clients are discussed. Evaluation of potential safety hazards in homes, an important responsibility that nurses should conduct during each visit, is examined in this chapter. The use of medical equipment in the home can greatly improve the safety of debilitated clients, but if inappropriately or inaccurately used can actually increase risks for injury. Actions that home care nurses can perform to ensure the careful and appropriate use of assistive devices are included. Ways for nurses to secure and to maximize their individual safety while carrying out their duties are explored in this chapter as well.

KEY CONCEPT

Home care nurses are primarily responsible for anticipating potential safety risks for their clients and providing appropriate interventions.

◆ Client Safety

The home care nurse is responsible for the assessment and ongoing evaluation of a client's potential risk for accident or injury and any issues that may impact physical, psychological, financial, and emotional integrity. Home care nurses are often the only healthcare professionals with an opportunity to observe clients in their own environments. Thus, nurses are responsible for acting as advocates for clients to promote health and welfare through interventions that facilitate safe surroundings.

NURSING ASSESSMENT FOR SAFETY

To maintain the safety of home care clients, nurses must have highly developed assessment skills to identify potential risks. Assessment of safety risks takes place during the routine environmental assessment conducted in initial visits to clients (see Chapter 13) and in subsequent visits by home care nurses (see Chapter 14). A heightened awareness of potential risks for clients increases the ability to identify possible problems.

KEY CONCEPT

Home care nurses need highly developed assessment skills to identify potential safety risks for their clients. Awareness of potential risks increases the ability to identify possible difficulties.

Assessment of Client's Condition

Thousands of defense mechanisms exist within the human body that detect subtle changes in the environment. These mechanisms provide individuals with early warnings of circumstances that may result in harm. The normal function of the senses helps the body to guard itself against a variety of environmental threats. The senses are often diminished, however, in clients receiving home care services due to advanced age, illness, the effects of medications, or as a consequence of other medical interventions. Impaired cognition, delayed response time, or limited mobility may inhibit an individual's ability to appropriately respond to perceptions of danger. As a result, many clients are especially vulnerable to injuries or accidents that are easily preventable for other people (Table 11-1).

Nurses should assess clients for decreased perceptive capabilities that may impede their ability to avoid unsafe circumstances and subsequent injuries. For example, a client with sensory loss resulting from a CVA may have a decreased ability to detect when water is too hot. While taking a bath, the client may experience a burn. Thus, a nurse should educate the client about the potential for injury and suggest necessary precautions to avoid such an outcome. Another client may have decreased visual acuity due to diabetes. If this client lives in a cluttered environment, the potential for tripping or falling is increased. The consequences of such an injury to a client with long-standing diabetes could be severe.

The Client with Cognitive Impairment. Clients with cognitive deficiencies face serious safety concerns. Confused clients or clients with Alzheimer's disease need constant supervision to protect their safety. Grollman and Kosite note, "As the perceptions of a person with Alzheimer's disease dim, previously safe parts of the house

TABLE 11-1. *Risks of Deterioration of Sensory Perceptions*

SENSE	POTENTIAL CAUSES OF DETERIORATION	CONSEQUENCES OF DETERIORATION
SIGHT	Medications	Falls
	Illness (i.e., diabetes, cataracts)	Taking wrong medications
	Aging process	Burns
	Head injury	
HEARING	Aging process	Unable to hear alarms
	Medications	
TASTE	Medications	Eating spoiled food
	Aging process	
TOUCH	CVA	Burns
	Head injury	Decubitus ulcers
	Neuromuscular conditions	Skin irritation
	Peripheral nerve damage	
SMELL	Head injury	Eating spoiled food
	Medications	Burns
	Aging process	Poisoning

can become dangerous" (1996, p. 150). Clients may burn themselves because they cannot distinguish the hot water tap from the cold. Lay caregivers must be instructed to lower water temperature to prevent this potential risk. Confused clients may turn an oven on and forget to turn it off. Lay caregivers must check appliances to be sure that they are not left running inappropriately. Clients may inadvertently lock themselves in bathrooms or closets and find themselves unable to escape. Locks should be removed from these doors to prevent such occurrences. Confused clients may also wander out of the house and become lost. Complex locks can often prevent these clients from leaving their homes without appropriate supervision and care.

The Client with Restrictions to Mobility or Functional Capacity. Most clients who require home care services have some restrictions to mobility and deficiencies in functional capacity. In fact, these issues often initiate referrals to home care. Mobility may be inhibited due to muscular weakness, decreased endurance, or impaired balance. If mobility is reduced, clients suffer from an inherent inability to respond quickly to environmental hazards. A misstep that could easily be corrected by someone with normal strength and balance can result in a disastrous fall for an individual with poor strength or balance.

Home care nurses are responsible for assessing a new client's ability to safely perform ADLs, because decreased functional capacity can present risks. For example, clients with Parkinson's disease may experience severe tremors of the upper extremities. This condition poses a risk for burns and other injuries for individuals who cook

Application to Home Care Practice
*Interventions to Assist a Client
with Mobility Impairment*

Clients who live alone are sometimes at risk for falls in and out of the
bathtub. Home care nurses can perform several interventions to address
this issue, depending upon a client's condition. Guard rails can be in-
stalled in bathrooms to improve a client's safety. The client can be encouraged to take sponge baths until strength improves. The nurse can also initiate visits by home health aides to assist the client in and out of the
bathtub.

or perform other ADLs for themselves. Clients who have difficulty swallowing or
adequately chewing food are at risk of aspiration or choking. When home care
nurses identify reduced ability to perform ADLs in clients, they must also identify
the potential safety hazards these limitations present and intervene to address
them appropriately.

Assessment of the Client's Environment

When nurses enter the homes of clients, an assessment of the physical environment
for safety is a routine component of every visit (see Chapter 13). The most carefully
developed plans of care for clients will not meet their needs if basic safety is lacking.
According to Whirret and Wooldridge (1992), "Injuries and accidents are among
the major causes of death and chronic debilitation for older adults. In addition to
the potential for traumatic loss of life or major disability, there are often substantial

Survival Alert:
*Environmental and Mobility
Safety Considerations*

- Clear pathways between bed, other resting areas, and bathroom.
- Use nightlights to keep paths visible.
- Secure or remove scatter rugs.
- Avoid slippery floors. Walk carefully on slippery floors, if necessary.
- Cover or remove sharp corners along pathways.
- Keep telephone and electrical cords out of pathways.
- Be sure to set the brakes on a wheelchair when client is getting in or
  out.
- If there is a chance that client may fall out of bed, be sure to use side
  rails.
- When you see something on the floor that does not belong there, have
  someone pick it up. If you see spilled liquid, wipe it up.

economic, ethical, legal, and family issues at stake with older persons at risk for such experiences". Nurses must evaluate the environment, considering each client's particular mobility limitations, functional capacity, medical conditions, and treatment plan. An environment that is perfectly safe for one individual may be extremely dangerous for another.

Nurses should assess walkways for frequent culprits of injuries: clutter, unnecessary scatter rugs, curled carpet corners, frayed spots, and electrical cords (Fig. 11-1). Poorly lit areas that present no threat to clients during the day create danger zones at night. Bathrooms and kitchens are also high-risk areas, because their floors often become wet and slippery. Clients often reach for items in bathroom closets and kitchen cabinets and lose their balance. Occasionally, medical care provided in the home can increase risks for other persons who reside there. For example, medical equipment and supplies (e.g., syringes) may present risks to children living in the home of adult clients (see below).

Some nursing interventions performed to address client safety issues require the removal of safety hazards. For a poorly lit walkway, a nurse may rearrange light sources or place a higher wattage bulb in a lamp that lights the area. If throw rugs represent a danger to an elderly client with an unsteady gait, a nurse may remove them with the client's permission.

Figure 11-1. Dark and cluttered walkways pose a safety risk to clients with mobility impairments.

Survival Alert:

Bathroom Safety Considerations

- ◆ Make sure tubs and showers have nonskid mats or strips.
- ◆ Make sure grab bars are in tub or shower and by the toilet as needed.
- ◆ Check that door lock has a safety release.
- ◆ Check that bathroom door does not block path to the toilet.
- ◆ Use tub bench and/or hand held shower when needed.
- ◆ Use nightlight in bathroom.
- ◆ To avoid burns, keep the water heater set to no hotter than 115°F.
- ◆ Wipe up any excess water on the floor.

The environments of clients consist of both their homes and their neighborhoods. Home care clients who live in areas with high crime rates may feel threatened walking outside to get their mail or answering the door for Meals on Wheels delivery. Clients may not leave their homes to seek appropriate medical treatment due to a fear of crime. Nurses have a responsibility to address these issues in order to maximize safety.

ABUSE OR NEGLECT OF HOME CARE CLIENTS

Home care nurses witness clients in their normal environment and thus are privy to situations and details that can be hidden from other healthcare clinicians. **Abuse** or neglect of clients may be undetected for years by family physicians who are

Survival Alert:

Kitchen Safety Considerations

- ◆ Keep a fire extinguisher in the kitchen.
- ◆ Do not leave grease on the stove. Clean it up.
- ◆ If you have a grease fire, do not put water on it. Use a chemical-type extinguisher or baking soda to smother it.
- ◆ Do not leave cooking pots unattended.
- ◆ Turn handles of pots away from the front edge of the stove.
- ◆ Have good lighting in the kitchen.
- ◆ Be alert when carrying hot liquid.
- ◆ Keep paper towels, napkins, and pot holders away from burners.
- ◆ Keep the kitchen floor clean and free of clutter and spills.
- ◆ Store knives so that blades are protected.
- ◆ Electric cooking does not produce a visible flame. Be sure to check that the dial is at the setting you want or off.
- ◆ If you have a pacemaker, stay out of the kitchen when a microwave is working.

unable to observe their natural interactions with family members and other lay caregivers. Moreover, physicians have limited opportunities to examine firsthand the circumstances in which clients live. As a result, home care nurses are often the first professionals to identify abuse or neglect in a home. Abusive or negligent behaviors include battering, verbal abuse, exploitation, denial of rights, forced confinement, ignored medical needs, sexual abuse, and other physical harm (Ebersole & Hess, 1994).

KEY CONCEPT

Due to the personalized nature of home care, nurses are directly exposed to the living conditions and situations of their clients. As a result, home care nurses are often the first professionals to identify abuse or neglect of clients.

Signs of Abuse/Neglect

Signs of abuse and neglect include poor grooming and hygiene, poor ventilation of a client's room, a room that is isolated from the rest of the house, contractures, excoriated skin, fecal impactions, decubiti, poor oral hygiene, cowering, passiveness, abrasions, bruises, burns, and dehydration. Abusive lay caregivers may not cooperate with medical treatment plans. For example, they may give medications to clients inconsistently, be unwilling to obtain necessary medical supplies and equipment, or unnecessarily discourage the mobility of clients by refusing to help them out of bed, into a chair, or to ambulate. Clients who are victims of abuse or neglect may receive no assistance from lay caregivers with dressing or bathing and may remain

Survival Alert:

Home Stressors That May Lead to Abuse or Neglect

- Alcohol abuse
- Marital problems
- Financial difficulties
- History of violence
- No respite for lay caregivers
- Decreased or interrupted sleep
- Incontinence
- Unresolved emotional issues between clients and lay caregivers
- Dementia
- Long history of condition with extended prognosis
- Heavy dependence on lay caregiver for ADLs
- Lack of outside social supports

in bedclothes all of the time. Nurses may perceive hostility or cynicism in the remarks of lay caregivers to or regarding clients. Occasionally, a lay caregiver accepts the responsibility of caring for an older or debilitated person solely for the purpose of receiving the client's extra income (e.g., social security). A home care nurse should be alert for signs that a lay caregiver is using a client's money inappropriately.

Reporting Abuse/Neglect

Most states have obligatory reporting mechanisms for healthcare providers in the event that nurses identify potential signs of abuse or neglect. Home care nurses must become familiar with these laws and reporting requirements. Verbal and written reporting are sometimes mandatory, and time frames for accurate reporting are usually very specific. After nurses file reports, employees of governmental agencies typically investigate the circumstances. In most instances, governmental examiners strive to maintain the confidentiality of the reporting source; however, lay caregivers often deduce that the source of information is the home care nurse. Therefore, to maintain a therapeutic relationship, home care nurses are wise to share their observations and concerns with clients and lay caregivers and explain their duty to report information ahead of time.

Respite for Lay Caregivers

The caregiving role can be exhausting and frustrating for even the most loving lay caregivers. Nurses can intervene in high-risk circumstances, even when actual signs of abuse or neglect are not apparent, in an effort to prevent future problems. They should provide lay caregivers with anticipatory guidance regarding medical conditions and how they may change over time (see Chapter 14). The need for regular, meaningful respite should be explained to lay caregivers. Nurses should encourage them to access resources and make specific plans for rest and personal time when caring for clients. In some situations, referral to social services may be indicated to provide counseling for clients and lay caregivers or to assist them with identifying helpful community resources (see Chapter 7).

CHILD SAFETY

Children present distinct safety concerns in home care. Children often live in the homes of adult clients (Fig. 11-2). Home care services are being provided to pediatric clients with increasing frequency as well. Services that are administered in home care may increase children's risks of accidents and injuries. Nurses are responsible for identifying these potential risks and must intervene to reduce the chances for misfortune.

Nurses can anticipate potential safety hazards in homes by identifying the developmental stages of the children who live there. Age alone is not always a good predictor of potential safety risks for children. For example, some pediatric clients experience developmental delays due to their clinical conditions and may exhibit the behavior or thought patterns of much younger children. Thus, home care nurses should anticipate the risks associated with different developmental levels, whatever a child's age may be.

Figure 11-2. Children often live with clients who are receiving home care services. Nurses must ensure that they protect the safety of the entire family.

KEY CONCEPT

The age of children is not always a reliable predictor of safety risks. Developmental and maturity levels may be more helpful indicators for nurses to consider when implementing safety interventions in homes with children.

Newborns may be at risk of falling off beds or suffocation. Toddlers normally like to explore and resist confinement from adults. Nurses must be prepared for dangers stemming from this behavior. If toddlers live in a client's home, medical equipment and medications must be appropriately stored. Adults must adequately supervise toddlers at all times. Home care nurses should also be alert for sibling rivalry. Supervised interactions between children may be indicated and recommended to parents. Teaching needs to be individualized to each client's home environment and to the specific needs of children living there (Display 11-1).

Safety Risks for Children

Typical childhood accidents include falls, suffocation, drowning, poisoning, and burns. Mishaps can occur even when conscientious parents or lay caregivers supervise. Children living with family members who require home care services experience increased risks. Less supervision for these children may be problematic, because lay caregivers are focusing much of their attention on clients. These children may also be exposed to hazardous environmental conditions, equipment, supplies (e.g., syringes) or poisonous materials (e.g., medications).

Young children should never be left unattended while they are awake. Small objects, such as safety pins, matches, syringes, thermometers, and small toys, must

Display 11-1:
Topics for Child Safety Education

- Appropriate foods for the child's development level to prevent choking
- Fences for stairwells or locks for doors to stairs to prevent falling
- Covering electrical outlets
- Appropriate storage of medications, household chemicals, and other poisons
- Appropriate use of restraints in cars
  - Car seats
  - Safety belts
- Toys appropriate for the child's developmental level
  - For small children, avoid toys with small pieces to avoid choking
- Supervision around any open water
  - Children can drown in just a few inches of water; adults should anticipate problems with buckets, toilets, etc.
  - Young children must *never* be left alone in a bathtub.
- Supervision of children when playing outside
  - Possible fencing to prevent wandering or running into streets with traffic
- Burn prevention by adjusting hot water temperature to no hotter than 115°F
- Keeping all pot handles on stove turned inward
- Avoidance of table cloths that hang over the edge (could be pulled down by a child)
- Careful storage and locking of any firearms in the home
- Keeping two single-vial doses of ipecac syrup in the home in the event of poisoning
- Poison control number to call in the event that ingestion of such substances occurs
- Safe cribs or bedrails

be kept away from them. Medical equipment must be kept away from small children at all times. The home care nurse must look out for Venetian blind cords, electrical cords, and other similar items that have caused strangulation deaths in children; adults must be reminded to keep these items out of children's reach. Families must also be educated regarding the poison control number to call in the event that a child ingests a toxic substance. Nurses need to teach adults about handling small children in the home, especially when nursing care is being provided.

Safety for the Pediatric Client

When children suffer from an injury, illness, or condition that reduces their mobility, perception, or cognition, their risk for accidental injury increases. Pediatric clients thus have special safety needs. The clinical condition for which a child is being treated by a home care nurse can present safety concerns that must be carefully evaluated. The nurse should anticipate potential safety issues associated with a child's disease process in the plan of care and identify interventions that can reduce hazards.

Medical treatments may present safety risks for pediatric clients. For example, children receiving infusion therapy face potentially greater risks than adults, because of their undeveloped judgment and impulsiveness. A child may inadvertently dislodge or remove a catheter, necessitating an additional invasive procedure and potentially delaying necessary treatment.

Nurses should assist a child's parent or other lay caregiver with identifying realistic functional goals. If lay caregivers experience denial regarding a child's limitations, they may not provide needed safety precautions. Medical equipment and assistive devices must be appropriately adjusted or changed as children grow. Inadequately sized equipment can increase the chances of accidents. For children whose mobility is impaired, precautions should be implemented to prevent falls (Fig. 11-3).

Children with cerebral palsy, muscular dystrophy, or skeletal deformities may wear braces or casts. Lay caregivers need instruction in the care and cleaning of this equipment, and must watch for skin breakdown. For babies sent home with cleft palates, home care nurses must enforce safe feeding to prevent choking and aspiration. Children with severe asthma may become seriously ill or die if their environment is not kept free from dust and other allergens to which they are sensitive. Lay caregivers must be reminded to keep these children's environments clean and dust-free. Children with perceptual disabilities (hearing loss, poor eyesight, or blindness) have obvious risks as they progress through their developmental stages, because

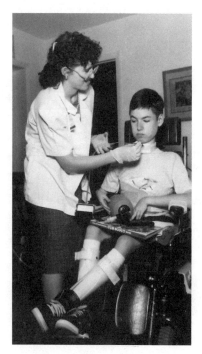

Figure 11-3. The nurse has many special safety concerns to consider when caring for a pediatric client. (Photo by Marilu Sherer, CARING)

they are unable to detect impending danger. Adequate supervision and careful modification of the home environment are indicated to prevent accidental injury. Pediatric clients may have conditions or receive treatments that increase their risk of bleeding and infection (e.g., hemophilia, chemotherapy, and AIDS). These children need to be carefully protected from falls or exposure to infectious agents that would have minimal effects or consequences for healthy children.

Child Abuse

Nurses should be alert for signs of physical, sexual, emotional, or psychological abuse and neglect of children in the home. The groups at highest risk for abuse include children, the elderly, the developmentally disabled, and the debilitated (Craven & Hirnle, 1996). Risks may be especially great for pediatric clients. A child's medical condition can contribute to strains in marital relationships and may cause financial problems, all of which exacerbate stressors within a household.

Signs of Child Abuse. Signs that a child may be a victim of abuse or neglect include poor hygiene, poor nutrition, inappropriate dress for weather, old or torn clothes, welts, small round burns (from cigarettes), circular abrasions around wrists or ankles (indicating restraint), slap marks, and bruises. Lay caregivers may give conflicting stories or explanations that do not match the degree of a child's injury. Children may be resistant to any type of physical contact. Infants may not cry or may cry very little; when they do, it is a helpless cry as opposed to a cry that expects a response. Parents may seem unable to comfort the child.

Dealing with Child Abuse. When questioned by a home care nurse about a child's signs of abuse or neglect, lay caregivers may become hostile and demand that the nurse leave. Abused or neglected children rarely answer questions posed to them about their situation honestly, and will usually defend their abusers. Most states have laws that strictly require the reporting of any suspected indications of abuse or neglect. Nurses must become familiar with applicable laws and reporting requirements in order to consistently comply with appropriate measures.

MEDICAL EQUIPMENT SAFETY

Medical equipment ordered to improve a client's safety can actually increase the client's risk for accidents and injuries. Frequently, clients who receive home care services use medical equipment to increase their functional status or to improve their safety. This equipment must be appropriately chosen for a client's individual needs, and used properly. Equipment that is poorly selected and misused can present increased safety risks.

Most equipment is designed for use by an average-sized person. Clients who are shorter, taller, heavier, or thinner than average may find the standard piece of equipment inappropriate. These clients require equipment sizing adjustments to meet their needs. Individuals who make equipment adjustments must have the experience and qualifications to do so. Home care nurses frequently have the opportunity to identify the need for new equipment or for changes in medical equipment that clients currently use. Nurses must become familiar with the special features of various

TABLE 11-2. *Equipment Features and Indications for Consideration*

FEATURE	CONSIDERATIONS
Wheelchairs	Width of the chair: necessary doorway accessibility (narrow and extra wide wheelchairs are available); portability (weight, fold-up ease, and removable arms); mobility of the client
Walkers	Walker height: height of client; front wheels feature, four wheels: ability to lift walker; seat: endurance; armrests: strength in arms
Crutches	Height of crutches: height of client; appropriate handgrips
Canes	Quad cane: client's balance; cane length: height of client; handgrip: amount of weight client places on cane
Hospital beds	Space available in client's home; half- or full-length siderails: alertness of client; whether the client will independently lower siderails
Bedside commode	For use over the toilet or at the bedside, or both
Lift	Strength and ability of person(s) using it

types of medical equipment in order to recommend the items most consistent with each client's individualized needs (Table 11-2).

KEY CONCEPT

Equipment that is poorly selected or misused can actually present increased safety risks for clients.

Wheelchairs

Wheelchairs are available in various widths, weights, and styles of portability. The wheelchair that a nurse selects for a client should meet the particulars of the client's circumstances. Clients who live in homes with narrow doorways require narrow wheelchairs. Obese clients require durable and wide wheelchairs. For clients who are very active and mobile in their communities, lightweight, compact wheelchairs that fold easily are most appropriate. Some wheelchairs have removable arm rests and leg rests. The nurse must determine whether a client will need to use a transfer board to enter the wheelchair, and specify the need for this feature very clearly when ordering the equipment.

Walkers

Clients with slow and unsteady gaits often use **walkers** (Fig. 11-4). Front-wheel or four-wheel walkers are available for clients who lack the strength to lift the walker. Arrests and seats are other available features on walkers. Walkers must be the appropriate height for the clients who use them. If walkers are too tall for clients, they will have difficulty lifting them to move forward. Because these clients already have unsteady gaits, the difficulty could cause them to fall. Walkers that are too short will

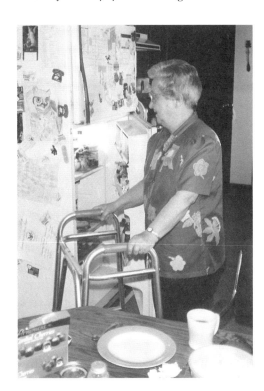

Figure 11-4. A walker helps this woman to perform many of her own ADLs and to function independently.

cause clients to bend over repeatedly. This movement will also hamper a client's ability to lift the walker.

Canes and Crutches

Clients with good balance often use **canes**. The type of handle and the height of the cane are important for nurses to consider when determining appropriate support for clients. **Crutches** need to be sized appropriately to prevent injury. Crutches that are too long can place pressure on and cause damage to nerves under a client's arms. Moreover, overly long crutches may cause clients to stand too straight, making it difficult for them to lift the crutches to move forward. If crutches are too short, clients will bend forward too far, impairing their gait. Inappropriate hand grips can result in nerve damage to a client's hands.

Transfer Equipment

Electric and manual beds are available with a variety of features. A **trapeze** is sometimes recommended for clients with difficulty repositioning themselves in bed (Fig. 11-5). Hospital beds are occasionally ordered for use in the home if clients need the ability to position the bed. Such beds are obviously bulky pieces of equipment; therefore, nurses must help clients to consider their most appropriate locations in the home. Floors must be durable enough to hold their weight. **Siderails** are a safety feature available in half or full lengths. If a client will independently lower

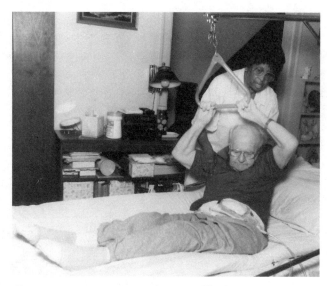

Figure 11-5. A trapeze and a special bed enable this client to receive services in the home. (Photo by Marilu Sherer, CARING)

the rails, half rails are appropriate. If a client is confused or has a lowered level of consciousness, full side rails should be selected.

Lifts are sometimes ordered when clients cannot be safely transferred to a chair or bedside commode. The space available in the home for this bulky piece of equipment impacts the type of lift nurses recommend. The number of people who will perform the lift transfers and their physical capabilities also affect the features of the lift that are needed. Clients or lay caregivers with complex needs may need a referral to a physical therapist for teaching. Nurses may also initiate calls to equipment vendors for someone to instruct clients about the appropriate use of equipment.

Liability

When home health employees use medical equipment to provide services, home care agencies have some liability for the safety of the equipment, even though clients independently lease the equipment from medical equipment companies. Therefore, agencies must ensure that their employees are knowledgeable in the use of medical equipment implemented in the home. Nurses must be able to recognize when equipment is functioning improperly and know appropriate follow-up measures. If equipment malfunctions and causes serious injuries or death, regulations mandate that agencies report these incidents to equipment vendors or manufacturers. Accidents, injuries, and safety hazards related to the care and services that nurses provide must be reported to their agencies and documented according to policy. Such incidents are investigated so that appropriate procedures are enacted to prevent future recurrences.

FIRE SAFETY

Fire safety is a concern for all home care clients. Because of the homebound status of many clients, leaving the home in the event of a fire is usually difficult, if not impossible. This household danger presents a greater threat in the homes of debilitated persons than in other settings. Clients in a weakened condition are unable to respond quickly to small household fires to contain them. Also, their ability to call for emergency assistance and to remove themselves from the physical location of the fire is often decreased.

Risks for Fire

The reduced functional capacity of clients can increase risks for fire. Individuals may not be able to maintain safety precautions around the stove due to weakness. Grease fires are common, particularly if clients have been unable to clean stove top spills and splashes between use. Rooms may be cluttered with trash when clients have limited assistance and decreased ability to maintain their homes. Excess paper and trash provide excellent fuel for fires.

Clients who smoke face a high risk for burns from fire. Those who smoke in bed or while relaxing in recliners may inadvertently fall asleep with burning cigarettes in their hands. Their clothing or furniture can then easily ignite. Clients may be unable to evacuate a burning area because of mobility limitations related to their medical conditions and, as a result, may suffer severe burns or die.

Medical treatments may increase risks for fire. Some home care clients require supplemental oxygen, which poses a safety risk (Fig. 11-6). Oxygen, although it does

Survival Alert:

Fire Safety Considerations

- ◆ It is important to have a fire extinguisher and an operating fire alarm in your home. Test alarms monthly.
- ◆ Keep matches and lighters out of children's reach.
- ◆ Do not smoke cigarettes if you are drowsy, have taken pain medication, or are resting in bed.
- ◆ Know all exits from your home and plan fire escape paths from all rooms.
- ◆ Keep passages and doorways clear.
- ◆ If a fire occurs, leave your home and do not reenter it. Call 911 (if available) or the fire department immediately from a neighbor's home.
- ◆ Unplug all appliances before attempting repair or touching with metal. Do not attempt repair of medical equipment.
- ◆ Keep flashlights and extra batteries handy in case of power failure.
- ◆ Do not plug more than two electrical cords into any outlet.
- ◆ Never use frayed or worn electrical cords.
- ◆ Use medical equipment only as instructed.

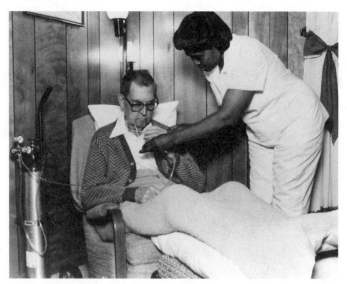

Figure 11-6. The use of oxygen at home requires great aware-ness of appropriate safety measures. (Photo by Marilu Sherer, CARING)

Survival Alert:

Electrical Safety Considerations

- Be sure all electrical equipment is in good condition. Keep it clean and dry.
- "Ground" large appliances with a three-prong plug.
- Never touch any electrical appliance when you are wet or when you are in or near water.
- If any appliance has a detachable cord, unplug cord from the outlet first, then from the appliance.
- Keep electrical cords away from heat, water, and pathways. Do not put cords under a rug.
- Unplug all appliances before attempting repair or touching with metal. Do not attempt repair of medical equipment.
- Keep flashlights and extra batteries handy in case of power failure.
- Do not plug more than two electrical cords into any outlet.
- Never use frayed or worn electrical cords.
- Use medical equipment only as instructed.

not ignite, creates a fire hazard because it enhances combustion. Thus, smoking while using oxygen presents an enormous safety threat. Nurses must carefully question clients who use oxygen and also smoke about their habits, and educate them regarding their behavioral risks. Nurses must stress the need for clients to turn off oxygen whenever they smoke. They must caution lay caregivers as well not to smoke in any rooms where oxygen is running. Electrical appliances, such as electric razors or heating pads, must never be used near running oxygen. In the event of a spark, oxygen can cause an explosion or facilitate flames if flammable materials are in the vicinity. When clients or lay caregivers use any flammable materials, nurses must instruct them to turn off oxygen. They should encourage the avoidance of materials that generate static electricity, such as wool and nylon, and the use and wear of cotton items as much as possible. Home care nurses must monitor oxygen equipment regularly for signs of leakage and report any problems immediately to equipment providers.

Fire Prevention Measures

Home care nurses should evaluate homes for functioning smoke alarms placed in appropriate locations. Fire extinguishers should be kept in rooms with high risks for fire (e.g., kitchens, rooms in which clients run oxygen). Clients and lay caregivers should be familiar with their use. Nurses should identify all potential exits, clearing passage as needed, and instruct clients and their lay caregivers in the ways to exit in the event of a fire. Lay caregivers should understand how to remove clients with severe mobility limitations from the home. Nurses may practice exiting the home with clients and lay caregivers. Nurses may also provide them with fire safety materials, such as pamphlets, for further instruction.

Fire While the Home Care Nurse Is Present

If a fire occurs while a home care nurse is working in a client's home, the safety of all those present depends upon the nurse's knowledge of appropriate responses. Home care agencies typically have specific policies regarding how their employees are to respond in the event of a fire (Display 11-2). Nurses must memorize the appropriate course of action to take well before they are faced with such a situation. This knowledge will enable them to respond quickly, calmly, and appropriately, protecting their own lives and the lives of their clients.

KEY CONCEPT

Home care providers must know rapid, appropriate responses in the event of a fire.

EMERGENCY AND DISASTER PREPAREDNESS

An additional safety issue for home care nurses to assess is the potential for emergencies and natural disasters. Nurses should discuss preparedness issues with clients regarding such events. Often, clients are dependent for a period of time upon home

Display 11-2:
Sample of a Home Care Agency's Fire Policy

1. When a small localized fire is discovered in a client's home, the employee will immediately remove the client from the vicinity of the fire and extinguish the fire with a fire extinguisher, if one is available in the home.

2. If the fire size cannot be assessed, is too large to handle with a fire extinguisher, or no fire extinguisher is available, the employee will take the following actions:
   a. Remove all those present in the home from the residence.
   b. Call the emergency phone number from a neighbor's home to report the fire, giving the exact address. The client's residence should not be reentered.
   c. Call the home care agency to report the incident.
   d. Remain with the client and lay caregivers or family until the fire department arrives and the fire is controlled or extinguished.
   e. Assist the client and lay caregivers or family in finding a place to stay, if needed. If necessary, notify a social worker or appropriate community organization to assist in this process.

care agencies to receive necessary medical services. If a natural disaster, such as a flood or earthquake, were to happen, nurses might not be able to make their usual visits. Thus, nurses should inform clients about actions they can take to prevent the deterioration of their health. A client may simply need to keep a wound covered with a clean dressing. If more critically ill, a client may require instructions to call for transportation to a hospital emergency room.

Nurses must be prepared to respond to any emergency in the home. They should be equipped and ready to provide appropriate interventions for medical emergencies, to activate the emergency medical response system, and to protect clients in the event of a fire or natural disaster. Nurses should have access to a face shield or mask at all times in the event that CPR or mouth-to-mouth resuscitation is indicated. They should also carry first aid supplies with them.

NURSING INTERVENTIONS AND ONGOING EVALUATION OF CLIENT SAFETY

All nursing interventions related to safety should be directed toward the goal of reducing a client's risk factors. The primary safety intervention that home care nurses perform is **education**. Communicating the importance of understanding potential risks and consequences of accidents is the first and most important step for nurses educating clients and lay caregivers. Instructing clients and their lay caregivers in ways to modify their homes to enhance safety is often indicated. Potential emergencies and appropriate responses to them is another important safety topic. Clients may require

Survival Alert:

Natural Disaster or Emergency Considerations

Before

Have on hand the following:

• Flashlights with spare batteries
• Portable radio with spare batteries
• First aid kit and fire extinguisher
• Food, cooking utensils, and a nonelectric can opener. Keep a supply of canned or dehydrated foods, powdered milk, and canned juices to last at least 72 hours.
• Water: at least three gallons per person for a 72 hour period
• Hygiene and sanitation supplies: toilet paper, plastic bags, soap, shampoo and toothpaste
• Heavy shoes and work gloves
• Tools: adjustable wrench for turning off gas and water

During

• Remain calm.
• If indoors, stay there. Get under a desk or table or move toward an interior wall. Stay clear of windows, bookcases, mirrors, and fireplaces.
• If outside, get into the open, away from buildings, trees, walks, or power lines. Sit or lie down and brace yourself.

After

• Remain calm.
• Check for injuries. Provide emergency first aid as needed.
• Do not use the telephone unless there is a life or death emergency.
• Turn on your battery-powered radio for reports and information.

---

education in exercises to improve their strength, endurance, and mobility. New glasses or hearing aides may be recommended to enhance a client's perceptual ability to detect high-risk situations. Nurses may instruct clients in available medical equipment that reduces safety risks.

Teaching alone, however, should not give nurses the false impression that they have adequately improved client safety. The home care nurse must also perform ongoing evaluations of a client's knowledge, response to recommendations, and ability to perform safety procedures. Nurses must verify that clients have learned and are able to demonstrate procedures (e.g., use of medical equipment). The ongoing evaluation of comprehension of safety measures aids nurses in identifying areas that require reinforcement. Home care nurses often intervene by making referrals to appropriate disciplines for follow-up of specific safety concerns.

Clinical Example
with Critical Thinking

Susan, a home care nurse, receives a referral for Mr. Barnhardt, who was recently discharged from the hospital with pneumonia. Mr. Barnhardt has a J-tube with which he has conducted bolus tube feedings for many years after a partial gastrectomy for cancer. The physician's order includes evaluating the client's home for safety.

When Susan knocks on the client's apartment door on her initial visit, she hears a voice inside yell, "Come in." When she steps in the door, Susan sees that the apartment is filled with boxes, paper, trash, and old food. She immediately smells a strong odor from the decaying food and trash. A narrow pathway between the trash and clutter leads her to Mr. Barnhardt, a thin, elderly gentleman sitting at a kitchen table, smoking a cigarette. On the kitchen counter are a blender, old food spills, and a few dirty 60-cc syringes used for the tube feedings. Mr. Barnhardt has an unsteady gait and a mild tremor from Parkinson's disease.

1. Identify all of the safety issues to be addressed in the nursing plan of care.
2. Prioritize the problems that Susan has encountered.
3. Discuss any personal safety issues that Susan should consider for herself while working in this environment.
4. Determine Susan's options if Mr. Barnhardt does not wish to make any changes in his environment to improve his safety.

DOCUMENTATION OF SAFETY INTERVENTIONS

Nurses must ensure that all safety assessments, instructions, and interventions are carefully documented in the medical record. The responses of clients and lay caregivers to teaching must be documented as well. In the event that a client experiences an accident or an injury, an agency must be able to demonstrate that a home care nurse took actions to anticipate and to prevent such an incident. Accurate documentation provides the information necessary for the agency to prove that their employees performed such measures.

KEY CONCEPT

All safety assessments, instructions, interventions, teaching, and responses to teaching must be carefully documented in the medical record.

◆ The Nurse's Personal Safety

Personal safety is of the utmost importance to nurses working within home care. Safety concerns should be discussed with individuals interested in the home care

Display 11-3:
Sample Home Care Agency Employee Safety Guidelines

- The nurse should consistently wear a name badge that clearly identifies the employee and the home care agency.
- Clients should be phoned in advance and alerted to the approximate time of the home care visit. If necessary, the nurse should obtain directions to the residence.
- If a client owns a pet known to be menacing, the client should be asked to properly secure the pet before the visit is made. If confronted with an aggressive dog, the nurse should back away, but not run.
- Home care nurses should keep change for an emergency phone call in a shoe or pocket.
- Vehicles should be kept in good working order, with plenty of gas.
- Cars should be kept locked at all times, with windows rolled up if possible.
- Cars should be parked in full view of the client's residence. Parking in alleys or on deserted side streets should be avoided, if possible.
- Home care nurses should be aware of their surroundings at all times while traveling in the community.
- When exiting the car, nurses should have the equipment they will need during the visit ready to go.
- Nurses should walk in a professional, businesslike manner directly to the client's residence.
- When passing a group of strangers, home care nurses should cross to the other side of the street, as appropriate, and keep eye contact with those in the group.
- In buildings, the nurse should use common walkways, avoiding isolated stairs.
- A nurse should always knock on the door before entering a client's home.
- Nurses should be aware of surroundings, including animals and other people, in the home.

field before they begin practice (Display 11-3). The work environment is controlled in almost every other clinical setting; such control, however, is not found in home care. Home care nurses usually perform their work alone. They are not accompanied by nor do they have ready access to other healthcare providers. Many factors influence a nurse's personal safety on the job. Complex issues surround home and personal safety for nurses, who must use common sense, keen observation, and assessment skills to determine and minimize risks (Whirret et al., 1992).

The family dynamics in a client's home may be volatile. Certainly, the clinical conditions that necessitate home care place additional stress on the family system. Clients or their lay caregivers may be mentally unstable or emotionally disturbed. These difficulties may not present themselves in other healthcare settings. Some people feel intimidated by institutions and thus do not display typical behavior indicative of psychosocial problems to the clinicians who refer them to home care. If a nurse ever feels uncomfortable in the home of a client, the nurse should immediately leave the premises. The nurse can create an excuse to leave the home (e.g., "I forgot some medical supplies in the car"). Nurses can later make arrangements to ensure that clients receive appropriate care by communicating such a situation to a home care agency supervisor and to a client's physician.

ENVIRONMENTAL SAFETY

When nurses enter a client's home for the first time, they face unknown circumstances. Some clients own pets that are menacing to strangers. When preparing for the first home care visit, nurses should ask clients if they have any pets. Nurses may appropriately ask clients or lay caregivers to restrain pets during visits.

Safety issues that nurses must consider when working within a particular community are frequently as unique as the community itself. In some communities, home care nurses use public transportation to visit their clients. In other areas, driving in snow and ice on country roads represents the greatest personal safety hazard for nurses. Some communities have serious crime problems. Most agencies have formal policies regarding safety precautions for employees working in the communities they serve, or informal protocols that should be learned and followed by all home care personnel.

Traveling to a Client's Home

Traveling to the homes of clients can pose risks to a nurse's personal safety. Most nurses use their own cars to perform their home care visits (Fig. 11-7). Automobile accidents are a risk for any driver. Nurses should religiously wear safety belts while

Figure 11-7. Ensuring personal safety while driving and traveling to the homes of clients is of particular importance for nurses.

driving. Nurses who use public transportation, such as buses or subways, face risks associated with waiting alone at stops and stations. Some home care agencies, particularly in high crime areas of large cities, provide security personnel to accompany home care nurses on visits to increase the protection of their employees.

Home care nurses should always park in busy, well-lit areas. They should keep personal automobiles in excellent condition and keep gas tanks at least half full. While driving, nurses should have their doors locked and windows closed. When nurses return to their cars after visits, they should look under and in their cars before entering them. Home care nurses must maintain a professional appearance. In some neighborhoods, however, nurses who wear uniforms or otherwise indicate by their appearance that they are healthcare professionals could attract crime from individuals who believe that nurses are carrying drugs or syringes. Employees at the home care office should always know their nurses' schedule of visits and route. If nurses intend to visit clients after normal working hours, this critical information must be communicated as well. Nurses should always be alert to their surroundings and above all trust their instincts—if a situation seems unsafe, the nurse should leave.

Traveling home care nurses should verify routes and know exact directions to a client's home. Although clients usually are able to provide good directions, nurses also benefit from checking routes on a map, particularly in dangerous neighborhoods (Fig. 11-8). Driving slowly, stopping to look at a map, or appearing lost may make home care nurses easy crime targets. When nurses are unable to find a client's address, they should drive to a secure location, where they can safely study a map or call the client or home care office to verify the address. Nurses should be alert to the possibility of crime in any area.

Nurses who work in rural areas experience increased risks due to the distances

Figure 11-8. A nurse studies a map at the home care agency in preparation for her visit to a client in an unfamiliar neighborhood.

they may travel. Areas with extreme temperatures present increased risks for nurses. In cold winter weather, a nurse should dress warmly and store blankets, extra clothing, boots, water, and food in the car, in case the car becomes stuck in snow or breaks down. In hot weather, nurses must protect themselves from hyperthermia and dehydration. Air conditioning is important to prevent dehydration from sweating. Nurses should carry plenty of water in the car and drink it throughout the day. Extra water should be stored in the event of a breakdown.

Leaving a Client's Home

Nurses should immediately leave a neighborhood if, for whatever reason, they feel unsafe. Home care supervisors should be quickly notified of problems so that other arrangements can be made to ensure that clients receive appropriate care. For example, a nurse can be accompanied by another home care employee or a police officer within the neighborhood. Nurses may feel more comfortable if clients or lay caregivers meet them at the door. Such provisions can be established after the nurse leaves the area. Employees should immediately report any unsafe conditions to the home care agency. The agency then has a responsibility to intervene to ensure the safety of its employee. Police departments in a community are excellent resources for determining areas of high-risk and appropriate precautions to be taken.

Emergency Measures

Home care nurses must know emergency phone numbers. The emergency plan developed for every client admitted to service should also include these phone numbers. Many home care nurses have car phones, which are excellent tools for increasing their personal safety. In the event of a car breakdown, it may be unsafe to leave the car to verify a location for supervisors, the police, or an auto garage. Nurses, therefore, must always be alert to their locations. Cellular phones that nurses can carry with them are the best option for home care nurses in many communities.

Survival Alert:

Signs and Symptoms of Dehydration

- Increased thirst
- Dry skin and mucous membranes; thick secretions; difficulty swallowing
- Weight loss
- Decreased amount of urine, dark in color
- Fever
- Constipation
- Weakness; faintness
- Mental confusion; drowsiness

Home Care Vs. Hospital:
Safety and Equipment Management

Issue	Home Care	Hospital
Scope of client safety assessment	Nurses work in highly uncontrolled environments. Most clients face mobility issues that increase risks for injury. They have limited access to professional assistance and supervision. Nurses must anticipate a wide range of potential safety risk factors, ranging from kitchen and bathroom safety, to crime prevention, to disaster planning.	Clients typically have fewer environmental risks, due the controlled environment, regular supervision of client activities, access to professional assistance for mobilization, and emergency response systems (e.g., call lights). Nurses have the opportunity to maintain a safe environment by identifying potential risks for clients, altering the environment as needed, and ensuring appropriate levels of supervision and support.
Identification of abuse/neglect	Nurses have a better opportunity to identify signs of neglect or abuse. They observe client and lay caregiver interactions in natural settings. Thus, they are more likely to witness typical behaviors. Home health plans of care often address multiple psychosocial and financial issues to achieve necessary health outcomes. A great opportunity exists for problem identification.	Nurses are limited in their opportunities to identify neglect or abuse of clients because their observations of interactions between clients and lay caregivers are few. They have no opportunity to witness clients in the home.
Accountability for equipment	Home care nurses usually identify the need for medical equipment. Nurses are responsible for ensuring that appropriate medical equipment is provided to clients.	The need for medical equipment is often identified by physicians or through ancillary services. If nurses identify the need for medical equipment, the type of equipment is usually specified or validated by appropriate ancillary personnel.
Personal safety	Nurses practice very independently in uncontrolled work environments. Risks are associated with commuting (e.g., driving on freeways, country roads and subways) in a variety of weather conditions. Nurses do not have ready assistance if they find themselves in a potentially unsafe situation. Clients' homes may present safety hazards (e.g., pets, unsafe communities or cluttered homes).	Nurses have ready access to other employees to assist them in the event of an unsafe situation. Safety features are built into the equipment they use (e.g., warnings about chemicals they may be exposed to are provided).

Home Products: Needle Sticks

Nurses should take great caution when using any product in the home. They should carefully read labels, follow directions, and avoid using products that are not in their original containers. Needle sticks are a particular concern in home care. Approved needle disposal containers must be available at all times to prevent recapping needles–a primary cause of needle stick injuries (see Chapter 12).

MEDICAL EQUIPMENT SAFETY

Equipment commonly found in hospitals and clinics that provides additional safety for healthcare workers is often unavailable in homes, unless furnished by the home care agency. Nurses need to anticipate equipment and supplies that may be needed during visits and bring these materials with them. Basic equipment and conditions that are taken for granted in hospitals and clinics include beds that can be raised to perform treatments without straining a nurse's back, needle disposal boxes, rubber gloves, good lighting, work areas free of clutter, inspected electrical equipment, appropriately labeled chemicals, fire alarms, and fire extinguishers. Therefore, home care nurses have a greater responsibility to ensure that relatively safe conditions are maintained.

OVEREXTENSION

Home care nurses must never attempt tasks that they are doubtful about successfully performing. Nurses are often tempted to try to perform tasks that are potentially beyond their capabilities—for example, lifting a client, or transferring a client to a commode. A nurse may feel that it is time-consuming to call the home care agency for additional help, or bothersome to ask for assistance from a lay caregiver who is taking advantage of the home care visit to get some rest. The results of nurses taking on dangerous tasks by themselves, however, could be disastrous; a nurse could suffer a serious back, neck, or shoulder injury requiring extensive medical leave and treatment. Occasionally, individuals are unable to return to nursing practice. Moreover, nurses put their clients' health at risk as well by trying to do too much by themselves.

◆ Summary

The safety of clients and their lay caregivers must always be a top priority of home care nurses. Nurses are often the first to identify signs of abuse in clients. They must recognize special safety considerations for children living in the homes of adult clients and for pediatric clients. Many factors should be considered when recommending medical equipment in order to meet the specific needs of clients and their lay caregivers. Nurses must ensure that they are prepared to handle fires and other emergencies in the home. Those who work in home care also need to take responsibility for maintaining their personal safety when they are providing services in the community. They must develop an awareness of the precautions that are most appropriate to the community they work within and consistently follow them.

References and Bibliography

All, A. (1994). A literature review: Assessment and intervention in elder abuse. *Journal of Gerontological Nursing, 20*(7), 25–32.

Chez, N. (1994). Helping the victim of domestic violence. *American Journal of Nursing, 94*(7), 32–37.

Craven, R.F. & Hirnle, C.J. (1996). *Fundamentals of nursing: Human health and function* (2nd ed.). Philadelphia: Lippincott.

Devlin, B. & Reynolds, K. (1994). Child abuse: How to recognize it, how to intervene. *American Journal of Nursing, 94*(3), 26–31.

Ebersole, P. & Hess, P. (1994). *Toward healthy aging: Human needs and nursing response* (4th ed.). St. Louis: Mosby.

Grollman, E.A. & Kosik, K.S. (1996). *When someone you love has Alzheimer's*. Boston: Beacon Press.

Hunter, E. (1997). Violence prevention in the home health setting. *Home Healthcare Nurse, 15*(6), 403–409.

Hyde, R.S. (1996). Home healthcare nurses' knowledge of Alzheimer's disease. *Home Healthcare Nurse, 14*(5), 391–397.

Krepper, R., Young, A. & Cummings, E. (1994). Pediatric healthcare. *Home Healthcare Nurse, 12*(4), 15–17.

Lachs, M. & Pillemer, K. (1995). Abuse and neglect of elderly persons. *New England Journal of Medicine, 332*(7), 437–443.

Lange, M. The challenge of fall prevention in home care: A review of the literature. *Home Healthcare Nurse, 14*(3), 198–205.

Leonard, B., Brust, J. & Nelson, R. (1993). Parental distress: Caring for medically fragile children at home. *Journal of Pediatric Nursing: Nursing Care of Children & Families, 8*(1), 22–30.

Meierhoffer, L.L. (1992). Nurses battle family violence. *American Nurse, 24*(4), 1, 7–8.

Milford, P. & Manser, A. (1995, February 8). Smoke detectors, best defense against fires. *News Journal* (Wilmington, DE), B1.

Morrison, B. (1995). Home health care: Staying safe in dangerous times. *Nursing, 25*(10), 49– 51.

Nadwarski, J. (1992). Inner-city safety for home care providers. *JONA, 22*(9), 42–45.

Rice, R. (1994). Safety in the community. *Home Healthcare Nurse, 12*(3), 70.

Smith, M. & Martin, F. (1995). Domestic violence: Recognition, intervention, and prevention. *MEDSURG Nursing, 4*(1), 21–25.

Whirret, T., & Wooldridge, P. (1992). Home safety and older adults. *Caring, 11*(12), 56–58.

Zang, S.M. & Bailey, N.C. (1997). *Home care manual: Making the transition*. Philadelphia: Lippincott-Raven.

POST TEST

1. List four examples of hazards for nurses to assess when performing home safety evaluations.

2. Determine how inappropriately sized walkers can present potential safety risks for clients.

3. Explain why oxygen used in the home presents a potential fire hazard, even though it does not ignite.

4. State the importance of reporting to home care agencies any accidents or incidents that create an injury or potential injury to nurses or clients.

5. Identify precautions that nurses can take when entering high crime neighborhoods.

6. Discuss personal safety issues that home care nurses face that are not encountered in other healthcare settings.

THINKING CRITICALLY IN HOME CARE

Consider the following situation:

Mrs. Sowolee, a 58-year-old widow, is the lay caregiver for her father, Mr. Taggart. Mr. Taggart, 81 years old, suffered a CVA approximately 6 months ago. He was living alone, but his safety was questionable due to an occasional unsteady gait and aphasia. Mrs. Sowolee provides excellent care for her father. He is always well-groomed, dressed, and kept active with various activities.

You receive a call from Mr. Taggart's son, who accuses his sister, Mrs. Sowolee, of taking money from Mr. Taggart's bank account. The son states that Mrs. Sowolee buys herself nice clothing and generally supports herself in a luxurious way—very different from how she lived before her father moved in with her.

1. Assess your initial feelings about the situation. Be able to identify and to explain your responses to Mr. Taggart's son.

2. Decide the steps that you would take to follow up on this accusation of financial exploitation of your client. Consider all of the factors that may be involved, including family dynamics. Be able to defend your conclusions.

12

Infection Control

LEARNING OBJECTIVES

After completing this chapter, the reader will be able to:

◆ Identify the importance of appropriate infection control protocols in home care today.

◆ Explain the process by which infections are transmitted.

◆ Give the rationale for reporting new client infections to the home care agency.

◆ Define standard precautions and transmission-based precautions.

◆ Describe appropriate client teaching related to infection control.

KEY TERMS

Acquired immune deficiency
  syndrome
Centers for Disease Control (CDC)
Cleaning
Contamination
Disinfecting
Durable medical equipment
Hepatitis
Human immunodeficiency virus
Infection
Means of transmission
Pathogen

Personal protective
  equipment
Portal of entry
Portal of exit
Reservoir
Standard precautions
Sterilizing
Susceptibility
Transmission-based
  precautions
Tuberculosis
Vectors

aintaining *appropriate* infection control procedures in home care is one of the nurse's most important functions. Using appropriate techniques maximizes the safety of clients, lay caregivers, families, and home care professionals. Infection control principles are especially important in the home setting today. Many clients now receiving services in the home are sicker than those traditionally served by home care. Often, these clients have compromised immune systems, making them susceptible to complications of infection. Home care clients are also receiving more invasive procedures than in the past. New technology that has enabled care to be provided at home also carries with it the burden of risk for infection. These infections can range from local inflammation of an intravascular site to life-threatening sepsis (Reese & Betts, 1996).

This chapter reviews the process by which infections are transmitted and ways for home care nurses to break the infection cycle. It discusses common infections that nurses encounter when treating home care clients. It addresses ways for nurses to identify and to report new infections in home care clients. This chapter covers standard and transmission-based precautions that act as infection control guidelines. Teaching regarding infection control measures is an important intervention for home care nurses to apply. This chapter includes information about infection control that nurses must express to clients and lay caregivers when providing services.

KEY CONCEPT

A thorough understanding of infection control procedures by home care nurses is especially important today because of the increased immunocompromised states and acuity of clients now being treated in the home.

◆ The Infection Cycle

An **infection** has been defined as a disease state that results from the presence of **pathogens**, or disease-producing organisms, in the body (Taylor, Lillis, and LeMone, 1997). Six components make up the **infection cycle** (Fig. 12-1):

- ◆ Infectious agent or pathogen
- ◆ Reservoir
- ◆ Portal of exit
- ◆ Means of transmission
- ◆ Portal of entry
- ◆ Susceptible host

Common pathogens include bacteria, viruses, parasites, and microbes. A **reservoir** is the natural habitat of an organism in which a pathogen grows and multiplies. Examples of reservoirs that hold pathogenic organisms for humans include other

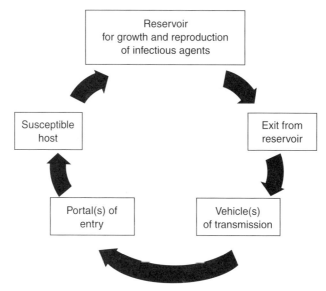

Figure 12-1. The cycle of infection.

humans, animals, contaminated food and water, and soil. The **portal of exit** is the means by which an infectious agent escapes from its reservoir. Common portals of exit for humans include the respiratory, gastrointestinal, and genitourinary tracts, and blood.

The **means of transmission** of an infectious agent to a human being is through direct or indirect contact with a reservoir. Direct contact includes touching, kissing, or sexual contact with an infected person. Indirect contact includes touching contaminated objects, ingesting contaminated water or food, and receiving contaminated blood. **Contamination** refers to an unclean condition where microorganisms are actually or potentially present (Craven & Hirnle, 1996). Infections are also transmitted indirectly through **vectors** (e.g., mosquitoes, lice, and ticks) that carry infections from one host to another. Airborne droplet transmission through coughing and sneezing also carries infections from the reservoir to the host.

Just as an infectious agent must find an exit route from its reservoir, it also must find a **portal of entry** into its new host. For humans, the portals of entry are the same as the exit routes. Once the infectious agent finds its entry route, it attempts to infect a new host, such as a person. The body's **susceptibility**, or degree of resistance, helps to determine whether infection is successfully accomplished. Chronic illness, poor nutrition, psychological stress, fatigue, and medical therapies such as immunosuppressive drugs, chemotherapy, radiation therapy, and steroids, can weaken an individual's immune system. Breaks in skin integrity can also increase susceptibility to infection. Internally placed tubing (e.g., nasogastric tubes), catheters (e.g., urinary, peripheral, or central nervous catheters), and tracheostomies place clients at additional risk, because these invasive treatments compromise natural barriers to infection. If a person's immune system is weakened, or the infectious agent is lethal enough to overcome the body's defenses quickly, the infectious agent accomplishes its mission of infecting a new host. The host in turn becomes its own reservoir, in which the infection multiplies. The cycle continues.

THE CLIENT AS THE SOURCE OF INFECTION

Treatment of infectious disease is often the rationale for the initiation of home care services. Clients may require intravenous antibiotics, dressing changes for infected wounds, or education to help them comply with medical treatment plans designed for infectious diseases. Occasionally, home care clients have undiagnosed infections while they are treated for other conditions. The stress of illness or injury often weakens the immune systems of clients. Symptoms of a client's primary diagnosis may mask an infection that remains undetected and untreated. Home care nurses should be constantly alert to signs of infection in all the clients they see, whether or not an infection has been previously diagnosed (Display 12-1). Individuals with undiagnosed infectious disease processes are more likely to spread infectious agents to friends and family unknowingly.

Home care nurses who have not taken appropriate precautions to prevent exposure to infectious agents may become infected as well. Healthcare professionals occasionally discover through skin tests in employment physicals that they have been exposed to tuberculosis. Pinpointing the source of exposure from within or outside the healthcare system may be almost impossible at that time. The probability is that healthcare professionals have unknowingly cared for clients with tuberculosis, who may still be spreading the disease to others.

Display 12-1:
Signs of Infection

CLASSIC SIGNS

Heat
Redness
Pain
Swelling

OTHER SIGNS/SYMPTOMS

Abnormal drainage
Painful urination
Sore throat
Cough
Aches
Tachycardia
Increased respiration
Diarrhea
Malaise

Psychosocial Considerations

Many clients with infections are adapting to the home care setting after discharge from hospitals. They may be used to clinicians and visitors entering their rooms gowned and masked. Some clients who have been hospitalized for extended periods experience not only the physical pain of their disease processes, but also the stress of alienation and social isolation from other people. Nurses must develop an awareness of these psychosocial issues when formulating plans of care for their clients. Nurses who show acceptance of clients as individuals promote a therapeutic relationship.

Clients with infectious diseases often fear spreading their illnesses to their loved ones. Education from home care nurses regarding appropriate infection control procedures, and the modeling of these techniques, helps to alleviate such anxiety. Most infection control protocols that hospitals and other acute care settings maintain can be less restrictive in the home. Strict isolation procedures in home care are usually unnecessary and impractical; moreover, they cause undue apprehension for clients and their lay caregivers.

Some infectious diseases cause exceptionally stressful responses. Many public misperceptions abound regarding the human immunodeficiency virus (HIV) and acquired immunodeficiency syndrome (AIDS) (see the following discussion). Clients may be unable to distinguish testing positive for HIV and being diagnosed with AIDS.

Home Care Vs. Hospital: *Infection Control*

Issue	Home Care	Hospital
Nosocomial infections	Low-risk, because home care clients are less susceptible to pathogens in their own home.	High-risk owing to large number of personnel giving care to clients.
Supplies	Supplies available inconsistently; nurse must ensure that needed materials are always available.	Nurses have regular access to all necessary supplies.
Environment	Inconsistent, uncontrolled environment.	Controlled environment, cleaned daily by professional housekeepers with commercial disinfectants.
Care providers	Lay caregivers perform clean or sterile procedures with supervision from clinical staff.	Licensed clinical staff perform sterile procedures.
Teaching	Teaching is critical to ensure that lay caregivers and clients maintain appropriate infection control precautions and proper disposal of contaminated medical waste and sharps.	Teaching infection control precautions and disposal of infectious waste are not typically emphasized in discharge instructions.

They may hold the belief that a diagnosis of AIDS means certain death within a short time. Diagnoses including tuberculosis, syphilis, and legionella infections often carry negative connotations with them. A diagnosis of genital herpes for sexually active adults can be emotionally devastating; however, these clients may feel unable to discuss their fears and concerns with anyone. Friends and family may not accept a client's diagnosis with Epstein-Barr viral infection as a legitimate disease. Clients with this diagnosis may feel misunderstood, ashamed, or crazy. Infectious diseases can cause disfiguring skin lesions, debilitating fatigue, and excruciating pain. Thus, many aspects of infectious disease can result in psychosocial stressors. Home care nurses should be alert to potential emotional reactions that clients may have about their diagnoses or symptoms, and incorporate these problems into plans of care.

THE NURSE AS THE SOURCE OF INFECTION

When immunocompromised individuals receive services from healthcare providers who travel from home to home, their risk of infection increases. Nurses and other personnel must recognize that they are likely to be sources of infection for their clients. In fact, home care nurses are probably more responsible for transmitting infections to clients than are inaccurate infection control procedures performed by clients and lay caregivers. Therefore, home care staff should display strict adherence to infection prevention protocols to avoid causing harm to clients.

KEY CONCEPT

Home care clinicians are sources of infection for clients and should strictly follow infection control protocols.

Home care nurses can transmit diseases to clients as carriers of infectious agents from other clients. They also sometimes carry infectious diseases themselves. Often, nurses know they have infectious diseases, but feel the need to report to work to prevent inadequate staffing. This practice can place clients at undue risk. Infectious diseases that are no more than a nuisance to otherwise healthy nurses can be extremely dangerous for clients with compromised immune systems. Employees with viral respiratory infections, influenza, herpetic lesions, and small infected wounds can infect clients through sneezing, coughing, touching during the process of providing care, or by using contaminated equipment. Most home care agencies have policies regarding the provision of services by sick employees. Nurses must follow these policies related to infectious diseases to ensure their personal health and the health of their clients.

◆ Common Infections in Home Care

Some of the most common communicable diseases seen in the home setting include tuberculosis, scabies, pediculosis, streptococcal pharyngitis, impetigo, and bacterial enteric infections. Tuberculosis, HIV/AIDS, and hepatitis are three infectious diseases that are of particular concern in the home care industry today. The incidence of each of these diseases is rising. Many individuals with these diseases are asymptomatic, particularly early in the disease process; therefore, they often remain undiagnosed for extended periods of time. Each illness is difficult to treat and often results in premature death. Home care providers should be aware of high-risk groups for these illnesses, early signs and symptoms, and precautions to take when treating those afflicted with these conditions.

TUBERCULOSIS

Tuberculosis is a highly communicable disease, and its appearance is increasing at alarming levels. "After a decades-long decrease in the number of TB cases reported in the United States, TB has reemerged as a serious national problem" (CDC, 1994, p.1). The bacteria that cause this infectious disease are classified as *tubercle bacillus*. High-risk groups for tuberculosis infection include people infected with HIV, foreign-born individuals, low-income populations, alcoholics, intravenous drug users, and residents in congregate care facilities. Symptoms can be indistinct, leading to delayed diagnosis. Home care nurses should suspect tuberculosis when clients report the following: night sweats, chronic chest pain, dyspnea, low-grade fever, malaise, progressive cough, and mucopurulent sputum. Nurses should test clients for tuberculosis when they exhibit these symptoms, particularly if they are members of a high-risk group. If clients are coughing, home care nurses should wear masks when treating

Survival Alert:
Conditions that Increase the Risk of Tuberculosis

- HIV infection
- Substance abuse (especially drug injection)
- Recent infection with *M. tuberculosis*
- Chest radiograph findings suggestive of previous TB (in a person inadequately treated)
- Diabetes mellitus
- Silicosis
- Low body weight (10% or more below the ideal)
- Cancer of the head and neck
- Hematologic and reticuloendothelial diseases
- End-stage renal disease
- Intestinal bypass or gastrectomy
- Chronic malabsorption syndromes
- Prolonged corticosteroid therapy
- Other immunosuppressive therapy

(Centers for Disease Control and Prevention. [1994]. Core curriculum on tuberculosis: What the clinician should know *(3rd ed.). Atlanta, GA: U.S. Department of Health & Human Services.)*

them until they can rule tuberculosis out as the cause of illness. If clients are found to be positive, they should be immediately isolated and treated. Infectiousness declines rapidly after effective treatment is initiated (CDC, 1994).

HIV AND AIDS

Infection with **human immunodeficiency virus (HIV)** can lead to the development of **acquired immune deficiency syndrome (AIDS)**. The severely compromised immune status of those infected with HIV characteristically leads to unusual opportunistic infections, malignancies, neurologic disorders, and wasting syndrome, among other conditions. Frequently, home care clients diagnosed with AIDS are receiving invasive medical treatment modalities, such as infusion therapy and inhalation therapy. These procedures pose a high risk of contracting life-threatening infections for these clients. Moreover, home care nurses are at increased risk of exposure to HIV as well.

The development of new treatment options has allowed healthcare professionals to view AIDS as a chronic condition instead of an imminently terminal disease. Although effective treatment has prolonged the life spans of those with AIDS, it is still considered a life-threatening disease. The disease process of AIDS results in a severely immunocompromised condition characterized by malignancies, unusual infectious diseases, wasting syndrome, and neurological disorders.

Exposure to infected blood, semen, vaginal secretions, or breast milk can cause transmission of HIV. The high-risk groups for HIV infection in this country are injecting drug users, homosexual and bisexual men, heterosexual partners of infected persons, and recipients of transfused blood and/or blood components. Home care nurses are primarily exposed to HIV through needle sticks (see below for further discussion). Nurses must take every precaution established within the policies of their home care agencies to avoid this occurrence.

Contact with other bodily fluids can also expose nurses to HIV. Home care nurses must practice standard precautions and transmission-based precautions consistently (see below). Nurses with any type of minor cut, abrasion, or inflammation of the hands should wear gloves while providing care to clients. Blood and body fluid spills are to be promptly cleaned with appropriate disinfectants.

HEPATITIS

Hepatitis is an inflammatory disease process of the liver caused by alcohol abuse or infectious agents (e.g., Hepatitis A, Hepatitis B). Hepatitis A is normally contracted through fecal-oral contact or exposure to blood or body fluids. Hepatitis B is usually contracted through blood contact. Individuals with hepatitis are frequently asymptomatic. Healthcare workers die every year from infection with Hepatitis B. Vaccines for this disease are available and are recommended to healthcare providers who are regularly exposed to blood. Home care nurses typically fit into this category; therefore, they should be appropriately protected with the vaccine.

KEY CONCEPT

Tuberculosis, HIV, and hepatitis are particular concerns for the home care industry today, because of their increasing incidence among client populations, delayed diagnoses, and the seriousness of these diseases.

◆ Reporting Infectious Diseases

Laws require home care agencies to report specified diseases to appropriate agencies. These agencies are responsible for identifying potential outbreaks of dangerous communicable diseases and for acting in the public's best interest to contain the spread of disease. Laws and regulations vary widely from state to state. Nurses should always report newly diagnosed infections in home care clients to their supervisors. Clinical managers within home care organizations should be knowledgeable of necessary reporting requirements. Agencies should also take the initiative to provide important verbal and written communication to appropriate parties. Home care nurses must develop an awareness of the infectious organisms plaguing their clients to ensure that appropriate reporting to home care agencies takes place.

Maintaining records of infections commonly found in the client populations of home care agencies can result in the discovery of practice patterns that are contributing to client infections. Nurses should be alert to new signs and symptoms of infection in clients whom they have not diagnosed. If they detect infections in clients, nurses must prioritize communicating abnormal findings to physicians so that they can initiate appropriate treatment. If they detect infection with an organism through a culture, nurses should provide appropriate follow-up to ensure that the organism is sensitive to the prescribed antibiotic therapy.

◆ CDC Guidelines

The **Centers for Disease Control (CDC)** is a federally funded program whose tasks are to study infectious diseases, make recommendations for their treatment,

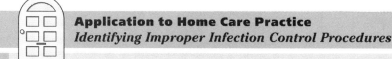

Application to Home Care Practice
Identifying Improper Infection Control Procedures

The Kennedy Home Care Agency determines that an abnormal number of *Pseudomonas* infections are occurring in the wounds of their clients. Through quality improvement efforts, the agency determines that one of their employees is spreading the infection through improper handwashing techniques. Follow-up activities, such as educating the employee, are initiated to prevent further spread of the infectious disease.

and publish guidelines for their prevention. The CDC conducts research studies on infectious diseases and publishes statistics in its **Morbidity and Mortality Weekly Report.** The CDC revised its recommendations for healthcare professionals in 1996. It has divided infections commonly found in healthcare and transmissible between clinicians and clients into two groups. Category I infections can be transmitted to or from clients and clinicians. Category II infections are primarily transmitted from infected clients to healthcare workers (Craven & Hirnle, 1996). The CDC recommends that **Standard Precautions** be used in the care of *all* clients, despite their diagnoses (Display 12-2). **Transmission-Based Precautions** are recommended in addition to Standard Precautions for clients diagnosed with diseases that can be transmitted by airborne, droplet, or contact routes. These standards were

---

Display 12-2:
Summary of Recommended Practices for Standard Precautions

STANDARD PRECAUTIONS

* Wash hands after touching blood, body fluids, secretions, excretions, and contaminated items, regardless of whether gloves are worn. Wash hands immediately after gloves are removed, between patient contacts, and whenever indicated to prevent transfer of microorganisms to other patients or environments. Use plain soap for routine handwashing and an antimicrobial or waterless antiseptic agent for specific circumstances.
* Wear clean non-sterile gloves when touching blood, body fluids, excretions or secretions, contaminated items, mucous membranes, and nonintact skin. Change gloves between tasks on the same patient as necessary and remove gloves promptly after use.
* Wear mask, eye protection, or face shield during procedures and care activities that are likely to generate splashes or sprays of blood or body fluids. Use gown to protect skin and prevent soiling of clothing.
* Ensure that used patient-care equipment that is soiled with blood or identified body fluids, secretions, and excretions is handled carefully to prevent transfer of microorganisms, or cleaned, and appropriately reprocessed if used for another patient.
* Use adequate environmental controls to ensure that routine care, cleaning, and disinfection procedures are followed.
* Handle, transport, and process linen soiled with blood and body fluids, excretions, and secretions in a manner that prevents skin and mucous membrane exposures, contamination of clothing, and transfer of microorganisms.
* Use previously identified techniques and equipment to prevent injuries when using needles, sharps, and scalpels, and place these items in appropriate puncture-resistant containers after use.

(Centers for Disease Control [1996]. Guidelines for isolation precautions in hospitals. Part II: Recommendations for isolation precautions in hospitals. American Journal of Infection Control, 24(1), 32–52.)

Display 12-3:
Summary of Recommended Practices for
Transmission-Based Precautions

TRANSMISSION-BASED PRECAUTIONS

The following precautions are recommended in addition to Standard Precautions:

Airborne Precautions

* Place patient in private room that has monitored negative air pressure in relation to surrounding areas, 6 to 12 air changes per hour, and appropriate discharge of air outside or monitored filtration if air is recirculated. Keep door closed and patient in room.
* Use respiratory protection when entering room of patient with known or suspected tuberculosis. If patient has known or suspected rubeola (measles) or varicella (chicken pox), respiratory protection should be worn unless person entering room is immune to these diseases.
* Transport patient out of room only when necessary and place a surgical mask on the patient if possible.
* Consult CDC Guidelines for additional prevention strategies for tuberculosis.

Droplet Precautions

* Use a private room, if available. Door may remain open.
* Wear a mask when working within 3 feet of patient.
* Transport patient out of room only when necessary and place a surgical mask on the patient if possible.

Contact Precautions

* Place the patient in a private room if available.
* Change gloves after having contact with infective material. Remove gloves before leaving the patient environment, and wash hands with an antimicrobial or waterless antiseptic agent.
* Wear a gown if contact with infectious agent is likely or patient has diarrhea, an ileostomy, colostomy, or wound drainage not contained by a dressing.
* Limit movement of the patient out of the room.
* When possible, dedicate the use of non-critical patient-care equipment to a single patient to avoid sharing equipment.

(Centers for Disease Control. [1996]. Guidelines for isolation precautions in hospitals. Part II: Recommendations for isolation precautions in hospitals. American Journal of Infection Control, *24[1], 32–52.)*

developed for hospitals but can be used in the home care environment as well (Display 12-3) (CDC, 1996).

◆ Infection Control Strategies

Some clients with infectious diseases being treated at home are unaware of their infections because they are asymptomatic. The advent of AIDS has forced healthcare providers to rethink infection control procedures. Universal precautions were developed in the 1980s out of concerns regarding care for clients with HIV. Revisions to these standards in 1996 further defined precautions that address risks associated with specific client populations. The increasing prevalence of infectious diseases such as tuberculosis and hepatitis presents risks to home care providers. Knowledge of appropriate techniques to prevent transmission will give home care nurses the tools to protect themselves, their families, and their clients. When conducted consistently, infection control procedures protect clients from potentially serious effects of infectious disease. Preventing exposure of clients to infections, cleaning reusable equipment, disposing of infectious waste correctly, using personal protective equipment, and adequate handwashing all interrupt the transmission of infectious agents.

HANDWASHING

Home care nurses are accountable for taking appropriate steps to prevent the spread of infection to protect the health of their clients. One simple procedure is the most effective preventive act that nurses can perform, yet they frequently neglect it: *handwashing* (Fig. 12-2). Handwashing has been recognized for more than a century as the *single most important strategy* to prevent the spread of infection by contact

Survival Alert:
Handwashing in the Client's Home

Often facilities for handwashing in the homes of clients are poor. Sinks and towels may be dirty. Soap may be unavailable. Some homes do not have running water. Home care nurses should always carry the following:

◆ Bactericidal soap in a plastic container and paper towels in a plastic bag to use in homes with available running water.
◆ Waterless antiseptic hand cleanser that does not require rinsing in a plastic container to use in homes without running water.

Bactericidal soaps and cleansers can be drying to the skin. Nurses should use lotions or emollients regularly to prevent the drying and cracking of skin on hands, which could provide portals of entry for infectious agents.

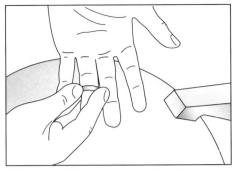

1. Remove all jewelry and dangling bracelets before washing. Bacteria can be hidden in these items.

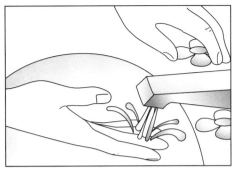

2. Adjust water temperature and keep it running while washing and drying hands.

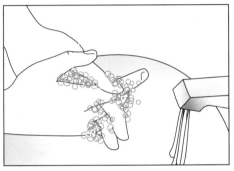

3. Wash your hands with bactericidal, fungi-cidal soap and water for at least 3 minutes. Be sure to scrub all surfaces of your hands starting from fingernails to wrists.

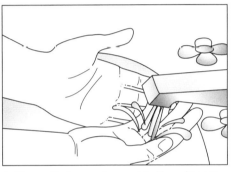

4. Rinse off all soap thoroughly. Keep fingers up higher than wrists to allow water to drain away from cleanest area of fingertips.

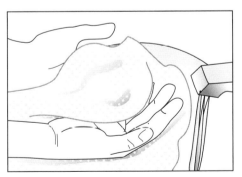

5. Dry hands completely with clean, dry paper towel.

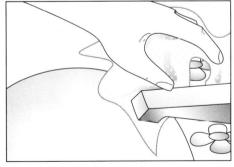

6. Use paper towel to turn off water and dispose of towel.

Figure 12-2. Handwashing technique. (Courtesy of Desert Hospital Home HealthCare)

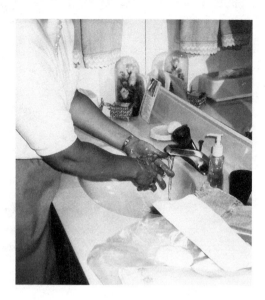

Figure 12-3. The nurse maintains appropriate handwashing to prevent the spread of infectious disease.

transmission. It is the cornerstone of all infection control efforts (Reese & Betts, 1996). Home care nurses must display appropriate handwashing to clients and lay caregivers and instruct them in similar technique. Handwashing instruction reinforces infection control teaching to clients and lay caregivers. Nurses thus display their professionalism and concern for the well-being of clients, and also enhance the home care nursing relationship (Fig. 12-3).

KEY CONCEPT

Handwashing is the most effective preventive act that nurses can perform to prevent the spread of infection.

BAG TECHNIQUE

Appropriate bag technique is a widely used infection control strategy that nurses implement in home care practice (Display 12-4). It helps to control transport of infectious agents from one client's home to another. Nurses designate and maintain "clean" and "dirty" areas of their nursing bags, which contain supplies and equipment that they access regularly. They typically carry these bags into every client's home. Without appropriate precautions, bags can become reservoirs for infectious agents, resulting in the transmission of nosocomial infections to clients.

Nurses should always carry a barrier, such as newspaper, on which to place their bags in a client's home. Nurses should set bags down on the barrier in a clean area of a client's home, far above the ground, if possible, to prevent access to children and pets. Before nurses open their bags, they should wash their hands.

Display 12-4:
Bag Technique

1. Place a newspaper or other barrier on a clean surface above the floor.
2. Place the nursing bag on the barrier.
3. Wash hands.
4. Remove only the items needed for the home visit.
5. When a visit is completed, clean reusable equipment and wash hands before returning items to the bag.
6. Do not return any unused disposable items to the nursing bag.
7. Close the bag.

They should then remove the items they will need during the visit and place them on a clean surface. They should clean reusable equipment, such as blood pressure cuffs or stethoscopes, before returning them to the nursing bag. These precautions keep materials inside the bag clean and help to prevent the inadvertent exposure of infectious agents to clients.

GLOVES, MASKS, GOGGLES, AND GOWNS

OHSA (1992) requires healthcare organizations to give employees **personal protective equipment (PPE)**, including gloves, masks, goggles, and gowns. Gloves do not preclude the need for handwashing before or after contact with clients. Nurses should use gloves once and then throw them away. For healthcare workers sensitive to latex, home care agencies should provide other types of gloves that are available for use.

Nurses should maintain an adequate supply of PPE at all times. Each piece of PPE should be immediately available to nurses working in homes, even when they do not anticipate the need for transmission-based precautions. Home care nurses must be able to respond quickly when needed. If supplies are not readily available, nurses may be unable to address urgent situations correctly and potentially may be exposed to pathogens.

PREVENTION OF NEEDLESTICKS

Nurses must take great caution when working with any sharps. Healthcare professionals are most commonly exposed to potentially serious bloodborne diseases (e.g., hepatitis, HIV) through needlestick injuries. Almost 40% of all needlestick injuries result from recapping needles after their contact with blood from a client (e.g., after an injection, drawing blood, or starting an intravenous line) (Craven & Hirnle, 1996). Nurses should carry puncture-proof plastic sharps disposal units always. They must never recap needles, but instead place them *immediately* after use into a puncture-resistant container. Anytime they use sharps in clinical procedures, nurses should place the sharps container in the immediate vicinity to allow for prompt disposal.

The sharps container can never become more than two-thirds full before replacement, and nurses should never stick their hands beyond the rim of a sharps container. If needle sticks occur, nurses should report them immediately to supervisors for appropriate follow-up procedures. Some healthcare organizations have adopted needleless systems or needle-housing systems to decrease the opportunity for needlesticks.

◆ Client and Lay Caregiver Education

Client and lay caregiver education is an important intervention performed by home care nurses that effectively prevents the spread of communicable diseases. Nurses usually include teaching of infection control principles within the plans of care for most home care clients (Displays 12-5 and 12-6). Reinforcement of these instructions as part of discharge planning helps to ensure compliance with these principles after home care is no longer necessary. Education should include concepts related to the transmission of infectious disease. Individuals often find it difficult to appreciate the nature of contamination, because pathogens are invisible to the human eye. Nurses should teach clients and their lay caregivers to develop a mental awareness or mental picture of the presence of microorganisms. They should be able to "see" places in the environment where infectious agents may exist and recognize ways these agents may be inadvertently transported to other locations. This awareness can help clients to identify opportunities to break the chain of infection.

PROTECTIVE INSTRUCTIONS FOR LAY CAREGIVERS

Home care nurses should teach standard precautions and transmission-based precautions to all lay caregivers of clients with infectious diseases. Typically, PPE primarily consists of gloves in home care; however, masks and gowns are occasionally necessary as well. Lay caregivers must understand the need to wear gloves if the possibility of contact with blood or body substances exists. Individuals may be tempted to use

---

Display 12-5:
Infection Control Teaching Plan for Clients and Lay Caregivers

- ◆ Appropriate handwashing technique
- ◆ Standard and transmission-based precautions
- ◆ Personal hygiene
- ◆ Concept of mode of transmission
- ◆ Laundering contaminated clothing and linens
- ◆ Washing and storage of dishes, utensils, personal care items
- ◆ Disinfecting contaminated surfaces and items
- ◆ Use of personal protective equipment
- ◆ Trash disposal
- ◆ Sharps disposal

Display 12-6:

Sample Agency Infection Prevention Guidelines for Clients and Lay Caregivers

SELECTION OF YOUR WORK AREA

You will need to select a specific section in one room of your home as your "supply area." It must be clean, well lit, quiet, free from dust and other activities, and not easily accessible to small children or animals.

CLEAN VERSUS STERILE

A "clean" area is one in which the area is clean and relatively free of germs. This is achieved by keeping your supplies in a dust-free, low-traffic area and by always washing your hands before handling any of the supplies.

A "sterile" area is one that is totally free of germs. When injecting or infusing a drug into the body, the medication and anything it touches on its way into your body must be kept sterile. Consequently, you must use the sterile technique taught by your nurse to prevent an infection.

DISPOSAL OF SUPPLIES: SHARPS CONTAINERS

Immediately after each use, it is important to place used needles, syringes, tubings, and empty vials of medication into the *sharps container*. Cap the sharps container when it is 2/3 full. Your nurse will gladly remove the container and replace it for you if you notify him or her when the container is ready. *Never throw the container into the trash. This could cause injury or spread disease to other people.*

If the nurse is no longer providing home health service to you and you continue to need a sharps container for your sharps in the home, you may take the full container to a local biohazard site disposal.

DISPOSAL OF SUPPLIES: SOILED DRESSINGS

Discard all soiled or used bandages, dressings, tubing, gloves, and other disposable items in a securely fastened plastic bag and place the bag in your trash container. If you should spill any blood or body fluids, immediately clean or wipe fluid and wash clothing in a 1 : 10 solution of bleach (this may cause discoloring of your clothing). Discard any other disposable items in a plastic bag, securely fasten, and dispose in your trash container.

(Courtesy of Desert Hospital Home Healthcare.)

---

gloves more than once to save money. Nurses should caution lay caregivers against this unsanitary practice and ensure that an adequate supply of gloves is available in a client's home. Even when gloves are worn, lay caregivers should carefully wash their hands. Nurses must stress this important concept to lay caregivers, who may be unaware of this requirement.

Survival Alert:
Reinforcing Handwashing for
Clients and Lay Caregivers

Home care nurses can help clients and lay caregivers to remember to
wash their hands by placing "reminder notes" in critical locations, e.g., by
wound care supplies, in the bathroom, and in the kitchen.

KEY CONCEPT

Client and lay caregiver education is an important practice of home care
nurses that effectively helps to prevent the spread of communicable dis-
eases.

Handwashing Instructions

Appropriate handwashing instructions should be part of every teaching plan for
clients and their lay caregivers. Communication of mode of transmission concepts
helps individuals to recognize indications for handwashing. Nurses should not assume that clients know how to wash their hands properly. They should explain
appropriate technique and remind clients and lay caregivers to make frequent handwashing a habit. They should encourage the use of antibacterial soap and clean
towels. If lay caregivers use gloves during care, nurses should educate them on the
need to wash their hands before and after using gloves. As lay caregivers demonstrate
appropriate decision making regarding handwashing while providing care to clients,
nurses should encourage them with positive reinforcement.

Laundering

Nurses need to include appropriate laundering techniques in teaching plans for
clients with infectious diseases. Generally, soiled laundry should be handled minimally and washed as quickly as possible. Nurses should instruct lay caregivers to
wear gloves when handling linens soiled with blood or body fluids. Soiled laundry
of clients should remain separate from the laundry of others in the household and
stored in a closed plastic bag until it can be washed. Hot water, one cup of bleach,
and strong detergent should be used in the washing machine. The wash cycle
should last a minimum of thirty minutes. Depending upon the extent of soiling and
contamination, home care nurses may recommend two laundry cycles. Linens and
clothing should then be placed in a hot dryer until completely dried. If a dryer is
unavailable, clothing should be dried in the sun.

Personal Items

Other household members should not use the personal items of clients with infectious
diseases, such as toothbrushes, hairbrushes, and razors. These items should be kept
separate. Dishes and utensils should be washed separately, in a dishwasher if possible,

and dried in the hot cycle. If a dishwasher is unavailable, the client's dishes should be washed separately in hot soapy water. The sink should be disinfected after use. Toys of pediatric clients should be kept separate from those of siblings or other children in the home. Nurses should encourage lay caregivers to clean personal items and surfaces in the rooms of home care clients frequently with soap, water, and disinfectant. Trash cans, bathrooms, bedpans, commodes, and other **durable medical equipment** (DME) should be disinfected regularly. The client's environment should be kept clean and neat with adequate supplies and circulation. Clients with infectious diseases should not prepare food, particularly for other household members.

Cleaning/Disinfecting/Sterilizing

Cleaning involves the physical removal of visible dirt or potentially contaminated material. Items are washed, dusted, or mopped. Soap or detergent and water may be used in cleaning. Cleaning must occur before items or surfaces can be disinfected or sterilized. **Disinfecting** is a process by which the presence of pathogens is reduced through chemical or physical means. Chemical disinfectants used most often in home care include isopropyl alcohol and bleach. Ten percent bleach solution is an appropriate disinfectant that can be used for many purposes; however, bleach is known to be caustic to metal. **Sterilization** is the complete elimination of all microorganisms. Sterile supplies and equipment are occasionally necessary in home care. Although nurses should use sterile technique when performing clinical procedures, clients and their lay caregivers can generally learn clean technique. Individuals are less susceptible to infection from pathogens in their own homes. Education regarding sterile vs. clean technique depends upon a client's condition, the abilities of clients or lay caregivers to learn, and the cleanliness of the home (Display 12-7).

Display 12-7:
Sterile Technique

- Bottles of sterile irrigation solution should be discarded every 24 hours.
- The nurse should check the integrity and expiration date of a sterile package before using.
- Moisture on a sterile field may indicate contamination.
- The nurse should never leave a sterile field.
- If the sterility of a field or a piece of equipment is questionable, the nurse should consider the object unsterile.
- The nurse should avoid sneezing, coughing, and unnecessary talking or air currents when working in a sterile field.
- The nurse should gather all supplies and prepare sterile fields in advance.
- Never reach across a sterile field.

(Craven, R. F., & Hirnle, C. J. [1996]. Fundamentals of nursing: Human health and function *[2nd ed.]. Philadelphia: Lippincott-Raven.)*

Trash Disposal

Some communities have laws regarding the proper disposal of known infectious waste. In many areas, these laws apply only to healthcare professionals disposing of medical waste. Home care nurses should educate clients and lay caregivers regarding the appropriate disposal of trash. Contaminated trash and supplies should be placed in a waterproof, plastic bag and disinfected with 10% bleach solution, tightly sealed, and then double-bagged (Figure 12-4). Sharps containers should never be placed in the regular trash disposal system. These containers should be returned to a pharmacy, hospital, or home care agency for proper processing and medical waste disposal. Laws and regulations change constantly regarding the disposal of medical waste. Home care agencies are responsible for compliance with current laws and should integrate these laws into their procedures. Nurses must become familiar with the trash disposal policies of their agencies.

Personal Hygiene

Clients and lay caregivers should maintain good personal hygiene. Keeping skin clean and dry helps to maintain its integrity. Regular oral hygiene maintains the integrity of the mouth's mucus membranes. Intact skin and mucus membranes provide the first line of defense against invasion from microorganisms. Nurses should teach clients and lay caregivers the importance of handwashing after using the bathroom and before any type of food preparation. Clients should be careful to cover their mouths when sneezing or coughing and to wash their hands afterward with soap and water. Appropriate care of fingernails and toenails can be very important for maintaining skin integrity and preventing a variety of skin infections. In general,

Figure 12-4. The nurse displays proper double bagging for disposal of infectious materials.

Ms. Campbell is a 41-year-old client diagnosed with AIDS. She has a history of IV drug use, which is the suspected source of her infection. Ms. Campbell receives antivirals intravenously. Evan is Ms. Campbell's home care nurse and has performed home visits for 3 weeks. The client has learned to self-administer her medications, and Evan now performs twice-a-week visits to monitor her disease process and draw labs. Evan has noted that the sharps container is not filling up as it should, based upon the number of infusions Ms. Campbell self-administers.

1. Explain the potential infection control concerns that could be responsible for the observations in this situation.
2. What questions might Evan ask Ms. Campbell to learn what is happening?
3. Elaborate a course of action that Evan should take if Ms. Campbell denies a problem.
4. Identify any potential risks posed to the public in this scenario. Assess Evan's responsibility to protect the public as well.

maintaining good personal hygiene is important for the psychological and physical well-being of clients and those who care for them.

◆ Documentation

Home care nurses must document all client and lay caregiver education they provide regarding infection control measures and the proper disposal of infectious waste. Documentation is particularly important for clients who have communicable dis-

Figure 12-5. The nurse reviews notes and documents to ensure that she has covered appropriate infection control measures with her clients.

eases, compromised immune systems, or medical treatments that involve the disposal of infectious waste. Nurses should also document any materials left in homes for maintaining appropriate infection control or waste disposal (e.g., a puncture-resistant container for the disposal of sharps). Documentation should note that nurses instructed clients and lay caregivers regarding safe disposal of sharps and how to dispose of containers when full (Figure 12-5).

Home care organizations may have printed teaching materials regarding infection control procedures for clients. Nurses should document the provision and review of these teaching materials. Documentation should also include responses from clients and lay caregivers to teaching, and their level of compliance in adequately performing necessary infection control procedures.

◆ Summary

Maintaining appropriate infection control techniques is a significant way for home care nurses to maximize the health and well-being of their clients. Understanding the mode of infection transmission, comprehending standard and transmission-based precautions, providing client and lay caregiver education, modeling appropriate infection control behaviors, assessing for and reporting infections, and performing follow-up as needed constitutes responsible professional behavior by home care nurses.

References and Bibliography

Bennett, G. (1994). Developing an effective infection control program for home care. *Caring, 13*(11), 50–53.

Bennis, S. & Davis, S. (1994). An effective approach to treating decubitus ulcers in home healthcare patients. *Home Healthcare Nurse, 12*(1), 47–52.

Boutotte, J. Protecting yourself against T.B. *Nursing, 23*(10), 64–66.

Centers for Disease Control and Prevention. (1994). *Core curriculum on tuberculosis: What every clinician should know* (3rd ed.). Atlanta: U.S. Department of Health and Human Services.

Craven, R.F. & Hirnle, C.J. (1996). *Fundamentals of nursing: Human health and function* (2nd ed.). Philadelphia: Lippincott-Raven.

Eggleston, B. (1994). Infection control update. *Nursing, 24*(3), 70–72.Free, K. W. Infection control and safety: Client education in the home. *Home Healthcare Nurse, 14*(12), 957–959.

Fraser, D. (1993). Patient assessment: Infection in the elderly. *Journal of Gerontological Nursing, 19*(7), 5–11.

Free, K.W. Infection control and safety: Client education in the home. *Home Healthcare Nurse, 14*(12), 957–959.

Friedman, M.M. (1997). Joint Commission on Accreditation of Healthcare Organizations' infection control requirements: Fact or fiction? *Home Healthcare Nurse, 15*(4), 236–238.

Gurevich, I. (1994). Preventing needlesticks. *RN, 57*(11), 44–51.

Korniewicz, D. & Garzon, L. (1994). How to choose and use gloves. *Nursing, 24*(9), 18.

Miller, C. (1995). *Nursing care of older adults* (2nd ed). Philadelphia: J.B. Lippincott.

Reese, R. & Betts, (1996). *A practical approach to infectious diseases* (4th ed.). Philadelphia: Lippincott-Raven.

Reiss, P. (1996). Battling the super bugs. *RN*, *59*(3), 36–40.
Sheldon, J. (1994). 25 tips on handwashing. *Nursing*, *24*(1), 20.
Taylor, C., Lillis, C. & LeMone, P. (1997). *Fundamentals of nursing: The art and science of nursing care* (3rd ed.). Philadelphia: Lippincott-Raven.
Walker, M. & Frank, L. (1995). HIV/AIDS: An imperative for a new paradigm for caring. *Nursing and Health Care Perspectives on Community*, *16*(6), 311–315.

POST TEST

1. Explain the increasing importance of maintaining appropriate infection control procedures in today's home care practice.

2. Describe the process for the transmission of communicable diseases.

3. Home care nurses should initiate strict isolation for immunocompromised clients.

   _____True   _____False

4. Discuss reasons why nurses must report newly discovered client infections to home care agencies.

5. Wearing gloves is the single most important strategy for preventing the spread of infection by contact transmission.

   _____True   _____False

6. Name the components of infection prevention.

THINKING CRITICALLY IN HOME CARE

1. Lucy Parsons is a 41-year-old woman diagnosed with breast cancer. She has recently completed a course of chemotherapy through a new central venous catheter. During a recent home care visit, Lucy had a temperature of 101.4°F. The nurse identified signs of an incisional infection at the surgical site.

   A. List additional assessment data the nurse should collect.

   B. Explain appropriate follow-up actions for the nurse to take.

   C. Describe Lucy's learning needs as they relate to infection control.

2. Fred Connors has just joined a new home care agency. He has recently observed one of the other nurses failing to maintain appropriate infection control procedures.

   A. Assess how Fred should handle this situation.

   B. Discuss potential consequences if Fred fails to address this problem.

UNIT 4

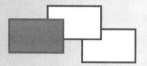

Home Care Practice

13

The Initial Home Care Visit

LEARNING OBJECTIVES

After completing this chapter, the reader will be able to:

◆ Explain the importance of the initial home care visit.

◆ List the required steps to take before making the first client contact.

◆ Discuss how to conduct the interview during the initial assessment.

◆ Identify the major components of an initial assessment.

◆ Consider specific issues related to the physical and environmental home care assessment.

◆ Evaluate nutritional considerations and their impact on home care services.

◆ Discuss ways to involve clients in planning care.

KEY TERMS

Advocacy	Mirroring
Assessment documentation tool	Name badge
Closed questions	Nonverbal communication
Cognitive interventions	Open-ended questions
The Health Belief Model	Psychosocial interventions
Interview	Technical interventions

The *initial* home care visit is the most significant meeting between clients and nurses. This contact introduces clients to the unique aspects of home care and creates a first impression that is likely to influence the quality of all subsequent services. Frequently, clients and their lay caregivers experience high levels of anxiety during the initial home care visit. Clients are usually the most ill and medically unstable at the beginning of home care services. Additionally, many clients have never received healthcare services in the home before; therefore, they are uncertain of what to expect. Nurses must remember that clients are allowing strangers to enter their homes to provide healthcare services. Clients and other members of their households are often unsure of the nurse's qualifications and of the reputation of the home care agency. Consequently, a nurse's ability to establish trust is pivotal at the beginning of the treatment period.

During the initial visit, nurses must build a solid foundation for a therapeutic relationship to be developed with clients and their lay caregivers. This chapter reviews the regulatory requirements that must be met within the initial home care visit. Preparation by nurses eases a successful and efficient initial home care visit; a discussion of appropriate preparation techniques is provided. The initial home care assessment must be comprehensive, consisting of several distinct components. This chapter examines each of these components thoroughly. This chapter also includes a discussion of the care planning process and ways in which home care nurses can involve clients in the development of goals. Interventions to assist clients in achieving these goals are covered as well.

KEY CONCEPT

During the initial home care visit, nurses need to establish a therapeutic relationship with clients and lay caregivers. Development of this relationship is essential for nurses to maximize the effectiveness of their care.

◆ Regulatory Requirements

Nurses must meet certain regulatory requirements within the initial assessment visit. Before beginning the visit, nurses must inform clients orally and in writing of their rights and responsibilities. Nurses conduct a comprehensive evaluation of a client's history, psychosocial condition, emotional status, functional abilities, support systems, environment, medications, equipment, and other factors influencing health and well-being to develop an effective plan of care. At times, nurses performing initial visits feel like detectives, compiling pieces of evidence from multiple sources to pull together a thorough analysis of a client's overall needs. Documentation requirements for the initial assessment are extensive: plans of care must be established; physician orders must be compiled and summarized in medical treatment plans; assessment data must be evaluated; and pertinent medical history must be obtained.

- ◆ Completely review the referral information regarding the client's status and initial physician orders.
- ◆ Phone the client.
  - ◆ Clarify that you are speaking to the right party.
  - ◆ Provide a full introduction, including your full name, the name of the home care agency, your professional status, and the purpose of the call (to schedule an initial client visit).
  - ◆ Inform the client of how the home care agency obtained the referral, the physician who prescribed the assessment visit, and the approximate length of the visit.
  - ◆ Request permission to schedule a visit.
  - ◆ Establish a mutually convenient time for the initial visit.
  - ◆ Verify the client's address.
  - ◆ Obtain specific directions to the client's home.
  - ◆ Ask about equipment or supplies that are needed to perform the initial visit.
- ◆ Collect necessary documentation tools to complete the initial visit.
- ◆ Gather medical supplies or equipment that will be needed during the initial visit.
- ◆ Verify directions as needed with a map.

◆ Preparation

When they prepare to perform initial home visits (Display 13-1), nurses must allow an adequate period to conduct the full assessment of new clients. Nurses must be careful to schedule any necessary visits to other clients accordingly to eliminate pressure and haste during their first visit to a new client's home. Generally, a home care nurse will receive some advance referral information regarding a client's status and orders from a physician. The extent of this information varies a great deal and depends on the reliability of the referral source and the willingness of a physician's staff to share detailed information.

REFERRAL INFORMATION

A complete referral includes recent laboratory studies, medical history, surgical reports, a hospital discharge summary, current diagnoses with dates of onset, pertinent hospital progress reports from nursing or ancillary services, emergency contacts, dates of last hospitalization, current medications, and physician orders for the first home care visit. Nurses carefully review all available referral information before scheduling initial visits. This information often provides clues to help nurses formulate pertinent questions. After reviewing this information, nurses are better able to decide whether they must visit clients at specific times (e.g., for a diabetic client who needs insulin injections) or whether they need certain supplies during a visit (e.g., for a client requiring wound care).

KEY CONCEPT

Nurses carefully review all available referral information before scheduling initial home care visits.

THE INTRODUCTORY PHONE CALL

When nurses phone clients to schedule initial home care visits, they provide clients with a full introduction. Nurses clarify that they are speaking to the appropriate person. They give their full names, the names of the agencies they work for, their professional status (e.g., registered nurse), and the purpose of the call (to schedule the initial client visit). Nurses tell clients how the home care agency obtained the referral, identify the physician who ordered the assessment visit, estimate the approximate length of the visit, and briefly overview procedures to be conducted. Nurses request permission to schedule the visit and obtain the input of clients to establish available times. Upon establishing a mutually convenient visit time, nurses ask for specific directions. Nurses also determine at this time whether clients have equipment or supplies in their homes that are necessary to complete the visit. If these supplies are unavailable, nurses obtain them and bring them when they call on clients.

◆ The Visit Begins

The visit itself begins with a knock on a client's door. Nurses greet clients or lay caregivers with warm smiles (Fig. 13-1). They should introduce themselves again,

Figure 13-1. The nurse greets the client with a warm smile. The client responds happily.

repeating their full names and professional status, the names of their home care agencies, and the purpose of the visit. This process reorients clients and lay caregivers to the reason for the visit and helps to set the tone for a professional relationship. Home care nurses wear appropriate identification, such as a **name badge**, to reassure clients that they are allowing authorized persons to enter their homes. During the initial visit, the badge also acts as a helpful reminder of a nurse's name, professional status, and affiliated agency. Nurses remember to ask permission to enter a home to make clients feel comfortable and to stress their respect for property.

KEY CONCEPT

Home care nurses wear appropriate identification, such as a name badge, to reassure clients that authorized persons are entering their homes. During initial visits, the badge also reminds clients of a nurse's name and professional status, as well as the agency's name.

Nurses start by informing clients of their rights and responsibilities (see Chapter 6), providing this information in writing as well. They review the procedures to be conducted during the visit and the expected length of time needed to complete them. Clients are sometimes hesitant to share information if they do not understand its purpose and use. Nurses must ensure that clients comprehend the reasons for the home care nursing visit and how information that is gathered during the assessment process will be used.

The nurse's ability to establish rapport with a client and lay caregivers is crucial at this time. Eye contact, active listening, positive facial expressions, and comfortable body language help nurses to express to clients and lay caregivers that they are nonjudgmental, trustworthy, and professional. The reluctance of nurses to answer questions truthfully and thoroughly can significantly hamper the development of trusting and therapeutic relationships with clients. Thus, nurses should answer any questions that clients or lay caregivers ask as directly and completely as possible.

◆ Assessment

Nurses spend a substantial portion of the initial visit gathering pertinent information to develop plans of care most appropriate to the needs of individual clients. Because of the breadth of information required, the use of a consistent methodology to acquire important facts is helpful to nurses. A systematized approach to performing the client assessment, frequently directed by the **assessment documentation tool**, ensures that they address all necessary components of the initial visit. Although documentation tools for initial assessments vary among home care agencies, most include the following elements: a medical history, a review of body systems, a psychosocial and environmental assessment, a review of prescription and nonprescription drugs, and a review of nutritional factors.

Issue	Home Care	Hospital
Primary objective and function	Establish trust through interpersonal skills and begin to develop a therapeutic relationship with client. Facilitate resolution of immediate safety and medical needs.	Perform a physical assessment and obtain medical history; triage medical and nursing needs, initiate admission MD orders.
Significance to client safety	Client reassessment will potentially not occur for several days. Failure to detect significant clinical findings can negatively impact client's health and safety.	Client will be assessed several times a day by MD and other nurses. If a significant finding is not identified by nurse during initial assessment, it is likely to be identified in subsequent assessments or by physician or other healthcare professionals.
Scope of assessment	Incorporates thorough physical, environmental, psychosocial assessment, evaluation of medication bottles and storage; interview re: client's access to food, prescriptions, and transportation for medical follow-up. Information provided by client is validated through personal observations of client's home and interactions with lay caregivers.	Incorporates thorough physical assessment and review of significant psychosocial issues and current medications. Assessment frequently conducted without lay caregiver present. Controlled safe environment for client.
Reliability of information	Home care nurse receives referral information that is often incomplete and sometimes inaccurate. During assessment, nurse relies heavily on client and lay caregiver for all information. Often receives from client an incomplete medical history. Client has sometimes not been evaluated by a physician for several days	Access to previous medical records within the institution. Recent physician admission assessment and orders based on recent assessment.

The comprehensive assessment is to be conducted in a continuum fashion. The least sensitive questions are asked first, and the least intrusive actions are performed at the beginning. Nurses gradually progress to asking the most personal questions and to performing the most intrusive procedures toward the end of the assessment. For example, the interview usually occurs before the physical assessment. During the interview, nurses first ask questions that are the most comfortable for clients to answer (e.g., about demographic information, medical history, and symptoms) and gradually move toward those questions that clients are likely to view as more personal (e.g., about financial worries, spiritual issues, and sexual concerns). This concept applies to the physical exam as well. Most physical assessments begin with the gathering of vital signs. Clients are then slowly introduced to the hands-on physical examination. By proceeding in this fashion, nurses provide clients and lay caregivers with a sense of familiarity, and develop trust with them.

KEY CONCEPT

The interview and physical assessment questions and procedures should progress from least to most intrusive. By proceeding in this manner, nurses develop trust with clients and lay caregivers.

THE INTERVIEW

The **interview** gives nurses an opportunity to obtain subjective information from clients about medical history, current symptoms, functional limitations, support systems, and psychosocial issues. Nurses must actively listen and pay attention to everything that clients and lay caregivers communicate during the interview. Learning to pay full attention to others as they communicate involves more than just listening to words. Nurses must absorb verbal messages, note gestures and subtle changes in voice inflection or facial expression, and register what clients fail to communicate (Hunt & Zurek, 1997) (Table 13-1).

TABLE 13-1. *Techniques that Facilitate and Block Communication During an Interview*

FACILITATORS OF COMMUNICATION	BARRIERS TO COMMUNICATION
Use broad opening statements	Make stereotyped comments
Give general leads	Give advice or state your opinion
Listen	Agree with the client
Acknowledge the client's feelings	Defend
Use silence	Give approval
Give information	Use reassuring clichés
Reflect or repeat the client's words	Request an explanation
Share observations	Express disapproval
Clarify	Belittle the client's feelings
Summarize	Change the subject
Validate	Disagree with the client
Verbalize implied thoughts or feelings	

(Craven, R. F., & Hirnle, C. J. [1996]. *Fundamentals of nursing* [2nd ed.]. Philadelphia: Lippincott-Raven.)

Nonverbal Communication

Nonverbal communication (including body language, and apparent discomfort with certain subjects) is often as important to a client's condition as what is spoken. Nurses clarify information by **mirroring** back to clients and lay caregivers what they perceive through all of their senses. For example, a nurse should ask a client who becomes fidgety when discussing a visit from a family member whether a problem exists or whether something makes the client anxious about the visit. Mirroring techniques allow nurses to obtain significant information that influences the effectiveness of the home care treatment plan.

KEY CONCEPT

Nurses must actively listen and pay attention to everything that clients and lay caregivers communicate during the interview. Nonverbal communication can be as significant as information that is spoken.

Nurses also display active listening to clients through their nonverbal behavior. Home care nurses are sometimes tempted to document throughout the duration of the interview, because extensive paperwork is needed at the conclusion of the initial visit. If nurses fail to maintain appropriate levels of eye contact, however, clients may perceive a lack of interest or concern. Clients will then be hesitant to respond to interview questions fully. Nurses show care and concern for clients by maintaining appropriate eye contact (Fig. 13-2). Nurses also communicate that they want input from clients through smiling, leaning toward clients, comfortable body gestures, and occasionally nodding after clients respond to questions.

Figure 13-2. During the interview, the nurse strives to maintain eye contact with the client.

TABLE 13-2. *Closed Versus Open-Ended Questions*

CLOSED	OPEN-ENDED
Do you live alone?	What kind of support do you get from friends, family, or others?
Do you have pain at the site of your incision?	What limitations in activity have you had since your surgery? What has caused these limitations?
Do you understand your medications?	How often and why do you take each of these medications?
Are you concerned about your finances?	What, if anything, concerns you about your finances?

Open-Ended Questions

Open-ended questions cannot be answered with a yes or no. Nurses must ask clients open-ended questions as often as possible, because they foster participation from clients in the interview process. These questions also increase awareness of the perceptions of clients regarding their condition and care, and issues affecting care. **Closed questions** (questions that can be answered with a yes or no) should be used to verify factual information only. Inappropriate use of closed questions expresses to clients that nurses want minimal information from them, do not value their perceptions, or find them unimportant (Table 13-2).

Home care nurses should clarify the perspectives of lay caregivers on pertinent issues as well. Occasionally, clients and lay caregivers answer the same question very differently. Nurses who listen for inconsistencies in messages can identify problems faced by clients that require further analysis. Nurses should also restate messages to clarify the information that clients give. For example,

> *Client:* "My daughter doesn't know what kinds of food to fix for this special diet I'm on."
> *Nurse:* "Are you saying that your daughter does not understand how to prepare a low sodium diet for you?"

Objectivity

Nurses must maintain objectivity and appear completely nonjudgmental of clients, lay caregivers, family members, and other healthcare professionals throughout the interview process. Nurses must become consciously aware of their personal prejudices and biases. For example, Phyllis, a home care nurse, has strong personal feelings about marriage, believing that spouses should play supportive and active roles for clients in times of illness. As Phyllis becomes aware of this personal bias, she can actively work to remain nonjudgmental when interviewing clients whose spouses do not wish to actively participate in their care.

PHYSICAL ASSESSMENT

Nurses ask clients where they prefer to have the physical assessment performed. If a lay caregiver is present, a client may wish to have privacy during the exam;

Home Care Conflict:
The Need for Effective Communication

Consider the following dialogue between a home care nurse and a client suffering from a back injury:

Client (angrily): "If I can't lift anything more than 5 pounds, how am I supposed to be able to do my chores? How will I be able to take care of my family?"
Nurse: "Can't you get your wife to help you with the chores?"
Client: "No wife of mine does chores!"

Problem: The nurse prematurely provides a solution to a poorly understood concern. The nurse's assumptions close down open communication. The client becomes wary of sharing his concerns, leading him to respond defensively. The nurse must assess what the client is really communicating. The client may be expressing anger about changes in family roles or concern regarding his ability to financially provide for his family. He may fear the loss of an enjoyable daily routine or of having a sense of purpose in his life.

A more effective response from the nurse is "It must be frustrating to have these new limitations on your activity. You sound like you're worried about how you'll be able to do the things you're used to doing for your family." Through mirroring techniques, restating the client's concerns, and responding objectively and nonjudgmentally, the nurse stimulates further communication with the client. The home care nurse can then evaluate the client's real issues of concern. The nurse displays recognition and acceptance of the client's emotional reactions, which helps to establish a therapeutic relationship and trust.

conversely, the client may feel uncomfortable without the lay caregiver's presence. Nurses request lay caregivers to leave or to remain during the physical exam in accordance with the wishes of clients. Nurses wash their hands before beginning a physical assessment. This necessary infection control procedure prevents the transmission of nosocomial infections to susceptible individuals (see Chapter 12). It also shows professionalism and concern for the well-being of clients.

Data obtained from examining the referral information, conducting the interview, and reviewing medications alert nurses to perform thorough examinations of especially compromised body systems. To demonstrate respect for privacy, nurses obtain permission from clients to conduct each component of the physical assessment, explaining its rationale. As the physical examination progresses, a nurse may observe a scar or auscultate an abnormal heart or lung sound. The nurse uses these findings to initiate further interview questions. Nurses should document brief notes of physical assessment findings and additional subjective data immediately. These notes should be comprehensive enough to adequately remind a nurse of a client's status so that full documentation can be completed after the visit. Failure to do this can result in an inaccurate recollection of information, which can negatively influence care delivery.

KEY CONCEPT

Failure to document physical assessment findings immediately can result in an inaccurate recollection of information, which can negatively affect care delivery.

Assessment of Functional Capacity and Activity Level

Assessing the functional capacity of a home care client is a significant component of the initial assessment. This assessment should include a client's ability to perform all activities of daily living (ADLs), including dressing, bathing, eating, toileting, oral hygiene, and general personal hygiene. A home care nurse must first establish what the client's functional level was before the acute event that led to the necessity for a home care assessment. Some individuals have contraindications that prevent them from conducting ADLs. For example, clients who are diagnosed with thrombophlebitis are ordered to remain on complete bed rest. If clients are unable to perform their own ADLs, nurses must establish whether these clients are receiving adequate assistance in the performance of these functions from lay caregivers, or whether some needs remain unmet.

The home care nursing assessment should also incorporate an assessment of a client's general activity level. Nurses should ask clients how far and how often they walk, what time they rise and dress in the morning, what time they go to sleep, and what other activities or exercises they regularly perform. Physicians prescribe exercise programs for some clients, and instruct other clients to restrict their activities. For example, clients recently discharged from the hospital after total hip replacements receive strict instructions not to flex at the waist more than 90 degrees, and not to cross their ankles or legs. Home care clients who are unaware of and thus do not follow these restrictions may experience joint dislocations. Likewise, clients who have recently undergone coronary artery bypass grafts receive specific activity prescriptions. Failure to follow specific exercise instructions can contribute to deterioration of cardiac status. Overexertion, or performing exercises more often than recommended, can be just as detrimental to a client's health as not being active enough.

ENVIRONMENTAL ASSESSMENT

Nurses must conduct an environmental assessment to determine the appropriate safe provision of home care services. This process also identifies many issues that are to be addressed in plans of care. Nurses perform many components of the environmental assessment during other portions of the initial visit. For example, a nurse treating a client who negotiated steps or used an assistive device to greet the nurse at the door is able to observe the client's gait and ability to safely use assistive equipment. A nurse led to the bathroom to examine a client's medications can determine whether the client is able to function independently in this environment, or whether assistive devices, such as tub handrails, are necessary (Fig. 13-3).

Should nurses not have the opportunity to make such observations during the routine course of the initial visit, they must deliberately gather this information to assess home safety and the appropriateness of the home environment for provision of care. Nurses need to ask clients for permission to look around their homes to identify environmental safety hazards (see Chapter 11). In neighborhoods with high crime rates, clients are to be questioned about safety precautions they have taken (e.g., installing a peephole, or home alarm system).

When factors in a client's environment impede the adequate provision of home care services, a nurse should attempt to rectify the situation. Some examples of measures that nurses take to improve home safety include obtaining appropriate assistive devices, removing throw rugs, providing for appropriate lighting of walkways, and asking lay caregivers to secure doors with locks. Occasionally, nurses conclude that they cannot safely administer services in a home due to environmental issues. For example, home care services are inappropriate for clients who require intravenous antibiotics but do not have adequate refrigeration for storing them. Sometimes, environmental elements present a danger to nurses. Some clients refuse to restrain animals that pose a threat to visitors in the home. Nurses must notify a supervisor of such circumstances. Home care agencies often have policies to guide appropriate measures when such environmental safety issues arise (see Chapter 11).

Figure 13-3. The home care nurse should assess the safety of the client's bathroom to see whether special safety devices are needed.

KEY CONCEPT

Performing an environmental assessment is an important responsibility of the nurse during the initial home care visit. Nurses are responsible for determining the appropriateness of providing healthcare in the home, identifying issues to be addressed within the plan of care, and removing any obstacles to the safe provision of treatment.

REVIEWING MEDICATIONS

Following the interview and the physical assessment, nurses obtain permission to examine the medications of clients. They scrutinize the bottles themselves, if possible. They document the exact prescriptions, dosages, and frequencies immediately. Nurses clarify with clients and lay caregivers that the dosages and frequencies printed on the bottles are consistent with what clients actually take. When looking at bottles, nurses check the dates of issuance, expiration dates, prescribing physicians, and issuing pharmacies. They frequently identify problems through this process.

During the review of medications, a nurse can learn a client's perception of the effects of different medications. Often, clients confuse the purposes of their medications; for example, they may confuse their antibiotics with their pain pills and incorrectly take the wrong medication to treat symptoms. Clients are to be questioned about their knowledge of side effects and the necessary precautions or requirements that accompany some medications—such as taking them with or without food. Nurses also question clients about any over-the-counter medications they

Survival Alert:

Problems to Identify When Reviewing Medications

- Expired drugs
- Drugs with negative interactions
- Two different medications with the same clinical effects
- The same medication prescribed by two different physicians (one may be generic, leading the client to mistakenly believe they are two different medications)
- Multiple pharmacies
- Multiple physicians
- Over-the-counter drugs the physician is unaware that the client uses
- Prescribed medications that the client does not have and reasons (i.e., too expensive, cannot get to pharmacy)
- Client not taking medications as prescribed and reasons (i.e., doesn't understand indications for use, is trying to extend use due to expense)

use (e.g., aspirin, laxatives, ointments, vitamins), and whether they take these medications regularly or on an as-needed basis.

KEY CONCEPT

Home care nurses identify many unresolved issues through careful review of client medications.

After reviewing all prescriptions, nurses clarify again with clients that they have discussed all medications. They ask clients about any old prescriptions kept in the house. Sometimes, clients maintain unused prescriptions in their medicine cabinets for years, "just in case" they ever need them again. A complete review of *all* medications often provides insight into additional diagnoses or clinical problems that are not indicated in the referral information and are not mentioned by clients (Display 13-2). Any of these possible problems are to be verified later with physicians.

REVIEW OF NUTRITIONAL FACTORS IN HOME CARE

Maintaining adequate nutrition and hydration is an important component of a healthy lifestyle. Nutrition issues are particularly important for individuals recovering from disease or injury. An adequate intake of a correct balance of nutrients can help individuals with compromised health status to maintain optimal functioning, and

---

Display 13-2:
Checklist for Reviewing Client Medications

- ◆ Obtain permission to look at the client's medications.
- ◆ Examine the actual bottles, if possible.
- ◆ Immediately document the exact prescription, dosage, and frequency of each medication.
- ◆ Clarify with the client and lay caregivers that dosages and frequencies printed on the bottles are consistent with what the client is actually taking.
- ◆ Check dates of issuance, expiration dates, prescribing physicians, and the pharmacy.
- ◆ Note multiple physicians, multiple pharmacies, expired drugs, drugs that interact, or two medications with the same clinical effects.
- ◆ Identify the client's perceptions of why each medication is taken.
- ◆ Question the client regarding knowledge of medication side effects and necessary precautions.
- ◆ Ask the client about any over-the-counter medications (e.g., aspirin, laxatives, ointments, and vitamins) used and ask how often they are used.
- ◆ Check with the client about any old prescriptions kept in the house.
- ◆ Verify with the client's physician any medications that indicate a diagnosis or problem not identified in the referral information.

can potentially slow the advancement of progressive disease processes. Conversely, inadequate nutritional intake can deplete an individual's strength and endurance, exacerbate a chronic condition, and potentially cause a general deterioration in health status.

Nutrition is an often overlooked aspect of the initial home care assessment, even though it tremendously affects the proper functioning of every body system. To be effective, medical treatments require individuals to have a satisfactory nutritional status. Nutrition impacts muscle strength, overall endurance, and functional capacity. Generalized weakness caused by malnutrition results in an increased likelihood of accidents and injuries. The body's immune system becomes weakened in persons with poor nutritional status, making them susceptible to a variety of diseases. Poorly nourished individuals do not feel "well." If poor nutrition becomes a chronic state for clients, they can become depressed because of ill health and loss of function.

Because of the uncontrolled environment inherent in home care, nurses face special challenges in assessing the nutritional status of clients and intervening to improve dietary problems. Many factors influence an individual's nutritional intake, including cultural practices, emotional connections to certain foods, financial issues, religious beliefs, and social support systems. These influences interfere with the ability of home care nurses to affect the nutritional intake of clients. Yet home care nurses must recognize the importance of assessing these influences and actively intervene to ensure optimal nutritional status (Table 13-3).

K E Y   C O N C E P T

Nutrition is an often overlooked aspect of the initial home care assessment, even though it has a tremendous impact on the proper functioning of every body system.

The Effect of Decreased Functional Capacity on Nutritional Intake

Home care nurses need to assess the functional limits of clients, identifying potential difficulties in accessing food. Clients receiving home care services are often homebound and unable to go to the grocery store by themselves. Family members, neighbors, or friends often purchase food for these clients; however, their support may be sporadic and irregular. Individuals with few social supports may find their ability to obtain food necessary for a healthy diet severely restricted. Some individuals resist asking others for assistance, resulting in decreased access to perishable food items such as fresh fruit, vegetables, and milk. Even those clients who have regular help in obtaining grocery items sometimes experience difficulties in getting the foods that they prefer. If an individual who is shopping for a client does not know the client's food preferences, the individual may purchase food that will not be used because it is not consistent with the client's preferences and habits.

Home care clients frequently have reduced energy, strength, and endurance. At a time when good nutritional intake is of great importance for these individuals,

TABLE 13-3. *Clinical Observations for Nutritional Assessment*

BODY AREA	SIGNS OF GOOD NUTRITIONAL STATUS	SIGNS OF POOR NUTRITIONAL STATUS
General appearance	Alert, responsive	Listless, apathetic, and cachexic
General vitality	Endurance, energetic, sleeps well; vigorous	Easily fatigued, no energy, falls asleep easily, looks tired, apathetic
Weight	Normal for height, age, body build	Overweight or underweight
Hair	Shiny, lustrous, firm, not easily plucked, healthy scalp	Dull and dry, brittle, loss of color, easily plucked, thin and sparse
Face	Uniform skin color; healthy appearance, not swollen	Dark skin over cheeks and under eyes, flaky skin, facial edema (moon face), pale skin color
Eyes	Bright, clear, moist, no sores at corners of eyelids, membranes moist and healthy pink color, no prominent blood vessels	Pale eye membranes, dry eyes (xerophthalmia); Bitot's spots, increased vascularity, cornea soft (keratomalacia), small yellowish lumps around eyes (xanthalasma), dull or scarred cornea
Lips	Good pink color, smooth, moist, not chapped or swollen	Swollen and puffy (chellosis), angular lesion at corners of mouth or fissures or scars (stomatitis)
Tongue	Deep red, surface papillae present	Swollen appearance, beefy red or magenta colored, swollen, papillae, hypertrophy or atrophy
Teeth	Straight, no crowding, no cavities, no pain, bright, no discoloration, well-shaped jaw	Cavities, mottled appearance (fluorosis), malpositioned, missing teeth)
Gums	Firm, good pink color, no swelling or bleeding	Spongy, bleed easily, marginal redness, recessed, swollen and inflamed
Glands	No enlargement of the thyroid, face not swollen	Enlargement of the thyroid (goiter), enlargement of the parotid (swollen cheeks)
Skin	Smooth, good color, slightly moist, no signs of rashes, swelling, or color irregularities	Rough, dry, flaky, swollen, pale, pigmented, lack of fat under the skin, fat deposits around the joints (xanthomas), bruises, petechiae
Nails	Firm, pink	Spoon-shaped (koilonychia), brittle, pale, ridged
Skeleton	Good posture, no malformations	Poor posture, beading of the ribs, bowed legs or knock-knees, prominent scapulas, chest deformity at diaphragm
Muscles	Well-developed, firm, good tone, some fat under the skin	Flaccid, poor tone, wasted, underdeveloped, difficulty walking
Extremities	No tenderness	Weak and tender, presence of edema

(continued)

TABLE 13-3. (CONTINUED)

BODY AREA	SIGNS OF GOOD NUTRITIONAL STATUS	SIGNS OF POOR NUTRITIONAL STATUS
Abdomen	Flat	Swollen
Nervous sytem	Normal reflexes, psychological stability	Decrease in or loss of ankle and knee reflexes, psychomotor changes, mental confusion, depression, sensory loss, motor weakness, loss of sense of position, loss of vibration, burning and tingling of the hands and feet (paresthesia)
Cardiovascular system	Normal heart rate and rhythm, no murmurs, normal blood pressure for age	Cardiac enlargement, tachycardia, elevated blood pressure
GI system	No palpable organs or masses (liver edge may be palpable in children)	Hepatosplenomegaly

(Adapted from Christakis, G. (ed) [1979]. *Nutritional assessment in health programs.* Washington, DC: American Public Health Association; and Williams, S.R. [1985]. *Nutrition and diet therapy* [5th ed]. St. Louis: Times Mirror/Mosby.)

they frequently have little motivation to plan meals and to prepare food. Food is an especially difficult issue for home care clients who live alone and require assistive devices such as walkers, wheelchairs, and canes for mobility. The ability of these clients to safely prepare meals in a kitchen and transport prepared food to a dining area is obviously impaired. Thus, the nutritional intake of these clients is often significantly compromised, because they tend to eat whatever is handy and easy to fix, despite its nutritional value. Some clients forget to eat, or eat only sporadically. Others ingest high-calorie, high-fat foods, resulting in high caloric intake with few valuable nutrients.

Home care clients occasionally have functional deficits that inhibit their ability to feed themselves. The functional impact of cerebrovascular accidents, arthritis, Parkinson's disease, and neuromuscular disorders can reduce manual dexterity to the point that individuals cannot adequately feed themselves. These clients require special utensils to increase their independence in eating. Sometimes, they need assistance from another person. The willingness of clients to use special utensils or to accept help from other people directly impacts their nutritional intake.

Special Diets
Special diets are often prescribed for home care clients as part of the treatment of their disease processes. Diabetes, hypertension, congestive heart failure, chronic liver disease, chronic renal failure, obesity, and malabsorption syndromes are among the conditions that require special diets. Instructions for special diets can range from general guidelines for clients regarding foods to avoid (e.g., a lactose-restricted diet) to highly complex and specific guidelines (e.g., a 2-gm-sodium, 1500-calorie-per-day

diet). Some individuals adapt easily to the particulars of their prescribed diets, needing only to limit certain food choices. Other home care clients, who need to dramatically alter their food intake to comply with a newly prescribed diet, can find the transition difficult. Lifelong food habits are difficult to change, causing significant quality of life issues for clients, and challenges for nurses to overcome in helping them.

Cultural, Ethnic, and Religious Influences on Food Choices

Cultural, ethnic, and religious influences can profoundly affect a client's nutritional intake and diet (see Chapter 4) (Table 13-4). Customs surrounding food choices are deeply ingrained in the lifelong behavioral patterns of clients because of their backgrounds. Dietary behaviors that a client acquires as a member of a group involve

TABLE 13-4. *Cultural Variations on Nutrition*

CULTURE	MILK	MEAT	BREAD AND CEREALS	FRUITS AND VEGETABLES	ADDITIONAL VARIATIONS
Italian	Seldom use milk; cheese is calcium source	Chicken, beef, veal, fish— baked, simmered, or browned in olive oil	Bread and pasta basic foods	Squash, tomatoes, salad; fruit used as dessert	Drink red or white wine with dinner; use garlic for seasoning
Chinese	Use little milk or cheese	Pork, lamb, chicken, fish— cooked in combination with vegetables	Rice with most meals	Cabbage, snow peas, squashes, mushrooms, fruit usually eaten fresh	Fresh foods prepared by stir-frying; unsweetened green tea
Japanese	Little milk or cheese	Seafood main protein source, especially raw fish	Rice is basic grain; white and wheat bread being increasingly used	Steamed and served with soy sauce; tray of fruit served at main meal	Soy sauce main seasoning; soybean oil main cooking fat; traditionally, dinners follow specific sequence of courses; tea is main beverage
Greek	Little milk; yogurt popular; cheese a favorite food	Lamb favorite meat, little beef eaten	Bread center of every meal; rice commonly served	Large amounts of vegetables, cooked and seasoned, preferably fresh; large quantities of fresh fruit	Meal is family ritual; holidays are special occasions with great variety of foods

(continued)

TABLE 13-4. (CONTINUED)

CULTURE	MILK	MEAT	BREAD AND CEREALS	FRUITS AND VEGETABLES	ADDITIONAL VARIATIONS
Puerto Rican	Little milk	Most cannot afford meat; may use dried codfish; legumes good protein source	Rice	Almost all eat viandas, which are starchy vegetables and fruits, such as plantain and green bananas; other fruits and vegetables used in limited quantity	Simple daily diet that contrasts with holiday meal; economy major factor in food selection
Mexican	Little milk	Little meat used	Corn basic grain used in bread and cereal; oatmeal popular cereal	Corn, fresh or canned, and chili peppers; fruit use depends on avail ability	Drink large amounts of coffee, common seasonings chili pepper, onions, and garlic; lard basic cooking fat
African American	Low intake of milk and dairy foods	Diet usually high in protein, favorite meats pork and chicken; most meats fried or barbecued	Sweet potatoes and hominy grits	High intake of dark, leafy green vegetables, fruits used in limited quantity	Diet high in fat and sodium because of methods of preparation

(Taylor, C., Lillis, C., & LeMone, P. [1997]. *Fundamentals of nursing* [3rd ed.]. Philadelphia: Lippincott-Raven.)

defining a meal versus a snack, everyday versus special foods, feminine versus masculine foods, and holiday foods. Food is used to express love and moral sentiments. It can be used to reward or to punish, to demonstrate piety, to symbolize identification with a group, or to display the separateness of a group (Dudek, 1997).

Tortillas and beans are food staples in many Mexican-American households and are incorporated into daily meal planning. Rice is a staple in the diets of many Chinese-Americans. Some clients avoid certain foods because of their beliefs; the notion of eating such foods may cause great emotional distress for these clients. Those who practice orthodox Judaism steadfastly avoid nonkosher meat and poultry. Hindus refuse beef, and Muslims will not eat pork. Nurses must remain sensitive to cultural influences on food choices and should attempt to develop diet recommendations that closely reflect a client's existing food beliefs and practices. For example, a nurse who is educating a Native American in diabetic food exchanges should incorporate familiar foods within each of the exchange categories. Failure to acknowledge and to integrate a client's firmly held beliefs will result in an ineffective plan

of care. Eschelman writes that "unless health workers understand the cultural influences on eating habits and can translate them into practical, culturally sensitive
recommendations, they cannot provide realistic, effective nutrition counseling"
(1996, 317).

KEY CONCEPT

*Lifelong, culturally-ingrained food habits are difficult to change and
often represent significant quality of life issues for clients.*

Alcoholism and Nutrition

Alcohol and other substance abuse is rampant in the United States, affecting 10.5%
of the population, or 19.2 million individuals (West, 1997). Alcoholism significantly
impacts an individual's nutritional status. Often, those who abuse alcohol fail to eat
properly and to care for other bodily needs during periods of excessive drinking.
Alcoholism is linked to numerous nutritional deficiencies. For example, thiamine
deficiency in America is largely related to alcoholism, because alcoholics often have
poor dietary intakes of thiamine as well as impaired thiamine absorption, metabolism,
and storage (Tierney, McPhee, & Papadakis, 1997). Heavy alcohol use produces and
aggravates numerous digestive system disorders, including ulcers. Excessive alcohol
intake also causes inflammation of the pancreas, destruction of liver tissue (parenchy-
mal necrosis), alcoholic hepatitis, and alcoholic cirrhosis. Each of these conditions
further undermines the alcoholic's compromised nutritional status.

The decreased function and mobility, and increased social isolation associated
with the postacute phase of an illness can lead to depression and increased alcohol
intake by home care clients. Home care nurses are often the first to identify alcohol
abuse in clients while treating them for unrelated diagnoses. Because of the high
incidence of alcoholism and its significant impact on overall health, home care
nurses must carefully assess clients for signs of alcohol abuse. Nurses should also

Survival Alert:
Alcoholism

Alcoholism is a disease that affects the entire family. Home care nurses
should help clients to recognize when their use of alcohol is problematic
and assist them with access to appropriate treatment. Helping clients to
acknowledge the need to seek help often requires the expertise of professional counselors. Treatment generally incorporates client and family therapy. When a home care nurse suspects alcohol abuse in a client, the
nurse should inform the client's physician of these findings and require authorization for psychosocial and counseling interventions by a medical social worker.

try to evaluate clients for the nutritional deficiencies and fluid or electrolyte imbalances often associated with alcohol abuse.

KEY CONCEPT

Because of the high incidence of alcoholism and its significant impact on a client's overall health, home care nurses should carefully assess clients for signs of alcohol abuse.

Financial Considerations

Home care clients who lack adequate financial resources may find it difficult to comply with prescribed diets. For example, liquid nutritional supplements are often recommended for clients needing increased caloric intake. These supplements are usually not covered by insurance plans and are quite expensive for clients on fixed incomes. Tremendous product development has taken place in specialized foods (e.g., sugar-free ice cream, fat-free crackers, and low fat chips). These products are good substitutes for favorite snacks for individuals on special diets. These foods, however, are often expensive and cost-prohibitive.

Financial issues can affect the nutrition of individuals who are following regular diets as well. Especially for many older and retired clients, money is sometimes so limited that resources needed for a basic diet are unavailable. To manage, individuals often purchase only certain food staples to stretch their food dollars. Fresh fruits, vegetables, meat, and other protein-rich foods are consequently sometimes lacking in the diets of home care clients. Thus, home care nurses should assess the nutritional intake of clients, as well as the economic reasons for their food choices. Failure to understand these influences can lead to ineffective nursing interventions.

Nutrition Assessment Strategies

Home care nurses can use several assessment techniques to identify nutritional issues for clients. Obtaining a client's height and weight is an important component of the physical assessment, but does not provide a complete picture of the adequacy of a client's intake. The interview, physical assessment, medication review, evaluation of functional status, and environmental assessment help nurses to identify existing or potential nutritional concerns and fluid and electrolyte imbalances. Nurses should establish any difficulties clients have with chewing or swallowing. Individuals with loose-fitting dentures, mouth pain, poor appetite, food intolerances and allergies, or no social support at meals are often at risk for developing nutritional problems.

Nurses can further evaluate potential nutritional problems by asking home care clients to recall their food intake over the previous few days. For individuals without the memory recall to perform this exercise adequately, lay caregivers can assist in this process. Nurses should request that clients or their lay caregivers keep a diary of food and fluid intake to provide an accurate picture. Actually looking in refrigerators and cupboards of homes can validate a nurse's findings and suggest the need for further investigation when inconsistent information is obtained. For example, a

Clinical Example
with Critical Thinking

Mr. Englehart, an 84-year-old gentleman, is referred to a home care agency for evaluation of needs after a 6-day hospitalization for acute congestive heart failure. The limited referral information indicates Mr. Englehart has had three previous hospitalizations in the past 6 months. He lives alone, but has a granddaughter who lives twenty miles away and visits him every weekend. COPD is listed as a secondary diagnosis. During the initial client assessment, Jan, the home care nurse, observes that Mr. Englehart's home is badly in need of repairs. It is cluttered and dark. The client's gait is unsteady, and he holds onto furniture as he walks through the house. Mr. Englehart almost stumbles while walking to the kitchen to get his medications. Jan notes Mr. Englehart's medications: Lasix 400 mg. q day; Lanoxin 0.25 mg. q day; Theodur 200 mg. q day; Verapamil 240 mg. q day; and ipratropium bromide 3 inhalations every 6 hrs. When asked about over-the-counter medications, Mr. Englehart reports using laxatives regularly. Upon performing a physical assessment, Jan observes that the client uses a pacemaker and has a large scar on his left flank. When Jan looks in Mr. Englehart's refrigerator, she observes the contents: some old condiments, beer, a stale loaf of bread, and a half dozen eggs.

1. What are some additional questions that Jan should ask Mr. Englehart after the physical assessment?
2. List information that Jan should report to Mr. Englehart's physician.
3. Provide additional information Jan should obtain during her conversation with the physician.
4. What information may Jan wish to obtain regarding Mr. Englehart's most recent hospitalization?
5. Based upon the client's history and medication review, assess the components of the physical assessment that Jan must complete thoroughly.

home care client reports regularly eating protein; however, when examining the kitchen, the nurse finds no sources of protein available. This data prompts questions to ask to find the reasons for the inconsistent information. Looking in the kitchen sink and trash also provides information regarding a client's recent food intake. Home care nurses must receive permission from clients or lay caregivers to perform such actions first.

◆ Nursing Diagnoses

To develop the most effective plans of care, home care nurses first identify problems that nursing interventions can affect. Nursing diagnoses provide a framework in which nurses can organize and summarize the extensive amount of data collected

Application to Home Care Practice
Nursing Diagnoses Developed From Findings During a Home Care Initial Assessment

Harriet Hudson

Assessment Findings:

62 y.o. female, adult-onset, insulin-dependent diabetes × 4 years, weight 162 lbs., height 5′2″. Lives with supportive husband. Recent episode of ketoacidosis requiring 4 day acute hospitalization. Client reports compliance with 1500-calorie diabetic diet, although when questioned about food intake reports having ice cream occasionally "to satisfy my sweet tooth." States: "I adjust my own insulin depending on how much I'm eating and how I feel." Per diet recall, estimate a daily caloric intake of approximately 2000–2200 calories, eating often, but sporadically, during the day. Client's activity/exercise consists of ambulating to restroom, bedroom, and kitchen as needed.

Nursing Diagnoses:

1. Altered nutrition (more than body requirements): related to excessive intake of high-calorie, high-fat foods and lack of exercise.
2. Knowledge deficit therapeutic regimen (diabetic diet, weight control, insulin therapy, exercise, S/S hyper- and hypoglycemia, and appropriate interventions): related to lack of understanding of disease process.

during the initial assessment (see Chapter 9). This framework allows nurses to evaluate information about clients in a meaningful way. Appropriate nursing diagnoses clearly identify actual or potential health problems to positively provide clients with necessary nursing interventions. The nursing diagnoses also help nurses to recognize intervening factors that positively and negatively affect problems. Nurses must priori-

Application to Home Care Practice
Integrating Client Strengths and Weaknesses in the Treatment Plan

After conducting Mr. Tilney's initial assessment, Stephanie, the home care nurse, attributes his condition to a poor understanding of medications. Stephanie identifies Mr. Tilney's **impaired memory** as a weakness related to his problems with effective medication scheduling. She also notes the strong social support available from Mr. Tilney's daughter, who lives near him. Armed with this information, Stephanie can develop a care plan for Mr. Tilney that will ensure that his prescriptions are appropriately administered with the help of his daughter.

tize nursing diagnoses to ensure that the most urgent problems receive prompt and appropriate attention. Nurses must develop effective nursing diagnoses after thorough client assessments; after reviewing assessment findings, nurses identify the strengths and weaknesses of each particular client.

KEY CONCEPT

Appropriate nursing diagnoses clearly identify actual or potential health problems, which are positively influenced by correct nursing interventions.

◆ Outcome Identification and Planning

Once they have formulated nursing diagnoses, home care nurses develop the initial plans of care for their clients. The plan of care may be very simple or highly complex, depending upon the nature of a client's problems. Eighty percent of individuals age 65 and older have at least one chronic condition. Many of these individuals have multiple chronic conditions (Montgomery, 1993). Multiple chronic diagnoses and their medical treatments can affect one another. They also may complicate psychosocial and family support issues. Each client has a unique set of circumstances; as a result, each plan of care is highly individualized.

CLIENT GOALS

Before they can propose interventions, nurses must actively involve clients and their lay caregivers in the development of goals and objectives for the plan of care. Nurses most effectively acquire this input by presenting a summary of assessment findings and nursing diagnoses and soliciting from clients and their lay caregivers desired outcomes. As in the assessment interview, open-ended questions are most effective in obtaining unadulterated responses. Clients and their lay caregivers sometimes feel uncomfortable responding to questions if the medical professional intimidates them or if they are unsure of whether certain goals are achievable. Nurses help clients to identify reachable goals by discussing the lifestyles they hope to resume after recovery. When a nurse truly obtains a client's goals for treatment, the nursing process is most effective. This process motivates clients and lay caregivers to participate fully in the development and subsequent implementation of the plan of care.

Withholding Judgment

Home care nurses are to remain objective and nonjudgmental throughout the process of establishing treatment goals and objectives. This fundamental concept of nursing practice is a principle that is often violated. In home care, more so than in other clinical settings, nurses are exposed to "whole" clients—including their cultures, belief systems, living conditions, etc. Sometimes, nurses find that client lifestyles are inconsistent with their own personal values and react emotionally. When clients detect this response, they may be unwilling to respond honestly when questioned about health and wellness goals related to their lifestyles.

Nurses may unconsciously promote goals and objectives that are consistent with their own personal belief systems, but are in conflict with their clients' beliefs. Such practices prohibit clients from actively participating in the creation and development of their individualized plans of care. For example, a nurse negatively judges the living conditions of a migrant farm worker because eight people live in a two-room home. The nurse identifies placement in a board and care or skilled nursing facility as a goal for the client. This goal addresses the nurse's own discomfort with the conditions of poverty. In actuality, the client's living conditions fail to affect the client's health negatively. In fact, separation from family causes emotional distress for this client, which in turn affects physical well-being. Goals established when a nurse projects personal values on a client's lifestyle can wind up harming more than helping the client.

KEY CONCEPT

Home care nurses should actively engage clients and their lay caregivers in the development of treatment goals and objectives. Nurses must remain nonjudgmental throughout this process. A plan of care is likely to be ineffective if it reflects the nurse's own values rather than a client's personal objectives.

Involving Clients

Occasionally, nurses develop goals they would like to see their clients achieve without appropriately involving their clients. Nurses then become frustrated when clients are not motivated to perform interventions necessary to achieve these goals. This scenario occurs regularly in the home setting. Nurses frequently become disillusioned about their personal effectiveness and become irritated with their clients. Clients become frustrated because they feel that their real treatment objectives are not being met. Home care nurses can avoid this conflict by developing and consistently using a client-centered approach in the goal development process. Through active listening, nurses have the opportunity to identify issues that are important to clients throughout the assessment process. The goal-setting stage of this process should incorporate information nurses have received regarding issues of concern for their clients and their clients' desires for recovery. Nurses should systematically ask themselves in the goal-setting process: "Is this a goal that I want the client to achieve or is this truly the client's goal?" Nurses can also gain perspective in identifying personal biases in the care planning process by collaborating with peers or a clinical supervisor.

Addressing Unrealistic Goals

Occasionally, a client's goals are unrealistic. Nurses need to educate clients and lay caregivers about reasonable expectations for recovery. Nurses should question clients regarding information they have received from other healthcare providers (e.g.,

Home Care Conflict:
Failure to Involve a
Client in Goal-Setting

Mrs. Suitt, an elderly woman, lives alone and uses a urinary catheter. During a particularly hot and humid summer, Audrey, a nurse new to home healthcare, visits Mrs. Suitt and finds that she has no air conditioning or fans to circulate air and to keep her home cool. These conditions make visits to Mrs. Suitt's home for any length of time almost intolerable for Audrey. Audrey believes that many clinical factors necessitate measures to cool the house. When Audrey discusses this situation with the client, Mrs. Suitt explains she has no financial resources to pay for a fan or air conditioner.

Audrey is determined to find a community organization to provide a fan for Mrs. Suitt at no cost. When Audrey shares this information with her, Mrs. Suitt tells her that she does not need a fan. Furthermore, the electricity costs to run the fan would be too much for her to afford. Audrey then researches the issue and finds that electricity to run a fan costs only pennies a day. After many phone calls, Audrey finds an organization willing to provide a fan for Mrs. Suitt. She triumphantly picks up the fan and delivers it to Mrs. Suitt, proud of her diligence in taking the necessary steps to meet her client's needs.

On her very next visit to Mrs. Suitt's home, Audrey finds that the fan is gone. Mrs. Suitt has called the donating organization to return it, and the organization has picked up the fan. Audrey feels incredibly frustrated and defeated by Mrs. Suitt's actions.

Outcome: Improving the temperature in the client's home met Audrey's need to place the client in a better living situation. This same goal, however, was unimportant to Mrs. Suitt, who resented taking charity. She considered Audrey's persistence to be interference. Unfortunately, the creative time and energy that Audrey used to obtain a fan for Mrs. Suitt would have been better used in directing efforts toward health improvement goals desired by Mrs. Suitt. Audrey did not appropriately engage the client in the development of goals. Strained relations and disappointment on both Audrey's part and Mrs. Suitt's negatively impacted Mrs. Suitt's plan of care.

physicians, or therapists) regarding their conditions, disease processes, or rehabilitative potentials. Nurses must be especially sensitive and empathetic in explaining realistic goals, and must understand clients' frustrations with limitations. Typically, clients experience many emotional reactions to changes in their functional status. They often experience a loss of self-esteem and increased dependence on others. Changes in functional ability often dramatically alter family roles, resulting in an array of conflicting emotions for clients and family members. Home care nurses can assist clients in accepting losses and limitations associated with their conditions by appropriately responding to reactions of anger and sadness with acceptance and empathy.

Stressing Safety

Clients sometimes fail to recognize that certain behaviors and attitudes threaten their health and safety. Home care nurses instruct clients about such risks. When possible, nurses should link health risks to important issues for clients. For example, an eighty-year-old client seems unconcerned when informed by a nurse that an unstable blood sugar level can result in ketoacidosis, coma, and potential death. Maintaining independence for as long as possible, however, is an extremely important issue for this client. Thus, the nurse should instruct this client about the potential debilitating effects of an uncontrolled blood sugar level (e.g., blindness, severe atherosclerosis, and kidney failure). The nurse should stress that these conditions can threaten the client's independence if the levels are not brought under control. By working within the context of issues important to each particular client, nurses achieve a consensus with clients about goals for their plans of care.

KEY CONCEPT

Occasionally, clients fail to recognize that certain behaviors and attitudes are negatively affecting their health. A home care nurse should link a client's health problems to issues of importance for the client, such as independence, participation in leisure activities, avoidance of pain, and disability. By focusing on these concerns, nurses motivate clients to actively participate in measures that will help them to meet the goals of their plans of care.

Documenting Client Goals

Home care nurses prioritize goals to reflect the urgency of a client's needs. The documentation of goals should include outcomes to be observed, not interventions to be performed by nurses. For example, "The nurse will instruct client on sterile technique while performing dressing change on (L) leg" is not a client goal. A more appropriate goal-oriented statement reads: "Client will demonstrate sterile technique without verbal cuing while performing dressing change on (L) leg wound." Appropriately documented goals allow the healthcare team, clients, and lay caregivers to easily evaluate the progress achieved. Nurses also need to consider a client's discharge plan when developing ultimate client goals. They must assess the outcomes to be reached to discharge clients from home care services safely.

◆ Implementation

The home plan of care frequently incorporates a broad spectrum of nursing interventions for nurses to implement. Nurses must determine the necessary interventions to actualize the goals of clients. Plans of care routinely include **cognitive interven-**

tions, such as client teaching and the supervision of the interdisciplinary team. Nurses frequently perform **psychosocial interventions** as well, such as reinforcing effective coping behaviors, evaluating social support systems, providing stress-reduction techniques, and encouraging clients to express their feelings. Nurses also perform **technical interventions**, such as wound care, irrigating a catheter, and administering drugs.

COGNITIVE INTERVENTIONS

A comprehensive plan of care usually includes client teaching on a variety of subjects (see Chapter 10). The assessment process results in a comprehensive list of needs and problems that should include any knowledge deficits clients have regarding their treatment plans. Identification of knowledge deficits is particularly crucial, because nurses must depend on clients and lay caregivers to carry out many parts of plans of care fully. Clients and lay caregivers must have a solid understanding of the disease process, including symptoms of exacerbation; interventions to perform to prevent the disease's progression; appropriate administration of medications; awareness of community resources and ways to access them; and knowledge of prescribed exercises or activity limitations. Educating clients and lay caregivers about modifications to the environment is another important cognitive intervention that

Application to Home Care Practice
Accessing Ancillary Services
for a Client

Mr. Dawson recently suffered a CVA with (L) hemiparesis and severe generalized weakness. Jim, his son and primary caregiver, has a medical history of back problems and is unable to lift more than 50 pounds. In an acute or subacute setting, a lift would be used to mobilize Mr. Dawson into a chair. In Mr. Dawson's small apartment, however, little space is available in the bedroom for the use of a lift. Moreover, the client's insurance does not cover the expense of a lift. Jim cannot afford to purchase one for his father. How will Paul, the home care nurse, creatively facilitate appropriate mobilization of the client?

Paul can assess any number of multidisciplinary resources within the home care organization itself. For example, a physical therapist would be able to recommend other ways for Jim to safety and effectively mobilize Mr. Dawson. The therapist could work directly with Mr. Dawson to build strength that would enable him to pivot transfer with minimal lifting. A social worker could assist Jim in finding a bigger, low-cost housing alternative, or other individuals who might assist in Mr. Dawson's care. A DME provider could identify a space-efficient lift to be used in the client's home. The social worker could help the nurse to identify other funding sources to assist Jim with the purchase of this necessary equipment.

nurses perform. These modifications frequently reduce safety risks in the home and promote speedy recovery.

Other cognitive interventions that home care nurses conduct include identifying the need for ancillary and community services, making appropriate referrals, and supervising the entire treatment plan. Frequently, the needs of home care clients extend beyond the scope of nursing care. As reviewed in chapter 7, clients often require the services of other disciplines and assistance from community services to meet specific needs. Because nurses are the primary coordinators of plans of care for home care clients, they must understand indications for referrals to such ancillary services. They also must continually ease and oversee these additional client contacts.

INTERPERSONAL INTERVENTIONS

Teaching and supervising by nurses are vital interventions for helping clients to understand the actions they must perform to optimize their own health. Increasing a client's knowledge base alone, however, will not lead to improved health unless the knowledge is appropriately applied. Home care nurses must also perform interpersonal interventions to develop therapeutic relationships with clients. Particularly in the home care setting, nurses frequently need to influence clients to change longstanding, destructive behaviors in order for treatment to have a positive impact.

A widely accepted model, **The Health Belief Model** (Rosenstock, 1966), discusses why individuals participate in wellness behaviors. According to the model, the concept of readiness and motivation to change is influenced by (1) perceived susceptibility to a specific condition, (2) perceived seriousness of the health problem, (3) benefits and obstacles to changes in behavior, and (4) cues that will stimulate a change in behavior. Often, psychosocial issues rather than knowledge influence clients to change their health behaviors. Home care nurses who have developed effective therapeutic relationships with clients can address issues of readiness from both a cognitive and interpersonal level.

One of the primary interpersonal interventions conducted by home care nurses involves being a client advocate. **Advocacy** involves helping clients to identify their needs and treatment goals, aggressively navigating healthcare and social systems to resolve these needs, and working with clients to meet their goals. Interventions include successfully communicating the needs of clients to physicians, insurance companies, and other involved disciplines. The success of a client's treatment plan depends upon a nurse's ability to build relationships and to maintain contact with the different individuals involved in a client's care. The nurse's effectiveness in communicating a client's needs to an insurance company can make a difference in whether reimbursement is provided for services. The nurse's ability to communicate the need for community resources often determines whether these resources are made available to a client.

Nurses occasionally identify dysfunctional communication that exists between clients and their families or lay caregivers. The stress of an illness or injury often exacerbates longstanding interpersonal conflicts. Dysfunctional relationships can inhibit a client's progress toward the goals of the plan of care. Nurses can intervene in these circumstances by helping to clarify communication among family members.

They can provide counseling and assist individuals to verbalize their needs, frustrations, issues, and concerns in a way that facilitates understanding and improved relationships.

TECHNICAL INTERVENTIONS

Home care nurses frequently perform specific technical nursing interventions in the care of clients (Display 13-3). Nurses in home care lack assistance from other nurses when they are uncomfortable performing certain procedures. Because of the generalized nature of home care nursing practice, nurses must be competent in a wide variety of technical procedures. Sometimes, nurses do not know beforehand that a technical intervention will need to be performed during a home care visit. For example, a client's nursing assessment shows signs and symptoms of an electrolyte imbalance. Upon reviewing findings with the client's physician, the nurse is instructed to conduct a stat venipuncture for laboratory studies. The nurse must be prepared to competently collect the specimen in the appropriate type of laboratory vial and transport it within recommended laboratory time frames and conditions. Failure to know and to competently perform this intervention can result in inaccurate laboratory results and subsequent inappropriate medical treatments. Therefore, home care nurses must be prepared at all times to competently and independently perform all technical interventions.

CREATIVITY IN THE PLAN OF CARE

Nurses must be creative in achieving client objectives with the limited resources that are available in many clients' homes. Solutions to client problems are often difficult to identify due to environmental or financial constraints. Home care nurses must investigate any and all potential solutions to these problems. Thus, they must be highly creative and resourceful when confronting problems with no readily apparent solutions.

Display 13-3:
Technical Interventions Performed by the Home Care Nurse

- Wound care
- Venipunctures and other laboratory specimen collections
- Insertion or irrigation of urinary catheters
- Administration of intravenous/intramuscular/subcutaneous medications
- Insertion and maintenance of peripheral or central venous catheters
- Tracheostomy care
- Maintenance and programming of equipment (e.g., infusion pumps, ventilators, or apnea monitors)
- Postural drainage and percussion
- Suctioning
- Emergency response procedures

Application to Home Care Practice
Care Plan Creativity

Mrs. Martinez hopes to achieve medication compliance. Poor eyesight contributes to her difficulty reading pill bottles; moreover, she often forgets to take her many medications because of an impaired memory. Bradley, a creative home care nurse, addresses this problem by creating a poster with large letters that includes a large picture of each pill and a clear time schedule. Bradley also educates Mrs. Martinez to take her medications in conjunction with various daily activities. He reminds Mrs. Martinez to take her white and blue pills when she brushes her teeth in the morning. Mrs. Martinez can keep her pill bottles near the sink where she brushes her teeth as a reminder. Bradley instructs the client to take her pink pill when her favorite game show airs. The nurse encourages Mrs. Martinez to place that pill bottle by her chair in the living room where she watches her program. Such triggers help Mrs. Martinez to remember her medications through their connections with daily living activities. This creative system facilitates the achievement of the goal of medication compliance.

Frustration is normal when nurses face client problems that do not seem to have any apparent solutions. Home care nurses should collaborate with nursing peers, other disciplines, a clinical supervisor, and resources in the community that work with similar client populations to come up with effective solutions. Although information must be kept confidential, reasonable professional discussion often leads to new perspectives in problem solving.

◆ Evaluation

During the initial visit, nurses determine issues that will require evaluation during subsequent home care visits. This determination corresponds directly with significant clinical findings, client goals, and the plan of care. Ongoing assessment and evaluation of abnormal clinical findings is critical to evaluate the improvement, stabilization, or deterioration of a client's physical status. Evaluation is also required for abnormal psychosocial and environmental findings. For example, during an initial visit to a client, a nurse discovers that the client lives with an emotionally unsupportive lay caregiver who increases the client's level of anxiety. On subsequent visits, the nurse must incorporate an evaluation of the client's anxiety level and the degree of emotional support given by the lay caregiver.

Nurses also must evaluate the effectiveness of all interventions that are performed in a client's plan of care. Nurses ask clients for their perspectives on the effectiveness of home care interventions. For example, a client's ability to retain knowledge regarding signs and symptoms of hypoglycemia can be tested by quizzing the client on information provided in previous visits. Occasionally, discrepancies in intervention effectiveness are found. For example, a client reports knowledge of the signs of an infection and appropriate actions (e.g., calling the home care nurse) to take in the event that a wound infection occurs. Yet, when the nurse conducts the physical assessment, obvious signs of infection are found. Clearly, a deficit in the client's understanding of appropriate measures is indicated and needs reinforcement.

Evaluation should occur through more than one source when possible. Nurses are to review the documentation in a medical record made by other professionals involved in the care of a client. For example, a nurse evaluates the results of assessments made by a physical therapist and the plan of care subsequently developed to address the identified needs of a client. This evaluation is reinforced by questioning clients and lay caregivers regarding interventions the therapist performed and their satisfaction with services received.

Evaluation should also include an ongoing analysis of the prioritization of interventions established during the initial nursing visit. Frequently, a client's physical condition, support systems, environment, and psychosocial status change during the course of home care services. Modifications to either the types of interventions required or the priority of these interventions are often needed. Home care nurses may recognize that the initially established plan of care is ineffective or more effective than expected in helping a client to achieve established goals. Nurses should actively involve clients in modifying the plan of care or adapting goals according to newly identified limitations or opportunities. For example, a client may progress further than had been anticipated with therapy. In this situation, the goals of a client are modified to reflect the higher level of function reasonably expected at the conclusion of the therapy treatment plan.

◆ Concluding the Initial Visit

Upon completion of the initial visit, nurses have a comprehensive awareness of significant client issues. Nurses should review assessment information and mentally develop and prioritize preliminary nursing diagnoses. Many new home care clients need immediate education regarding medication scheduling. When clients are discharged from an acute healthcare setting, they often receive new prescriptions. Although teaching occurs in the acute care setting, frequently clients are highly stressed or simply not feeling well enough to absorb this new information. Home care nurses can prevent inaccurate dosing by assisting clients with developing an administration schedule for medications.

Other home care clients have been prescribed nursing interventions that need to be performed during the initial visit. For example, a physician prescribes a nurse to intravenously infuse 1000 cc D5W 1/2 NS over 8 hours for a high-risk antepartum client recently diagnosed with dehydration caused by hyperemesis. Although a comprehensive initial assessment is still required for this client, the nurse should initiate the infusion soon after reviewing rights and responsibilities with the client and conducting a condensed interview and physical assessment. A more comprehensive assessment can be completed once the infusion has started.

Home care nurses often identify other critical client teaching needs to be addressed during the initial visit. For example, a client who is performing wound care on a surgical incision requires teaching regarding signs and symptoms of infection if a knowledge deficit exists. Clients also need to be educated as to how to contact home care nurses in the event that they have a question or experience a problem. Nurses must prioritize teaching that truly needs to be accomplished during the initial visit. Clients are frequently overloaded with information during their initial contacts with home care nurses. Nurses should not try to incorporate more than clients are able to absorb; doing so may result in client anxiety and failure to learn the most critical information.

The end of the initial visit is the time to summarize findings and conclusions with clients and lay caregivers. Nurses share this information as openly and sensitively as possible, and request that clients share their objectives for home care as well. Together, they can jointly develop a plan of action. Afterward, the client's physician should be contacted as soon as possible so that the nurse can relate pertinent findings, clarify uncertainties, and discuss the client's objectives for home care and the tentative plan of treatment.

DOCUMENTATION

After the initial visit, assessment findings and the physician-approved plan of treatment must be documented. Nurses must complete documentation as soon as possible, while objective information and subjective impressions are fresh, to ensure the accuracy of their conclusions. Nurses should only take short notes during the interview and assessment in order to appropriately listen and maintain maximum awareness of the information communicated to them (Fig. 13-4A). Specific data, such as vital signs, measurements, and locations of abnormal lung sounds, scars, or breaks in skin integrity must be documented during the visit. Often, documentation of

Figure 13-4. (A) The nurse writes notes of important clinical findings during the initial session with the client. (B) She completes full documentation at the home care office.

general, elaborated observations about a client's condition is best performed after the visit (Fig. 13-4*B*). Otherwise, clients may feel that nurses are more interested in filling out paperwork than in attending to their needs.

Many home care agency operational issues depend upon the timely submission of documentation (see Chapter 5). The treatment plan is used to initiate physician referrals to ancillary services. If documentation is not submitted quickly, a delay in service can result, or an ancillary service may visit a client without the benefit of information obtained during the initial visit. When a nurse fails to submit documentation of an initial visit in a timely manner, the signed authorization of a treatment plan by a physician may be inappropriately delayed as well.

KEY CONCEPT

Home care nurses should complete documentation of initial visits as soon as possible, while the objective information and subjective impressions are fresh. Timely documentation helps to ensure the accuracy of conclusions and the quality of client care.

◆ Summary

The initial visit to a client is a comprehensive overview of multiple factors that impact the client's health. Nurses who communicate respect and a nonjudgmental attitude encourage their clients to develop trust in them. This trust is important for the effectiveness of the mutually established treatment plan. Nurses must use a holistic approach in the initial assessment of clients. Information must be meticulously verified for accuracy against information that may not be as obvious. Failure to do so may result in wasted time, energy, expense, and, at worst, an unnecessary deterioration in a client's condition. Home care nurses act like detectives, searching for clues that provide definitive solutions to a client's problems. Some of the most satisfying moments in home care occur when nurses follow hunches based on obscure information that positively impact a client's health.

References and Bibliography

Bailey, A., Ferguson, E. & Voss, S. (1995). Factors affecting an individual's ability to administer medication. *Home Healthcare Nurse, 13*(5), 57–63.

Bennett, E.G. & Woolf, D. (Eds.). (1991). *Substance abuse* (2nd ed.). Albany: Delmar.

Capozza, C. & Sousa, A. (1994). Preventing malnutrition in the home care patient. *Caring, 13*(11), 68–71.

Davidhizar, R. & Dunn, C. (1996). Malnutrition in the elderly. *Home Healthcare Nurse, 14*(12), 948–954.

Dudek, S.G. (1997). *Nutrition handbook for nursing practice* (3rd ed.). Philadelphia: Lippincott-Raven.

Eschelman, M.E. (1996). *Nutrition and nutrition therapy* (3rd ed.). Philadelphia: Lippincott-Raven.

Fink, S. (1995). The influence of family resources and family demands on the strains and well-being of caregiving families. *Nursing Research, 44*(3), 139–146.

Gillespie, J. (1995). Five things you should know about medicine cabinets. *Nursing, 25*(1), 29.

Holzmeister, L.A. (1996). Diabetes: Nutrition therapy in home care. *Home Healthcare Nurse, 14*(3), 179–184.

Hunt, R. & Zurek, E. (1997). *Introduction to community based nursing.* Philadelphia: Lippincott-Raven.

Kelly, M. (1996). Medications and the visually impaired elderly. *Geriatric Nursing, 17*(2), 60–62.

McCaffrey, M. (1994). Home health care update 94: Pain control— keeping current. *Nursing, 24*(6), 51–52.

Mills, E. (1994). The effect of low-intensity aerobic exercise on muscle strength, flexibility, and balance among sedentary elderly persons. *Nursing Research, 43*(4), 207–211.

Montgomery, P. (1993). Starting a hospital based home health agency: The service and its environment. Part 1. *Nursing Management, 24*(8), 39–41.

Rice, R. (1995). *Handbook of home health nursing procedures.* St. Louis: Mosby.

Rosenstock, I.M. (1996). Why people use health services. *Milbank Q, 44,* 94–127.

Stulginsky, M. (1993b). Nurses' home health experience. Part II. The unique demands of home visits. *Nursing & Healthcare, 14*(9), 476–485.

Tierney, L.M. Jr. McPhee, S.J., & Papadakis, M.A. (Eds.) (1997). *Current medical diagnosis and treatment.* Stamford, CT: Appleton & Lange.

Varrichio, C. (1994). Human and indirect costs of home care. *Nursing Outlook, 42*(4), 151–157.

Wendt, D. (1996). Building trust during the initial home visit. *Home Healthcare Nurse, 14*(2), 92–98.

West, J. (1997). Alcoholism fits into list of mental disorders. *Desert Sun,* February 1, B4.

POST TEST

1. Explain the importance of the initial client visit.

2. List the steps that nurses should perform before they contact clients to schedule the initial visit.

3. Determine appropriate actions nurses should take when performing an interview.

4. A review of over-the-counter medications that the client takes only occasionally is unnecessary.

    _____True   _____False

5. Assessment of only those body systems with which the client has a problem is necessary.

    _____True   _____False

THINKING CRITICALLY IN HOME CARE

1. In addition to the clients' addresses, phone numbers, referring physicians, emergency contacts, and general demographic information, the following information is included in these referrals received by Acme Home Care:

    Mr. Dophene is a 75-year-old male, recently discharged from a skilled nursing facility. He suffered a CVA 2 months ago. He lives with his wife.

    MD orders home health evaluation: check home for safety, administer a Foley catheter, provide wound care for decubitus on coccyx, and evaluate for referrals to physical and occupational therapy.

Mrs. Sosa, an 87-year-old woman, is diagnosed with adult onset diabetes. She is new on insulin and was discharged from Healthy Hospital yesterday.

MD orders home health evaluation: teach insulin administration, evaluate need for medical social worker and community services.

A. Establish any additional information that home care nurses should obtain before making initial contacts with these clients by phone.

B. Determine questions for nurses to ask the clients and lay caregivers during the initial phone contacts.

2. Fred Carney is 82 years old, has a diagnosis of COPD, and lives alone. His granddaughter visits regularly and assists him when necessary. Karen, the home care nurse, suspects Mr. Carney is not receiving a nutritionally adequate diet. Karen is finding it difficult to assess Mr. Carney's intake because of his poor short-term memory.

A. Determine other ways in which Karen can asses Mr. Carney's nutritional intake.

B. Explain possible ways for Mr. Carney's granddaughter to assist the nurse in helping to ensure a good diet for her grandfather.

3. Francis, a home care nurse, is questioning his ability to be nonjudgmental of a client. What is the most appropriate course of action for Francis?

14

Subsequent Visits, Recertification, Transfer, and Discharge From Home Care

LEARNING OBJECTIVES

After completing this chapter, the reader will be able to:

◆ Understand the importance of subsequent home care visits.

◆ Identify critical elements in the recertification process.

◆ Discuss the significance of planning long-term care for clients.

◆ Review the process of transferring home care clients to other settings.

◆ Identify clients who may benefit from alternative care settings, e.g., skilled nursing facilities, rehabilitation facilities, and hospices.

◆ Explain why discharge planning begins with admission to home care and includes the participation of clients and their lay caregivers.

KEY TERMS

Anticipatory guidance	Recertification
Certification	Rehabilitation centers
Conservatorship	Skilled nursing facilities
Discharge planning	Supplemental
Hospice	physician orders

T*he initial* home care visit (Chapter 13) begins the nursing process and creates the foundation for all future client contacts. Nurses provide most home care services, however, during subsequent visits. Through subsequent visits, nurses carry out and adjust plans of care as appropriate to the evolving needs and conditions of clients. The effective performance of subsequent visits is critical to stabilizing the health of clients and helping them to reach their goals. Nurses must determine a suitable frequency of visits to meet each client's individualized needs. Establishing appropriate visit frequency is critical to ensuring safe provision of care. Visits that are too frequent may result in an overly dependent nurse-client relationship and denial of reimbursement for services. Visits that are too infrequent may result in preventable deterioration in clients and acute exacerbations of conditions. Nurses may need to schedule visits as often as twice a day or as infrequently as once a month. Home care nurses must be able to anticipate the potential needs of clients to establish suitable intervals between contacts with them.

Similarly, nurses must schedule an appropriate duration for home care services. Third party payors usually find indefinite provision of skilled home care services to be inappropriate for most clients. In fact, some payors deny any home care services that lack a finite duration and end date. Therefore, nurses must always consider the long-term needs of clients and attempt to decide the most appropriate care settings for them. Payors and agencies usually consider home care services to be limited, and appropriate for clients with subacute care needs—not with chronic long-term problems. Nurses have a responsibility to anticipate long-term care needs and to help ensure that they are met. Many clients have chronic illnesses that cause the gradual deterioration of physical health. By the time these individuals require home care, their disease processes are often advanced. Clients and lay caregivers need anticipatory guidance about disease progression to prepare them for the future. Clients must consider many issues, including finances, supportive care, advance directives, and emotional issues associated with these decisions. Educating clients about potential long-term options can ease their acceptance of disease and promote planning to address important issues.

The process of anticipating the needs of clients at discharge should begin with their admission to home care services. The conditions of clients, however, often change during treatment. Nurses must constantly reconsider and update plans of care. Some clients require a long duration of skilled home care services. Although payors will still consider the care limited, some clients have conditions that warrant extended lengths of stay in home care programs. When home care medical certification plans near completion, nurses must reevaluate the ongoing needs of clients. They must decide whether continued home care is appropriate. If necessary, nurses will complete a recertification process and develop another medical certification plan. If continued home care is inappropriate, nurses must determine whether they should transfer clients to another care setting. Occasionally, nurses must refer clients to long-term care settings, rehabilitation hospitals, or, for terminally ill clients, hospice programs.

This chapter contains an in-depth consideration of follow-up care for clients and ways for nurses to use subsequent visits to help clients achieve their health goals. It reviews the process for recertifying home care clients. It discusses strategies for long-term planning with clients who appear to have indefinite needs that are inappropriate for continued home care. This chapter concludes with a discussion about coordinating discharge planning at the end of home care services—an important function of home care nurses.

◆ Subsequent Visits

While planning care, nurses target interventions to perform and establish schedules that will most effectively help clients to meet their goals. Follow-up or subsequent nursing visits are important for ensuring that information gathered during the initial visit is still relevant and that clients are progressing toward established goals. Before each subsequent contact, nurses must reacquaint themselves with details of the clinical conditions and needs of their clients. This process consists of reviewing clinical notes from previous visits, identifying significant clinical findings, reestablishing treatment goals, and noting goals that clients have achieved. By continually reviewing and updating information about each client, nurses can best determine issues and interventions to address during a subsequent visit.

KEY CONCEPT

Follow-up or subsequent nursing visits are important for ensuring that information gathered during the initial visit is still relevant and that clients are progressing toward established goals.

Application to Home Care Practice
Establishing Visit Frequency

Mrs. Sacks has received chemotherapy and has a newly placed central line. Her physician orders the home care nurse to instruct Mrs. Sacks in the management of her newly placed central venous catheter and to take appropriate actions if signs and symptoms of infection occur. The nurse schedules daily visits until Mrs. Sacks can independently perform the procedure with excellent technique and can verbalize signs and symptoms of infection. Daily visits are required in this situation, because the client's reduced immunity places her at high risk for infection and adverse events within 24 hours of the procedure. If the nurse visits this client less frequently, early identification of a problem is compromised.

Conversely, Mr. Schick was discharged from the hospital with an exacerbation of COPD. Mr. Shick was diagnosed four years ago and is knowledgeable of his disease process. In this situation, a home care nurse may schedule an initial visit frequency of three times a week to perform respiratory assessments because the probability of a rapid deterioration of Mr. Shick's condition is minimal.

REVIEWING FINDINGS FROM THE INITIAL VISIT

To perform subsequent home care visits adequately, nurses should first review findings from the initial home visit, client goals, and the plan of care. Because the initial home care visit is the most comprehensive assessment that nurses perform, this review process reacquaints nurses with the conditions and needs of clients to allow appropriate planning for subsequent care. Nurses should familiarize themselves with priority needs. They should reexamine the strengths and weaknesses of clients to strategize objectives and to target necessary interventions. Nurses may not consider certain findings from an initial visit to be significant; as they carry out a plan of care, and further information becomes evident, however, data from the initial visit may become more relevant. Therefore, reviewing findings from the initial visit before subsequent visits can enhance the effectiveness of nurses in helping clients to reach their health goals.

ESTABLISHING VISIT FREQUENCY

When establishing visit schedules for clients, home care nurses must determine the needed frequency of interventions in a plan of care. They should consider many factors, including the acuity level of clients, the stability of their conditions, and the availability of reliable lay caregivers to perform procedures. Nurses can clearly identify the frequency of visits for some clients. For example, Mr. Burns, who lives alone and needs daily dressing changes on his coccyx, requires daily nursing visits until a lay caregiver can be found to perform the wound care. Nurses should evaluate the probability of an adverse event occurring within various time frames when establishing schedules. Generally, clients require visits most frequently when first admitted to home care. Learning needs for clients are greatest at this time because their medical conditions are usually the most unstable, community resources are not yet involved, and clients and lay caregivers are most anxious. Nurses should reduce the frequency of visits when clients have stabilized conditions, recognize early signs of problems, and understand appropriate responses; lay caregivers exhibit skills necessary to meet client needs; and community resources start providing support. Table 14-1 outlines indications for different types of visit frequencies, with examples.

KEY CONCEPT

Nurses should consider many factors, such as acuity level, condition stability, and the availability of reliable caregivers, when determining the frequency of nursing interventions.

Nurses usually develop a plan of care for a period of sixty-two days. Nurses must anticipate what visit frequency clients will require, and include this information in the medical treatment plan. They must reach a consensus about interventions with clients and their physicians. Physicians must authorize the frequency of visits estab-

TABLE 14-1. *Scheduling Visits*

INDICATION	EXAMPLE
INDICATIONS FOR DAILY VISITS	
Treatments or procedures need to be performed daily and the client and/or lay caregiver have not demonstrated competency in performing them independently.	A new diabetic client who has not yet learned how to self-inject insulin
A client's clinical condition is unstable, with a moderate to high probability of change that could have negative clinical consequences.	A client with indications of unstable congestive heart failure who is presenting with lung congestion, pedal edema, and a five pound weight gain in three days
A client requires a daily complex medical treatment that is too high risk for the client and/or lay caregiver to learn.	A client with cancer who is receiving daily infusions of a cytotoxic drug that requires thorough clinical assessments and venipunctures for blood chemistries
A client is in an unsafe environment and at high risk for injury. **Note:** Daily skilled nursing visits for this reason must be relatively short-term while interventions are actively taken to resolve the unsafe situation. An agency that cannot resolve this problem should discontinue the client from services.	A client who lives alone, and has recently experienced two serious falls
INDICATIONS FOR VISITS 3–5 TIMES A WEEK	
A client's clinical condition is unstable, but the probability of a significant change within 24 hours is unlikely. A significant change, however, could begin in 48–72 hours.	A client discharged from the hospital after treatment for pneumonia who presents with rales auscultated in the lower lobes of the lungs
A client or lay caregiver has critical teaching needs for early signs and symptoms of clinical deterioration to report to healthcare personnel, or care activities that need to be performed regularly and appropriately to prevent an adverse client outcome. Daily teaching is not necessary to prevent an adverse outcome.	A client with congestive heart failure who needs to learn dietary restrictions and an activity program to gain endurance
A client or lay caregiver is suspected of being noncompliant in following a treatment plan.	A lay caregiver for a client with a recent CVA with left hemiplegia is suspected of not performing prescribed exercises to prevent contractures
Nurse needs to evaluate the effectiveness of a new medical treatment.	A client with a new prescription or new dressing change order
Client or lay caregiver has recently received instructions regarding medical treatment plan. Nurse needs to evaluate understanding and implementation of new information.	A client who has been taught medication scheduling, effects, and adverse reactions for newly prescribed drugs
INDICATIONS FOR VISITS 1–3 TIMES A WEEK	
A client's condition is unlikely to change significantly within 3–5 days, or the client or lay caregiver is knowledgeable and competent to assess signs and symptoms of impending problems and apply learned interventions, or access appropriate healthcare personnel.	A client with stabilizing congestive heart failure

(continued)

TABLE 14-1. (CONTINUED)

INDICATION	EXAMPLE
A client or lay caregiver has moderate to minimal teaching needs.	A client who has had multiple sclerosis for many years who has received a change in prescribed medications to control symptoms
A client requires a nursing intervention that must be performed with this frequency.	Clients who require duoderm dressing changes or a weekly protime
INDICATIONS FOR VISITS 1–2 TIMES A MONTH	
A client is relatively stable with moderate potential for deterioration but cannot reliably report changes in condition.	A client lives alone and unreliably reports changes in condition
A client will deteriorate if the long-term care plan is inconsistently implemented. A moderate to high probability exists that the client's plan of care may be followed inconsistently.	A client has multiple lay caregivers and/or community agencies involved in the plan of care. The efforts of multiple agencies need overall coordination. The plan of care needs regular supervision to ensure services are rendered appropriately.
A client requires a treatment to be performed with this frequency.	A client who requires venipuncture for protime and assessment of S/S bleeding, or Calcimar injections
INDICATIONS FOR VISITS ONCE EVERY TWO MONTHS	
A client requires a treatment that needs to be performed with this frequency.	A client who requires changes of indwelling urinary catheter
A client's condition is stable, but will deteriorate if the long-term plan of care is inconsistently implemented. A moderate to high probability exists that the client's plan of care may be followed inconsistently.	Plan of care is relatively stable, but due to multiple involvement of community organizations and caregivers, requires regular review, coordination, and revision

lished when clients are admitted to service. If changes to the frequency are required, nurses must obtain additional physician orders.

CONDUCTING SUBSEQUENT VISITS

The administration of subsequent visits occurs most efficiently and effectively when nurses use a systematic process. Nurses need to review pertinent information about the clients that they plan to visit on any particular workday. They need to establish approximate schedules in which to space their visits to allow for adequate travel time. They must phone clients to confirm visits and establish mutually agreeable appointments. Finally, they must carry out the visits themselves, incorporating interventions and making any revisions to the plan of care as necessary.

Establishing a Daily Schedule

Home care nurses typically begin their workdays by reviewing a list of scheduled clients. They review each client's initial visit documentation, plan of care, and as applicable, documentation from subsequent visits. Nurses also evaluate the geo-graphic proximity of the homes of clients to determine the best order in which to make their visits. Each day's schedule should incorporate, in order of priority, the clinical needs of the scheduled clients, locations, and client preferences. Location is an important consideration when determining visit times. Nurses who must drive long distances to meet the preferences of many clients will find their time to conduct thorough visits diminished. Usually, nurses can establish their schedules without any conflicts with clients. Occasionally, however, clients strongly prefer specific visit times and are disappointed when nurses cannot accommodate their requests. Nurses should evaluate the rationales behind the preferences of clients. If they cannot meet these preferences because of the clinical needs of other clients, nurses can offer a variety of options. They can volunteer to visit a client on another day, at a preferred time, if the client requesting a preference has no immediate or critical needs. Or, they can offer to have another home care nurse perform the visit at the preferred time. Nurses should discuss such issues with the home care agency's supervisor or scheduler, and coordinate appropriate follow-up.

KEY CONCEPT

Location is an important consideration when determining visit times. Nurses who must drive long distances to meet the preferences of many clients will find their time to conduct thorough visits diminished.

Phoning Clients

Nurses phone clients to confirm visits, and ideally, to agree upon mutually satisfactory times for them. During these contacts, nurses should take the opportunity to gather additional information that can help them prepare appropriately. They should ask clients or lay caregivers about any needed supplies, new symptoms, or results from physician visits, and about the status of specific problems. A nurse also may wish to contact a client's physician or a member of the interdisciplinary care team to evaluate progress and to ask questions before visiting a client (Fig. 14-1).

Reassessment

Nursing interventions in subsequent visits follow the written plans of nursing care established after the initial visits with clients. As discussed in Chapter 9, the plan of care incorporates anticipated client needs for the duration of home care services, along with a discharge plan (see below). It provides a flexible blueprint for interven-tions to help clients with goal achievement. The needs and conditions of clients, however, often change during services. Nurses can reassess clients by reviewing new laboratory reports, examining the clinical notes of personnel from ancillary services, and questioning clients about their subjective reporting of issues. They complete reassessment by interviewing clients and lay caregivers, observing family dynamics and the environment, and conducting components of the assessment again.

Figure 14-1. The nurse phones a client to schedule a visit.

Typical Interventions

Home care nurses can perform many interventions, depending upon the client populations they serve. Most interventions, however, focus upon the need for clients and lay caregivers to carry out necessary aspects of the medical treatment plan independently. Nurses prioritize interventions based upon their impact on stabilizing or improving a client's condition. Teaching is a critical component of most visits (see Chapter 10). Nurses teach clients and their lay caregivers about concepts as simple as following a schedule of oral medication, or as complex as infusion of TPN through a central venous catheter. They also teach clients to recognize problems early and to intervene appropriately. Home care nurses also perform many technical interventions. In the past several years, technology has advanced the number and types of procedures that can be performed in the home (see Chapter 1). These interventions may include diagnostic testing (e.g., the electrocardiogram, or uterine monitor), the administration of therapeutic agents, wound care, or the maintenance of a variety of intravenous lines.

Nurses often counsel clients and lay caregivers through therapeutic communication. They encourage clients to identify their personal priorities. Nurses attempt to empower clients to make behavior choices based upon these priorities. They may contract with clients to perform specific behaviors that will influence their clients' recovery and health. They may need to confront clients about inconsistencies in stated priorities or behaviors that do not support these priorities.

Unconventional Care. As discussed in Chapter 7, home care nursing interventions include referring clients to appropriate community organizations or to alternative types of care, and coordinating the care of all involved personnel. Home care nurses also perform interventions that are less conventional than in other settings. To ensure a client's safety, a nurse may need to adjust the client's home (e.g., remove throw rugs, clear cluttered hallways, rearrange lighting to illuminate a dangerously dark walkway, or move items in the kitchen to eliminate a potential fire hazard). Home care nurses have been known to pick up prescriptions for clients to ensure that they receive medication to relieve pain or discomfort or to treat an infection. A nurse may prepare a meal upon discovering that a client has not eaten for 24 hours because a paid lay caregiver never arrived to cook. Many nurses in home care have gone to grocery stores to purchase food for clients who have nothing in the house to eat.

Such nursing interventions cannot be incorporated into long-term plans of care. Continual performance of these types of activities can encourage dependent client relationships. Home care nursing is unique, however. When they discover that clients have urgent or critical needs that no one else is available to fulfill, nurses are obligated to do whatever is necessary to meet them. The primary responsibility of home care nurses, however, is to empower clients and available lay caregivers to perform a variety of health behaviors independently. Through interventions directed toward this objective, nurses can simplify the achievement of both short- and long-term goals.

K E Y   C O N C E P T

Home care nurses perform a number of interventions that are less conventional than in other care settings. Many of these interventions cannot be incorporated into long-term plans of care, however, because continual performance of these types of activities can encourage dependent relationships with clients.

IDENTIFYING NEW CONCERNS OR ISSUES

During subsequent visits, home care nurses sometimes identify new concerns or issues that they have not incorporated into a plan of care. Nurses may not have recognized an issue during previous visits (e.g., dysfunctional relationships with lay caregivers), or clients may be facing entirely new problems (e.g., new diagnoses). In either case, nurses must restart the nursing process. A nurse should assess new problems or issues in the context of each of the client's other needs, and the client's strengths and weaknesses, to develop an accurate nursing diagnosis, a realistic outcome, and an effective plan of care. New data may result in the revision of previously established nursing diagnoses, which would require the revision of corresponding outcomes and plans of care.

◆ Recertification

When clients are first admitted to home care services, physicians must certify them. **Certification** is a process by which a physician sanctions a comprehensive medical treatment plan for a client. The treatment is for a limited period, and the physician confirms that the client is homebound and requires skilled, intermittent home care services. Clients who require services beyond the certified period must be **recertified** intermittently to meet regulatory requirements. A nurse must systematically evaluate a client's overall condition and critique the plan of care to ensure that continued home care is the most appropriate type of service for the client. This process occurs comprehensively during the recertification process.

KEY CONCEPT

Clients who require services beyond the certified period must be recertified intermittently to meet regulatory requirements.

DURATION

Physicians normally certify home care clients to receive services for 62 days—which is specified as the maximum duration of services in the Medicare Conditions of Participation and in many state licensing regulations. Many licensed or Medicare-certified home care agencies follow this standard for all of their clients. Often, agencies do so even when they do not expect clients to require home care for the full 62 days. Accurate predictions of necessary lengths of stay are difficult to determine. Clients often develop new problems during the course of their care—or problems that were previously not identified on admission may become evident. By certifying clients for the entire allowed period, home care agencies have the flexibility to continue to provide services if new needs arise, without repeating the extensive certification process.

SUPPLEMENTAL ORDERS

The medical treatment plan can be updated with **supplemental physician orders**. Physicians can update treatment plans by providing telephone orders to home care agencies when clients require medication changes, increases or decreases in the frequency of visits, or the addition or discharge of ancillary services. Usually, home care nurses send transcribed telephone orders to physicians for signature; however, they can usually implement the change in orders before a physician returns the signed orders.

SHORTENED OR EXTENDED SERVICES

Frequently, clients do not require services for the entire certification period, because they have met their treatment goals. Sometimes a client may no longer be homebound and can therefore receive services in other, less costly settings (e.g., a physician's office or an outpatient rehabilitation clinic). Under these circumstances, physicians provide orders to end home care, which abbreviates the 62-day certification period.

Sometimes, clients require services that surpass the 62-day certification period. Care coordinators (i.e., home care nurses) must then complete the process of recertification. Nurses complete a thorough evaluation of progress toward goals and identify goals that clients have not yet achieved. They should carefully review nursing diagnoses, objectives, and interventions to consider the continued appropriateness of existing plans of care. They should make alterations to plans of care as needed.

PAPERWORK

After finishing an evaluation, a nurse completes the new certification/recertification document, which includes a client's primary diagnoses (which the home care agency has been treating), pertinent surgeries or procedures, a comprehensive list of medications, the client's prognosis, goals for treatment, and specific orders for home care services. For Medicare clients, the certification/recertification document includes a statement in which the physician "certifies" that a client is homebound and requires intermittent skilled services. Home care nurses usually create this document, which a physician then reviews and approves. Recertification provides an opportunity for nurses to review with physicians services that they have provided over the previous 2 months, goals that clients have achieved, and plans to address ongoing needs and goals.

KEY CONCEPT

Recertification provides an opportunity for nurses to review with physicians services that they have provided over the previous 2 months, goals that clients have achieved, and plans to address ongoing needs and goals.

Survival Alert:

Plan of Care Considerations During Evaluation for Recertification

◆ Would missing assessment data (e.g., diagnostic testing, psychosocial information) modify the nursing diagnoses?
◆ Are the nursing diagnoses accurate and complete?
◆ Are the outcomes reasonable?
◆ Are the interventions appropriate for the nursing diagnoses?
◆ Do the interventions appropriately consider the client's strengths and weaknesses?
◆ Are there additional interventions that may be useful in achieving the established outcomes?
◆ What would be the appropriate frequency of home visits during the next certification period?

◆ Long-Term Planning

Many clients who require home care services are in a subacute phase of illness. For these individuals, complete recovery is fully expected and their need for healthcare services will be routine. However, 99 million Americans suffer from chronic disease. This number is expected to increase. Such individuals incur healthcare costs that are four times higher than those incurred by the rest of the population (Healthcare Leadership Review, 1997). Many of these persons require home care services and are likely to have extended healthcare needs.

KEY CONCEPT

99 million Americans suffer from chronic disease. Many of these persons receive home care services and are likely to have extended healthcare needs.

As chronic diseases progress, clients typically experience more functional deficits and therefore often require long-term supportive care. Clients may need to consider medical equipment to maximize their independence. To help them prepare appropriately for the future, nurses should assist clients with advanced chronic disease processes in long-term planning. Nurses should identify clients who can benefit from this type of planning, identify potential issues they may need to address, and target ways to address them.

ANTICIPATORY GUIDANCE

Nurses are responsible for identifying clients who require long-term planning. They can educate these clients about their disease processes and provide **anticipatory guidance** to help them realize future needs (Table 14-2). Nurses can answer clinical questions regarding probable symptoms, functional deficits, and compensatory mechanisms. Anticipatory guidance for clients with chronic disease assists them to prepare for and cope with predictable problems. Chronic progressive diseases that often result in functional deficits will limit a client's independence. Clients with diabetic retinopathy may gradually lose visual acuity and their ability to drive. Clients with multiple sclerosis may lose their ability to walk independently. Congestive heart failure often results in weakness and shortness of breath that may reduce an individual's ability to perform ADLs. Clients who receive anticipatory guidance can consider how to address these needs while they are relatively "well" and can better consider all of their options.

Anticipatory guidance can empower clients to control important areas of their lives. Often, as a client's condition worsens, a sense of helplessness and lack of control sets in. Clients can become severely depressed. They may have unsubstantiated fears and anxieties. Individuals need to understand their disease processes and the typical issues that individuals with certain diseases must face. Nurses should discuss likely

TABLE 14-2. *Anticipatory Guidance*

AREA OF CONCERN	HELPFUL HOME CARE NURSING INTERVENTIONS
Long-term planning for chronic illnesses	Nurses can educate clients about their disease processes and answer clinical questions regarding probable symptoms, functional deficits, and compensatory mechanisms. They can assist clients to prepare for and cope with predictable problems and possible limits to independence. For complex long-term planning, consultation with social workers is appropriate. Medical social workers can evaluate the need for conservatorship, perform financial counseling, and assist in finding appropriate long-term placement.
Financial considerations	Medical insurance often does not completely cover many needs of chronically ill individuals. Some clients with chronic disease also experience increased expenses in areas not typically considered to be health-related. Nurses can help clients to plan appropriately for financial issues they may have to address when choices are still available. Informed clients can investigate their insurance benefits and options like Medicaid, food stamps, and reverse mortgages. For clients with complex financial issues to evaluate, referrals to social workers can be helpful.
Emotional issues	As their clinical conditions worsen, clients may experience a sense of helplessness and lack of control. They can become severely depressed or have unsubstantiated fears and anxieties. Nurses can discuss functional deficits that may occur and compensatory mechanisms available to assist clients (e.g., medical equipment, or community resources). Examples of people with similar diagnoses who have successfully adapted to their limitations to lead satisfying lives can offer realistic models of success. Specialized support groups are also extremely helpful.
Advance directives	Anticipatory guidance helps clients to make appropriate choices about their healthcare. Nurses will often find reviewing advanced directives worthwhile for individuals with mid- to end-stage chronic diseases. For clients with the potential to lose the ability to live independently, nurses can provide information about board and care facilities, skilled nursing facilities, and private duty companies.

functional deficits that may occur, and compensatory mechanisms available to assist clients (e.g., medical equipment, and community resources). They should also address potential financial issues with clients. Clients should also be educated in emotional issues they may deal with as their independence decreases. Nurses should recognize the importance of discussing typical or common issues; discussing highly unusual cases may cause clients unnecessary anxiety, or may raise false hope.

Depending upon the progression of a client's disease, giving examples of people with the same diagnosis (while maintaining confidentiality), who have successfully adapted to their limitations and lead satisfying lives, can offer realistic models of success and assist clients to develop goals. When they are able to participate, support groups are often extremely helpful to clients with chronic disease (see Chapter 7).

Counseling and Social Services

Occasionally, long-term planning can become complex (involving multiple family issues, potential legal problems, poor coping skills, convoluted financial worries, etc.). In these circumstances, nurses will find consultation with social workers appropriate. They may want to obtain physician orders for the referral of clients to social services. Medical social workers have the experience and education to provide clients with necessary psychosocial counseling (Fig. 14-2). They can evaluate the need for **conservatorship** (legal guardianship), perform financial counseling, and assist in finding appropriate long-term placement. Nurses often work hand in hand with social workers to address long-term care issues for clients; nurses identify future clinical needs and provide anticipatory guidance, and social workers counsel clients to address other specific needs and issues.

Financial Considerations

Advanced chronic disease often results in many financial issues for clients to consider. Medical insurance often does not completely cover the many needs of chronically ill individuals. Some health plans do not cover prescriptions. Some insurance policies do not cover custodial care, board and care, or skilled nursing facilities. Clients with chronic disease also have increased expenses in areas not typically considered to be health-related. For example, individuals may need to cover the costs of gardeners, housekeepers, or repair persons to perform tasks that they once performed independently. Clients may need to pay others to drive them to grocery

Figure 14-2. A medical social worker provides anticipatory guidance for this couple. (Photo by Marilu Sherer, CARING)

stores or doctor's offices. Dependence upon others can be very costly in a number of ways; for individuals with limited resources, these additional costs can be devastating.

Anticipatory guidance enables clients to appropriately plan for financial issues they may have to address when choices are still available. Informed clients can investigate benefits they have with existing insurance policies. They may look into options such as Medicaid and food stamps. **Reverse mortgages** are a new concept in which individuals who own their homes sell them back to mortgage companies and receive monthly payments. Some life insurance policies pay out benefits before death. For clients with complex financial issues to evaluate, referrals to social workers can be helpful.

Emotional Issues

Clients with debilitating chronic diseases that become progressively worse over time must also deal with a number of emotional issues. As physical status deteriorates, clients endure many losses. Even individuals with relatively good functioning must cope with the knowledge of a diagnosis, and the awareness that a condition may advance. As functional skills decline, discomfort and pain increase, or exacerbations occur more frequently and are more severe, clients will confront changes in their social life, the inability to maintain hobbies, the loss of privacy, and the loss of activities that helped to define them as people. They may feel shame over dependence upon family or for causing financial difficulties for their loved ones. They often see the people most important to them endure anxiety about the future and grief over losing a lifestyle they enjoyed together.

Educating clients about their disease processes enables them to make decisions regarding their personal relationships and lifestyles. Individuals may wish to scale back work schedules to enjoy active hobbies as long as they are able. Some people decide to plan vacations they had intended to take much later. Some are motivated to repair personal relationships. Individuals may choose to develop hobbies they will be able to enjoy as a disease progresses. Home care nurses can simplify active decision making regarding these types of issues while performing anticipatory guidance. These types of decisions may have a tremendous impact on the quality of life and may result in greater acceptance of disease.

Advance Directives

Providing anticipatory guidance also enables clients to make appropriate choices regarding their healthcare. Nurses discuss advance directives (Fig. 14-3) with clients upon home care admission. They share so much information with clients at that time, however, that nurses will often find it worthwhile to review this issue again—especially for individuals with mid- to end-stage chronic disease. These clients, particularly, should actively make choices about the healthcare they want to receive when they can no longer express their wishes. Nurses should inform clients regarding options for dealing with specific issues. For example, if a client has a great potential to lose the ability to live independently, the nurse can provide information about board and care facilities, skilled nursing facilities, and private duty companies. The positives and negatives of each choice should be explained to allow the client the ability to make informed decisions. Clients may also wish to discuss treatment options

DECLARATION

I, *Mildred Jones*, being of sound mind, willfully and voluntarily make this declaration to be followed if I become incompetent. This declaration reflects my firm and settled commitment to refuse life-sustaining treatment under the circumstances below.

I direct my attending physician to withhold or withdraw life-sustaining treatment that serves only to prolong the process of my dying, if I should be in a terminal condition or in a state of permanent unconsciousness.

I direct that treatment be limited to measures to keep me comfortable and to relieve pain, including any pain that might occur by withholding or withdrawing life-sustaining treatment.

In addition, if I am in the condition described above, I feel especially strongly about the following forms of treatment. **I realize that if I do not specifically indicate my preference regarding any of the forms of treatment listed below, I may receive that form of treatment.**

◆ Cardiac resuscitation:	I do want (*x*)	I do not want ( )
◆ Mechanical respiration:	I do want ( )	I do not want (*x*)
◆ Tube feeding or any other artificial or invasive form of nutrition (food):	I do want ( )	I do not want (*x*)
◆ Any artificial or invasive form of hydration (water):	I do want ( )	I do not want (*x*)
◆ Blood or blood products:	I do want ( )	I do not want (*x*)
◆ Any invasive diagnostic tests:	I do want ( )	I do not want (*x*)
◆ Any form of surgery:	I do want ( )	I do not want (*x*)
◆ Kidney dialysis:	I do want ( )	I do not want (*x*)
◆ Antibiotics:	I do want (*x*)	I do not want ( )

Other instructions:

I (*x*) do ( ) do not want to designate another person as my surrogate to make medical treatment decisions for me if I should be incompetent and in a terminal condition or in a state of permanent unconsciousness.

Name and address of surrogate (if applicable):

> *Jonathan Jones*
> *423 Main Street*
> *Crossroads SC*

Name and address of substitute surrogate (if surrogate designated above is unable to serve):

> *Trudy Conover*
> *619 Wyoming Drive*
> *Crossroads SC*

I made this declaration on the *21* day of *10/95* (month, year).

Declarant's signature: *Mildred Jones*

Declarant's address: *423 Main Street*
Crossroads SC

The declarant or the person on behalf of and at the direction of the declarant knowingly and voluntarily signed this writing by signature or mark in my presence.

1. Witness's signature: *Mary Martin*
   Witness's address: *818 Hill Drive*
   Bayside CA

2. Witness's signature: *Rosa Diax*
   Witness's address: *1043 River Road*
   Summit SC

Figure 14-3. Sample advance directive.

354

that their physicians have explained to them. By using therapeutic communication and active listening skills, nurses can help clients to identify priorities and to make decisions that are consistent with issues most important to them.

◆ Transfers

Occasionally, nurses must transfer home care clients to other care settings. The chronic conditions of clients may deteriorate to the point that they can no longer live independently in their own homes. Clients may require more aggressive therapy than they can receive in the home to achieve full rehabilitative potential. Those who no longer wish curative treatment for terminal illness may join a hospice program to receive necessary services. Clients are also occasionally transferred to other home care organizations, if, for example, they are moving closer to family members. When they transfer clients to other clinical providers, nurses should act accordingly to ensure that all clinical needs are met.

Clients should always be actively involved in the decision to transfer their care. Soon after home care nurses identify the potential advantages of transferring clients, they should inform clients of their observations and conclusions. Nurses should discuss all options objectively, reviewing the advantages and disadvantages of each (Fig. 14-4). If they are required to move—even temporarily—from their own homes, clients may meet these suggestions with resistance. Nurses should not force decisions, but should allow clients to consider options over time. Doing so reinforces the need to discuss such concerns with clients early in the home care treatment period. Frequently, clients overcome their initial emotional responses to leaving their homes or changing existing care settings and focus upon the advantages and benefits.

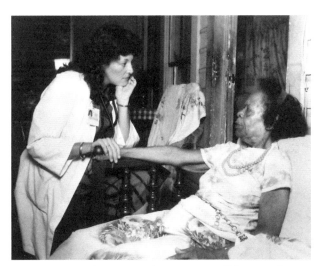

Figure 14-4. The nurse discusses possible transfer to another care setting with a client. She comforts and reassures the client, who is distressed by the change. (Photo by Marilu Sherer, CARING)

KEY CONCEPT

Clients who are asked to consider moving—even temporarily—from their own homes may resist such suggestions from nurses. Nurses should not force decisions but should allow clients to consider options over time.

Nurses must often obtain information from potential care providers to educate clients about their options appropriately. For example, they may need to verify that providers accept specific insurance policies. They may want to establish the types of clients that certain care centers accept. To protect confidentiality, clients must allow nurses to communicate information about their needs to other potential providers. When clients consent to such communication, nurses can give specific data to appropriate individuals from the healthcare organizations in question. Nurses and organizational representatives can then evaluate the appropriateness of potential transfers. Nurses must inform potential providers of all of the significant care needs of clients. Failure to reveal all pertinent client information may result in the refusal of a client before the completion of a transfer or denial of insurance coverage for care provided.

When clients agree to transfer their care to another healthcare provider, home care nurses must ease the transfer of their medical records. Nurses should follow the established policies of their agencies regarding the release of medical records. They should review records to ensure that they are complete before transfer. If possible, they should communicate directly with care providers who will treat clients in the new setting. By doing so, nurses have the ongoing opportunity to address each client's particular condition and needs. Such communication prevents gaps in care that can occur during transfer. This interaction also gives new care providers someone to contact if questions about clients arise after transfer. Nurses most commonly transfer home care clients to skilled nursing facilities, rehabilitation centers, and hospice programs.

SKILLED NURSING FACILITIES

Skilled nursing facilities provide 24-hour nursing care to clients who require extensive assistance with their ADLs or their routine medical care. They employ licensed nurses to perform skilled nursing services and to supervise procedures by nonlicensed caregivers, primarily nursing assistants. When considering transfer to a skilled nursing facility for clients, nurses should encourage them to remain independent for as long as possible. Skilled nursing facilities are usually inappropriate for clients whose needs can be met by facilities that provide lower levels of care (e.g., board and care facilities). The inappropriate transfer of clients to skilled nursing facilities can result in unnecessary healthcare expenses. Moreover, such a setting is unlikely to meet a client's comprehensive needs (e.g., may require leaving the facility regularly to perform personal errands). A skilled nursing facility must meet a client's social and physical needs. For example, a facility that primarily cares for clients with Alzheimer's disease would be unsuitable for a mentally alert and active client.

Short-Term Care

Many clients are biased against receiving care in skilled nursing facilities. Some clients have negative perceptions of "nursing homes"; they may view such centers as places where individuals go at the end of their lives, to remain alone and ignored until death. Some skilled nursing facilities, however, give care for short periods only. Nurses should educate clients who require short-term care in such facilities that their stays will be of limited duration. For example, an individual may require care in a skilled nursing facility while recovering from a CVA. During the stay, a client receives therapy and regains strength until able to function independently at home again. Other individuals may need care from a skilled nursing facility if they require services that are too frequent or irregular for home care nursing. For example, clients who need wound care six times a day or injections of pain medications every 3 to 4 hours are best served in skilled nursing facilities for a limited time. When their conditions improve, the clients can transfer to home care until they can function independently.

Long-Term Placement

Many clients require long-term placement in skilled nursing facilities. These individuals must carefully consider their options when choosing a provider. Some clients may wish to be close to family members to ease visitation. Others may desire facilities that can provide a number of interesting social activities. Financial considerations

Survival Alert:

Questions to Ask When Considering Long-Term Residential Care

- What are the client's current housing situation and living conditions?
- What services does the facility provide?
- What are the client's nutritional and exercise requirements?
- Are social interaction and companionship available?
- Does the client have any special safety concerns or psychological needs?
- Is the transfer affordable?
- Will the client be close to family, friends, and other visitors?
- Is the residence appropriate for the client's health status, mental and emotional state, and functional capacity?

(Adapted from Hunt, E.L., & Zurek, R. [1997]. Introduction to community based nursing. *Philadelphia: Lippincott-Raven.)*

Clinical Example
with Critical Thinking

Mr. Miles is an 84-year-old client with Parkinson's disease. He lived independently until a recent fall resulted in a hip fracture requiring surgical repair. After hospitalization, Mr. Miles was transferred to a skilled nursing facility and was discharged after 30 days. Mr. Miles received home care nursing therapy services to help him to return to his previous independent level of function. Kristin, the client's daughter, moved in with her father on a temporary basis to assist him until he can function independently.

Mr. Miles's Parkinson's disease has progressed, and independent function no longer appears realistic. Kristin must return to her home in another state in 3 weeks. The home care nurse has briefly discussed the possible need for long-term placement in a skilled nursing facility with Mr. Miles and Kristin. The client adamantly refuses, because he was very unhappy with the skilled nursing facility where he stayed after his hospital discharge.

1. Identify Mr. Miles's discharge options.
2. Target ways for the home care nurse to ensure an appropriate level of care when home care services are no longer appropriate.
3. Describe the anticipatory guidance that the nurse should provide for Mr. Miles.
4. Consider the information that the nurse should include in the documentation regarding the discharge plan.
5. Decide how the multidisciplinary home care team can work together to ensure a safe discharge.
6. Explain ways for a social worker to assist Mr. Miles in making appropriate decisions.

may limit the choices of some clients. Long-term placement in a skilled nursing facility can be very expensive. Social workers can help clients who require long-term placement to explore all options and provide financial counseling.

REHABILITATION CENTERS

Many clients who receive home care therapy need to continue **rehabilitation** services following their home care discharges. Home care therapy is valuable because it addresses the specific functional needs of clients in their own homes; however, therapists have limited access to equipment that could potentially advance strength and mobility. Clients who have had orthopedic surgery, for example, can often improve functional ability through continued therapy even when they are no longer homebound. When such clients can leave their homes, referrals to outpatient therapy clinics are often appropriate. Outpatient therapy programs have many pieces of exercise equipment; as a result, they can often provide more aggressive therapy for clients than programs in the home setting.

Some clients with multiple functional deficits can benefit from inpatient rehabilitation centers. Clients suffering from head injuries, neurological surgeries, or CVAs, with good rehabilitation potential, require extensive therapy (e.g., several hours a day) to achieve ultimate functional ability. Home care is limited in its ability to assist such clients, because it lacks the equipment to provide intensive therapy. In such cases, home care builds the tolerance of clients for the extended therapy they will receive in an inpatient rehabilitation center. When a client can tolerate several hours of therapy on a daily basis, transfer to an inpatient rehabilitation center is appropriate.

HOSPICE

Hospice programs provide specialized supportive services in the home to clients diagnosed with terminal illnesses who no longer wish to receive treatment designed to cure or to prolong life. Hospice is designed to keep terminally ill clients in their own homes as long as possible. Many home care agencies, skilled nursing facilities, and hospitals provide hospice care. Organizations that provide hospice care exclusively also exist. Home care agencies typically have designated teams of clinicians who care for hospice clients. Hospice is considered a specialty form of home care. Concepts of nursing practice in home care are generally applicable to the care of hospice clients. Hospice is distinguished by the specific client populations served, and the philosophy of hospice that permeates the care provided.

Hospice is a concept of care, not a place (Display 14-1). The hospice philosophy encourages clients and their lay caregivers to live each day fully. It focuses on the quality of life of clients and their families. Supportive personnel assist clients and their lay caregivers through the stages of dying to achieve acceptance. Hospice programs have medical directors who oversee clients' care. They provide medical

---

Display 14-1:
Principles of Hospice

- ◆ A client's quality of life is more important than the quantity of life.
- ◆ Clients and their families are units who require care.
- ◆ Most needs of dying clients can be met in their homes.
- ◆ Because the needs of clients cannot always be filled in the home, inpatient services must also be available.
- ◆ Hospice services must be available 24 hours a day, 7 days a week.
- ◆ An interdisciplinary team serves hospice clients and families to fulfill their many complex needs.
- ◆ Hospice interventions focus on management and control of the physical, emotional, and spiritual needs of clients and families.

(Adapted from Craven, R.F., & Hirnle, C.J. [1996]. Fundamentals of nursing: Human health and function. *Philadelphia: Lippincott-Raven)*

guidance to the hospice team to manage the symptoms of terminal diseases aggressively. Nurses within hospice programs have specialized training in symptom management, pain control, and the psychosocial aspects of care needed by terminally ill clients and their loved ones. Experts in spiritual and emotional counseling are members of the interdisciplinary team who view clients and their lay caregivers as a unit. Care is highly comprehensive and holistic. Assessment and care planning for hospice clients attempts to address the extensive physical, emotional, psychological, and spiritual issues associated with death and the dying person.

KEY CONCEPT

Hospice is a concept of care, not a place. The hospice philosophy encourages clients and their lay caregivers to live each day fully. It focuses on the quality of life of clients and their families.

Although the most common diagnosis treated by hospice programs in this country is cancer, the philosophy of hospice is appropriate for any terminal illness. Clients with end-stage respiratory disease, cardiac disease, renal disease, Alzheimer's disease, AIDS, and other chronic conditions benefit from services that hospice offers. Dying is considered a process, not an event. Clients and their significant others endure incredible physical and emotional changes during this process (Gurfolino & Dumas, 1994). Hospice assists individuals through these changes and empowers them to make decisions consistent with their values in aspects of their lives over which they retain control.

Hospice Nursing

Nurses in home care who choose to specialize in the provision of hospice care must become comfortable with death as a stage of life. Most nurses and healthcare providers usually spend their entire careers helping clients to prolong life. The concept of accepting death without actively attempting to delay it is foreign to many nurses. The hospice philosophy views death as a natural phase of life that can be emotionally, spiritually, and physically challenging. Individuals enduring this life phase need the professional support of clinicians who assist them with confronting unresolved emotional and spiritual issues. The clinicians also address physical needs. The ability to form therapeutic relationships is extremely important for hospice nurses. Aside from pain and symptom control, these nurses focus interventions upon helping clients to accept death while living fully, one day at a time. As Fisher explains, "What people near death do need is to be free of pain and fear, to be comfortable and relaxed. They need to be listened to no matter how subtle or even obscure their means of communication may be . . . (The client) needs to hear words of love and reassurance" (1996, p. 57). Hospice nurses are supportive and caring toward clients and their significant others. They encourage loved ones to provide support for clients during an emotionally charged and draining period of their lives.

The cornerstone of hospice care is teaching clients and lay caregivers to empower themselves and to feel in control of suffering and pain. Hospice nurses support clients and lay caregivers and help them to face the enormous physical and emotional changes encountered during the dying process. Process is a critical concept to understand when caring for dying persons. The phases of dying continually change and overlap and finally culminate in death (Gurfolino & Dumas, 1994).

Reimbursement
Medicare covers hospice services for beneficiaries who have received a prognosis of 6 months or less and no longer desire curative treatment. Hospice services are broader in scope than those services provided in the Medicare home care benefit. They usually include care from nurses, volunteers, social workers, pastoral care personnel, home health aides, and medical directors. Medicare covers all professional and paraprofessional services, equipment, medications, respite services for lay caregivers, and medical services (e.g., diagnostic services, and acute hospitalizations) associated with the care of terminally ill clients. Medicare reimburses hospice programs at a flat rate: a per day charge for every day the client receives the hospice benefit. Reimbursement covers all of the expenses for services rendered through the program. Most insurance companies mirror the Medicare hospice benefit in their coverage guidelines. When nurses transfer home care clients to hospice organizations, home care services are discontinued. Care is transferred to the hospice provider.

Volunteers
Volunteers are an important component in hospice programs. Medicare-certified hospice programs are required to maintain specific levels of volunteer hours and ensure that volunteers are adequately trained if they provide services to hospice clients. Volunteers perform a variety of functions. Lay caregivers of hospice clients have demanding physical and emotional responsibilities. These individuals may be awake several times a night to administer pain medications or provide company for their loved ones. They are facing their own issues of grief, yet may not want their loved ones to see their pain. They may hide their feelings and attempt to maintain cheerful countenances to avoid worrying clients. Volunteers can provide tremendous assistance. They can perform errands for family members who do not want to leave their loved ones alone. They may stay with clients whose families need a day of respite to relax and to visit friends (Fig. 14-5). Volunteers may spend time with clients and allow them to talk about issues of concern that they are uncomfortable sharing with lay caregivers. Volunteers actively participate in the care planning process and are an integral part of the team. All activities hospice volunteers perform provide tremendous assistance to clients, their lay caregivers, and the professional hospice team.

Early Referrals to Hospice
Hospice is most beneficial for clients and their significant others when nurses refer terminally ill clients early. Clients who have the opportunity to understand their limited prognoses can go through the emotional work of grief and ultimate acceptance. The hospice team can develop trusting, therapeutic relationships with clients and loved ones that are effective in managing the end stage of terminal illness. They

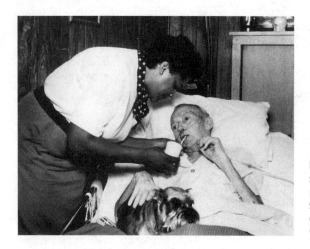

Figure 14-5. This volunteer spends some time with a hospice client, providing needed respite for his primary lay caregiver. (Photo by Marilu Sherer, CARING)

can help clients and families to accept emotional and spiritual assistance and to cope with the stress of dying. Too often, clients do not enter hospice programs until pain and symptoms are out of control. Physicians may have difficulty discussing limited prognoses with clients out of fear that they will become depressed and lose the will to stay as well and as active as possible. Some physicians have difficulty accepting death because they view it as a failure to fulfill the obligation to make clients well. Waiting until clients are in crisis to discuss limited prognoses, however, can create tremendous emotional turmoil for clients and their families, exacerbating symptoms even further. Home care nurses are often the first clinicians to identify the potential advantages of a hospice referral. Nurses should discuss this option with physicians before addressing this sensitive issue with clients.

◆ Discharge From Home Care

Nurses should gradually prepare home care clients for their eventual discharge from services. They initiate this process during the first home visit, and continue it with all subsequent visits. Nurses give all services with the ultimate goal of ensuring each client's maximum wellness and safety after clients no longer receive services.

PLANNING

As care coordinators, nurses initiate discharge planning with a client's admission to home care services, and continue the process throughout treatment. When clients assist in the development of their goals, they are better able to recognize their readiness for discharge. Nurses must continually update clients about milestones suggesting progress toward these goals. Clients and lay caregivers must be ready to assume care independently upon discharge. They should agree to the discharge, knowing whom to contact with problems or concerns. They should contact any private resources available to them, and be aware of their eligibility for support

Home Care Vs. Hospital:
Discharge Planning

Issue	Home Care	Hospital
Responsible party	Home care nurses are primarily responsible for developing an appropriate discharge plan for all home care clients.	Designated individuals within the acute care setting are responsible for performing discharge planning.
Psychosocial elements	Clients and their families can become anxious with a pending home care discharge. For them, discharge means the loss of social support from their home care providers and the loss of helpful services. Clients who have received services for extended periods may have developed dependent relationships with nurses. As a result, they may unconsciously attempt to delay discharge by developing ambiguous symptoms or regressing in their knowledge and skills.	Multiple nurses care for clients in acute care settings. Dependent relationships are less likely to develop. Hospitalizations are relatively short, and clients expect to be discharged as soon as possible. Clients may be anxious because of recent acute illness, fear of recurrence, and doubts about their ability to care for themselves at home. Discharge, however, is based upon rigid guidelines. Hospital personnel have little discretion in delaying discharge without objective clinical findings.
Identification of discharge criteria	Home care nurses are primarily responsible for identifying indications for the appropriateness of discharge from home care. Nurses determine when clients have knowledge of health information and are proficient in skills. They communicate this information to physicians, with recommendations to discontinue home care services, to receive physician orders.	A client's nurse is generally not accountable for identifying the need for discharge. The physician, utilization review nurse, or case manager is primarily accountable for identifying that discharge criteria are met.

from community programs (Esposito, 1994). When multidisciplinary teams devise comprehensive discharge plans upon admission, clients are better prepared for the eventual discontinuation of home care services.

REFERRALS TO COMMUNITY ORGANIZATIONS

Often, appropriate home care discharge includes referrals to community organizations that fulfill long-term needs for clients (see Chapter 7). Ethical, legal, and regulatory guidelines mandate that home care agencies prevent the premature or inappropriate discharge of clients from services. Moreover, agencies must give clients information about appropriate resources. Nurses must perform reasonable interventions to ensure that they have maintained home safety after services are discontinued. Clients must receive appropriate follow-up measures for any outstanding problems. Nurses can accomplish these objectives by instructing clients and lay caregivers regarding necessary ongoing physician visits, educating clients about outpatient laboratories they may need to contact, providing information about adult day care centers, and alerting clients to services offered by senior centers and other community organizations. Clients and their lay caregivers should be able to verbalize clearly how to contact assistance if problems develop. These actions help to ensure maximum wellness for clients long after home care services end.

Display 14-2:
Indications for Discharge From Home Care Services

The treatment objectives are obtained or are no longer attainable:

- The client has regained a maximum level of physical, social, and emotional functioning and independence.
- The client and lay caregivers have learned to provide safe, effective, and efficient methods of care.
- The client has been hospitalized, institutionalized, or sent to an outpatient service.
- The client dies.
- Changes in the home or support situation make home care impossible for the client.

Purposeful and ongoing lack of cooperation from the client and/or lay caregiver in attaining treatment objectives have rendered multiple efforts by multidisciplinary home care staff ineffective. The client has neglected his or her responsibilities in the implementation of the home care service plan. This lack of cooperation may be exhibited as follows:

- Client repeatedly refuses home care visits.
- Consistent failure of client, lay caregiver, or responsible party to follow treatment plan prescribed by the physician.
- An able client refuses to visit the physician, rendering the physician unable to continue to prescribe an effective medical treatment plan.
- The client moves out of the geographic area of the home health agency, and care must be transferred to another provider.

The client's physician orders a home care discharge or refuses to renew home care orders for continued home care.

- The client requests termination of home care services.
- Home care is no longer medically necessary
- The client is no longer homebound and can receive necessary healthcare services through his physician or through outpatient services.

INDICATIONS FOR DISCHARGE

When clients meet discharge criteria (Display 14-2) before the certification period ends, physicians must authorize the discontinuation of home care services. Care coordinators submit written discharge summaries that include a client's progress during home care services, the client's status at the time of discharge, and any referrals made to community resources to physicians. Discharge summaries typically provide brief synopses of the types of interventions performed for clients, and client health outcomes.

KEY CONCEPT

When clients meet discharge criteria before the end of the certification period, a physician must authorize the discontinuation of home care services.

Psychosocial Elements for Clients and Lay Caregivers

Home care professionals must realize that clients and their lay caregivers sometimes become quite anxious when faced with a client's impending discharge from service. Clients who have received services for many months are likely to become distressed at the prospect of such services ending. Clients often develop strong relationships with nurses and other personnel. For them, discharge means the loss of social support from their home care providers and the loss of helpful services.

Clients or lay caregivers may unconsciously attempt to delay or to prevent discharge from home care. Clients may suddenly develop ambiguous symptoms. Lay caregivers may decompensate and become unable to perform procedures in which they had previously shown competency. Home care nurses should recognize the anxiety many clients face at discharge and provide the appropriate emotional support and reassurances they need during this difficult transition.

KEY CONCEPT

Home care professionals must remember that clients and their lay caregivers may become anxious when faced with an impending discharge from service. For these clients, discharge represents the loss of social support and helpful services.

Encouragement of Independence

Home care nurses should encourage independence as much as possible throughout the duration of service. Occasionally, nurses lose their objectivity concerning clients that they have worked with for long periods. They may unwittingly encourage a client's dependence. Nurses may unconsciously exaggerate the significance of clinical findings to rationalize a delay in a client's discharge. When they unreasonably postpone discharge, nurses waste resources; moreover, they encourage unhealthy, dependent relationships with their clients. All clients, including those with extended treatment periods, deserve to be prepared for eventual discharge from services when they are admitted to home care. Nurses should discuss discharge throughout the duration of home care services to reduce the trauma of separation for clients and for themselves.

KEY CONCEPT

When they unreasonably delay discharge from home care, nurses waste resources and encourage unhealthy, dependent relationships with clients. Encouraging the independence of clients and preparing them for discharge from services help nurses to avoid these pitfalls.

◆ Documentation

Home care documentation must reflect the appropriate frequency of subsequent visits. If documentation reflects stability in a client's status, and that the client and lay caregiver(s) have knowledge of critical health information, the frequency of visits should correspond with the minimal needs of the client. Conversely, if the medical record reflects an unstable medical condition, and learning needs regarding critical health issues, the frequency of subsequent visits should be appropriate to meet the client's more urgent needs. A lack of consistency between documentation of needs and visit frequency can result in regulatory and payor investigation and potential penalties.

Home care nurses must also carefully document performed interventions related to long-term care planning, anticipatory guidance, transfers to other care settings, and discharge planning. This documentation reflects the home care nurse's efforts to ensure appropriate continuity of care when home care services are no longer indicated or appropriate. Documentation is particularly significant when clients exercise the right to choose discharge options that do not fully address their rehabilitation potential or other needs.

◆ Summary

Nursing interventions that help clients reach their goals are predominantly achieved through subsequent home care visits. Nurses must learn skills to perform subsequent visits efficiently and effectively. They must develop an effective system for implementing home visits and performing skills necessary to assess clients' needs. Clients with extended home care needs require nurses to complete a recertification process to conform with regulatory and payor standards. Occasionally, home care cannot effectively meet a client's needs, and the home care nurse must transfer the client to another care setting. Home care nurses need to develop skills related to long-term care planning and anticipatory guidance. Effective discharge planning should start with the initiation of a client's home care treatment plan. Personnel from all disciplines should involve clients and lay caregivers in discharge planning throughout care. Clients and their caregivers will feel a sense of accomplishment as they progress toward goals and established objectives. Home care teams are rewarded with the accomplishment of helping clients to achieve optimal health and safety.

References and Bibliography

Amado, A.J., Grow, V. & Nofziger, J. (1995). An evaluation of hospice care with terminally ill cancer patients. *Caring, XIV*(11), 27–30.

Bergevin, P.R. (1995). Hospice techniques: Creating the story of a life. *American Journal of Hospice and Palliative Care, 12*(6), 11, 27.

Bramwell, L., MacKenzie, J., Laschinger, H. & Cameron, N. (1995). Need for overnight respite for primary caregivers of hospice clients. *Cancer Nursing, 18*(5), 337–343.

(1997). Chronic care crisis predicted. *Healthcare Leadership Review, 16*(2), 15.

Durour, D. (1989). Home or hospital care for the child with end-stage cancer. *Issues in Comprehensive Pediatric Nursing, 12*(5), 71–83.

Esposito, L. (1994). The home care nurse as case manager. *Caring, 13*(4), 30–33.

Fisher, R. (1996). Dealing with death. *American Journal of Nursing, 96*(7), 56–57.

Fryback, P. & Reinert, B. (1993). Facilitating health in people with terminal diagnoses by encouraging a sense of control. *MEDSURG Nursing, 2*(3), 197–201.

Gurfolino, V. & Dumas, L. (1994). Hospice nursing: The concept of palliative care. *Nursing Clinics of North America, 29*(3), 533–546.

Hirsch, M.A. (1995). Uniquely hospice: Policies and procedures of terminal care at home. *Caring, XIV*(11), 20–26.

Hull, M.M. (1991). Hospice nurses: Caring support for caregiving families. *Cancer Nursing, 14*(2), 63–70.

Kammer, C. (1994). Stress and coping of family members responsible for nursing home placement. *Research in Nursing and Health, 17*(2), 89–98.

Lumsdon, K. (1993). Bridging the gap: Home- and community-based programs integrate acute and long-term care. *Aging Today, 76*(23), 44, 48.

Malone-Rising, D. (1994). The changing face of long-term care. *Nursing Clinics of North America, 29*(3), 417–430.

Mitchell, S. (1994). Facilitating transitions across care settings. *Canadian Oncology Nursing Journal, 4*(2), 104–106.

O'Rawe Amenta, M. (1996). Hospice nursing and managed care. *Home Healthcare Nurse, 14*(10), 815–816.

Stulginsky, M. (1993). Nurses' home health experience. Part II. The unique demands of home visits. *Nursing and Healthcare, 14*(9), 476–485.

Yost L. (1995). Cancer patients and home care. *Cancer Practice, 3*(2), 83–87.

POST TEST

1. Discuss the importance of subsequent nursing visits and steps that nurses should take when preparing for them.

2. Explain why most home care agencies certify all clients for 62 days, regardless of whether their conditions seem to warrant longer or shorter stays initially.

3. Determine the role of anticipatory guidance in long-term planning for clients.

4. Name common transfers that home care nurses make for clients.

5. Identify important concepts of hospice care.

6. Explain ways for nurses to ease the discharge of clients from home care.

THINKING CRITICALLY IN HOME CARE

It is 4:00 p.m. on Monday. Helen, a home care nurse, has just reviewed her schedule for the following day. She needs to determine an appropriate order for her appointments with clients. The following clients are slated for visits tomorrow:

	PRIMARY NEED	*STATUS*
Mr. Loomer	Newly insulin-dependent diabetic requires education on injections, S/S hyper- and hypoglycemia	New client referral: initial assessment visit
Expected length of visit: 2 hours		
Mrs. Thorp	Wound care of Stage III decubitus at coccyx	Client has been receiving services for 4 weeks; son is a competent lay caregiver; receives daily dressing changes—dressing usually saturates and leaks by early morning.
Expected length of visit: 45 minutes		
Mrs. Perez	Assessment of CHF status and lung sounds; evaluate medication compliance	Client has been on home care service for 5 weeks; called previous afternoon to report increased LE edema, HH supervisor moved weekly nursing visit up 2 days.
Expected length of visit: 45 minutes		
Mrs. O'Meary	Teach and assess medication compliance—multiple prescriptions and history of noncompliance; resulting in exacerbations of respiratory distress and hospitalizations. Dx: COPD	Client has been on home care service for 2 weeks; lives alone. Question client's ability to continue to live alone.
Expected length of visit: 45 minutes		

(continued)

	PRIMARY NEED	STATUS
Mrs. Paxton	Home health aide supervisory visit	Client has been on service for 3 months, receiving intermittent nursing visits every 4 weeks for urinary catheter changes. Home health aide visits three times a week. 36-year-old woman with multiple sclerosis, wheelchair bound. The client prefers a morning home health aide visit to receive her personal care.

Expected length of visit: 30 min.

Total Visit Time: 4 hours 45 min.

Total Expected Travel Time: 1 hour

Total Expected Documentation Time: 1 hour 30 min.

Total Miscellaneous Office Time, e.g., Phone Call/Gather Supplies. 45 min.

Total Work Day: 8 hours

1. Based on the above information, arrange a tentative schedule for Helen to follow. The schedule should begin at 07:30 and end at 16:00. Be sure to factor in time for lunch and breaks as well.

2. Provide a rationale for the order in which you schedule Helen's visits to each client.

Post Test Answers

◆ Chapter 1—Home Care Overview

1. a. St. Vincent de Paul organized a group of women who visited the sick in their homes, and with Mademoiselle Le Gras formed the Sisterhood of the Dames de Charité. They contributed to the development of home care as a practice that provided health education and supervision to caregivers of the sick. Their philosophy of service was unique for its time—De Paul and Le Gras believed that interventions should focus on the causes of health problems, and that the best way to serve people was to help them help themselves.

   b. Florence Nightingale's work dramatically influenced the provision of community health nursing. She believed that individuals were responsible for their health. Nursing was not just attending to the sick, but also educating individuals in ways to best promote their health. These premises are basic to home care nursing.

   c. William Rathbone worked closely with Florence Nightingale to establish a school to train home care nurses in England. He successfully created a program in which trained personnel provided home care services in the city of Liverpool.

   d. Lillian Wald raised the public's awareness of the significant impact of home care. She wrote two books about her experiences caring for impoverished, urban populations afflicted with illness: *The House on Henry Street* (1915) and *Windows on Henry Street* (1934). Wald worked with Mary Brewster to provide healthcare services in poor, immigrant neighborhoods. They gave nursing care to the needy and worked for legislative and social reforms to improve the living conditions of their society. Wald is considered the founder of "public health nursing" and actually coined the term.

2. Regulatory bodies that have developed standards of quality for home care services include state licensing departments, the Joint Commission of Accreditation of Healthcare Organizations (JCAHO), the Community Health Accreditation Program (CHAP), and the Health Care Finance Administration (HCFA).

3. Trends that are significantly changing the home care industry include technological improvements, pursuit of cost-effective health plans, the aging American population, changes in family status—including less family-based social support, increased personal responsibility for health, and increased demands for lay caregivers to learn complex healthcare concepts and procedures.

4. Nurses depend heavily upon the participation and support of lay caregivers, because home care professionals are usually present in each client's home for only 1 to 4 hours per week. During the remaining time, clients and their lay caregivers must understand critical information to manage disease processes independently. Often, the most important lesson for them to master is knowing when to call nurses for help or advice, because serious complications related to disease can occur at any time. Clients and lay caregivers must recognize beginning symptoms of problems and know early interventions to perform to avoid serious complications.

5. Preceptors can help nurses entering home care practice to adapt to independent practice and broad accountability. They can explain the need to learn about community resources, indications for ancillary services, pressures from managed care companies, heavy documentation requirements, client/caregiver conflicts, and productivity expectations. Preceptors help nurses adapting to home care through a period of reality shock, providing expert advice as nurses learn how to problem-solve difficult situations independently. Preceptors provide basic information about accessing supplies, submitting documentation, coordinating client schedules to reduce travel time, and introducing oneself to a new client; such information helps to advance nurses from learners to independent practitioners. This assistance improves client care, decreases burnout, and increases job satisfaction.

◆ Chapter 2—Comparison of Home Care and Acute Care Nursing

1. Nurses in hospitals and other acute care settings have many conveniences at their fingertips: beds that elevate, necessary medical supplies, comprehensive and updated medical records, and clean sheets and gowns. The environment belongs to the providers of healthcare. Clients often feel uncomfortable in acute care settings. They must ask someone where to find a bathroom. Clients are frequently dependent upon nurses for many needs that they cannot meet themselves. Meals are served "on schedule." Baths are given when nurses or nursing assistants are available for assistance. Clients wear hospital gowns instead of their own robes. In home care, clients are in their own environments—their homes, and their "castles." Home care personnel are guests within the homes of clients. Clients know where the bathrooms are and where to find their medications. Clients determine when they will eat and bathe. Nurses have very limited control over most environmental factors that may affect the health of home care clients. Clients with financial concerns may not control the temperatures of their homes appropriately. They may be at risk for dehydration in hot areas, or hypothermia in cold environments. Clients may not be able to afford medications, or medical equipment to maintain environmental safety. Clients may have trouble leaving their homes and may miss ap-

pointments with their doctors. Doorways that are too narrow for wheelchairs may make it difficult for clients to reach their own bathrooms.

2. Unique relationships often develop between home care nurses and their clients. Nurses get to know the "whole" client. Photographs in clients' homes give nurses insight about the individuals they are treating. Home care nurses are exposed to the hobbies and relationships of their clients. They have the chance to touch the lives of their clients and to experience a sense of professional leadership and independence.

3. Assessment skills needed by nurses working in acute care settings change when they move to home care. Unlike in hospital practice, home care nurses must comprehensively evaluate a client's status based on their own observations and the reports of clients and their lay caregivers. In home care, nurses must perform a holistic assessment, considering not only physical, but psychological, emotional, economic, and environmental factors affecting their clients and lay caregivers. They must create plans of care that address critical issues of health and safety that clients and lay caregivers can manage independently.

4. In home care, education to enable clients and lay caregivers to be independent in skills and knowledgeable in important concepts is often critical for safety. Clients and lay caregivers who do not possess necessary skills or knowledge may perform medical treatment plans incompletely or incorrectly. Disastrous consequences to health and well-being can result. When clients are in their own homes, they are usually less anxious and less acutely ill. Such factors enhance their readiness for learning. Barriers to learning still may exist, however. As in hospitals, these barriers include the effects of medications, a client's diagnosis, pain, and anxiety. Additionally, illness often exacerbates psychosocial issues in family systems that may contribute to learning difficulties. Sometimes, the home environment itself is not conducive to learning. Distractions, such as clutter, many visitors, and children, can impede the learning process. Teaching materials are not as readily available in homes as they are in hospitals; therefore, home care nurses must carefully plan instructional sessions to decide whether they need any items.

5. Home care nurses must be able to identify client issues that community resources can resolve, and have a working knowledge of ways to contact these resources. Nurses in home care become aware of comprehensive and holistic issues of clients that may not be evident in hospitals (e.g., alcohol abuse, financial hardships, or strained family relationships). Such issues are often difficult to detect during a short hospitalization. Home care nurses must assess the client for all potential community resource needs. Developing friendly, professional relationships with contact people within community organizations can help home care nurses simplify client access to many free or low-cost services of nonprofit organizations. Therefore, the nursing advocacy role in home care demands that effective nurses network with organizations that can help clients in need.

6. Significant others can greatly influence the quality of care that clients receive; their influence can be negative or positive. Lay caregivers can be verbally, physically, or emotionally abusive or neglectful, negatively influencing a client's health. They may not administer medications, provide treatments, or prepare meals as directed. Lay caregivers may incorrectly carry out physician orders because of a lack of understanding, or because of cultural or language barriers. Most lay caregivers are eager to learn how they can help promote the recovery of their loved ones. These lay caregivers can provide emotional and spiritual support, laughter, memories, and sometimes physical care unmatched by any healthcare professional.

◆ Chapter 3—Managed Care

1. Traditionally, financial incentives existed to increase the use of expensive healthcare services. When Medicare was initiated in 1965, the federal government reimbursed healthcare based upon the use of services and the cost to healthcare providers to perform such services. Medicare imposed few limits on spending, and the healthcare industry grew rapidly. This system encouraged organizations to charge high rates and to use resources excessively. In 1982, the Tax Equity and Fiscal Responsibility Act attempted to contain the uncontrolled costs of hospital services. It started a prospective payment system in an attempt to decrease the growing tax burden. Within this system, hospitals were forced to accept some financial risk for providing inpatient services to clients. A flat reimbursement schedule for established Diagnostic Related Groupings (DRGs) would be used to establish reimbursement provided to hospitals each time a client was admitted. Hospitals thus initiated earlier discharges for clients and decreased their use of expensive and unnecessary ancillary services and supplies. Initially, increases in the cost of health insurance premiums were merely passed on to the customer. As competition and price sensitivity of products continued to grow, however, businesses could no longer accept rising health insurance expenditures and remain viable. They demanded lower cost insurance products. Insurance companies responded to these demands with the advent of managed care.

2. Managed care is often criticized for directing large amounts of money away from care-related activities to administrative functions; discriminatory practices; restrictions regarding the healthcare providers available to clients; gag rules; and conflict of interest issues that arise from financial incentives for healthcare providers to withhold services. Responses to the many criticisms of managed care include legislative processes on both the state and federal levels; accreditation processes and market forces; businesses choosing MCOs based upon data regarding quality of services; employers managing employee healthcare themselves; and point of service plans.

3. Critical pathways can be exceptionally useful to home care nurses because of the generalized nature of home care practice. Home care nurses see a variety

of client populations; they are unlikely to know the best practice patterns for every diagnosis they encounter. Critical pathways can guide nurses to perform necessary teaching, verify correct medical treatment plans, and initiate appropriate referrals to ensure that their clients achieve expected clinical outcomes cost effectively.

4. The role of the home care nurse changes in the managed care environment. A home care nurse must fulfill the role of client advocate. When managed care plans cover clients, the care coordinator role of home care nursing becomes extremely important. Nurses will need to cross train, appeal decisions, and cooperate with MCOs to serve their clients best.

5. The home care nurse fulfills the role of client advocate when the nurse understands how to ensure approval and payment for needed services from MCOs—who often require regular reports about their clients' progress toward established goals in medical treatment plans. These reports must be provided in a timely way, or payment of services may be denied, causing clients or home care agencies to be financially liable for the cost of care.

6. Overall, home care agencies will find their best interests served by developing partnerships with MCOs that are motivated to achieve the same objectives: positive outcomes, prevention of physical deterioration, and satisfaction of clients. Relationships with MCOs should be collaborative, as nurses and organizational representatives work together to develop the most cost-effective plans of care to achieve client outcomes. Efforts to achieve cooperation with MCOs, however, should never compromise the primary responsibility of home care providers to ensure safe and effective care for clients.

◆ Chapter 4—Cultural Adaptability

1. The composition of American society is changing rapidly. The United States Census Bureau predicts that by the year 2080, over half of the American population will consist of individuals currently labeled minorities. Between the years 1990 and 2030, the American Association of Retired Persons (AARP) predicts that the white population will increase by 93%, compared with a projected increase of 328% for older minorities. The influence of new social groups is being felt most strongly in the sprawling urban areas of the East and West Coasts and in the growing metropolitan areas of the South.

2. To provide effective home care, nurses must develop a strong set of skills to guide and direct their practice. The development of communication skills for assessment and teaching, and creativity to incorporate cultural beliefs into care planning is essential for providing quality care. Nurses in home care often see a broad range of problems and work with many physicians whose practice patterns vary. As a result, nurses often need to develop a tremendous range of assessment, interviewing, and procedural skills.

3. The more a home care nurse knows about a client's culture even before the first visit, the more likely the plan of care will be successful. One of the best resources for home care nurses to consult is the supervisor or experienced peer. Many community service agencies also have staff experienced in working with culturally diverse populations. As a group of staff members work with a particular population, they may want to meet regularly to share ideas and to develop a journal of tips related to that particular group. Nurses may also want to examine materials that address cultural issues.

4. As nurses work with different cultural groups and talk with peers who have had similar work experiences, understanding of cultural variations becomes clearer and more comprehensive. Home care nurses within an agency may find it beneficial to "pool" cultural information in written form, creating a handbook of suggestions and references specific to the populations that the agency serves.

◆ Chapter 5—Documentation

1. Documentation in home care is necessary for financial, regulatory, quality control, legal, and communication purposes.

2. Inaccurate documentation has a direct impact on the receipt of reimbursement for the care provided to home care clients. Insurance companies obtain facts about clients and care provided to them to determine whether coverage guidelines are met. Vague documentation can cause payors to have an inaccurate picture of a client's status, and may result in the denial of payment for home care services.

3. Organizations that evaluate home care documentation are JCAHO, CHAP, Medicare, Peer Review Organizations, and state licensing authorities.

4. Teaching is probably the most underdocumented skilled service performed by nurses.

5. Much of the communication among professionals involved in a case is written, because of the relatively infrequent opportunities for personal interaction. Incomplete or inaccurate communication of a client's care can result in inappropriate care and negative client outcomes.

6. The old adage, "if it's not documented, it wasn't done" is one that continues to apply in the courts today. The complete recording of a client's assessment and all actions taken to address client issues is the nurse's best defense in court.

7. In home care, various third party payors depend heavily upon the documentation of nurses to determine whether interventions are covered according to the criteria established in insurance plans. Failure to appropriately record a client's clinical findings can result in denial of coverage for services.

8. Home care nurses must understand Medicare criteria for home care services. Medicare is currently the largest payor for home care, and most other payors use Medicare guidelines as a model for their coverage criteria.

9. Care is ordered by a qualified physician; services are required on an intermittent or part-time basis; the client is homebound; services are skilled; and services are medically necessary.

10. Three disciplines that are considered to provide skilled services under Medicare are nursing, physical therapy, and speech pathology.

◆ Chapter 6—Client Rights and Responsibilities

1. Laws regulating the maintenance of client rights for home care agencies are outlined in the Omnibus Reconciliation Act of 1987. Failure to comply with these laws will result in serious consequences for agencies. JCAHO and CHAP are accrediting bodies that also stipulate measures home care agencies must take to ensure maintenance of client rights.

2. The client right that is more significant in home care than in hospitals is the right to respect for a client's property.

3. Educating

4. False

5. Home care agencies have an obligation to provide care only if they have adequate resources to meet the needs of clients. Care must be provided in accordance with physician orders. Appropriately trained personnel must perform the required care. Clients must be educated about potential emergencies and what actions they should take should an emergency occur.

6. Responsibilities of clients include giving accurate and complete information about their health; assisting with the development of a safe environment; informing home care agencies when they are unable to keep scheduled visits; participating in their care planning; adhering to their plans of care; requesting additional information if they lack understanding; sharing concerns and problems with staff members.

◆ Chapter 7—Coordination of Care and Interdisciplinary Communication

1. Conditions that warrant a need for rehabilitative therapy include fractures or dislocations; orthopedic surgeries (joint replacements or reconstructive surgeries); degenerative joint or disc disease; rheumatoid arthritis; amputations; new prostheses; burns with joint involvement or other involvement that reduces function; cerebral vascular accidents; multiple sclerosis; head injuries; spinal cord injuries; Parkinson's disease; amyotrophic lateral sclerosis; neuropathies or myopathies that cause functional limitations; chronic obstructive pulmonary disease; chronic cardiac disease; functional limitations that require utilization of special assistive devices; laryngectomies or glossectomies; dysphagia; hearing loss; and blindness.

2. Developing an awareness of community resources often can make the difference between helping clients remain safely independent in their own homes and institutionalization or injury.

3. Failure to coordinate a home care treatment plan can result in conflicting interventions by personnel from involved disciplines. Lack of coordination can result in frustration, increased morbidity, lack of progress toward treatment goals, or rehospitalization. If instructions from involved healthcare professionals repeatedly conflict, clients may lose confidence in their judgment.

4. Home care professionals may rarely see the other providers involved in the delivery of a client's treatment. The chances of providing services simultaneously, or meeting other providers in home care offices are remote. Home care professionals tend to be unavailable when paged. Professionals are generally with clients, and unable to fully discuss the circumstances of other clients over the phone because of the need for confidentiality; also, when they are traveling, stopping to use a phone may be inconvenient and time consuming. Medical records within home care agencies are usually not as current as hospital medical records. Frequently, community agencies or organizations outside the control of home care organizations fulfill components of plans of care. They do not formally document in home care medical records or communicate pertinent information to primary physicians. Yet, their interventions can be equally important to the success of a home care treatment plan.

◆ Chapter 8—The Home Care Nurse as Supervisor

1. Home health aides are trained to provide "hands on" supportive services to clients, including assistance with bathing, toileting, ambulating, transferring, range of motion exercises, and meal preparation; they also assist in feeding patients, perform light housekeeping to maintain a client's health and safety, and perform simple skin care. Homemakers are not required to have any formal specialized training, and they provide services that typically do not require them to "touch" clients. These services may include housekeeping, simple meal preparation, performing errands, shopping, and companionship.

2. Home health aide duties may include assisting clients with simple exercises to supplement therapy services, ambulation, personal care, household services essential to health care at home, and administration of medications that are ordinarily self-administered; they also may report changes in a client's condition and needs, and complete appropriate records.

3. Nurses perform supervisory visits to evaluate the continued appropriateness of home health aides' assignments and to ensure that clients are achieving their goals. Supervising aides in the home can allow nurses to ensure that aides use appropriate technique, perform duties completely and accurately, and treat clients with respect.

4. In home care, nurses must accept the role of supervisor or manager of the care that aides give to clients. For many nurses, this role is the first supervisory responsibility of their career. Home care nurses must understand basic concepts of management to fulfill this responsibility successfully. Management consists of four primary functions: planning, organizing, directing, and controlling. The management process is very similar to the nursing process (see Chapter 9). During the **planning** phase, home care nurses complete a client assessment and identify the need for specific home health aide services. Nurses should prioritize the client's needs, establish goals, and determine the types of interventions necessary for the client to achieve these goals. **Organizing** requires nurses to express the needs and goals of a client's plan of care to home health aides; to identify the sequence of interventions to be performed; and to establish regular opportunities for interaction and discussion about the client's progress. **Directing** involves a nurse's supervision of a home health aide's performance of responsibilities. Home care nurses should instruct and demonstrate procedures as needed to ensure quality care for clients. The management function of **controlling** involves the nurse's review of home health aide documentation to ensure that care is provided as planned. Controlling also means assessing the progress of clients toward their preestablished goals. If clients do not progress as anticipated, home care nurses revise the plan of care and initiate the management process again.

5. Nurses should provide feedback to home health aides in an educational way to improve technique in the performance of duties. Nurses must be as specific as possible. Most aides are anxious to learn how to take care of clients more effectively. Nurses who take time to explain not only what should be done for clients and how—but also why—help aides to increase their knowledge and effectiveness.

◆ Chapter 9—The Nursing Process and Home Care

1. The following phases constitute the nursing process: systematic assessment of a client's health and factors influencing the client's health; diagnosis of the client's health problems and responses to actual or potential health concerns; outcome identification, or the formulation and documentation of a client's strengths, weaknesses, and goals to plan strategies to reduce client problems effectively; implementation of planned interventions; evaluation of the effectiveness of the plan of care, the responsiveness of the client to interventions, and progress toward goals.

2. Activities that nurses complete during the preparation phase of the home visit include reviewing clinical records of clients; collecting necessary supplies, equipment, and paperwork; reviewing the overall schedule, incorporating each client's scheduling needs and efficient travel to establish approximate visit times; and phoning clients to obtain their permission to make visits, to agree

on approximate visit times, and to inform them of any actions they should take before the visits.

3. In home care, nurses can actually observe a client's routine in the home and identify actual needs during assessment. Thus, they can develop more effective plans of care than in institutional settings. In most other healthcare settings, nurses formulate interventions based upon needs that they assume clients will have in their day-to-day functioning. These assumptions may or may not be accurate, which influences their effectiveness. Nurses can also identify probable causes and contributing factors of actual or potential problems more easily in home care than in other settings when formulating nursing diagnoses. Clients and lay caregivers are usually less anxious in their own homes. Additionally, nurses can observe them in their natural settings and, as a result, witness their honest and customary interactions with and reactions to one another.

4. In home care, a client's ongoing decisions, actions, and behaviors affect the attainment of goals more than nursing procedures do. Thus, clients and their lay caregivers must actively participate in plans of care if clients hope to regain full health. Home care nurses who achieve the most positive client outcomes are usually effective agents of change for clients. Involvement of clients in decision-making related to their health goals is an essential change strategy. If a client is unwilling to adopt wellness behaviors, or refuses to practice strategies to better manage health, the client's status will most likely fail to improve. Nurses expect many home care clients to take their medications regularly, to follow prescribed diets, to be alert for signs and symptoms of disease, to report problems, to maintain established exercise programs, or to perform any number of medical interventions. Clients will not achieve the goals and objectives established in their plans of care unless they execute such activities.

5. Nurses conduct follow-up activities that include the following: calling physicians if indicated to report any unexpected assessment findings and to collect any additional treatment plan orders; revising plans of care to reflect the changing needs of clients; making referrals to community organizations as needed to access appropriate support systems for clients; communicating pertinent information to other healthcare providers to coordinate efforts; documenting findings, interventions, and client responses; and cleaning equipment as needed.

◆ Chapter 10—Client Teaching

1. In home care, nurses spend relatively short periods of time with clients. Most of the time, clients and lay caregivers need to provide any necessary care and to identify changes in the conditions of clients that warrant immediate interventions. Client teaching by nurses allows individuals to safely meet their needs when nurses are unavailable to assist.

2. Adult learning principles include the following: adults need to participate in and direct the learning process; adults are motivated by practical reasons to learn new information; adults learn more effectively if past experiences are integrated into the instructional process; adults who put new information to imme-

diate use can retain it better; adults need clear, specific feedback in the instructional process.

3. Steps of client teaching sessions include preparation, learner assessment, development of learner outcomes, development of the teaching plan, implementation of the instructional session (subject introduction, instruction, and summary), evaluation of learner outcomes, and documentation.

4. Techniques that nurses can use to stimulate the senses during learning and to enhance retention include providing written instructions, having clients write down verbal instructions, demonstrating procedures, supervising return demonstrations, asking open-ended questions, and using pictures or simple diagrams.

5. False

◆ Chapter 11—Safety and Equipment Management

1. When performing home safety assessments, nurses must evaluate walkways for clutter. They need to look for unnecessary scatter rugs, and examine electrical cords, curled carpet corners, areas that are not well lit, and dangers in kitchens and bathrooms.

2. Walkers that are too short will cause clients to bend too far forward. Walkers that are too tall will cause clients to stand too straight, so that they cannot easily lift the walkers to move forward.

3. Although oxygen itself does not ignite, it can create a fire hazard because it enhances combustion.

4. Nurses should report all accidents and incidents to their home health agency supervisors for investigations into potential causes. Nurses can thus ensure that appropriate interventions will assist in preventing further occurrences.

5. Nurses who use public transportation, such as buses or subways, face risks associated with waiting alone at stops and stations. Some home care agencies, particularly in high crime areas of large cities, provide security personnel to accompany home care nurses on visits to increase the protection of their employees. Home care nurses should always park in busy, well-lit areas. They should keep personal automobiles in excellent condition and keep gas tanks at least half full. While driving, nurses should keep their doors locked and windows closed. When nurses return to their cars after visits, they should look under and in their cars before entering them. Employees at the home care office should always know a nurse's schedule of visits and route. If nurses intend to visit clients after normal working hours, this critical information must be communicated as well. Nurses should always be alert to their surroundings, and above all, trust their instincts: if a situation seems unsafe, a nurse should leave. While traveling, home care nurses should verify routes and know exact directions to clients' homes. Although clients usually are able to provide good directions, nurses also benefit from checking routes on a map, particularly in dangerous neighborhoods. Driving slowly, stopping to look at a map, or appearing lost may make home care nurses easy crime targets. When nurses are unable

to find a client's address, they should drive to a secure location, where they can safely study a map or call the client or home care office to verify an address.

6. Nurses who work in home care must recognize personal safety issues that are seldom encountered in institutional settings. Examples of issues for home care nurses to consider include travel in dangerous neighborhoods, homes with potentially dangerous pets, clients and lay caregivers with histories of violent behavior or with unstable psychiatric conditions who exhibit threatening behavior, and clients who openly display weapons in the home.

◆ Chapter 12—Infection Control

1. Using appropriate infection control techniques maximizes the safety of clients, their lay caregivers, and home care professionals. Infection control principles are especially important in home care today because sicker clients are being treated in these settings. Their immune systems are more compromised, making them more susceptible to complications of infection. Clients are also receiving more invasive procedures in home care today, which necessitates nurses' use of appropriate measures.

2. Common pathogens include bacteria, viruses, parasites, and microbes. A reservoir is the natural habitat of an organism, in which a pathogen grows and multiplies. The portal of exit is the means by which an infectious agent escapes from its reservoir. Transmission of infectious agents to human beings occurs through direct or indirect contact with reservoirs. Just as an infectious agent must find an exit route from its reservoir, it also must find a portal of entry into its new host. Once the infectious agent finds its entry route, it attempts to infect a new host. The body's susceptibility, or degree of resistance, helps to determine whether infection is successfully accomplished. If a person's immune system is weakened, or the infectious agent is lethal enough to overcome the body's defenses quickly, the infectious agent accomplishes its mission of infecting a new host. The host in turn becomes its own reservoir, in which the infection multiplies. The cycle continues.

3. False

4. Laws require home care agencies to report specified diseases to appropriate agencies that are responsible for identifying potential outbreaks of dangerous communicable diseases and for acting in the public's best interest to contain the spread of disease. Nurses should always report newly diagnosed infections in home care clients to their supervisors. Home care nurses must develop an awareness of the infectious organisms plaguing their clients to ensure that appropriate reporting to home care agencies takes place. Maintaining records of infections commonly found in the client populations of home care agencies can result in the discovery of practice patterns that are contributing to client infections.

5. False

6. Components of infection prevention include appropriate handwashing technique; practicing standard and transmission-based precautions; maintaining good personal hygiene; understanding concepts of mode of transmission; laundering contaminated clothing and linens; washing and storing dishes, utensils, and personal care items of infected individuals; disinfecting contaminated surfaces and items; using personal protective equipment; appropriate trash disposal; and appropriate sharps disposal.

◆ Chapter 13—The Initial Home Care Visit

1. The initial home care visit is important because it provides clients with their first impressions of a home care agency, and it establishes the foundation for the therapeutic relationship that a nurse needs to develop to provide effective care.

2. Steps that nurses should take before contacting a client to schedule the initial visit include carefully reviewing all referral information; evaluating the need for a specific visit time to perform a medical treatment; and assessing the need for supplies or equipment necessary to complete the visit.

3. Appropriate actions for nurses to take when interviewing include active listening, demonstrating a nonjudgmental attitude, and maintaining eye contact.

4. False

5. False

◆ Chapter 14—Subsequent Visits, Recertification, Transfer, and Discharge From Home Care

1. Subsequent nursing visits are important for ensuring that information gathered during an initial visit is still relevant and that a client is progressing toward established goals. Before each subsequent contact, nurses must reacquaint themselves with details of the clinical conditions and needs of clients. This process consists of reviewing clinical notes from previous visits, identifying significant clinical findings, reestablishing treatment goals, and noting goals that clients have achieved. By continually reviewing and updating information about a client, a nurse can best determine issues and interventions to address during the next visit.

2. Accurate predictions of necessary length of stay are difficult to make. Clients often develop new problems during the course of their care, or problems that were previously not identified on admission become evident. By certifying cli-

ents for the entire allowed period, home care agencies have the flexibility to continue to provide services if new needs arise, without repeating the extensive certification process.

3. Nurses can educate clients about their disease processes and provide anticipatory guidance to help them realize future needs by answering clinical questions regarding probable symptoms, functional deficits, and compensatory mechanisms. Anticipatory guidance for clients with chronic disease helps them to prepare for and cope with predictable problems. Chronic progressive diseases that often result in functional deficits will limit a client's independence. Clients who receive anticipatory guidance can consider how to address their potential needs while they are relatively "well" and can better consider all of their options. Anticipatory guidance can empower clients to control important areas of their lives. Often, as a client's condition worsens, a sense of helplessness and lack of control sets in. Clients can become severely depressed. They may have unsubstantiated fears and anxieties. Individuals need to understand their disease processes and also typical issues that individuals with their diseases must face. Nurses should discuss likely functional deficits that may occur and compensatory mechanisms available to assist clients (e.g., medical equipment, and community resources). They should address potential financial issues with clients. Clients should also be educated in emotional issues they may deal with as their independence decreases.

4. Nurses most commonly transfer home care clients to skilled nursing facilities, rehabilitation centers, and hospice programs.

5. Hospice is a concept of care, not a place. The hospice philosophy encourages clients and their lay caregivers to live each day fully. It focuses on the quality of life for clients and their families. Supportive personnel assist clients and their lay caregivers through the stages of dying to achieve acceptance. Hospice programs have medical directors who oversee clients' care. They provide medical guidance to the hospice team to manage the symptoms of terminal diseases aggressively. Nurses in hospice programs have specialized training in symptom management, pain control, and the psychosocial aspects of care needed by terminally ill clients and their loved ones. Experts in spiritual and emotional counseling are members of the interdisciplinary team who view clients and their lay caregivers as a unit. Care is highly comprehensive and holistic. Assessment and care planning for hospice clients attempt to address the extensive physical, emotional, psychological, and spiritual issues associated with death and the dying person.

6. Nurses should gradually prepare home care clients for their eventual discharge from services. They initiate this process during the first home visit, and continue it with all subsequent visits. Nurses give all services with the ultimate goal of ensuring each client's maximum wellness and safety after the client no longer receives services. Nurses help to ease discharge through appropriate planning and referrals, and by encouraging the independence of clients.

INDEX

Page numbers followed by f indicate figures; those followed by t indicate tables.